About the Author

Glen Oglaza is an award-winning television news reporter and political correspondent with more than twenty-five years' experience with ITN and Sky News. At ITN, he covered many of the biggest stories of the 1980s and 1990s, was part of the award-winning ITN teams covering the fall of the Berlin Wall, the plight of the Kurds in the wake of the first Gulf War, and the massacre in Dunblane. He was BAFTA nominated for his coverage of the London poll tax riot. As a political correspondent, he covered the governments of Tony Blair, Gordon Brown and David Cameron.

More When I Stories
From the front line of television news – and beyond.
Covering politics for Sky News

Glen Oglaza

More When I Stories
From the front line of television news – and beyond.
Covering politics for Sky News

PEGASUS

© Copyright 2024
Glen Oglaza

The right of Glen Oglaza to be identified as author of
this work has been asserted by him in accordance with the
Copyright, Designs and Patents Act 1988.

All Rights Reserved

No reproduction, copy or transmission of this publication
may be made without written permission.
No paragraph of this publication may be reproduced,
copied or transmitted save with the written permission of the publisher, or
in accordance with the provisions
of the Copyright Act 1956 (as amended).

Any person who commits any unauthorised act in relation to
this publication may be liable to criminal
prosecution and civil claims for damages.

A CIP catalogue record for this title is
available from the British Library.

ISBN 978 1 80468 010 0

*Pegasus is an imprint of
Pegasus Elliot Mackenzie Publishers Ltd.*
www.pegasuspublishers.com

First Published in 2024

**Pegasus
Sheraton House Castle Park
Cambridge England**

Printed & Bound in Great Britain

Dedication

For Maddie and Seb

Acknowledgements

So many people have helped me over so many years. You know who you are, so just a few special mentions.

My sister, Sue, for all the typing, fantastic support and keeping me to deadline. Elaine Wadsworth and all at Pegasus. The late and much lamented Tony Cartledge and all at Metro Radio. All those at ITN and Sky News who were such a pleasure to work with. The camera crews and VT editors who taught me so much. Sandy Gall, who first aroused my interest in becoming a television news reporter. Andy Reeds and all at Crown Media, so much unsung talent. Marion, for all the good times. My parents, for putting up with me. Most of all this is for my children. This is some (but by no means all!) of what we got up to. And you, dear reader. I hope you enjoy sharing my reminiscences.

Finally, apologies if I've forgotten or misremembered anyone or anything although, as I kept and still keep a diary, this is unlikely.

Introduction

In *When I Stories* I reminisced about my ten years at ITN covering some of the biggest stories in the world, joining Sky News and starting to focus on exclusively covering politics. This is the sequel, covering my years working as a political correspondent for Sky News during the administrations of three prime ministers, Tony Blair, Gordon Brown and David Cameron. During my ITN days, a bag was always packed and passport at the ready, a great life when you're young and single. But married with a child, as I now was, needed a more manageable lifestyle. As I'd always been something of a political nerd but also keen to have as many adventures as possible, the new glove fitted perfectly.

CHAPTER 1

2003: Total Politics. The 'Sexed Up' Dossier. Dr David Kelly. Saddam Captured

Finally, after six years as a freelance I was a full-time staff political correspondent for Sky News. Even though I had been reporting politics for Sky News for almost all of those six years, this had so many advantages. It meant I was fully a part of the team. It also meant that I would be sent on more foreign assignments and would enjoy Sky's generous annual paid leave. The only downside was that it meant, in effect, taking a cut in income as I would have to stop my media training and consultancy, although I got permission from head of news Nick Pollard to continue with the military and some charity work in my own time. The Sky News salary was generous enough, but it didn't fully compensate for the loss of so many corporate clients. What was most important, though, was that I was back doing what I most enjoyed full time, reporting the news based in Westminster. It felt like a whole new phase in my life.

First up was the Criminal Justice Bill, then a plan to reform the House of Commons, then packaging all day on a Home Office crackdown on gun crime. Next day, David Blunkett announced a ban on replica guns. His announcement came at five forty-five p.m., so I had to hastily scramble together a package for six p.m., with re-cuts every hour all evening and reaction interviews with Simon Hughes, Oliver Letwin, Chris Mullin and others. A YouGov poll revealed that people had very little faith in Labour's crime policy. I packaged that and, the next day, a piece on the Labour split on whether or not to go to war in Iraq. Former Argentine military dictator, General Leopoldo Galtieri, who had invaded the Falklands, died at the age of seventy-six. He was not much lamented. I did a couple of lives about him before returning to Iraq and Labour Party politics.

David Blunkett gave a speech about ID cards, he wanted them, and also talked about the stabbing of a Special Branch officer in Manchester. We were in Cardiff for a meeting of the Welsh Assembly and to cover an IDS speech on asylum seekers but, in a rare cock-up, no one back at base had booked a satellite feed or worked out how would we feed our package. We had to drive it to Bristol and feed it from there. We were still back in Millbank in time to watch the package run on *Live at Five*. We had stayed the previous night at the five-star St David's hotel with superb views across Cardiff Bay, but had had to drive through some pretty rough areas to get there. Of course, it wasn't anything like as bad as driving through the Bombay (Mumbai) slums to get to the Kempinski Hotel back in 1990, but the contrast between the five-star luxury and the streets around it wasn't so entirely dissimilar.

Tony Blair met Hans Blix, head of the UN inspectors looking for evidence of WMD in Iraq. For me, this meant endless lives outside Number Ten. Geoff Hoon announced details of the British military deployment to the Gulf. Thirty-six thousand soldiers, sailors and airmen, a huge deployment by British standards. The Americans were sending more than ten times as many. The aircraft carrier, *HMS Ark Royal*, and helicopter carrier, *HMS Ocean*, were already on their way. 7th Armoured Brigade and 16 Air Assault Brigade, both of whom I knew well, were among the troops being deployed. War now looked inevitable.

The same day, my package also included Jack Straw at the UN in New York. The Security Council had passed UNSCR 1441 the previous November, offering Saddam Hussein a 'final opportunity' to comply with UN inspections and surrender any weapons of mass destruction. Iraq, it pointed out, was also in breach of previous UN Security Council Resolutions on importing prohibited missiles and other weapons. The diplomatic route had clearly run its course.

I was getting my own insights into how the military was viewing the apparently imminent invasion of Iraq, for example, when I was a member of a panel taking a Q&A session at the UK Defence Academy in Shrivenham. My fellow panellists were Glyn Mathias, formerly of ITN, the soon-to-be-notorious Andrew Gilligan of the BBC and Professor Chris Bellamy. Although the session was ostensibly about Afghanistan, with Royal Marines Brigadier Roger Lane who was about to take over command there from Brigadier John Riley, the subject quickly switched to Iraq, the justification for action and, more importantly from their point of view, the practicalities of such an operation.

Then it was off to Brussels, where EU foreign ministers were meeting Hans Blix. I interviewed Jack Straw, the EU's High Representative for Foreign Affairs Javier Solana, and the Greek foreign minister (Greece currently held the EU Presidency). The foreign ministers backed the Americans, demanding that Iraq comply with UNSCR 1441.

On to Paris for a very quirky story and well away from the politics of invading Iraq. An Iranian refugee, Mehran Karimi Nasseri, had been living in the departure lounge of Charles de Gaulle airport for the previous fourteen years! Known as 'Sir Alfred', one of his parents was British, but he was stateless. Airport staff fed him. I persuaded him to do an interview and lots of posing, eating, sleeping, brushing his teeth etc. He ended up staying at the airport for another three years. In 2004, he published his autobiography, *The Terminal Man*, and there was a Steven Spielberg film starring Tom Hanks.

I was also doing lives in Paris on the French attitude to the Iraq crisis and the French position ahead of Colin Powell's address to the UN Security Council which was due the following week.

From there, we drove to Le Touquet for a Blair-Chirac bilateral summit. It took hours to get there through a heavy snowstorm, mostly doing less than ten miles an hour in heavy traffic. The news that day was dominated by the disintegration of the space shuttle Columbia and the deaths of seven astronauts.

The night before the summit, I got our satellite truck to park right outside Le Touquet's town hall. We had already done several lives from outside the aptly named Westminster Hotel where Tony Blair was staying. When we returned to the town hall the next morning, the police had cordoned off the area. Every other broadcaster's satellite truck was still at the Westminster Hotel. We got some fantastic exclusive shots of Blair and Chirac doing a walkabout in a massive scrum of people waving little plastic Union Jacks and French flags (I still have a couple somewhere!). I moved the truck again, to the Palais de L'Europe. Again, no one else had moved their satellite trucks, so we had that to ourselves as well.

Adam (Boulton) and I were alternating the live two-ways, helped by producer Clare Parry, while I was also packaging the day's events. The Le Touquet summit had been billed as a confrontation, High Noon for Blair and Chirac over Iraq. Although Chirac was his usual overbearing and patronising self, in fact they agreed on a lot of the issues and finished with a joint press conference before and after which I did long (very long!) live two-ways. They agreed on the need to reform the European Union, but not on reform of the Common Agriculture Policy. They simply agreed to differ on Iraq, although they did agree that they wanted to disarm Saddam Hussein. Chirac believed UNSCR 1441 meant more time for the UN weapons inspectors to do their job, and that another resolution would be required to sanction military action. This was not the American interpretation of 1441, but it was the Blair government's position to get a second resolution if possible, although Tony Blair still hoped that Saddam Hussein could be pressured into full compliance with resolution 1441. Both agreed to listen to what Colin Powell had to say to the UN Security Council.

George Galloway had visited Saddam Hussein in the mid-90s, after the first Gulf War. He came out with this, "Sir, I salute your courage, your strength, your indefatigability. We are with you until victory. Until Jerusalem." This to a dictator who had gassed and murdered thousands of his own people. It had beggared belief. Now, Tony Benn had done a television interview with Saddam Hussein which was almost as nauseatingly sycophantic. I had always admired Tony Benn, though hardly ever agreed with his politics, but this really lowered him in my estimation. Of course, I couldn't say this on air at the time, simply reporting the story with excerpts from the interview.

US Secretary of State Colin Powell delivered his presentation to the UN Security Council on February 5th, and argued in favour of military action. He rather theatrically held up a model vial of anthrax, saying he had no doubt that Saddam had biological weapons and was on the brink of producing nuclear weapons. Powell had initially been against intervention to overthrow Saddam Hussein, preferring a policy of containment, but he was the Secretary of State and therefore had to present the Bush administration's arguments. Powell referred to the British dossier, which Tony Blair had used to justify invading Iraq, as evidence for his assertions.

Just two days later it emerged that the 'dodgy dossier' had included entire sections lifted from a graduate student's thesis paper.

This was, of course, a huge story. I was live in Downing Street almost constantly. Number Ten had no choice but to admit the plagiarism while insisting that it only covered areas of accepted facts (the structure of Iraq's secret police and so on), and did not dilute the central argument that Saddam Hussein had ready-to-use WMD.

The French and the Germans were back-pedalling. Chirac had always been against military action in Iraq, now the Germans seemed to be leaning the same way. There were anti-war marches in London as well as in Paris and Berlin. On February 10th, I did a substantial package and lives from Downing Street on the fracturing support for the American-led coalition. The danger for the British government is that they were being painted into a corner, with Tony Blair portrayed as America's 'poodle'.

Next stop was Brussels and lives all day outside NATO HQ. A deadlocked EU meeting on Iraq was postponed. Next day we were in Paris. Sky head of news, Nick Pollard, wanted lives from the capitals of all five UN Security Council permanent members (the US, UK, France, Russia and China) on the day chief UN weapons inspector Hans Blix reported to the Security Council. Blix also appeared to be softening his position. He was non-committal. He criticised Colin Powell's presentation, and seemed to be saying that he believed weapons inspections could still succeed.

The central problem was that the Americans were hell-bent on regime change, deposing Saddam Hussein, rather than only taking out his WMD capability. Support for this stance in Europe was far from enthusiastic, to say the least. The lives from the capitals looked good. We were live from the Place de la Concorde every hour for most of the day explaining the French government's position, which was diametrically opposed to that of the British government.

There was a huge anti-war demo in London when we returned the next day, around a million people marched. The police said seven hundred and fifty thousand, the organisers claimed two million. Troops and tanks had been deployed to Heathrow Airport as a show of force and enhanced security. Tanks! Not sure what use a tank would be against an attack by a surface-to-air missile, which was the fear at the time, but from our point of view the tanks at Heathrow provided fantastic pictures and a very good story. At one point, the government had even considered closing the airport, but very quickly rejected that option.

I knew there was an avalanche of work coming our way, so I took the opportunity to take the family on holiday for a week to Lanzarote, where a friend owned a house. In Spain, an opinion poll showed just four per cent were in favour of invading Iraq, even though the Aznar government was supporting the American position.

As soon as we got back, I was off to Madrid where Tony Blair was having a bilateral summit with Spanish Prime Minister José María Aznar. We were live all evening at Moncloa Palace, the Spanish prime minister's official residence. Aznar was supporting Tony Blair, but clearly had an even bigger problem with public opinion than the British government had. We continued doing lives the next day before and after a joint Aznar-Blair press conference.

Back in Britain, I interviewed David Blunkett and covered an anti-terrorism rehearsal exercise in Harrogate. How well prepared was the UK? Next day, it was Jack Straw when he hosted the Russian foreign minister, Igor Ivanov. The day after, and another anti-war demo. I interviewed Jeremy Corbyn and comedian Mark Thomas for my package, the lead story, which also took in PMQs and the French, German and Russian foreign ministers standing side by side in Paris saying they were against any military action in Iraq.

Tony Blair went on MTV to talk about Iraq (trying to court the youth vote!). Geoff Hoon spoke at Chatham House. The Chatham House rule is a strange one. You're allowed to report what was said, but not who said it. I was at one event when the guest speaker was John Bolton who at the time was US ambassador to the UN and later went on to serve Trump as national security advisor until he could stand it no longer and resigned (in September 2019). As I was live reporting outside Chatham House, he came out of the front door just behind me. I was live. "I'm not allowed to say who delivered the speech under the Chatham House rule. Oh look, there's John Bolton!"

I was live in Downing Street for several days before the Azores summit. It was felt that military action against Iraq could start very soon. Chirac was saying France would oppose it whatever the circumstances, and would veto any second UN resolution calling for such military action. In effect, France was saying don't even bother trying for a second UN resolution. The Americans were clearly itching to get on with it, with or without UN support. As well as standing in Downing Street doing lives explaining the latest developments, I covered Tony Blair meeting the Romanian prime minister. The Eastern European countries were supporting Blair's position to call for a second UN resolution (after 1441) to justify war. The day before the Azores summit, Blair held a press conference laying out what he would be saying to George W Bush.

We flew to Lisbon and on to the island of São Miguel to connect with a short flight to the island of Terceira where the summit would be held, a trilateral summit between Blair, Bush and Aznar, hosted by Portuguese Prime Minister Jose Manuel Barroso. Ostensibly, the summit was to discuss a second UN resolution. In fact, they took the decision to go to war.

As is often the way with these summits held in inaccessible places, the press were kept miles away. When we first landed at the US base in Terceira on the eve of the summit, we had just one hour of daylight to get pictures for a preview package. The Azores are very green, a bit like Devon only with good weather, palm trees and the brightest of flowers, the names of every one of which ITN cameraman Alan Downes would no doubt have known had he been there! Our package featured churches, children, the fishing harbour, rural scenes and a PTC at the US airbase. Not bad for an hour's work.

Next morning, I blagged my way onto the airbase, claiming to be from Azores Portuguese TV! Not once, all day, was I ever asked to show any ID. Our satellite dish, provided by the EBU, was stuck outside the airbase perimeter along with the rest of the media, creating a logistical problem. We filmed Blair's plane arriving and George W emerging from Air Force One. I managed to do live two-ways as they arrived by using a local satellite dish which had been allowed in position though only to cover the end of summit press conference. Sky News political editor, Adam Boulton, and producer Clare Parry were on Tony Blair's flight, and I got Adam in front of a camera live as soon as they touched down. Security moved the dish we were using to a so-called 'sterile location', no lives permitted, so we relocated to the EBU dish. My 6p.m. live spot was shared with Keith Graves in Washington and David Chater in Baghdad.

It was felt that the war could start as soon as the next day. At the press conference ending the summit, Bush said, "Tomorrow is a moment of truth for the world." And called for, "The immediate and unconditional disarmament of Saddam Hussein." Tony Blair said Saddam had been playing games with the international community and would continue to do so, but he also called for a last and final round of contacts but added that we were in, "The final stages... now is the time when we have to decide".

Three days later the coalition invaded Iraq and the second Gulf War began.

The press conference ended in time for me to do a last live of the day into *Sky News at Ten*. And my suitcase, which had gone missing from the flight from London to Lisbon finally turned up. I had been wearing the same clothes for three days. Not pleasant.

As we arrived home from the Azores, Robin Cook resigned from the Cabinet. Unlike Clare Short, he had stuck to the principal of collective Cabinet responsibility. That is that you aired your differences in Cabinet but, once a decision was taken, that became the position of the Cabinet and therefore of the government. He said his opposition to military action against Iraq meant that he could no longer do so. By contrast, Clare Short, who was Secretary of State for International Development, had been all over the airwaves for weeks attacking the policy of her own government. She eventually resigned from the Cabinet on May 13th.

Tony Blair made his historic speech to the House of Commons justifying going to war with Iraq based on UNSCR 1441 but without a second resolution. Technically, he did not need the approval or agreement of parliament. The sovereign has the power to declare war. Blair told MPs if he didn't win the debate he would resign. He delivered one of the most persuasive performances in modern parliamentary history. Although around a quarter of Labour MPs voted against him, as did the Lib Dems, the Conservatives backed the prime minister and the government won the vote convincingly, 412 votes to 149. Next day Operation Telic, the British military campaign, began.

There was a large and noisy demonstration outside parliament and the anti-war demonstrators were back the next day for PMQs, which I packaged all day, taking in the voices of the protestors.

That night, the Americans launched forty cruise missiles into Iraq. They apparently had intelligence revealing where Saddam Hussein was hiding and this was their attempt to kill him. He appeared on television soon afterwards to say they had missed. I was helping with a theatre war game at the UK Defence Academy in Shrivenham. I should really have been in Brussels for Sky News, but it was a long-standing commitment. However, it gave me a unique perspective, the senior military view of the campaign. At 4.30 p.m., coalition ground troops invaded Iraq from Kuwait. I had dinner that evening with Royal Marines Brigadier Roger Lane (of Afghanistan fame) and three others. They spoke to me in strictest confidence and were completely frank but I'm honour-bound not to reveal what was said. They were, however, already considering what would happen once Saddam was overthrown, some sort of 'exit strategy' which neither the American nor the British government appeared to have even thought about.

We watched the BBC *Ten O'clock News*, their choice not mine, which was embarrassingly poor. They had phonos (live reports on the phone) from Baghdad and from the Iraq/Kuwait border. Phonos! Sky had live cameras at both locations. There was a report, by an old friend of mine now at the BBC, about how they, the hacks, had to wear gas masks. Really! And it included a PTC in a gas mask. "Pure Monty Python," remarked one of the senior army officers I was working with. I told them they should have watched Sky News instead.

The next day saw the start of the massive bombing of Baghdad, and speculation that Saddam Hussein was already dead. As the fighting continued I was covering the politics from Westminster. A typical package, on March 31st, had interviews with Geoff Hoon, Gordon Brown (on the cost of the war), IDS and Charles Kennedy and was fairly comprehensive. I also interviewed anti-war Labour rebels including Glenda Jackson, and George Galloway who described Tony Blair and our armed forces as 'wolves', not a popular view. To attack Blair was one thing, but to so describe our troops when they were fighting a war was considered completely unacceptable.

We got the shocking news that our friend and colleague, Terry Lloyd, and his ITN team were missing in Iraq. Their cars had been shot up, caught in crossfire near Basra. Their two cars were both clearly marked as press vehicles. Then we heard that Terry was dead. We were numb. It later emerged that Terry had initially been shot and wounded, and transferred to a minibus that was picking up casualties. American forces had blasted the minibus killing everyone inside.

Terry and his team had not been embedded with coalition forces. The reporters and crews who were embedded were sending back images straight out of a Hollywood war movie. There are many problems with embedding, not least that we surrender objectivity for access. We see the tank rounds being fired, but not their effect at the receiving end. So, as well as having teams embedded with the coalition forces, it was vital to have other teams reporting on where the tank shells landed, and to give the perspective of those, especially civilians, who were suffering in war. This was a brave thing to be doing, but was essential if we were to get a fuller picture and tell a more faithful story. This is what Terry and his team were doing, the finest, bravest journalism, and it had cost him his life. Terry was universally popular. Clever, funny, sometimes hilariously sarcastic, he was also one of the very best television news reporters of his generation. He had revealed Saddam's massacre of thousands of Kurds in Halabja in northern Iraq in 1988, the first evidence of Saddam Hussein's slaughter of his own people. We were numb with shock.

Muhammad Saeed al-Sahhaf, Iraq's information minister, became known as Comical Ali for his series of outlandish claims in the face of reality. He said American troops were committing suicide in their hundreds and there were no American tanks anywhere near Baghdad. In the background, you could clearly hear the sound of the fighting as coalition forces took the Iraqi capital. His finest moment came during a live on Sky News when he claimed the Americans were nowhere near Baghdad airport. "We crushed their forces at Saddam International Airport and cleared the whole airport," he claimed, as Sky News showed a split screen with him on the left and on the right our reporter with the Americans at that very moment securing the airport.

Chemical Ali, Ali Hassan al-Majid, former defence minister and now head of Iraq's Intelligence Services, was not funny at all. Saddam Hussein's cousin, he had become notorious in the 1980s and 1990s for the mass deportations and genocide of the Kurds in northern Iraq and the Marsh Arabs in the south, and the gassing of five thousand Kurdish villagers in Halabja, a story broken by Terry Lloyd in 1988. Unlike Comical Ali, he was prosecuted for war crimes and genocide in 2007 and sentenced to death. He was hanged in January 2010.

At Westminster, I was getting on air fairly frequently, usually after a lobby briefing in Downing Street, or interviewing Defence Secretary Geoff Hoon, or reporting on the activities and utterances of Tony Blair.

April 9th was Budget Day. I cut a substantial package but it didn't make it to air (although you could 'press the red button' if you really wanted to see it). It was the first and only time Budget coverage has been abandoned because this was also the day that Baghdad fell. My friend and fellow Sky News correspondent, David Chater, had bravely stayed in Baghdad throughout the 'shock and awe' bombing. Now, he was in his element, welcoming the American troops into the centre of Baghdad live on air. His team's coverage included the iconic toppling of the giant statue of Saddam Hussein, erected just a year before to celebrate the dictator's sixty-fifth birthday, and its 'dismembering' by locals. It was the symbolic moment, the Berlin Wall moment of the war. The pictures from Baghdad were incredible.

As is the way with news, even as we were watching them the questions were being asked: Where was Saddam Hussein? And where were his two genocidal sons? And what would happen next? The Kurdish cities of Kirkuk and Mosul were still, nominally at least, in the control of Saddam Hussein as was his hometown, Tikrit. And what next politically? The Kurds were clearly hoping for sovereignty, their own country, once again a futile hope. And what for the rest of Iraq? Who could form a functioning government? How would the humanitarian effort be coordinated? What, in short, were the plans for a post-Saddam Iraq?

The Kurds took Kirkuk the next day, April 10th, without a fight. The scenes of celebration were similar to those we had seen in Baghdad the day before, including the toppling of another Saddam statue. The Turkish government expressed its alarm. Then, as now, the Turks were determined to deny the Kurds their own country. I packaged a television broadcast to Iraq by Bush and Blair called *Towards Freedom*. Few people, including the two leaders, realised that the conflict in Iraq was far from over. My package ran all evening and, unusually, all the next morning as well.

Clare Short, who still hadn't resigned, was guest speaker at the Foreign Press Association, but refused to give me an interview afterwards. Of course, she knew what I would be asking her. Later that day, I interviewed Dr Fadhil Chalabi, the former secretary general of Opec and, more pertinently, cousin of Ahmed Chalabi, founder of the Iraqi National

Congress who was being touted by the Americans as a future leader of Iraq. His cousin was keen to make the case, but the general view, and certainly the view from Downing Street, was that it was never going to happen, not least because Chalabi was an exile who would be seen in Iraq as nothing more than an American puppet. In fact, he did go on to serve as deputy prime minister for a year, 2005-06.

Slowly, we were beginning to cover news other than Iraq. I interviewed Alistair Darling for a package on government plans to use motorway hard shoulders to ease congestion, but Iraq was never far away. That same day, I did a live after Jack Straw and David Blunkett said they would have resigned if the government had lost the March 18th Iraq war vote, and that Tony Blair would have gone too.

The great thing about covering Westminster politics is that there are always stories happening, sometimes very big ones. So, a typical day, April 30th: the Labour PLP (Parliamentary Labour Party) met, and I did a PTC in the corridor outside the committee room they use. Commonplace enough these days, but not so much back then. PMQs that day, and another feeble performance by IDS. I also packaged around an Alan Milburn speech on foundation hospitals, interviewed the Metropolitan Police Deputy Assistant Commissioner Andy Trotter on his plans to contain the next day's expected May day demos and, finally a Jack Straw press conference on the day the Middle East 'road map' was published, the two-state solution.

The road map was rejected by Hamas and failed to stop the second Intifada. Over the next month (and, of course, beyond) the killings in Israel-Palestine continued almost unabated, despite the efforts of Ariel Sharon and Mahmoud Abbas, the newly-elected Palestinian prime minister.

The next day, I packaged an announcement from Belfast that the Stormont elections, due on May 29th, had been postponed because the Unionists didn't think that the IRA statement on the decommissioning of all their weapons was clear enough. Tony Blair held a press conference, and we had reaction from Gerry Adams and the DUP. I did a live on the UK local elections and then a story, embargoed until nine p.m., that Tory MP Crispin Blunt was to table a motion of no confidence in Iain Duncan Smith's leadership. I interviewed Crispin: Would he be the stalking horse? We ran the story at 9p.m., and I updated for the Ten to include interviews with Shadow Secretary of State for Trade and Industry Tim Yeo and Labour's

John Reid, who could hardly contain his glee at the Conservative Party's woes.

In the local elections at the end of April, Labour lost more than 800 seats, losing control of Birmingham and Coventry.

The next day, Friday, was flat out doing lives and packages on the local election results, the first at seven a.m. For the first and last time I did live phonos for South African radio who, for some reason, were interested in a British local election! I was live at 11.50 a.m. as IDS arrived at Conservative Central Office to deliver his 'victory' statement. We took it live and the second he finished I was back in front of the camera. The Tories had gained 600 seats, but their share of the votes remained at 34%. Would it be enough to save his leadership? Turned out it wasn't, he was gone less than six months later.

Crispin Blunt did a live two-way into Sky News. He began with, "As I told Glen Oglaza last night". I loved it when that happened.

The euro was still very much a story. I covered it again for two days in May after a lobby briefing with Tom Kelly, the new PMOS, in which he briefed that Tony Blair and Gordon Brown were completely unified in their approach to joining the euro. Strangely, no one believed him.

The parliamentary press lobby held its bi-centennial dinner that May at the London Metropole Hotel. We were each asked to bring an MP. I invited Theresa May. I thought she might one day be in the Cabinet, though I never imagined she would become prime minister. I don't think anyone else did either. Guest of honour, Tony Blair, gave a very funny speech, as did Press Association veteran and doyen of the lobby, Chris Moncrieff. We had a great table, gossip central, with Adam Boulton and Anji Hunter, Tom Kelly, Jane Bonham-Carter, Baroness Liz Symons and Lord Tim Razzall. I sat between Theresa May and Amanda Platell. We laughed, a lot, but getting conversation out of Theresa was like getting the proverbial blood out of a stone. She was very guarded. It seemed she really did not do small talk.

There were a few of the old ITN faces there, including Dave Mannion and Stewart Purvis. Dave said, "You don't look a day older", which was patently untrue but very charming of him. Mostly, though, he was singing the praises of ITN's political editor Nick Robinson, who he had poached from the BBC. Nick had become something of a bogey man to the Labour Party, which scrutinised his every utterance for any pro-Tory bias. It didn't help that he had once been the national chairman of the Young Conservatives.

Overnight on May 22nd, the police erected concrete blocks outside parliament as added security. We hadn't been told this was going to happen. I was live every hour all morning, and also doing lives for LBC radio, plus a package to run all afternoon. The things looked ugly, and still do, but if they prevented any deaths or injuries the aesthetics were a very small price to pay.

At the end of May ,US Secretary of Defence Donald Rumsfeld let the cat out of the bag (and among the pigeons!) when he declared that WMD might never be found in Iraq and that Saddam Hussein may never have had any in the first place! Great timing for Tony Blair as he was on his way to visit Kuwait and Iraq. Rumsfeld's comments cut to the very core of the prime minister's integrity.

John was being John again! No violence this time, just a two fingered salute to the assembled media in Downing Street. It gave us all a laugh and a short piece for the news. That second weekend of June, I was back doing lives in Downing Street ahead of what was billed as a crucial meeting in Brussels on Britain joining the euro. In Brussels on the Sunday afternoon, we recorded a headline tease in the Place de Luxembourg before dinner with the crew near La Grande-Place. As a city, Brussels gets a bad press, it's dull, boring, bureaucratic etc. But La Grande-Place is spectacular, and was particularly so on this warm June evening. And there are moules and Belgian white beer, so what's not to like?

We were very hard at work the next day with lives all day. As expected, Gordon Brown gave a speech in which he set out five economic tests for joining the euro which had not yet been met. So it was yes to joining the euro, but not yet. The tests were so stringent that not yet really meant never. I continued doing lives in the evening with guests including Conservative MEPs' leader Jonathan Evans and Lib Dem leader Graham Watson. Fourteen hours of live two-ways in all, but it was a huge story. It felt like Gordon Brown had well and truly put the idea of joining the euro to bed.

After lunch and a stroll around beautiful Bruges we headed to Paris, where Tony Blair was visiting Chirac for another bilateral. After lives in the Place de la Concorde with guests Pierre Rousillon of *La Figaro* and Andrew Freeman of the *Economist*, I tried to get our satellite truck into the courtyard of the Élysée Palace. I knew there would be no chance of success but it was worth a try and at first it was looking good. The security guards were almost persuaded when orders came from above. We couldn't get a signal from the road outside, despite the best efforts of the satellite truck crew, JJ and Erez, and the police would not let us cable across the main road. So we had to record the Blair-Chirac meeting and tape feed it. It would have been so much better live. We did do lives from the truck outside the palace before and after the two leaders held a Q&A session.

We had more luck the next day at the Hôtel Matignon, official residence of the French prime minister. I got our truck into the courtyard. When he found out what we were up to, the French prime minister's press secretary gave a Gallic shrug and said, "This is the first and last time".

So, we had the only live position and got exclusive live shots of Tony Blair's arrival as I was live on air, and a live doorstep with him as he departed. I did two more live two-ways, all of this was exclusive and looked fantastic just by virtue of our location. Sometimes, television news is 80% or more logistics. It is always 100% fun to scoop the opposition.

Back in Downing Street the next day Tony Blair reshuffled the government at sub-Cabinet level. Nick Brown, Barbara Roche, Lewis Moonie and Michael Meacher were among the ministers sacked to make way for new talent in the shape of Hazel Blears, Tim Howells, Margaret Hodge and Malcolm Wicks among others. As ever, for us this meant endless lives in Downing Street and trying to get advance notice of the various comings and goings. I was live all day starting at 7 a.m. Tony Blair did a lot of the hiring and firing by phone, which made life difficult for us. It's always easier when we see the various ministers coming out of Number Ten looking either dejected or pumped up and that, of course, made much better television.

There was some confusion over the role of the new Department for Constitutional Affairs, which sounds like something from *The Thick of It*! This was to replace the Lord Chancellor's office, and take responsibility for prisons and the probation service away from the over-burdened Home Office. It was also to incorporate the Scotland office and the Wales office, which seemed very odd. At the lobby briefing at eleven a.m., Godric Smith, who shared the role of PMOS with Tom Kelly, was unable to shed much light. A career civil servant, Godric always played a straight bat, remarkably free of party spin. This meant his briefings could be rather dull, without the verbal jousting we enjoyed with Alastair Campbell and to a lesser extent Tom Kelly, but it also meant that he was credible and trusted. On this occasion, he didn't appear to know any more than the rest of us. The department eventually became the Ministry of Justice in 2007 with a much more clearly defined role.

The "dodgy dossier" was dominating the news and, a few days later, I was in Downing Street doing lives and packages on that when I was asked to do a live two-way for Fox News in New York. Once I'd finished, Fox asked for a one-minute monologue on David Beckham! He had just been sold to Real Madrid for twenty-five million pounds. He was flying to Tokyo as the news broke, so he left Heathrow a Manchester United player and landed in Japan as a Real Madrid Galactico. Fortunately, I knew enough about football and about David Beckham to pull this off, although I was surprised that an American audience would be so interested in this story about what they call 'soccer'.

By June 23rd, Tony Blair was under a lot of pressure and I did a piece on Tony's troubles (we didn't actually call it that, though it was tempting). First and foremost was the 'dodgy dossier' and the claim by BBC correspondent Andrew Gilligan on Radio Four's *Today* programme that the government had 'sexed up' the dossier. The House of Commons was debating tuition fees for students in higher education with fresh debates coming up on fox hunting and foundation hospitals. Tuition fees and foundation hospitals were not at all popular with Labour MPs and the government was skating on thin ice despite its huge majority.

News broke at midday that Alastair Campbell was to give evidence on Iraq's supposed WMD to the House of Commons Foreign Affairs Select Committee. Gilligan's jibe, that the government had 'sexed up' the dossier, was squarely aimed at him and he would continue to deny it. Gilligan had even accused Alastair Campbell directly, by name, in an article for the *Mail on Sunday*. Alastair Campbell gave his evidence for nearly three hours, using the opportunity to bash the BBC's coverage in general. He'd been at war with the BBC for some time.

At the end of June, I covered the Campbell-BBC row for three days. It had been running on and off for almost a month, since Gilligan's 'sexed up' claim at the end of May. On June 27th, the BBC replied to Alastair Campbell in a letter, refusing to apologise and accusing him of intimidation. I was live at five o'clock with the letter hot off the printer and, later, with Alastair Campbell's vitriolic response. I worked that day from 8 a.m. until midnight.

During those few days at the end of June, the war of words between Number Ten and the BBC continued to hot up. At the centre of it was BBC reporter Andrew Gilligan, who I thought was something of a kite-flyer. On June 29th, my package included interviews with John Reid, Baroness (Valerie) Amos and Martin Bell. The BBC sent over an on-camera statement by director of news Richard Sandbrook and Number Ten faxed me another missive from Alastair Campbell to the BBC, much softer in tone, saying to wait until the Foreign Affairs Committee report. I had been on air every hour and more for three days on the same story.

Tony Blair gave a speech in Liverpool. I talked into it live and had to keep going. He was twenty minutes late! Fortunately, there was plenty to say.

The Foreign Affairs Select Committee reported on July 7th. It exonerated Alastair Campbell, clearing him of any 'sexing up' of the dossier while, at the same time, saying that 'undue prominence' had been given to the claim that Saddam Hussein could have launched a WMD attack within forty-five minutes. Which rather begged the question of who had been responsible for giving the claim undue prominence and, semantics and good taste apart, what was the difference between that and 'sexing up'? Of course, the real issue was that Iraq's weapons of mass destruction, if they had ever existed, had never been found.

Gilligan's source was finally revealed to be weapons expert, Dr David Kelly. He had been one the UN's weapons inspectors working in Iraq. The softly-spoken Dr Kelly gave evidence to the Foreign Affairs Committee. He said he believed he must be Gilligan's source but denied saying the things Gilligan claimed his source had said. Labour MP, Andrew MacKinlay, known for being direct to the point of rudeness, was particularly brutal, accusing Dr Kelly of being 'chaff' and 'the fall guy'.

"I reckon you are chaff. You have been thrown up to divert our probing. Have you ever felt like a fall guy? You've been set up, haven't you?"

The next day, Dr Kelly gave evidence to the House of Commons Intelligence and Security select committee. He described the dossier as accurate and, "A fair reflection of the intelligence that was available, presented in a very sober and factual way." A day later, Dr Kelly's body was discovered near his home in Oxfordshire. He had taken his own life.

It was one of those absolutely jaw-dropping moments. I was on air almost continually from Westminster, including a live phono with American Public Service radio whose presenter, and presumably audience, had no idea who Dr Kelly was, so I had to do a new-readers-start-here to fill in the background for them. The government announced the Hutton Inquiry to be chaired by Lord Hutton, former Lord Chief Justice for Northern Ireland, into Dr Kelly's death but not into the whole WMD/intelligence dossier affair. It was to report within two months.

Tony Blair had been on a flight from Washington to Tokyo when the news came in of Dr Kelly's suicide. In Washington, he had triumphantly addressed both houses of Congress, an honour rarely afforded a foreign leader. As he emerged from the plane in Tokyo, he was white. He looked shattered. At a press conference in Japan he seemed drained and exhausted. The travelling press, including Sky's Adam Boulton, asked the questions that needed to be asked. They boiled down to whether or not David Kelly had been driven to suicide and, if so, was the government to blame. His death also begged the question of whether or not the BBC was entirely blameless. Tony Blair called for 'respect and restraint' and for us to wait until Lord Hutton's inquiry reported. The intense, hostile questioning culminated in a *Mail on Sunday* reporter shouting as Blair left the room, "Is there blood on your hands? Are you going to resign?"

While Adam was in Japan with the prime minister, back at Westminster everyone was still shocked by Dr Kelly's death, but the blame game was in full swing. I was doing lives every hour. Not surprisingly, Glenda Jackson called on Tony Blair to resign, while loyal Labour MPs were blaming the BBC.

On July 20th, the BBC officially confirmed what we already knew, that Dr Kelly had indeed been Gilligan's source or, as they put it, his 'principal source'. In a statement read by Richard Sambrook, the BBC maintained that they had accurately reported and interpreted what Dr Kelly had said, in effect accusing him of lying. Needless to say, this kept me busy doing lives and packages all day, for twelve hours. It was difficult to fathom just why the bosses at the BBC were defending Gilligan so robustly. Dr Kelly had explicitly said that he had not told Andrew Gilligan that the government had 'sexed up' the intelligence dossier, nor had he mentioned Alastair Campbell, but he was no longer with us to defend himself. The bigger issue was whether or not the BBC should have admitted earlier that he was their source. His local MP Conservative Robert Jackson told us that, in his opinion, Dr Kelly might still be alive had they done so.

It seemed that Tony Blair and Alastair Campbell were off the hook, at least for the time being. The question being asked, and not only by Robert Jackson, was whether Gilligan was going to drag the BBC down with him. Would there be resignations, and how high up the BBC hierarchy would they go?

The twists and turns of this story kept me busy for days. On July 24th, Andrew Marr of the BBC was putting it about that Alastair Campbell would resign the next day, which would be seen as an admission of guilt. However, on the BBC news that evening he said that Campbell was expected to leave his Downing Street job in the autumn, which we knew anyway. That same day, the Americans released gruesome images of Saddam Hussein's sons Uday and Qusay, who had been killed in a fire fight.

The Alastair Campbell not resigning non-story resulted in me doing lives, doughnutting my own package, in Downing Street every hour for most of the next day.

At the end of the month, the House of Commons Foreign Affairs Select Committee released a report claiming that the Iraq war had made the world a more dangerous place and had increased rather than reduced the threat from al-Qaeda. I also did a preview piece on the Hutton Inquiry which was to begin the next day, August 1st, and would dominate political coverage for the next two months.

And then the Walter Mitty story broke.

The *Independent* newspaper was reporting that a senior Whitehall official had compared Dr David Kelly to James Thurber's 'The Secret Life of Walter Mitty'. This was just two days before Dr Kelly's funeral. At the lobby briefing, Downing Street said it had not been anyone from Number Ten. By early evening, they were admitting that it had, indeed, been someone from Number Ten but speaking out of turn and not expressing the view of Tony Blair or the government. By mid-evening rumours were rife that it had been the PMOS, Tom Kelly. I was live every hour updating this farrago as it unravelled. Next day, Tom Kelly admitted that it had been him, but said that he had been quoted out of context in an off the record briefing on lobby terms, and apologised 'unreservedly'. I did lives doughnutting my own package all afternoon and evening. Tom Kelly had described Dr Kelly as a 'Walter Mitty character' in an aside to the *Independent*'s Paul Waugh. What a daft thing to say.

The Hutton Inquiry was dominating our lives. On Friday evenings, I would package a lookahead piece previewing the potential highlights of the following week. A succession of BBC bosses, including Director General Greg Dyke, traipsed into the Royal Courts of Justice on the Strand to be grilled. So too, of course, did Andrew Gilligan and Alastair Campbell, both twice. Alastair Campbell used the witness box as a platform to bash the BBC. Gilligan was, in my view, unconvincing. Tony Blair was treated with deference. The inquiry lawyers were meticulously probing, but the sessions were far from dramatic.

The inquiry gave our audience a detailed insight into the workings of both the government and the BBC. It was focused on the circumstances leading up to Dr Kelly's suicide, how his name got into the public domain and whether, once his name was known, he should have been given more support, but it did not address the question of the 'dodgy dossier' and the justification for going to war. That would be for the Chilcot inquiry some years later.

Away from Hutton, other stories I covered that September included Sweden voting in a referendum not to join the euro, Labour losing the safe seat of Brent East in a by-election to the Lib Dems, overturning a previous Labour majority of 13,000. Sarah Teather took the seat which had been Labour for twenty-nine years. Lord Williams of Mostyn, leader of the House of Lords, died suddenly at the age of just sixty-two. I covered the Hutton Inquiry's lawyers summing up, and then it was off to the Labour Party conference in Bournemouth.

Not for the first time, the conference became something of a stand-off between Tony Blair and the unions. For me, it was the usual mad few days of lives and packages, gossip, drinking and political intrigue. Gordon Brown gave his usual rousing performance, ending his speech with: "Best when we are boldest, best when we are united, best when we are Labour."

His omission of the phrase 'New Labour' in this speech and throughout the conference did not go unnoticed, and was seen as an afront to Tony Blair even though he, Gordon Brown, had been one of the principal architects of New Labour. As usual, Blair's speech the next day was calm and measured. It was, though, dramatic by his standards. Against a staged backdrop of supporters, who applauded enthusiastically at every opportunity, there was a passage listing the values of New Labour. His most memorable line was: "I can only go one way. I've not got a reverse gear."

This was seen as a response to the unions, to Gordon Brown, and to anyone else who had attacked him. It also seemed to me to be Thatcheresque, 'the lady's not for turning', a prime minister utterly convinced he was doing the right thing whatever anyone else might think.

Back from Bournemouth, a weekend of doing lives every hour on the Conservative Party leadership. How much longer could IDS survive? In one bulletin, at four p.m. on a quiet Sunday afternoon, I had a package at the top of the hour, a live two-way at four thirty p.m. and, at four forty-five p.m., a full length four-minute interview I'd recorded the previous Friday with Felicity and Susannah Miller, mother and sister of Dan Miller who had been one of the two hundred and two people killed in the Bali bombing precisely a year earlier. Sky News was certainly getting its money's worth out of me!

The undermining of Iain Duncan Smith's leadership of the Conservative Party was building with what felt like unstoppable momentum. At the Tory Party conference in Blackpool, he had delivered the worst conference speech by the leader of any party I have ever seen. "The quiet man is turning up the volume," he declared, but he really didn't have the voice to carry that line. For some reason, his glass prompting screens, on which the speech is written, had been placed on the floor instead of at eye level, which meant he kept having to look down. It was painful to watch. It was dull, insipid and uninspiring. The knives were out.

The 1922 committee of Tory backbenchers met at 5 p.m. on October 22nd. The meeting lasted barely ten minutes and avoided the leadership issue but, privately, Conservative MPs were telling us that IDS was finished. There had, apparently, been something of an outburst at Shadow Cabinet in which he had asserted, petulantly, "I am the leader". I reported all that and, most significantly, major party donor Stuart Wheeler saying that the case for removing IDS was 'overwhelming'.

The next day, another big party donor, Reading FC Chairman John Madejski, demanded a leadership contest. The dye was cast, but for a vote of no confidence 25 Conservative MPs, 15% of their total, had to write to the chairman of the 1922 committee, Michael Spicer, demanding a vote. It took a few days. On Monday 27th, IDS did television interviews saying his opponents should either get their twenty-five letters by Wednesday or give up. However, there was absolutely no reason why they should adhere to his timetable. He was basically saying put up or shut up. He also said he would fight a vote of no confidence if one materialised.

I was doing seemingly endless lives and packages from Westminster and from Chingford, Duncan Smith's constituency. Within twenty-four hours of his challenge, the answer came. It was put up rather than shut up. At lunchtime on October 28th Michael Spicer announced that he had received the twenty-five letters required to trigger a vote of no confidence. IDS emerged from Conservative Central Office to say he would fight the no confidence motion. We all knew he was going to lose. It was obvious. He must surely have realised it himself.

He was gone the next day, by 90 votes to 75. It had been much closer than expected. If just eight votes had gone the other way, he would have survived, though mortally wounded. Like most other journalists at Westminster, I had expected him to get fifty at the very most. Iain Duncan Smith passed into history as the first Conservative Party leader not to fight a general election since Neville Chamberlain.

His successor was named very quickly. Within hours, David Davies said he would not be standing for the leadership and declared for Michael Howard. Liam Fox, Oliver Letwin and Stephen Dorrell quickly followed suit. Two days later, Ken Clarke also announced that he wouldn't stand. A week later, Michael Howard was elected unopposed.

Michael Howard had many fine qualities. He was good in the Commons, and is a much kinder, warmer man than his public image suggested. But the public image was the problem. Ann Widdecombe's disloyal remark that there is 'something of the night' about him had stuck. The *Daily Mirror* wasted no time with a front page depicting him as Dracula. He had also supported unpopular policies in the past, including Clause 28 and Margaret Thatcher's poll tax. His refusal to answer the same question fourteen times during an interview with Jeremy Paxman on the

BBC's *Newsnight* had left him with a reputation for being a bit of a slippery customer, clever but manipulative. Because of all this and more, I thought he had no chance of winning a general election. Surrounding himself with Ken Clarke and others who were seen as more empathetic and less abrasive might help but it wouldn't be enough.

It was an exhilarating week of political intrigue and I was very happy to be in the thick of it. Charles Kennedy did a live two-way with us in which he warned Michael Howard that the Lib Dems would be targeting his Folkestone and Hythe seat. On the Sunday, my package included interviews with Liam Fox, Michael Portillo, Cecil Parkinson and Oliver Letwin. No one, it seemed, would be standing in Michael Howard's way. The week culminated on Thursday 6th of November and the announcement from the 1922 committee in committee room fourteen that the party had a new leader.

While Adam was live with various senior Conservatives on Abingdon Green, I went to the Alton community centre in Roehampton, (in the marginal constituency of Putney) for Michael Howard's acceptance speech at four thirty p.m. An hour earlier, I had done a live from the podium where he was due to speak and I was supposed to talk live into the speech just before it began, but Sky News took a long and very unflattering live from Ann Widdecombe instead which was irritating. For the evening, I cut a package on Howard's day. Another Conservative leader, Blair's fourth.

The other big story that day was that Michael Fawcett, Prince Charles' senior valet, had won an injunction against the *Mail on Sunday* forbidding the paper from reporting an unspecified allegation. I had friends phoning all evening, asking what the allegation was. I was happy to fill them in, though of course we could not disclose it on air. I'm delighted to say I had no involvement in covering that story.

I spent two days covering the CBI annual conference at the International Convention Centre in Birmingham. Sky News business unit were doing most of the work, this was very much their story. My task was to do lives and packages around speeches by Tony Blair, Gordon Brown and Michael Howard. Business Unit colleagues were amazed that I knew precisely what Tony Blair was going to say before he said it. Simple: I had phoned Dave Hill, Alastair Campbell's successor as Downing Street director of communications, to get a full briefing. In their world, they saw this as the equivalent of insider trading!

The following Sunday, I was reporting on the terror threat at home and abroad in the wake of the bombings by al-Qaeda at the British Embassy in Istanbul and the HSBC building in Beşiktaş, while Jonny Wilkinson was writing himself into the pages of rugby history. I managed to catch the end of the Rugby World Cup final. With ten minutes to go in extra time, England and Australia were level at seventeen all when Wilkinson scored a drop goal. England won 20-17, and Jonny became a sporting legend.

On December 1st, Sky News Westminster hosted Christmas drinks for MPs at the Cinnamon Club, the old Westminster library in Great Smith Street. I met James Murdoch for the first time, he had his charm on full beam, and chatted to Michael Howard, David Davies, Tony Banks, Austin Mitchell and many, many others. Some were charming and refreshingly indiscreet, others were more guarded. As far as I was concerned, all conversations were confidential (except for unattributable background and for my own enlightenment and amusement), and the occasion was a chance to behave like human beings.

Tuition fees kept me busy for the first few days of December. It was the theme of a Tony Blair press conference with a supportive speech by Gordon Brown, and dominated PMQs that Wednesday. Students mounted a noisy demonstration outside Parliament. My generation had been very lucky. Tuition fees were paid for by the government and we also received a maintenance grant. I studied English so, basically, I was being paid to read books! Subsequent generations of students have not been so fortunate. We probably shouldn't forget that, despite all the vitriol heaped onto the Lib Dems after 2010, it was a Labour government which introduced tuition fees for students in higher education.

On December 14th, Saddam Hussein was captured hiding in a hole in the ground, bearded and looking totally deranged. What began as a rumour was confirmed by Tony Blair, first in a written statement then in a statement on camera, and by an American press conference in Baghdad at which President Bush's man, Paul Bremer, Provisional Coalition Administrator of Iraq, told the world triumphantly: "Ladies and gentlemen, we got him." That got me doing lives in Downing Street all day. The pictures of Saddam were extraordinary. Now, the questions were what happens next, when would he face trial, where and how? And who would judge him?

On December 17th Ian Huntley was convicted for the murders of Jessica Chapman and Holly Wells in Soham. I was covering the last PMQs before Christmas when the verdict came in from the Old Bailey. He got two life sentences while his girlfriend, Maxine Carr, got three and a half years for perverting the course of justice. She had given him a false alibi. I interviewed David Blunkett at the Home Office on the lessons to be learned from these awful, awful murders. The local police had not exactly covered themselves in glory, and social services had failed to spot Huntley despite his history of child abuse. I am against the death penalty, there have been too many miscarriages of justice, but Huntley made me wonder why.

Christmas at Westminster is an endless round of drinks parties, including at Number Ten the evening of the Huntley sentencing. I managed to get to five in a fairly typical evening. The first two were with Adam, the Department of Constitutional Affairs party hosted by Charlie Falconer, and the Foreign Office where we lost count of the number of ambassadors attending. I collected fellow Sky News correspondent, Tim Marshall, and our politics producer, Peter Diapre, at the Reform Club. Boring party, great location. Walking past the Foreign Press Association, we noticed a party was in full swing so, of course, we invited ourselves in. Finally, at The Red Lion pub in Whitehall, leaving drinks for two DTI press officers, Nicola Savage and my friend Richard Darlington. It is testament to my alcohol tolerance at the time that I was still absolutely coherent and perfectly able to walk in a straight line at the end of the evening. These days, I would barely make it past the first couple of drinks!

Just before Christmas, a story on speed cameras. The Conservatives were calling for penalty points to be abolished, and were asking: Why were there so many of these cameras? Good question.

They also had strong opinions on speed bumps, which they had introduced when they had been in government. They were supposed to be for accident black spots only. Ken Clarke once told me that if he had known they would be used in almost every street and road in the country, he would not have supported the wretched things.

CHAPTER 2

2004: The Hutton Inquiry. Morecambe Bay Cockle Pickers. Kathy Gun. Flour Bombs in the Commons. 'Gobby'. UKIP surge in the European Elections. The Butler Report. Ken Bigley. George W Re-elected. Boris Johnson Sacked. David Blunkett

The end of January was dominated by the Hutton Inquiry report. But first, there were plenty of other stories to cover.

The year began with an internal squabble, a mini turf war. Tony Blair was due to visit Basra. When the prime minister goes abroad, a political correspondent goes with him or her. There are two reasons for this. Firstly, that there will almost certainly be something, some event or development, that we need to talk to the prime minister about. Secondly, in case something happens during the trip. The foreign desk had assigned a general reporter without consulting the political unit. There was a small row. We won.

Michael Howard took out two pages in *The Times*, 'I believe', a Maurice Saatchi inspired assertion of values. Much of it was bathetic. For example: I believe everyone should be happy, healthy and wealthy. Well, er, yes!

Education Secretary Charles Clarke made a statement to the House on tuition fees. I interviewed him and the provost of University College London, Malcolm Grant, for a preview piece the evening before for *Sky News at Ten*. The proposed introduction of tuition fees for students in higher education was deeply dividing the Labour Party. MPs were due to vote on tuition fees on January 27th, definitely one of Tony's Troubles!

PMQs on January 14th was dominated by the forthcoming Hutton Inquiry Report. Michael Howard was not letting it go, despite Tony Blair's pleas to wait until Lord Hutton actually reported. I had already prepared a Hutton Inquiry preview piece, so I simply added the exchanges in the House of Commons to the top of it. From PMQs to Church House for a Tony Blair speech advocating tuition fees. I vox popped several university vice-chancellors who had been in the audience, not something that happens every day. Top quality vox pops!

David Kay resigned. He had led the weapons inspectors searching for WMD in Iraq. He now said he believed there hadn't been any, hugely embarrassing for both Bush and Blair. I was linking live from Downing Street into my packages on both David Kay's resignation, and on tuition fees. My David Kay effort was our lead story all day. The David Kay package and live was at the top of every hour, with the tuition fees story on the half hour. Rather oddly, a group of visiting teenagers asked for my autograph! Even more oddly, they got me to pose with them for a photo on the doorstep of Number Ten. My father had done the same when I was seven or eight years old. My parents may have been just a tiny bit over-ambitious.

We had most of the Hutton Report's findings before they were officially delivered. It leaked big time. The *Sun* had most of it and we had the rest. Gilligan's claims were 'unfounded', and the BBC's editorial and management processes were 'defective' in as much as they sprang to Gilligan's defence without properly checking the accuracy of his allegations. Nobody could have anticipated Dr Kelly's suicide and there had been no covert, underhand government strategy to name him as the BBC source. The dossier had not been 'sexed up', but accurately reflected the available intelligence at the time.

It was a Wednesday. PMQs was immediately followed by Lord Hutton's long statement followed by Tony Blair's statement in the House. I was busily packaging the story, with updates every hour, in a nice, warm studio in Westminster. Adam was doing the lives in Downing Street in a snow blizzard without an umbrella, which must have been distracting for the viewers. It certainly distracted and entertained us! I suggested to our producers that someone really should take Adam an umbrella, but no one did.

Of course, the newspapers screamed WHITEWASH (not Adam, but the Hutton Report!) but, within twenty-four hours, both the BBC Chairman Gavyn Davies and Director General Greg Dyke had resigned. Andrew Gilligan also resigned from the badly bruised BBC.

President Bush ordered an inquiry into the failure to find WMD in Iraq. Tony Blair followed suit and announced the Butler Inquiry to look into the intelligence that had taken the country to war. Former Cabinet Secretary Robin Butler would be digging far deeper than Lord Hutton, whose remit was restricted to the events directly leading to Dr David Kelly's death. I was live in Downing Street talking about the Butler Inquiry and waiting for it to be officially announced, an announcement which was delayed for twenty-four hours. When it came, I was cutting substantial packages on the inquiry's remit, to look at the veracity of the intelligence. The Lib Dems told us they would boycott the inquiry because it wouldn't question the role of politicians, the political process or any political interference. Like others, I felt the inquiry report, due in July, would just blame the intelligence services, not tell us anything we didn't already know, and that I could probably write the report myself now, in early February.

Next day, and more Hutton. The Commons was disrupted by protestors shouting from the public gallery when Tony Blair opened the debate on the Hutton Inquiry Report. The sitting had to be delayed for ten minutes. Other protesters daubed the word 'Whitewash' on the Downing Street gates. I packaged the story all day, with the luxury of having a producer, and a very good one, Jonathan Levy. My four-minute package was followed by live two-ways at 8 and 9 pm and into *Sky News at Ten*.

That evening, Baroness Emma Nicholson told me that she had some exclusive video of Saddam Hussein giving money to an Iranian terrorist group, the MKO. I asked her to sit on it until the next day, and not to tell anyone else. I got the pictures the following morning and interviewed Emma Nicholson about them. There were hours of tapes, some it very good material, but it was a bit of a nightmare transferring the poor-quality VHS. I cut a package for *Sky News at Ten*, which *Sunrise* also ran the next morning. A proper exclusive.

February 9th was the first relatively quiet or at least non-frenetic day for months. I covered a Michael Howard speech at Bloomberg's swish offices in Finsbury Square, 'The British dream'. I have to say I found it platitudinous. One live at 5.30 p.m. and a package which ran all evening, but only by virtue of him being the Leader of the Opposition.

In Morecambe Bay, at least twenty-one Chinese cockle pickers were drowned by the incoming tide. They were being paid far less than the local cockle pickers, spoke very little English, and were unfamiliar with the times of the tides. It emerged that they had been illegally trafficked into the country in ships' containers and been hired out by criminal gangs. The disaster, which I regarded as murder (a gang master was later convicted of manslaughter) made front page news, of course. The political angle, which I covered, centred on illegal immigration and their exploitation.

St Valentine's Day was also Michael Howard's one hundredth day as Conservative Party leader. I resisted a request to cut a package with no preparation at all (there had been no forward planning), and did lives all afternoon instead with a package for the evening, topped and tailed with two long PTCs, a sort of recorded doughnut. I was with Michael Howard at Morecambe Bay a few days later. Lives there, and at Lancaster police headquarters where he had a meeting. I was happily waffling away live on air when he emerged and we did an impromptu live interview. Perfect timing. We also interviewed the Bishop of Morecambe, local Chinese community leaders and local MP Geraldine Smith.

The next day, Michael Howard gave a speech in Burnley. We had been booked into a very shabby two-star hotel, which was two stars too many, so I transferred us to the splendid Dunkenhalgh country hotel just outside Accrington. It was my first and only time in Burnley, which gave me a chance to look at Turf Moor and to point out in future to Alastair Campbell that it really isn't a Premier League stadium!

Back in London, and the news that five Britons had been released from Guantánamo Bay. I had covered the story the previous month when it had first been suggested that they might be released so it came my way again. Foreign Secretary Jack Straw held a press conference to respond to two international events, the Libyan prime minister denying responsibility for the Lockerbie bombing and for the murder of WPC Yvonne Fletcher, and Vladimir Putin dismissing the Russian prime minister and government three weeks ahead of a presidential election. As so often with these press conferences, which we took live, I made sure I got to ask the first question.

The government suddenly and without explanation dropped the court case against Kathy Gun, a translator at GCHQ who had leaked information to the *Observer* newspaper and was being prosecuted under the Official Secrets Act. She had told the *Observer* that the Americans had requested compromising intelligence on diplomats from member states of the UN

Security Council ahead of a vote sanctioning the invasion of Iraq. Allegedly, the Americans were planning to bug the UN offices of several countries whose votes they needed, and were asking help from British intelligence to do so. Kathy Gun became the poster girl for anti-war activists. Her defence was that she wanted to stop any loss of life in a war she considered illegal. When her case came to court, on February 25th, it was dropped within half an hour because the prosecution, the government lawyers, failed to offer any evidence.

Of course, during my live two-ways, I was asked why the government had so suddenly and dramatically dropped the case. I had no idea! I could only speculate about the potential embarrassment if, during the trial, the documents she had revealed became exposed to public scrutiny, that the government did not want the whole issue of the legality of the war dragged through the courts, and that the government would probably say that our national security could in some way become compromised. To this day, I have seen no official explanation.

In 2019, Keira Knightley played the role of Kathy Gun in the film *Official Secrets*.

Clare Short waded into the story the next day with the astonishing claim that MI6 had tapped the phone of UN Secretary General Kofi Annan. Even in the extremely unlikely event of this being true, Short was a privy councillor and bound to secrecy rather than compromising MI6 operations. To have tapped Kofi Annan's phone would have been against international law, or at least two major international conventions, so Tony Blair was able to deal with her claim simply by saying that the UK always acts within the law, and branding her allegation as 'deeply irresponsible'. Short was portrayed in the press as being bitter and possibly slightly unhinged. I did lives into Sky News every hour all afternoon, a live for the now notorious Fox News in New York and, for some reason, another live two-way for Egyptian TV who had collared me while I was doing lives for Sky on Abingdon Green.

Another government whistle-blower emerged just two weeks after Kathy Gun's trial had ended in such confusion. Steven Moxon was a Home Office civil servant at the Immigration and Nationality Directorate in Sheffield. He claimed that immigration checks were being waived for anyone coming from the Eastern European countries which were due to join the European Union in May. It was a Wednesday, and I was packaging PMQs. His allegations were political dynamite because they suggested that, in effect, the figures were being massaged to disguise the anticipated mass migration from Eastern Europe after May. The ascension of the Eastern European countries to EU membership without any limits on immigration into the UK was extremely controversial. It still is.

On May 11th, one hundred and ninety-one people were killed and two thousand injured when terrorists attacked commuter trains in Madrid, three days before the Spanish general election. It was the worst ever terrorist attack in Spain and the worst in Europe since Lockerbie in terms of loss of life. The pictures coming in from Madrid were horrific. Of course, Sky News sent a team to the Spanish capital. My job, as a political correspondent, was to be live in Downing Street. The Spanish government was quick to blame ETA, the Basque separatist group, but the scale and coordination of the bombings seemed to me to be far too big for ETA, way beyond their capabilities and simply not their modus operandi. No warning had been given, and the attempt to kill as many people as possible looked far more like the work of al-Qaeda, although I also suggested that it was just possible that ETA and other terror groups had upped the ante, that a terrorist atrocity now had to be on a much larger scale to get attention. Frightening if true. ETA denied it and, by the evening, al-Qaeda admitted they had done it or, in the parlance of the time, 'claimed responsibility'. By the next day, Sky News was being anchored from Madrid and I was doing live two-ways with presenter Jeremy Thompson, another ex-ITN colleague.

Apart from the politics of the Spanish government, mid-election campaign, being so swift to blame ETA, the burning question for us was would something similar happen here? And if so, when and how? The answer came a year later in July 2005.

The Spanish government lost the election as the socialist opposition came to power claiming that the government had been weak on terrorism and still accusing ETA of carrying out the Madrid bombings. Whereas Aznar had had a close relationship with Tony Blair and had supported the overthrow of Saddam Hussein, the new Spanish government was cut from a very different cloth. One of the first acts of the new socialist prime minister, José Zapatero, was to announce the total withdrawal of Spanish forces from Iraq saying the war had been illegal, and to denounce Bush and

Blair who he said had gone to war based on a lie. I interviewed David Blunkett, Baroness (Liz) Symons and Robin Cook to get their reaction. I also interviewed Tony Benn who, of course, regarded Zapatero as a comrade in the struggle!

The government won a second vote on tuition fees at the end of March by a majority of 28, comfortable enough though hardly convincing given Labour's huge House of Commons majority. But it was enough. The decision had been made. I did lives before and after the vote, and interviewed NUS President Mandy Telford twice live during the debate. The Lib Dems had voted against the introduction of tuition fees, but that wouldn't be enough to save them in 2015.

Speculation was rife that the government would announce a referendum on the proposed new EU constitution. The BBC had 'breaking news' that they 'understood' that Tony Blair was about to announce a referendum. They were wrong, but I had to walk something of a tightrope between Downing Street's denials and speculation by a rival news organisation. We believed the source to be John Prescott. We also believed that the BBC may have 'sexed up' whatever he had said. By using a Michael Howard interview I had done earlier, I was able to speculate about when such a referendum might be held, and how the question might be framed. Did this add fuel to the fire of speculation that Tony Blair might go to the country in October? Could this be an election issue? Would it be in Labour's manifesto? Although I was fairly certain that the next general election would not come for another year, Gordon Brown's Budget had certainly felt like pre-election seduction.

Downing Street was also denying speculation that Tony Blair would stand down after a year or two if Labour won the next general election. Some Cabinet ministers were quietly briefing that, if re-elected, he would serve a full third term. It seemed absurd to me that he would go to the country saying, 'vote for me, but I'll only serve for a year or two' and become a lame duck prime minister. But that is precisely what he did do ahead of the 2005 election campaign which he fought on a sort of de facto joint leadership platform with Gordon Brown.

After the last PMQs of April, Jack Straw hosted a reception at the Foreign Office to celebrate the new Eastern European countries joining the EU. Tony Blair made a speech, which we took live. I had the pleasure of meeting the actress Rachel Weisz and of interviewing Egon Ronay, Hungary being one of the new EU members. He was very charming but also very old and rather deaf. It was a long interview! He was supposed to do a live down-the-line interview but he couldn't hear anything, so we scrapped that idea.

Tony Blair held a joint press conference with Italian Prime Minister Silvio Berlusconi. We were more intrigued by Berlusconi's bizarre hair than by anything he said. Jack Straw held another with the governor of Basra. I managed to negotiate getting the first question. Tony Blair launched Labour's local election campaign in Leeds. Press officer Matthew Doyle briefed me on the train from London. Arriving in Leeds mid-evening, I went for a stroll around the city centre. The streets were full of drunken yobs, and I quickly retreated back to our hotel. I had been to Leeds many times and had often stayed out late in pubs and clubs, but I had never seen it like this. Maybe Leeds United had lost that day.

Next morning, and lives ahead of Tony Blair's speech launching Labour's local election campaign. He arrived at the venue behind me during my ten a.m. live, perfect timing. I voiced live into his speech at ten forty-five a.m., and was back on air once he'd finished. By 1.40 p.m., I was on the train back to London, and home. A good morning's work.

Adam thought Tony Blair was in trouble with the PLP, some of whom thought he had become an electoral liability in the wake of the Iraq war. I thought it very unlikely that he would be going anywhere. He still seemed in good shape to win a third election victory. I had all day to cut a three-minute package for *Live at Five*, a luxury, including a PTC in Downing Street timed to coincide with Tony Blair's departure for PMQs.

Next day, it was off to Coventry where Tony Blair was doing a 'Big Conversation' event at the headquarters of Jaguar cars. I listened and did a live afterwards, but my attention, like everyone else's, was focused on Armed Forces Minister Adam Ingram telling the House of Commons that *Daily Mirror* pictures of British soldiers supposedly abusing Iraqi prisoners were fake. Given that Donald Rumsfeld was also making a surprise, unannounced visit to Baghdad, there was little further interest in my story from Coventry. The correct decision.

I was doing lives the next morning when the Queen's Lancashire Regiment held a press conference at which they said that the *Mirror*'s fake pictures put our soldiers' lives at risk. As soon as they said that, I suggested that *Daily Mirror* editor, Piers Morgan, was toast. I was right. He was sacked later that afternoon. Days later, the *Mirror* admitted that the pictures were fake, claiming to be the victims of a hoax. The pictures had apparently been set up in north west England and not in Iraq at all, but Piers Morgan refused to apologise, claiming the pictures illustrated the kind of abuse that was happening at the time.

A few days later, Tony Blair was in Ankara for bilateral talks with the Turks, while speculation about his leadership was still doing the rounds. Bizarrely, Gordon Brown and David Blunkett were in north Kensington, appearing on something called Youth Culture TV. They didn't look at all comfortable, down with the youth! I doorstepped Gordon Brown on his way in and out. Not surprisingly, he was saying nothing about the party leadership. But in a one-to-one interview, David Blunkett gave me something he hadn't given the BBC or ITN, who had gone before me while I was trying to see if Gordon Brown would support Tony Blair's leadership. A very full answer, totally and unequivocally supporting Tony Blair. Excellent. The BBC and ITN were most satisfactorily annoyed!

Peter Fiddich once wrote a piece in *The Financial Times* in which he suggested that most journalists' ambitions were firstly to impress their editor, secondly to confound the opposition, with informing the audience/readership coming a very poor third. I put the third ambition first, but it was always fun to beat the opposition.

Fiddich also wrote, in the same article, about how newsrooms had changed. From noisy, smokey places, with people shouting, phones ringing, typewriters clattering away, half empty bottles of whisky ready to hand, they had become like 'the Bradford and Bingley on a quiet Monday afternoon', full of earnest young things in suits typing away at silent computer keyboards. I empathised with this as it had been my experience over the past twenty years.

There was more disruption in the House of Commons during PMQs when Fathers 4 Justice protesters threw purple dye flour bombs from the West Gallery aiming at Tony Blair. Several MPs dived for cover. Blair didn't react. PMQs was suspended. The flour bombs were harmless, but the incident could have been far worse. There had been a serious breach of security. I went straight to St Stephen's entrance to do lives. How had they got in without proper searching? What were the security implications? Should the public be excluded from the House of Commons? I was doing live interviews with MPs on these and other questions. Subsequently, Perspex screens were erected in front of the public gallery to prevent such an attack from happening again.

In the evening I was live in Downing Street. German Chancellor Gerhard Schroeder was coming for dinner, but there was only one story, the House of Commons security breach. For once, Tony Blair answered my shouted question.

I disliked shouting questions, unless a politician was being deliberately evasive or had done something terrible and hadn't resigned or at least spoken about it. We were blessed with the BBC's Paul Lambert, known universally and affectionately as 'Gobby'. He was the undisputed master of 'the shout', his dulcet cockney tone booming on the news shouting at politicians, usually along the lines of, "Will you resign, minister?" Despite being from rival organisations, he would often have a mischievous conversation with us. "So, what's the shout?" he would ask, and we would discuss what was most likely to get a response or at least a reaction. He smoked like a chimney and would often sidle up to me. "Got a fag mate?"

Government ministers would frequently breeze past him as he shouted an often quite rude question at them with a cheerful, "Good morning, Gobby".

Such was the universal use of his nickname that when he was prime minister, David Cameron, taking questions at a press conference, pointed at him to ask the next question. "Gobby. Er, I mean Paul." In common with everyone else at Westminster, I was very sad to hear the news that Paul had died in April 2020. He was only sixty-one. As Gobby, he was a Westminster legend.

Between 1995 and 2002, four British Army Logistics Corps trainees had died in obscure circumstances at Deepcut Barracks in Surrey. They had been fatally shot, apparently self-inflicted. One such incident might be understandable. Four was not. Had the army failed in its duty of care? Was bullying endemic at Deepcut? In short, what the hell was going on? The families of Sean Benton, Cheryl James, Geoff Gray and James Collinson wanted answers. After initial investigations, coroners' verdicts had been suicide in the case of Sean Benton with open verdicts on the others, who were only seventeen and eighteen years old. The newspapers had exposed what they reported as widespread abuse of trainees at the barracks. Now, on May 24th, the government was to decide whether or not their deaths warranted a public inquiry, something their families had been demanding. I interviewed them outside the Ministry of Defence before a statement in the House by Armed Forces Minister Adam Ingram. There was to be no public inquiry. The angry families held a press conference immediately afterwards. We took that live, and I packaged the story. To this day, and despite subsequent inquests, the deaths of their children have still not been explained to the satisfaction of their families.

It was ten years to the day since the deal, non-deal or misunderstanding between Tony Blair and Gordon Brown at the Granita restaurant in Islington. The deal, or non-deal or misunderstanding was, supposedly, that Gordon Brown would give Tony Blair a clear run at the Labour leadership but that, if elected prime minister, Blair would only serve two terms and then hand over to Brown. That time was almost up. Although both men denied that a deal had been agreed, Blair had conceded to Brown at around that time if not at that actual meal more or less free rein over large swathes of domestic policy. The story was well worth a package.

For local elections night I was in Hastings, a marginal council where, as expected, Labour lost control. Labour had 15 seats, the Conservatives had 13 and the Lib Dems 4, so no overall control. Lives every hour from 8 p.m. until 3 a.m. Unusually, we managed to get the result before it was announced, so we were able to break it citing party activists as our source. They weren't!

From the local elections to Brussels for the European elections. We got ourselves an excellent live position inside the parliament chamber. We did lives every hour as the results came in from four p.m. until two thirty a.m. the next morning. On a very low turnout, the Conservatives won twenty-seven seats and Labour nineteen, but what was most newsworthy was the UKIP surge from just three seats to twelve, the same number as the Lib Dems. After a few hours' sleep, we were back doing lives the next morning, including a live interview with European Parliament President Pat Cox. John Reid, sent out to spin for Labour, described the election as 'disappointing' for Labour but 'disastrous' for the Conservatives. In truth, it was pretty bad for both of them.

Back in Westminster the next day, the spin went into overdrive. Michael Howard made a speech, Tony Blair held a press conference, and I interviewed Charles Kennedy at the European Parliament office where he was posing with the newly-elected Lib Dem MEPs. The Lib Dems hadn't done badly, up from ten MEPs to twelve, but it had hardly been the breakthrough they had been hoping for.

Tim Henman lost his Wimbledon quarter-final against an unseeded Croat, Mario Ancic, and in straight sets. The three saddest words in the English language at the time? "Come on Tim!"

Home Secretary David Blunkett was having a very public row with Humberside Chief Constable David Westwood. He accused the Humberside force of failing to alert anyone about the previous crimes of Soham killer, Ian Huntley, which included police investigations into indecent assault and rape. The Bichard Report, launched the day after Huntley was convicted, led to the introduction of CRB checks, now the norm.

After a few days working at the UK Defence Academy in Shrivenham, I did preview lives and packages looking ahead to the Butler Report on Iraq, expected the following week. Would he criticise the government as well as the spooks? And how strongly? The previous day, the US Senate Security Committee had crucified the CIA. I did lives, packages, and doughnuts all day, up to including 10 p.m., with a fresh package for the following morning's *Sunrise* programme. And this was just the preview!

When the Butler Report was published, its main criticism of the government was Tony Blair's tendency toward informality, which the report labelled 'sofa government'. This suggested that too many discussions were being had and too many decisions taken in informal meetings rather than at Cabinet. I found this perplexing. Which prime minister has not had meetings, on the sofa or otherwise, with his or her inner circle to thrash out policy and strategy?

As for the intelligence services, Butler concluded that Saddam Hussein had intended to renew the development of WMD once the UN weapons inspectors were out of the way.

The day after the Butler Report, I was back in Leicester for the second time in just over a month for the Leicester South by-election, triggered by the death of popular Labour MP Jim Marshall. The by-election was being seen as a referendum on the Iraq war, and Blair was duly punished when the Lib Dems won the seat, overturning a Labour majority of more than 13,000. On the same day, in another by-election, Labour held on to the seat of Birmingham Hodge Hill, but only just. Future Cabinet minister Liam Byrne's majority was a mere 460, down from more than 11,000.

Tony Blair liked to boast that he had never lost a by-election to the Conservatives during his ten years in office. He could not say the same about the Liberal Democrats. Liam Byrne achieved a level of notoriety when he left his job as chief secretary to the Treasury after Labour lost the 2010 general election. He left a note for his successor, Liberal Democrat MP David Laws: *I'm afraid there is no money. Kind regards, good luck!* It was a joke, and not at all untypical of the humorous notes outgoing Cabinet ministers left their successors from a rival party, but that didn't stop the new coalition government making hay, using it to justify the austerity cuts they were introducing. It was light-hearted, a joke and private, but politics can be a dirty business.

It had been a good night for the Lib Dems, not too bad for Labour, but fairly awful for the Conservatives who were down from second to third place in both seats. Having done the usual election night workload of live two-ways from 10 p.m. until 3 a.m. with live guests including Patricia Hewitt for Labour, Sarah Teather for the triumphant Lib Dems, Sir Peter Soulsby, the defeated Labour candidate, and the rather odd Yvonne Ridley who had stood for George Galloway's Respect Party, it was wheels up at six o'clock the next morning for the aftermath. Our first live was at 7 a.m. I had sent an elaborate and comprehensive package for *Sunrise* the previous night, so they were happy with that for the first hour of their programme which began at 6 a.m. We grabbed some breakfast before our next live at 8 o'clock and then headed to local Lib Dem HQ for a live interview with Party leader Charles Kennedy. It was an enormous bun fight, but I asked all the questions. I didn't let anyone else get a word in! We took it all live, and so did the BBC who had two live cameras, one on Charles and the other on me, so BBC viewers were treated to the Sky News correspondent asking all the questions, which must have annoyed the BBC bosses. I certainly hoped so.

A couple of days later, we had fun chasing Robert Kilroy-Silk around the European Parliament building in Strasbourg. He was actually a good sport, and stopped to speak to us on camera whenever we popped up after lying in wait for him. It was the first session of the newly elected European Parliament. The UKIP MEPs walked out. They held a press conference at eleven thirty a.m. The UKIP leader was a former Conservative MP, Roger Knapman, but Robert Kilroy-Silk was the star turn. We took the press conference live, and I'm afraid I hogged the first half dozen questions. We did a live with Kilroy-Silk at midday, sent a package to Sky News, interviewed outgoing President of the European Parliament Pat Cox for Sky News Ireland, and that was it. The producers back at Sky News were happy with our package and didn't require any more lives. So we had a chance to see Strasbourg and look around the cathedral.

We had a slightly bizarre experience that evening. We had slipped over the border into Germany for dinner in Offenburg (which we renamed Sodoffenburg). It was a quiet civilized meal, cameraman, producer, one of the satellite engineers who had brought his girlfriend, and me. The food was very good but the wine was off. We sent it back. The poor waitress returned to tell us her boss had said the wine was fine. Eventually, she agreed to let us order another bottle, but failed to bring it. Finally, midway through dinner, she told us that we weren't allowed to have wine! "It is not permitted." Very strange.

Cameraman Colin Hamilton told her we would not be paying. Colin has a dry, wicked sense of humour but doesn't suffer fools. He's also Irish, and not averse to a row. The waitress went away and returned again to tell us that if we wouldn't pay they would call the police. Fine, we said, go ahead and call them. She was back two minutes later with a most bizarre proposition. "OK, don't pay. But if you don't leave at once, we'll call the police." Er, we could live with that! It was very odd. I have no idea of the thought process or the psychology behind such a decision. Maybe it was just a kind of bourgeois, quiet town in Germany mentality, anything to avoid a row or any kind of conflict or confrontation? We were completely perplexed.

Next morning, as we were leaving, there was a bomb scare at Strasbourg airport which was evacuated for an hour. Maybe the fear gripping Europe had affected the owner of the restaurant in Sodoffenburg. Perhaps he thought we might be Irish terrorists? Who knows?

Back in London, we heard that Peter Mandelson was to be the next European commissioner for trade before his appointment was officially announced. I was live in Downing Street, so I missed a drinks reception with Gordon Brown at the Treasury. Government departments held summer drinks receptions every year as well as Christmas parties. While I'd been in Strasbourg, I had also missed Michael Howard's drinks reception at Conservative Central Office. On this day, July 22nd, the Conservatives moved out of their beautiful building in Smith Square to an ugly office block in Victoria Street.

Michael Howard's leadership of the Conservative Party, eight months in, appeared to be having very little effect on the opinion polls. Labour remained comfortably ahead. That gave me a story to package for the evening on a quiet Monday at the end of July. I did a package on the sixtieth anniversary of the Warsaw uprising, a subject about which I knew a lot, and another the next day when John Scarlett began his new job as head of MI6.

The England football manager, Sven-Göran Eriksson, who was married, was in trouble after the *News of the World* claimed that he had had affairs with, among others, TV presenter and fellow Swede, Ulrika Jonsson. At FA headquarters, I interviewed Swedish reporters who were doorstepping the building. They thought the story was nonsense, that a person's private life should remain private, and asked me, "why are the British so weird?"

It was summer holiday time and we headed for Morocco, staying in Agadir, Marrakech and Essaouira, where my wife Marion's friend Peter had a house. In Marrakech, we stayed at the fabulous La Mamounia hotel set in lavish royal gardens. Once Winston Churchill's favourite winter retreat, when we arrived our room wasn't ready so they very kindly upgraded us to the suite next to the Churchill suite. Result!

In early September, Tony Blair conducted a small Cabinet reshuffle. At the beginning of the week, Andrew Smith had resigned as work and pensions secretary. He was a Gordon Brown supporter, so there was the usual speculation about what had become known as the TB-GBs, the power struggle at the top of government. The speculation was fuelled by the expected return to Cabinet of arch-Blairite Alan Milburn, the former health secretary. after fourteen months out of government to 'spend more time with his family'. Tony Blair dodged all reshuffle questions at his monthly press conference on the Tuesday, telling us to wait until Friday, when the expected change was announced and Alan Milburn returned to Cabinet as minister for the Cabinet Office and chancellor of the Duchy of Lancaster.

On that Friday, I did a very long live into the lunchtime news on the reshuffle and on the TB-GB issue. It was a quiet news day, the bulletin was short of stories, so they kept me talking, filling airtime, by throwing in random questions about fox hunting and about Northern Ireland. A classic example of why, as a specialist correspondent, you need a hinterland of knowledge.

Andrew Smith, by the way, was the thirty-fifth and final MP to nominate Jeremy Corbyn for leadership of the Labour Party in 2015. With just minutes to spare, his nomination meant that Corbyn reached the thirty-five nominations needed. Andrew Smith did not support Jeremy Corbyn but, like others, had said he wanted a 'broad debate' about the direction of the party. It was a decision that would come back to bite him and the others when Corbyn was so unexpectedly elected party leader.

That autumn, party conference season began with the Lib Dems in Bournemouth. I did a preview piece on the eve of conference with my by now usual stunt of a PTC at the podium on stage. The first two days of the conference were predictable enough, interviews with Charles Kennedy and the obligatory shots of the party leader walking along the promenade, but day three was completely overshadowed by news from Baghdad.

Ken Bigley was a civil engineer who had been kidnapped in Baghdad, along with two American colleagues, Jack Hensley and Eugene Armstrong. Their captors, an Islamic terrorist group headed by Abu Musab al-Zarqawi, released a video of the three men kneeling. They threatened to behead them if their demands for the release of Iraqi prisoners were not met. They killed Eugene Armstrong on September 20th and released a video of his murder. From Bournemouth, we were doing lives and getting reaction to this awful news. Within hours, they released a second horrific video of the second American, Jack Hensley, being beheaded. Sky News did a live interview with Ken Bigley's distraught brother Paul. I had spoken to a contact at the Ministry of Defence who told me they believed all three men had been beheaded and that al-Zarqawi was simply releasing the videos one by one. I did not report that on air.

Ken Bigley was murdered on October 7th. Al-Zarqawi didn't get his just desserts until June 2006, when he was killed by a laser-guided bomb from an American jet.

Meanwhile, the Lib Dems conference continued. Charles Kennedy delivered an uncharacteristically dull speech and fluffed a few critical lines but, of course, he got a standing ovation anyway. I had done a profile of him the day before, focussing on his health which I thought didn't look that great. On the day, I did lives and packages before and after his speech, and vox popped his rapturous Lib Dem audience.

From Bournemouth, after two days off at home in north London, it was off to Blackpool for the Labour Party conference. On the eve of conference, I doorstepped Foreign Secretary Jack Straw, who stopped to give me a very good, and exclusive, interview about Ken Bigley. It was September 25th, and Ken Bigley's fate was still unknown. I did several other interviews that evening, including a very good one with Neil Kinnock on TB-GB. We had Ken Bigley's brother Paul live on the phone. He said he had new information that his brother was still alive and criticised the government, and Tony Blair specifically, for not doing enough. He used emotional language, accusing Tony Blair's policies and the invasion of Iraq as the 'kiss of death' for his brother.

It was an early start the next morning for lives before and after Gordon Brown's conference speech. This kept me busy from 7 a.m. until 3 p.m. After that, I had to go to a Progress fringe meeting to get Alan Milburn. The meeting was very boring and went on and on for more than two hours in a very hot, stuffy room. I was happily contemplating taking a short break when some video emerged of Jack Straw shaking hands with Robert Mugabe in New York. I knew where Jack Straw would be that evening, at the Asia Night reception. It fell to me to go there on the basis that I was the one he was most likely to talk to. I had to wait for nearly two hours as he was very late arriving, but there are worse fates. Asia Nights were always fun and with excellent food. We also filmed a bit, the pictures being far more eye-catching than the visually boring debates from the conference hall. And Jack Straw gave me the sound bite I had been waiting for, as he almost always did.

Tony Blair's conference speech was as good as ever, a kind of calming vicar's homily to balance Gordon Brown's fiery, passionate sermon of the day before. He was interrupted twice by anti-war protestors. They must have been accredited to have got in, security was tight with endless checking of passes. Having said that, I had got onto the conference floor without once having to show any ID. I did live vox pops afterwards, a by now regular practice which had been dubbed back at base, 'Glen's friends', my live vox pops being cued by the director in the gallery as, "… and cut to Glen's friends"!

There were five days between Labour in Blackpool and the Conservatives' annual conference in Bournemouth. I had some time off but also did some work, including a live two-way with Fox News about Ken Bigley on October 2nd. Tony Blair was recovering at Chequers after treatment for his irregular heartbeat. His condition was easily treated and not in any way debilitating but, of course, the health of the prime minister was important news. Although Tony Blair's health was of interest, it was of no great concern. That didn't stop some members of his own party muttering darkly about his health being another reason to change leader, although they didn't do so on camera. The party was restive and still deeply divided over the invasion of Iraq.

I did a couple of lives on the Sunday afternoon before the conference. My colleague, Jon Craig, was doing most of them, he'd arrived in Bournemouth before me and already had his feet firmly under the table, as it were. I did the eve of conference package, including interviews with Liam Fox and Oliver Letwin, Michael Howard's arrival at his hotel and, yes, a PTC at the podium on stage. Again!

Opposition party conferences are generally less intense than those of the party in government. They are not announcing government policy. On day one, I packaged a not very interesting Liam Fox speech, interviewed Malcolm Rifkind, David Cameron and, at his book signing, William Hague and did a preview piece looking ahead to Michael Howard's first leader's speech.

In the evening, our Sky News team were eating in the Red Panda Chinese restaurant, a vast, cavernous place which was packed. Suddenly, Jimmy Saville appeared. He proceeded to visit every table, shaking hands and posing for pictures. Every table except one. We didn't want him anywhere near us, and he must have caught the vibe especially from me and our politics producer Peter Lowe. I thought there was something very creepy about him and found him repulsive. There had been rumours, but this was years before his exposure as a serial child sex offender following his death in 2011.

On the morning of Michael Howard's speech, Paul Sykes withdrew his financial support for UKIP, which was obviously very good news for the Tories. Howard's speech went well. Iain Duncan Smith wasn't exactly a hard act to follow. I packaged it, long packages which were the lead story all afternoon and evening. Parties that evening included the *Telegraph*, Bloomberg and the BBC. The *Telegraph* parties usually had the best gossip and the highest headcount of Conservative MPs. Bloomberg's were the most lavish and generous, and the BBC people were usually open and friendly despite our rivalry.

It was crime the next day. Shadow Home Secretary David Davis gave his conference speech and he and Michael Howard visited a drugs rehabilitation centre which, as intended, provided good pictures for my package of the day. I also did a piece on Young Tories, which included a picture sequence set to music, Cliff Richard's 'The Young Ones'. I wasn't taking the mickey. Well, not much. I liked to think that, if he'd seen it, Rik Mayall would have been amused.

Back in Westminster, post conference season, and a Tony Blair speech on welfare reform, 'The Opportunity Society'. I packaged that for *Live at Five*, and did just one live after a meeting of the PLP that evening. They appeared to have calmed down, the anti-Blair sentiment was receding.

Next day, and to Downing Street for an interview with Tony Blair, who had been meeting European Commission President José Manuel Barroso. A fairly long interview in which he revealed very little. In the afternoon, a Pensions Commission report that basically said we're all doomed, and a Jack Straw statement in the House finally admitting that the claim that Saddam Hussein had had WMD ready to launch 'within forty-five minutes' had been wrong. At the lobby briefing that afternoon, we spent forty minutes trying to get the PMOS Tom Kelly to explain why Tony Blair wouldn't apologise for the intelligence being so inaccurate. Tom's favourite phrase when he couldn't or wouldn't answer a question was 'we don't discuss processology', whatever the hell that was supposed to mean.

The very next day, Tony Blair did, indeed, apologise at PMQs for the inaccuracy of the intelligence while maintaining, of course, that Britain had gone to war in good faith.

The following Monday was my birthday, and a busy day in Westminster. In the morning, Jack Straw held a press conference with the Palestinian foreign minister. I did a live on that and another after the eleven a.m. lobby briefing. Geoff Hoon announced that more British troops would be deployed to Iraq to support the Americans fighting the insurgency. I packaged that and did live doughnuts at 5, 6 and 7 p.m. I still managed to escape in time to celebrate my birthday in the evening with Marion and daughter Maddie, friends, champagne and chocolate cake.

On October 22nd, the kidnappers of aid worker Margaret Hassan released a video of her in captivity. She was forced on camera to urge Tony Blair to withdraw British troops from Iraq. She had been taken three days earlier. Margaret Hassan worked for CARE International and had been doing fantastic work in Baghdad for many years. I did lives every hour all afternoon and evening. Jack Straw issued a statement calling for her immediate release which I managed to get twenty minutes before the Press Association. In Baghdad, hundreds of people took to the streets demanding her freedom. Many of them were or had been her patients. She had helped many Iraqi children suffering from leukaemia and spinal injuries. It was thought that the murderer of Ken Bigley just two weeks earlier, Abu Musab al-Zarqawi, was behind her kidnap. Despite increasing hopes that she would be released, her fate remains officially unknown. It is believed that she was murdered by her kidnappers two weeks later.

Much closer to home, we got the terrible news that day that our former ITN colleague, Owen Smith, had collapsed and died of a suspected heart attack. He was just fifty years old. A home news editor during my time at ITN, Owen was not only a brilliant journalist but also one of the funniest people I've ever met, with a razor-sharp Liverpool wit and a joke for every occasion. Working with him had always been an absolute joy.

MPs voted in favour of the introduction of Las Vegas-style super casinos. Twenty-nine Labour MPs rebelled, claiming that they would encourage gambling and result in more gambling addiction, but several cities had been lobbying hard to get a super casino which they saw as a money spinner and a way of rejuvenating run-down areas. At first, there were no restriction on the number of these super casinos but, as the bill passed through the committee stage, Culture Secretary Tessa Jowell was persuaded to limit the number to eight, down from the original proposal of around forty. Anti-gambling and church groups remained absolutely opposed to their introduction.

George W Bush was re-elected. He had won the popular vote, which he had failed to do in 2000, even though John Kerry had got over four million more votes than Al Gore had managed. It all came down to the twenty electoral votes of Ohio. I commented at the time, though not on air, that the fate of the free world depended on a bunch of redneck farmers from Ohio! Family, Faith and Flag had been the three Fs that had delivered victory for Bush. Sky News was anchoring from Washington, I was live in Westminster although, of course, I would far rather have been in the States. Tony Blair did a statement at 8pm congratulating George W, and I packaged British political reaction.

The *Daily Telegraph* was ecstatic about Bush's victory, while the *Mirror*'s front page was US election disaster see pages two, three, four, five, six and seven and asked, how can 59, 054, 087 people be so dumb? But that was not my story. Yasser Arafat was very ill in hospital in Paris, and I was live all afternoon on rumours that he had died. He hadn't, but he did pass away a week later at the age of seventy-five. He had been one of my first interviews with a major foreign leader back in 1991.

After a few days training at the UK Defence Academy in Shrivenham on the topic of Op Telic (the Iraq operation), back at Sky News there were two stories for me to cover. Yasser Arafat's funeral service was held in Cairo, after which he was buried in Ramallah. The Israelis would not allow him to be buried in Jerusalem. The scenes were chaotic, with tens of thousands of people turning out. They mobbed his coffin. British and other foreign nationals were evacuated from Sierra Leone.

Then came the big political news of the day: Michael Howard sacked Boris Johnson. He had lied about an affair with Petronella Wyatt. As always, it was the lie and attempted cover up which led to political downfall. The *Mail* and the *News of the World* had got the story and were about to splash it all over their front pages. I did lives all evening and put together a Boris Johnson political obit which was, as we now know, a little premature!

Nevertheless, the Boris Johnson story kept me busy all the next day with lives and packages leading the news every hour. One of the most colourful if gaffe-prone politicians, it seemed his political career was over. No one imagined for a moment that he might one day become prime minister. No one except, perhaps, for himself.

I put together another political obit, that of Home Secretary David Blunkett. This was also premature, but only by a few weeks.

Fox hunting was debated, yet again. I was live with Countryside Alliance leaders at their demo outside Parliament. Eventually, after much to-ing and fro-ing between the Commons and the Lords, known at Westminster as ping-pong, the Commons speaker invoked the Parliament Act meaning the Lords could no longer block the will of the Commons and that fox hunting would become illegal the following February. That same evening, Tony Blair was meeting the Hungarian prime minister at Number Ten and taking questions. I got some very good answers on fox hunting, Iraq and the Olympics. The big story of that day in mid-November was that the British bid to host the 2012 Olympic Games had been formally submitted.

A few days working at the Royal College of Defence Studies at their magnificent mansion in Mayfair. The RCDS, the most prestigious arm of the UK Defence Academy, is a unique institution with a one-year course in defence diplomacy for senior military officers, diplomats and civil servants from the UK and allied nations. It has been a privilege to support the course for nearly twenty years and counting.

David Blunkett was under increasing pressure. The allegation against him was that he had helped to fast-track the renewal of a work permit for his ex-lover's nanny. Details were emerging slowly. On December 5th, I did lives and packages on the story every hour for ten hours. It was the only political story making headlines. David Blunkett would survive in office for just another ten days.

In Belfast, a power-sharing agreement had reached an impasse, with Ian Paisley demanding to see photographic evidence of the IRA decommissioning its weapons. Gerry Adams and the Sinn Féin leadership had talks with Tony Blair in Downing Street. I did lives before and after the meeting and we took Gerry Adams live when he emerged from Number Ten. I did a live two-way for Sky News Ireland, but then switched back to the David Blunkett story. To add to his troubles, he had been rather rude about the competence of some of his Cabinet colleagues. Michael Howard had had fun with this at the previous Wednesday's PMQs.

Worse was to come for Blunkett. The *Mail* had a story that his ex-lover Kimberly Quinn's nanny had also been fast-tracked for a second visa application so that she could go on holiday to Austria.

Next day, December 15th, the *Mail* broke its story. Although the Austrian ambassador said it wasn't true, Michael Howard was relentless at PMQs, at one point hurling a copy of Stephen Pollard's biography of Blunkett across the dispatch box at Tony Blair for dramatic effect. The pressure on David Blunkett seemed unstoppable. The only question at Westminster was whether or not he could survive until Christmas.

By mid-afternoon, the rumour mill was out of control. At four p.m., David Blunkett failed to appear at a meeting of senior police officers he had been supposed to chair and which had been flagged up as 'business as usual'. This set alarm bells ringing. I dusted off the political obit I'd prepared in November, and headed over to the House to see what I could glean. He resigned at six p.m., not only because he had been so publicly rude about Cabinet colleagues and had become an embarrassment but also, crucially, because an email had revealed that the nanny's residency application had, indeed, been fast-tracked.

David Blunkett protested his innocence but said he took responsibility for the actions of Home Office officials. It felt almost Shakespearean, that he had given up his political career for the sake of his two-year-old son and Kimberly Quinn's unborn child. She was seven months pregnant. There was a lot of personal sympathy for him, but also a large majority of opinion in Westminster that he had to go. Of course, the story kept me busy doing lives and packages all that day and the next.

David Blunkett had been a successful Home Secretary. Crime had fallen to an all-time low, the rise in the number of asylum seekers had been reversed. The Sangatte refugee camp in France had been closed, and refugee numbers had dropped from one hundred and ten thousand to fewer than thirty thousand. He had also updated the archaic laws still governing homosexuality, while also increasing protection against paedophiles, rapists and other sex offenders. Although it felt like it at the time, this was not the end of his career at the political top table. He was back in Cabinet after the following May's general election as secretary of state for work and pensions.

Lobby journalists had a lock-in to read Sir Alan Budd's report into the Blunkett affair at eleven forty-five the next morning before it was officially released. I did a live before Sir Alan's press conference at midday, breaking the story. He concluded that there had been no cover up, the nanny's residency application had been fast-tracked but there was no trace of Blunkett's fingerprints, no evidence that he had personally intervened. However, there was, 'a chain of events linking Mr Blunkett to the change in the decision'. It was, in effect, an open verdict, case not proven. Once again, I was doing lives on David Blunkett's resignation.

I had a whole week off for Christmas. On Boxing Day, Phuket in Thailand was hit by a tsunami. I knew Thailand fairly well, I had been there several times. I had visited Phuket on a press trip in the early 1980s when there had been just one hotel and a lot of rubber plantations. Now, Phuket's seafront was wall to wall hotels and packed with tourists. Sky News was very well covered very quickly and, although as a political correspondent I had no role in covering natural disasters, I called the foreign desk in case they needed extra reporters. I was back working in Westminster a couple of days later. The number of dead had reached one hundred and twenty thousand, up to five million people were homeless and there were fears of an outbreak of cholera with awful images of decomposing bodies, especially in Sri Lanka. I interviewed International Development Secretary Hilary Benn, and the high commissioners of India, Sri Lanka and the Maldives. A huge international relief operation was under way and I reported on that, but I really wanted to be in South East Asia.

CHAPTER 3

2005: Blair's Third Election victory. Gleneagles Summit. Winning the 2012 Olympics. 7/7. The King of Bosnia

2005 was election year. Could Tony Blair win Labour an historic third term? Or would he be scuppered by the invasion of Iraq? Would the Lib Dems finally break the two-party stranglehold in the House of Commons, the two-party system? Could Michael Howard win, or at least force a hung parliament? And what of Gordon Brown? Would he make a move for the party leadership? Before or after the election?

All these questions and more would be resolved in May, but first we had to get there.

I returned to work on January 3rd. The Foreign Office revealed that one hundred and fifty-nine Britons were missing following the South East Asian Tsunami. Most of them had been in Thailand. Tony Blair returned from a holiday in Egypt. I was live at the Foreign Office every hour all afternoon and evening. The total number of people confirmed killed by the Tsunami had reached almost 145,000 and was still rising. Foreign Secretary Jack Straw was due to go to Indonesia and Thailand. I was keen to go with him if there was any room on his plane, but the Foreign Office told me he would be going by scheduled flight and there would be no arrangements for the press. The government offered to send a company of Gurkhas to Indonesia to help.

I had a day in the Hatfield and Welwyn Garden constituency to see if anyone there actually cared about TB-GB or if this was simply of interest only within the Westminster bubble, and to see if the Iraq war really was an election issue.

Hatfield and Welwyn Garden was a Labour marginal held by Public Health Minister Melanie Johnson. We interviewed her, the Conservative candidate, Grant Shapps, the editor of the local newspaper and a lot of local voters, vox pops. It appeared that neither TB-GB nor the Iraq war were anywhere near the top of peoples' concerns. Local issues prevailed. Nevertheless, Grant Shapps won the seat for the Conservatives in May.

The next day, Gordon Brown, John Prescott and Alan Milburn launched Labour's election campaign poster in Billingsgate. I talked live into and out of this somewhat unspectacular event before heading to Downing Street where Ian Paisley was once again having a meeting with Tony Blair.

The Foreign Office announced that Jack Straw would go to Auschwitz for the sixtieth anniversary of the liberation of the Nazi death camp. I had been there as a child and as an adult, but the job had already been assigned by the foreign desk. I did lives all afternoon and evening. I would go again, some years later, with Prime Minister Gordon Brown.

It had been an intense few days, so it came as a bit of light relief to go to Toulouse for the launch of the A380 Airbus super jumbo. We were spoilt by Virgin Atlantic, who flew cameraman Martin Smith, producer Nick Ludlam and me first class. In the Virgin lounge at Heathrow, I chatted at length with Richard Branson about fighting malaria, Blair-Brown, etc. He only chatted with us, rather than working the room. I put this down to his shyness. He was more gregarious at the superb dinner he hosted that evening in Toulouse.

Although this sounds like a Virgin Atlantic PR freebie, the launch of the A380 super jumbo was, without doubt, a legitimate story. Next morning, we drove from the hotel in convoy with Richard Branson, who did the first live into Sky News at seven a.m. I took over from eight a.m., a live with Airbus boss, John Leahy. The launch itself was slightly naff, not to my taste, a lot of razzamatazz. I continued doing lives while, in between, Martin, who was more used to war zones and covering natural disasters than champagne freebies, got some great shots of the aircraft from every conceivable angle. We fed a package and did our last live doughnut at six o'clock. Our efforts were very well received back at base, thanks largely to Martin's pictures. Our EasyJet flight home that evening was something of a come down, literally back to earth with a bump.

The day after we returned from our little French jaunt, Robert Kilroy-Silk quit UKIP and launched a new political party, Veritas. So far as I could see, this was a one-way ticket to political oblivion. Next day, I covered

Michael Howard visiting a training centre for the unemployed in Southwark, a Charles Kennedy press conference, and Tony Blair out and about in Watford. I had all three party leaders out campaigning, but my package only just squeezed onto the news. It was inauguration day for George W Bush in Washington, and Sky News had gone completely Bush-tastic!

Next day, Culture Secretary Tessa Jowell announced a crackdown on loutish, drunken behaviour ahead of allowing pubs to set their own opening and closing times. Twenty-four-hour pubs! I did lives all morning, including one with Minister of State for Policing Hazel Blears, and a package for *Live at Five* with a PTC in our favourite Westminster watering hole, The Marquis of Granby. In my diary, I condensed all this to 'binge drinking with Hazel Blears'!

I covered a Michael Howard speech on immigration, a big issue in the 2005 election and even more so in 2010. The Tories had launched a controversial campaign poster: It's not racist to talk about immigration. Below were the words they were putting on all their posters: Are you thinking what we're thinking? I thought putting 'racist' and 'immigration' in the same sentence was, in itself, racist. Immigration wasn't about race. Or did they think it was?

A YouGov opinion poll at the end of January still had Labour a long way ahead. Labour's election coordinator, Alan Milburn, found himself at the centre of a row over a poster showing Michael Howard as a flying pig. Another poster showed Howard swinging a stopwatch. Anti-Semitic according to the Tories, a 'Fagin smear'. It was nothing of the sort, but Labour prudently removed the images from its website.

On February 1st, Irish Prime Minister Bertie Ahern was back in Number Ten for more talks with Tony Blair. I did lives for Sky News and Sky News Ireland. After my last live at ten p.m., news broke that Pope John Paul II had been taken to hospital with breathing difficulties. I did very long lives outside Westminster Cathedral at midnight, twelve thirty a.m. and one a.m. Everything you ever wanted to know about the Pope, and more! Fortunately, I actually knew a lot about the Polish Pope and was easily able to talk at length about him. Reporter Barbara Serra, who spoke fluent Italian, and cameraman Martin Smith were sent to Rome. The Pope recovered, although he died two months later.

London Mayor Ken Livingstone put his size tens in his mouth again when he accused an *Evening Standard* reporter of being like a Nazi concentration camp guard. The newspaper pumped up the story as much as possible. Apparently, the 'Jewish community' was very upset. Livingstone was accused of anti-Semitism. Apparently, the reporter was Jewish. I very much doubt that Livingstone knew that. I did lives on the story all day and my only ever live phono for Talk Sport.

As the Ken Livingstone story was rumbling on, I went to a community centre in Fulham for a Gordon Brown speech. We weren't covering it, I just went to chat about the general election with Gordon Brown and his special advisor, Ian Austin. In the afternoon, I cut a package on Tony Blair encouraging school trips, and a photo-op messing about with school children on a dinghy in Worcestershire. Election? What election?!

Tony Blair held a 'terrorism summit', inviting Michael Howard and Charles Kennedy to Number Ten to discuss the government's 'control orders' proposal, i.e. house arrests. Home Secretary Charles Clarke was making sure that the government's tough stance on terrorism was getting through to the voters. He launched the new Anti-terrorism Bill in the Commons the following Tuesday, which kept me busy doing lives and packages all afternoon and evening, with a four-minute piece for *Sky News at Ten*.

I was media training the NSPCC at Hillside Studios in Bushey, Hertfordshire, when a Sky News team turned up to do interviews. They spotted me and we had a chat. Having prepared them, I left the NSPCC people doing TV interviews. They also did some radio lives. They were re-launching their Full Stop campaign: Child abuse must stop. Full Stop. To support the campaign they had small, round green badges. I had been training them back in 1999 and they had asked me to take a box of the badges and give one to as many MPs as possible. I was happy to do so, but it was too soon after the Good Friday agreement and the colour green was too political. It is the Fenian colour. So, I had very little success. In any case, green is the colour for go, red is the colour for stop. I couldn't understand why their badges were not red. I still don't. I told them that back in 1999 and I told them again now. Having said that, the campaign was a huge fundraising success.

At the end of February, Attorney General Lord Goldsmith insisted that his legal advice to parliament on invading Iraq almost two years earlier had been written entirely by him without any interference from Downing Street. I had been doing lives after Tony Blair's monthly press conference when we broke the story just before 6pm and I switched to covering it with lives and a package. Two years on. To me, it felt like the invasion was already passing into history even though the Iraqi insurgency was still costing lives and for many in the Labour Party it was still a very raw issue.

I was doing yet another TB-GB story on the last Sunday in February, a quiet news day. I was about to go live at 11am when the Pope appeared at the window of his hospital room and waved to the adoring crowd outside. Of course, we switched to the live pictures from Rome. Being big-footed by the Pope was a first!

Margaret Dixon was a pensioner whose shoulder operation had been cancelled seven times. She said she had written to Health Secretary John Reid but had received no reply. The Conservatives jumped on the opportunity to highlight government failings in the management of the NHS. Tory press officers were camped out at her home, Michael Howard invited her family for breakfast. It felt to me that she was being politically exploited, but it worked. Soon after her shoulder became a national story, she had her operation. The newspapers dubbed it 'the battle of Margaret's shoulder'. At least they spared us 'Shouldergate'.

From Margaret's shoulder to Harrogate for the Lib Dems spring conference, held over a long weekend. We did the usual eve of conference piece on the Friday evening with a live doorstep with Charles Kennedy when he arrived. The conference, really a rally for the troops, was all about Charles Kennedy's speech the next day. We milked it for all it was worth, with lives before and afterwards and live interviews with Lord (Tim) Razzall and Tim Farron, a future party leader but who knew that at the time? A couple of lives the next morning, and a one-to-one sit-down interview with Charles Kennedy which we cut down to four minutes and which Sky News ran all day.

The next day, the Lib Dems had a rare triumph in the Commons when the government's new Anti-terrorism Bill was defeated. A Lib Dem amendment was passed which gave the power to impose Control Orders to judges rather than the Home Office, and also set a greater burden of proof.

Lives and doughnuts all evening, and again the next day when the Lords threw out the proposed new Prevention of Terrorism Act. This became another ping-pong when, the following day, the Commons rejected every House of Lords amendment with majorities of around a hundred for each vote on each amendment. The government made one concession, a sunset clause, an annual review of the Act which was still draconian and almost certainly in contravention of the Human Rights Act and the European Convention on Human Rights. The Lords held its longest ever sitting, more than thirty hours, and for the first time Tony Blair's mentor and erstwhile Lord Chancellor, Lord (Derry) Irvine, voted against the Labour government.

The ping-pong continued for the rest of the week. Thursday was insane. In the afternoon, the Lords voted not once but twice to reject the bill. I was doing lives around those votes and a big package for *Sky News at Ten*. More lives at midnight and one a.m. The Commons resumed its sitting at one twenty a.m.! I had to cut a new package and do more lives at 2, 2.30 and 3am for anyone who was still awake! After a heated debate, the Commons adjourned just after 3am So, another live at 3.30 which ran as an 'As Live' for what was left of the night.

Friday was just as crazy. The Lords had convened again at five a.m. to reject the Commons rejection. For me, it meant lives all day. At 4.30pm I was summoned to Downing Street along with Andrew Marr of the BBC and ITN's Nick Robinson. We were told in a live statement from Tony Blair that a compromise had been reached. Simultaneously, Charles Clarke announced the agreement in the House of Commons. I did lives in Downing Street before and after Tony Blair's statement, and more back in the studio. The Lords met and voted for the compromise at 6.30, the Commons returned forty-five minutes later and Commons Speaker Michael Martin announced that the Bill had received Royal assent.

I did a pooled interview at the Home Office with Charles Clarke for us, ITN and The BBC, and a final live at 10pm. Phew! It had been quite a week. The sunset clause had proved to be enough of a compromise to avoid a potential constitutional crisis, with both sides claiming victory. It was one hell of a way to get legislation through parliament.

I had been due to go to Brighton on that Friday for the Conservatives' spring conference. I went on the Saturday, but not before a couple of lives on the Anti-terrorism Bill at 7 and 8 seven o'clock. Having set up the camera for my live two-way, cameraman Aaron Scott had to grapple with a deranged drunk who was trying to interrupt as I was live on air! The man was lucky. Aaron is a karate black belt, but he simply restrained the idiot until I'd finished.

Like all party spring conferences, and unlike the main annual conferences in the autumn, this was more of a rally, the centrepiece being the party leader's speech to his/her troops. I did three lives before Michael Howard's speech, a very long live afterwards summarising what he had just said, and another three after that. We finished at 6pm. It was a warm day, the sea air was glorious, and I would happily have stayed to do more, but the decision was to up sticks and head back to London, which was actually just as well as Marion and I had a friend's wedding reception to go to in the evening.

After a few days supporting another theatre war game at the UK Defence Academy in Shrivenham, thirty officers of colonel rank and above, I had one day off, just one, part of which I spent researching ahead of the general election and, of course, watching television news almost constantly. Workaholic? Moi? My long-suffering wife certainly thought so.

I was back at work just as Howard Flight resigned as Conservative Party vice-chairman. In a speech, he had suggested that the Tories were planning far deeper cuts in public spending than they had so far revealed in public. It was a speech to Conservative Way Forward which, unfortunately for him, had been secretly recorded. I was live every half hour from six a.m., including a live with George Osborne, who said Flight was wrong and had to go. Labour hastily arranged a press conference to take full advantage of this latest Tory misery. John Reid, Alan Milburn and Ruth Kelly, three Cabinet ministers, claiming Flight's gaffe had let the cat out of the bag and revealed the Conservatives' true intentions. Michael Howard gave an on-camera statement. Not only was Flight sacked as vice-chairman, he would also have the whip removed and would not be allowed to defend his Arundel and South Downs seat as a Conservative.

Three days later, Flight was refusing to go quietly and demanding an emergency meeting of his local Conservative association. Michael Howard held a press conference on childcare policy. We had been told by party press officers that he would not take any questions on Howard Flight. Sky News was taking the press conference live and I got the first question. No prizes for guessing who I asked about! He replied that he would not discuss that, wanted questions on childcare and invited another question. There were about fifty journalists in the room. Silence. I thought that any moment now someone would pipe up with a question. The silence continued for almost ten seconds, which is an eternity of dead air on live television. I felt some sympathy for him, but eventually said, "Perhaps now you could answer my question". And he had to. He had nowhere else to go.

Howard Flight was elevated to the House of Lords in 2010. A week after his peerage was announced he was at it again, saying that cuts to child benefit would 'discourage the middle class from breeding'. Breeding!

Tony Blair went to Buckingham Palace at 11am on April 5th. The day before, I had cut a package on the election starting gun. We went to a running track and got someone to fire a starting pistol. Corny, but it worked. At 11.30 I did a long live on Abingdon Green with Teddy Taylor, Tony Banks and Jenny Tonge, three of the eighty-five MPs who were retiring. I cut the lead package, with aerial shots of Tony Blair going to the palace, and speeches by Blair, Michael Howard, Charles Kennedy and Gordon Brown. I got a very warm, congratulatory note from head of news Nick Pollard. An historic day. Opinion polls that day suggested the Tories were narrowing the gap. Surely not!

We had teams with the three party leaders, but part of my election coverage remit was to cover Gordon Brown. The election had already become a kind of TB-GB joint offer by Labour, and Tony Blair had already said he would not be serving a full third term. So, the next day, I was in Battersea where Gordon Brown was visiting a Sure Start centre. In my live at eleven a.m., he was behind me meeting the Sure Start people and he did a live with us afterwards. I had a quiet word with him about covering his campaign and he told his press officer Jo Dipple to bring me up to speed on 'the beautiful parts of the country we plan to visit'.

We were back in time for a very lively PMQs, the last of the parliament. We were live at a joint Tony Blair and Gordon Brown press conference, a visual underlining of the fact that we were now in the realms of joint leadership. I did a long live afterwards, also taking in the highlights of a Michael Howard press conference which had been held at the same time. Poor planning by the Conservatives. If they had held their press conference before or after the Labour one, we would have taken it live. As it was, we stayed with Tony Blair and Gordon Brown and the drama unfolding at the top of the Labour Party, at the apex of government.

On April 8th, Tony Blair flew straight from the Pope's funeral to Birmingham. Rover cars had called in the administrators. Gordon Brown was there too, another example of the de facto joint leadership, at least for the purposes of the campaign. I packaged the story for *Live at Five*, with lives all evening.

Much of the following week was mired in arguments over Conservative tax and spending plans. A Conservative candidate in a tight Labour marginal had doctored a photo in his election leaflet. It was impossible for Michael Howard to sack him so close to the general election. At a press conference, a cheeky newspaper reporter asked Michael Howard if he was turning into Victor Meldrew, the grumpy old man in the TV sitcom *One Foot in the Grave*.

On the Thursday, I covered the launch of the Respect Party's election campaign and did lives with the effervescent George Galloway. I was supposed to spend the next day on the Prescott battle bus, but his advisor Beverley Priest cancelled with just twenty-four hours to go. Perhaps they feared, probably with some justification, that I might not take it or him too seriously. In any event, the main Labour event that Friday was a Gordon Brown speech, so I was perfectly happy covering that instead. The BBC ran a very boring piece on the Prescott battle bus. I had been asking for such access for more than a week. We would have had a lot more fun with it, which is presumably precisely what they didn't want.

That evening, Gordon Brown flew to Washington for an IMF meeting. My producer, Jane Elston, another ex-ITN colleague, phoned Sky News managing editor Simon Cole, to only half-seriously suggest we go too and he agreed to send us, so we flew out ahead of the Brown entourage.

Sky News and ITN are in the same building in Washington. We do our lives from the roof. The backdrop is the Capitol building, so they always look good. With cameraman Andy Nicholas, I did lives all the next morning and a long, sit-down interview with Gordon Brown on the IMF, Rover, the election and his role in the campaign. I used excerpts from that interview in my subsequent live two-ways.

After the fairly tortuous process of getting IMF accreditation (we had come on impulse, so nothing had been arranged in advance), we interviewed Gordon Brown on Conservative tax plans which were due to be unveiled two days later but had leaked to the papers and to us. We had got a lot on air with some good stories, so it had been well worth sending us. After a second night at the George Hotel (modest, but with the most comfortable pillows in the world!), we had a free morning in Georgetown and I played at being the old Washington hand, showing Jane one or two of the city's most famous landmarks and walking from the Washington Monument to the Lincoln Memorial before flying home in the afternoon.

Chrissie Hynde of The Pretenders was in the taxi queue at Heathrow. I had booked her band for a university gig in my student days, back when I was responsible for such things. I had at one stage considered dropping out of university and becoming a music agent, I had had a couple of job offers. Getting The Pretenders had been one of my triumphs. Booked months ahead, they played our gig just as their first number one, 'Brass in Pocket', hit the top of the charts! Of course she wouldn't remember, so I spared myself and her the embarrassment of talking to her.

Straight back to work the next day, and a Gordon Brown speech in Hatfield which we took live with live two-ways from me afterwards. The problem with following the same politician on the campaign trail is that you get to know the supposedly off the cuff, impromptu speech they make at every location almost by heart, especially the jokes. I often had to stop myself blurting out the punch line before it had been delivered.

Bethnal Green and Bow was the constituency where it was felt George Galloway's Respect Party had the best chance of winning a seat. I had already done some filming in advance, vox pops in Brick Lane and Whitechapel Road and interviews with George and the Labour and Tory candidates. All four candidates, including the Lib Dem, were at a hustings meeting in Mile End. It was a proper old fashioned very lively hustings meeting, none of this modern stage-managed-for-television nonsense. There was cheering, jeering, booing and heckling in the packed hall. Three people were forcibly ejected. It made a very good package for *Sky News at Ten* and, unusually, the piece also ran every hour the next day from early morning into the evening.

George Galloway went on to win the seat at the election, defeating Labour's Oona King. He was succeeded by Rushanara Ali, who took the seat back for Labour in 2010 when normal service was resumed.

Sky News' interest in covering Gordon Brown's every move was waning, so I switched to covering Reginald Keys who was standing against Tony Blair in Sedgefield. Reg Keys was the father of a soldier, Royal Military Police Lance Corporal Tom Keys, who had been killed in Iraq. He was standing as an anti-war independent candidate.

We went to Newton Aycliffe where Reg Keys was campaigning in the marketplace. We interviewed him, former independent MP and BBC reporter Martin Bell, who was supporting him, and did some vox pops and a PTC for our package. We filmed him door to door campaigning in Ferryhill. Local bookmakers were giving odds of 50-1 on Reg Keys winning the seat. It might just as well have been fifty million to one. On May 5th, he got just over 4,000 votes, not far behind the Conservatives and Lib Dems. Tony Blair got more than 24,000. At the vote declaration, Reg Keys spoke movingly about his son Tom and urged the prime minister to say sorry to the bereaved families. Tony Blair's expressionless face as he listened to what was basically a father's lament became one of the abiding images of the 2005 election.

The attorney general's legal advice on the Iraq war was published in full at the end of April, two years on. He concluded that the war was lawful but, international law being as vague as it is, its legality could in theory be challenged in court. Gordon Brown led the Cabinet ministers who sprang to Tony Blair's defence, saying the decision to go to war had been a collective Cabinet decision.

Gordon Brown's press officer, Jo Dipple, told me he kept asking where I was, since I was supposed to be covering his campaign. "He misses you." By happy coincidence, I was back with them the next day.

The Liberal Democrats had a 'decapitation' strategy, meaning they were targeting the seats of leading Tory MPs. To me, this seemed daft as they ought to be laser-focused on protecting their own seats and targeting marginals where they had come second in 2001. To illustrate this aspect of the election campaign we went to the Haltemprice and Howden constituency in Yorkshire, the seat of Shadow Home Secretary David Davis. It was the second safest Conservative seat in the country. To be fair to the Lib Dems, they had come second in 2001, losing by just under 2,000 votes. We only spent a few hours in the constituency, a long interview with David Davis and interviews with the Lib Dem and Labour candidates. In May, David Davis held his seat comfortably, increasing his majority over the Lib Dems to more than 5,000.

Two days before the election, Coldstream Guardsman and father of three Anthony Wakefield was killed during a routine patrol in Iraq. His death elevated the Iraq war issue back up the political agenda. My package included interviews with Tony Blair and Charles Kennedy.

Gordon Brown's press officer, Jo Dipple, told me they had two seats available on a helicopter the next day, and we could spend the day flying around the country with them as the pool crew. They should probably have included the press association as is normal for such pool arrangements, but we weren't complaining.

So it was that cameraman Ed Bayliss and I travelled to Elstree the next morning in the prime minister's convoy, blues and twos and police motorcycle outriders. There were two executive helicopters, one for Tony Blair the other for Gordon Brown, another example of a kind of joint leadership. There had been many examples of it during the campaign, one of the most memorable being Tony Blair chasing after Gordon Brown carrying two ice cream cones, one of which he had bought for the chancellor.

I had been on many helicopters, but none like this. We could not see the pilots from our luxury cabin which was equipped with very comfortable armchairs. We buzzed around the country making several stops, including meeting party workers in Great Yarmouth (raining, poor visibility) and a school visit in Goole (clear visibility, blue skies), ending the day at Leeds-Bradford airport. It had been great fun but also quite exhausting, the final push before the election. Mostly, it was a fantastic opportunity to spend time with the future prime minister. Gordon was upbeat and very cheerful.

I could barely believe that the election campaign was finally over and tomorrow would be election day. 05/05/05.

As always, election day meant we could not legally report any politics until the polls closed at ten p.m. A few weeks earlier, we had a sweepstake in our Westminster newsroom on the result. I had put my fiver on a Labour majority of 85. The BBC and ITN exit polls gave Labour a majority of 66, and they were absolutely spot on. It was a big drop from the 167 majority of 2001 but still a handsome majority, and Tony Blair became the first Labour leader to win three consecutive general elections.

Through Gordon Brown's people, I had arranged access to Labour's victory party at the National Portrait Gallery. I did a live from there before Tony Blair arrived at 5.30am. When he did, I was the only reporter inside with the party activists, a Sky News cameraman and live shots.

At 6.40am I interviewed Alan Milburn live outside, at the entrance to the gallery. John Prescott was in his battle bus parked across the road and tried to drown us out! As I was talking with Alan Milburn live, John Prescott was bellowing over the bus's loudspeaker: "The election's over, Alan, you don't need to talk to them any more!" I don't know if he was drunk. He was certainly drunk on victory.

John Prescott had always been good value for the media, especially the newspapers, and usually for all the wrong reasons. Originally dubbed 'Prezza', that changed to 'Two Jags' after it emerged that he owned a Jaguar and had the use of another as his official ministerial car, then to 'Two Jabs' after the 'John is John' incident. Then it was 'Two Shacks', a reference to his having a grand official residence, Dorneywood, and culminated in 'Two Shags' after his affair with his diary secretary Tracey Temple was exposed in 2006. Pathetic really, but a great game for mischievous newspaper hacks.

Some vignettes from that night: George Galloway defeated Oona King in Bethnal Green and Bow, and Stephen Twigg lost Enfield and Southgate, his own Portillo moment. Enough Labour voters had switched to the Lib Dems to allow the Conservatives to retake the seat. In my own constituency, Hornsey and Wood Green, Lib Dem Lynne Featherstone took the seat from Labour's Barbara Roche, overturning a Labour majority of more than 10,000. The Lib Dems' decapitation strategy failed. David Davis, Oliver Letwin and Theresa May all held their seats.

After the Alan Milburn live interview and John Prescott's contribution, I headed to Downing Street to do more lives. I did two long lives in the eleven o'clock news hour, another two for the midday news, and another at one o'clock so I was there, live, for Tony Blair's historic third term mission statement and the pose on the doorstep of Number Ten with his family. Adam took over the Downing Street lives for the afternoon and I headed back to Millbank to cut a Labour Party package for *Live at Five*. I finally escaped at 5.30pm, twenty-two hours after I'd arrived at work.

Back to work early the next morning for a Cabinet reshuffle. The headline was the return to Cabinet of David Blunkett after just six months in the political wilderness. Alan Johnson was to head a new department, Productivity, Energy and Industry, David Miliband became Communities and Local Government minister, John Reid replaced Geoff Hoon at Defence, and Peter Hain became Northern Ireland secretary. Live doughnuts in Downing Street every hour from 7am until 2pm when I handed over to my colleague, Jon Craig, although my package continued to run all afternoon.

Michael Howard fell on his sword, not a dramatic resignation but an announcement that he would stand down as Conservative Party leader once a successor had been chosen. He reshuffled his Shadow Cabinet on the Tuesday after the election, another busy day doing lives and packages all evening.

It was live two-ways again the next day when the PLP met. The anti-Blair rebels were well and truly seen off. That evening, Arsenal were at their sublime best, playing silky football to thrash Everton 7-0 in the final game of the season. Seven-nil!

On the Thursday, George Galloway was accused by a US Senate sub-committee of taking money from Saddam Hussein as part of the food for oil programme. He denied it. I broke the news that he would be going to Washington the following Tuesday to give evidence. I immediately began planning to go with him. I cut a package on the story which ran all evening with a couple of live two-ways.

George Galloway had been in Egypt. On the Sunday, I met him off his flight at Heathrow. No other reporters were there, so I got a good and exclusive interview.

It was a very different story at Heathrow at five the next morning, a huge media scrum as George Galloway headed to Washington. I had to hang around the airport in Washington for nearly three hours before another mad media scrum around Gorgeous George. I got to our Washington bureau at 4pm (nine o'clock BST) to do a live, with another at 5pm local time for *Sky News at Ten*, and a final live at 6 o'clock before cutting a package for the next morning's *Sunrise* programme. I finally got to bed sometime after 9pm, 2am in the UK, another twenty-two-hour day!

I caught up with George Galloway the next morning and interviewed him live as he strode down the street towards the Senate sub-committee. His entrance was little short of gladiatorial. I stopped at the entrance to the building. To my amazement, around one hundred reporters, photographers and camera crews, including my American cameraman, just kept going, right into the committee room. At Westminster, we were not allowed inside committee rooms during hearings, which were filmed by remote cameras. In Washington, they do things differently. Photographers and camera crews were literally clambouring all over the tables and chairs to get the best shots.

George Galloway lived up to his billing. At his pugnacious best, he went on the attack. The members of the US sub-committee, accustomed as they were to deference from anyone giving evidence, didn't know what had hit them! He made absolute mincemeat of them. Sky News took his forty-five minutes of evidence live, and ran it again in the evening at full length. It was great theatre, almost a blood sport, and I did lives before and after his testimony and got him to our live point first, ahead of ITN and the BBC, to do a live two-way with Sky News. I did further lives at nine, ten and eleven p.m BST, six p.m. local time.

In the evening, I was kindly invited to Sky's Washington bureau's farewell dinner for producer Dan Williams. I spent much of the evening drinking Mojitos and chatting with the incomparable Mick Deane, cameraman and legend.

We got fulsome herograms from back at Sky News HQ. At Sky News Westminster, Jon Craig was apparently calling me 'Gorgeous Glen', while Adam Boulton was referring to me as 'Glen O'Galloway'!

Returning to Westminster, another story on Tony Blair's health. He had a slipped disc. I have five of them so I felt his pain. A package for *Live at Five*, and lives every hour after that on Blair's health, the UK's EU rebate and the Tory leadership. Foreign Secretary Jack Straw was going to Brussels two days later. I gently suggested that we (meaning I!) should go with him.

Arsenal won the FA Cup in a penalty shoot-out with Manchester United. They/we didn't deserve it. We had played badly, showing little ambition, while Manchester United missed chance after chance. It was all one-way traffic. The number of corners told the story: Manchester United had twelve, Arsenal just one. But we won.

Next day, Sunday, and it was off to Brussels for the foreign ministers meeting. John Williams, head of the FCO press office, was on the same Eurostar train so I had a chat with him about the UK rebate. In the evening, with Sky News cameraman Neil Morris, I did doorstep interviews with Jack Straw and several other EU foreign ministers and sent a package for *Sunrise* and *Live at Five*. Dinner was in the Grande-Place with very large beers and cacophonic live 'jazz'.

Next morning I doorstepped Jack Straw again and was then ushered into the inner sanctum for an exclusive one-to-one sit-down interview. So the quick trip to Brussels had been very worthwhile.

I didn't have to travel too far from home the following morning. Gordon Brown and John Prescott were visiting an affordable housing project in, of all places, Hampstead. After lives before and after PMQs that Wednesday, I talked live into the Queen's speech Treasury debate, George Osborne's debut against Gordon Brown. Osborne looked and sounded like an undergraduate student debater, way out of his depth, with a small and slightly high-pitched voice and seemed very nervous. Brown welcomed his 'seventh Shadow Chancellor'. It was a walkover.

At the end of May, a day trip to Blaenau Gwent where there had been a Labour Party rebellion. At a by-election caused by the death of Labour MP Peter Law, Dai Davies had taken the seat, representing the Blaenau Gwent's People's Voice. This was Labour's safest seat in Wales, once the constituency of Nye Bevan and Michael Foot. Sky News cameraman Mostyn Price met me off the train at Newport. We got shots of the valley, the former coal mine which was now a museum and the site of what had once been the Ebbw Vale steel works. If you wanted a symbol of how parts of Britain had been neglected this was it. We interviewed the new MP and the losing Labour candidate, did a PTC in Ebbw Vale and some vox pops before I headed back to London where I cut a package with some black and white archive footage and very tight sound bites. It made a good piece for *Sky News at Ten*. The piece also ran all the next day and received a lot of compliments.

In early June, I was back in Brussels. In a referendum, the Dutch had just rejected the new EU constitution. We did lives all day. At three thirty p.m., Jack Straw announced in the House of Commons the suspension of the second reading of the EU bill, which meant there would not be a British referendum. First the French, now the Dutch. The Blair government was off the referendum hook.

In the evening, we drove to Luxembourg for a Gordon Brown/EU finance ministers meeting the next day. Cameraman Colin Hamilton and producer Julian Morrison regaled me with funny stories about the life and times of Sky's Europe bureau. They weren't overly impressed by their new correspondent. Apparently, during the Dutch referendum, she had asked them when the Netherlands had changed its name to Holland!

The EU finance ministers meeting was as dry as ever but we got the Gordon Brown arrival shot, did lives for three hours, and then got a sit-down interview with him at which he announced that the EU was to double aid to Africa. This was breaking news on Sky, and I did lives doughnutting a Gordon Brown grab. We weren't needed for the evening, which meant I caught the last flight from Luxembourg to London's City airport. Excellent. The flight afforded some perfect views over Buckingham Palace, St Paul's Cathedral, The Imperial War Museum etc.

It had been Colin Hamilton's last day in the Brussels bureau, not the most exciting but at least it had been the lead story. We had not been wanted for the evening because both Blair and Bush had spoken about Africa aid, trade and achieving one hundred per cent debt relief.

At the end of the week, G8 finance ministers met in London to discuss the debts of developing nations. I was live on that every hour for twelve hours, including a mid-afternoon live with Gordon Brown, who was pushing hard for one hundred per cent debt relief. I covered the same story in the same way for the next two days, eleven hours of lives from Downing Street on African debt relief, another Gordon Brown interview, and packages. It was our lead story and, at half past every hour, Sky News aired a cut down version of my interview with the chancellor. Eighteen countries had agreed to a one hundred per cent debt write-off immediately, with more to follow. It had been a very productive three days. Dozens of lives, several packages, and three sit-down interviews with Gordon Brown as the story developed. I deserved a pay rise! Fat chance!

I was in Paris the following week where Tony Blair was meeting Jacques Chirac and Kofi Annan to discuss G8 issues. Britain was to host the G8 meeting in Scotland the following month. The evening before, we were supposed to do lives but, in California, pop superstar Michael Jackson was found not guilty of all ten child abuse charges against him after a four-month trial. Sky went Jackson-tastic! Big-footed by Michael Jackson. Fair enough.

The Jackson mania had subsided enough by the next day. I somehow managed to persuade the authorities at the Élysée Palace that this time we could park our satellite dish in the palace courtyard. We cabled across the courtyard to the palace steps for live coverage, with palace bureaucrats fluttering around us muttering about health and safety! I did live two-ways as Blair, Chirac and Kofi Annan arrived. The opposition, ITN and the BBC, were nowhere in sight.

I did a long live into Tony Blair's speech on the G8 summit. Sky News political editor Adam Boulton and producer Peter Lowe had travelled on Blair's plane, so Adam took over the lives. They were suitably astonished at our location inside the Élysée Palace. We relocated to the British Embassy, no issues parking the satellite truck there, they were happy to see us. We sent a package for *Live at Five*. I wrote the script in the embassy's beautiful garden, a fabulous working environment. Tony Blair held a press conference at the embassy at five forty-five p.m. and was very upbeat about the forthcoming summit in July. I did lives at 6 and 7pm, and we relocated to the Place de la Concorde for a final live at 8 o'clock with a new package to run all evening.

The G8 summit that July was held in the Gleneagles Hotel in Auchterarder. I had been doing lives for days looking ahead to the summit issues. Top of the UK's agenda were aid to Africa and global warming/climate change. For once, access to the leaders was comparatively relaxed once we were inside the security cordon.

On our first morning there, we were all distracted. All eyes were on Singapore. The International Olympic Committee was going through the final bids to host the 2012 Olympic Game. Paris was the bookies' favourite. I did lives all morning from six a.m. The decision came at twelve forty-five p.m. London had won! There were loud cheers in the media centre and at the Gleneagles Hotel next door where Tony Blair was jumping up and down and hugging the nearest people. He had been to Singapore to support

Britain's Olympic bid. So too, to support the French bid, had Chirac, probably not such a good idea from the point of view of Paris!

At four p.m., after a lot of hanging around and a ludicrous amount of security, a pooled press conference with Tony Blair, Bob Geldof and Bono. Geldof had organised the Live 8 concerts, twenty years on from Live Aid. There were only five reporters present: Jon Snow of Channel 4 News, the BBC's Andrew Marr, Bill Neely for ITN, Andy Bell of 5 News and me. Only two questions were allowed. I managed to get the first. It undoubtedly helped that Sky News was taking the press conference live.

I did more lives later, including some 'Make Poverty History' protestors around two hundred of whom had stormed the security fence and been marched away by the police after a bit of a punch-up. Ten thousand police officers, many of them armed, had been deployed to Scotland. They included sharp-shooters and also in attendance, it was rumoured, were SAS snipers. There was some light relief when we heard that George W had fallen off his mountain bike. He was waving at some police officers at the time, shouting, "Hey you guys". He was unhurt, but what an image!

The contrast with the next day could not have been greater. From the euphoria of winning the Olympic Games bid to the awful terrorist atrocities of July 7th. With Sky News anchor, Jeremy Thompson, who was presenting from Gleneagles, I did lives at 7, 7.30 and 8 am on Britain's agenda for the G8 summit. The first news came at 8.50 of an explosion at Liverpool Street in London, which was reported at first as a 'power surge'. Then there was a second, in Russell Square, followed by a third, in Edgware Road. It was clearly terrorism and, when a fourth bomb destroyed a bus in Tavistock Square, we realised that this was what we feared, London's Madrid, and that many people would be dead or injured.

Tony Blair made a statement. Totally gone was the Tiggerish Tony of just twenty-four hours earlier. Now, his jaw was set. I don't think I've ever seen someone's mood change so suddenly and dramatically. Less than twenty-four hours earlier, the prime minister had literally been jumping for joy when London won the bid to host the Olympics and had had a spring in his step for the rest of the day. Now, he looked in shock. From the euphoria of the day before we were now all in despair.

52 people died and more than 700 were injured in what had been the worst terrorist attack in Britain since Lockerbie in 1988 and the most devastating attack on London since the Second World War.

Shortly afterwards, the prime minister made another on-camera statement, surrounded by the other G8 leaders and the leaders of the other countries who had been invited to attend the summit in a show of solidarity. He would return to London but the G8 summit would continue in defiance of the terrorists. Foreign Secretary Jack Straw would deputise for Tony Blair in his absence.

There was really nothing we could do from Gleneagles that day but watch the awful story unfold on Sky News. Tony Blair returned to Gleneagles that evening in a Chinook with an escort of army helicopters, but he seemed to be with us in body only. It was obvious that his thoughts and focus were hundreds of miles south, in London.

On the phone that evening, seven-year-old Maddie asked me, "Daddy, why are there bombs?" I had no reply.

The summit continued. It seemed a lot less important or relevant. July 8th was the final day. Jeremy Thompson and Adam Boulton were hoovering up all the lives, I was packaging. We had a lot of material. I cut a piece for lunchtime and another for *Live at Five*. Tony Blair's speech was applauded by the world leaders present, another act of anti-terrorist solidarity, and we had sound bites with the South African and Nigerian presidents as well as Bob Geldof and Bono. It all made for a strong package, but hardly seemed to matter after what had just happened in London.

The following Monday, I was doing lives before and after Tony Blair's speech to the Commons on the London terror attack. Our head of politics Peter Lowe was leaving us. He was off to a management job at Sky News HQ in Osterley. Steady, calm and unflappable, he would be a great loss. I chatted for an hour over coffee with Jonathan Levy who would replace him in the following month. Jonathan was energetic, a go-getter, fizzing with ideas and very ambitious. I anticipated, correctly, a very different style of leadership.

Next day, a complicated package on electronic security which involved me doing three PTCs which were fed through graphics and as if by magic I appeared to be inside a mobile phone, a computer screen and an ATM cashpoint. All very clever, it worked well and looked good.

That Wednesday I packaged an understandably subdued PMQs. At midday the next day, a two-minute silence was held around the country and throughout much of Europe. There was a vigil at six p.m. in Trafalgar Square. In between, I did lives in Downing Street as the Cabinet met to discuss even tougher anti-terrorism legislation.

The following week began hectically. Lives all morning on the new anti-terrorism laws and a live in the afternoon with Shahid Raza of the British Muslin Council who told me he believed there could be 'thousands' of young British Muslims considering engaging in acts of terrorism. This became our lead story. I interviewed Shadow Home Secretary David Davis and his Lib Dem counterpart Mark Oaten together as they emerged from the Home Office after cross-party talks at five p.m. A long fifteen-minute live, followed by a live interview with Home Secretary Charles Clarke at 6pm and a final live an hour later pulling it all together.

On the Tuesday, lives in Downing Street all day. Tony Blair had invited Michael Howard and Charles Kennedy to a meeting he was having with British Muslim leaders and, later, I covered a live press conference with Tony Blair and Afghan President Hamid Karzai. A second day of lives more than once an hour for ten hours.

On the Thursday, there was another attempted multiple terrorism attack, bombs on three London Underground trains and a fourth on a bus. It was clearly an attempt to copy July 7th. This time, the bombs failed to detonate. The would-be suicide bombers ran away. Some had almost been caught.

The next day police shot dead Brazilian student Jean Charles de Menezes at Stockwell station in south London. They suspected that he was one of the previous day's failed bombers, wrongly as it turned out. He was shot in the head seven times. Initially this was not a political story and the Sky News political unit didn't get involved, but that was to change very soon. Within twenty-four hours, the police admitted that they had killed an innocent man and apologised. Obviously, this completely changed the narrative. How had the police got it so badly wrong? And was there now a de facto shoot to kill policy?

In fact, head shots were policy when it came to suspected suicide bombers, the theory being that a shot to the chest could detonate a hidden bomb. There were, however, several inquiries into police competence. By the following evening, I had taken over the lives outside Scotland Yard from Sky's excellent crime correspondent, Martin Brunt. MPs had already begun to ask questions.

Next morning, there was a terrorist attack in Egypt at the holiday resort of Sharm el-Sheikh. Tony Blair had holidayed there the previous Christmas. I had also recently been there, though not at the same time. Eighty-eight people were killed by three bombs. It was almost certain that British tourists would be among them. I did lives at the Foreign Office as soon as the news came in and for the rest of the afternoon and evening on the Sharm el-Sheikh attack and the Metropolitan Police admission that they had shot dead a completely innocent man, Jean Charles de Menezes.

Sunday was much quieter. All I had to do was interview Metropolitan Police Commissioner Sir Ian Blair, who we used to refer to as Sir Ian No Relation (to Tony). Then it was off the next day to Salisbury for the funeral of former prime minister, Sir Edward Heath. Years before, at university, he had been the first former prime minister I had ever met. He had died a week earlier at the age of eighty-nine. The cathedral was the perfect setting, just a stone's throw from Ted Heath's home. Our satellite truck arrived late, so I did my first live using the BBC truck, which was very courteous of them. There were often times when we helped each other, others when the rivalry could be cut-throat. An occasion like this demanded collaboration rather than confrontation. My next live, with our own truck this time, was a long voiceover of the pictures of the coffin arriving. I did another live once the service had ended, and cut a package for *Live at Five* before heading back to London.

Two days later, Tony Blair had meetings at Number Ten with the king of Bahrain, the prime minister of Turkey and the prime minister of Spain, José Zapatero, who had been so critical of Blair's role in the 2003 invasion of Iraq. I did lives in Downing Street and, for the evening a very different story. The police had found bomb parts and bomb-making equipment used on July 7th in a car in Luton.

The next day, Thursday July 28th, the IRA announced the end of all military activity. The end. Finally. I did lives on that including lives for Sky News Ireland, and interviewed John Major, whose role in securing the Good Friday agreement is still not fully recognised to this day.

September the 7th was Maddie's first day at Highgate school. It was also my first day back at work after a break taking in Lisbon, Barcelona and Rome. She was very excited, I was a lot less so although I soon got back into the swing of things.

Never, or rarely, did what I was doing feel like work. Work was something you went to do in an office, factory or whatever, probably Monday to Friday, nine to five. I felt so lucky, blessed even, that I was actually being paid to do something I enjoyed so much. It could be incredibly stressful, meeting deadlines and staying ahead of the opposition, but I thrived on the stress.

Next morning, I interviewed Gordon Brown ahead of a press conference announcing more money to fund British immunisation programmes in the world's poorest countries. I did lives from the Treasury before and after the press conference and interviewed the Ugandan health minister.

I covered Liam Fox launching his Conservative leadership campaign and went to a Malcolm Rifkind leadership rally, One thousand, two hundred people at Westminster Hall. I thought he was very impressive but also, like Liam Fox, had little if any chance of becoming party leader.

The Liberal Democrat annual conference in Blackpool that September was unmemorable but as busy as always. I did lives and packages for three days. I interviewed Charles Kennedy several times, Sir Menzies Campbell twice and other leading Lib Dems including Simon Hughes, Mark Oaten, Alan Beith and Sarah Teather who, at the time, was actually being touted as a possible future party leader.

On the day of Charles Kennedy's leader's speech, I was live every hour and didn't emerge from the Winter Gardens or see daylight all day. It was a relief to cut and send a package for the early evening news programmes and get out of there! As for the content, the only really notable issue was Charles Kennedy's leadership. He hit back at critics who had accused him of being 'asleep at the wheel', and gave a rousing conference speech which, in itself, was enough to convince most Lib Dems that they had the best leader available to them.

From Blackpool to Brighton for the Labour Party conference. This time, Gordon Brown's speech was far more conciliatory, focusing on the 'renewal' of New Labour. I packaged that while Adam did the lives.

The parties that evening included the *Guardian* party at The Grand, a chance to catch up with Gordon Brown, Neil Kinnock, Peter Mandelson and Northern Ireland Secretary Peter Hain. Earlier that day, the de Chastelain Commission, the independent international body established to oversee the decommissioning of paramilitary weapons in Northern Ireland, confirmed that the IRA had indeed decommissioned all of its weapons. The Unionists remained suspicious. Among the IRA arsenal reported to have been destroyed were one thousand rifles, several tons of Semtex, two dozen heavy machine guns, seven surface to air missiles, mortars, flame throwers, detonators, twenty RPG launchers, one hundred handguns and more than one hundred grenades. Apparently, they had even had a Second World War Bren light machine gun!

The leader's speech, and Tony Blair received his first standing ovation before he had even uttered a word. He clearly wasn't going anywhere anytime soon. I packaged five minutes for *Live at Five*, with a re-cut with more reaction and a live with four Labour Party delegates for *Sky News at Ten*.

I had the usual early start the next day. I did a package on school food, which the government thought should be healthier. It would have been news if they had said the opposite! An eighty-two-year-old anti-war protestor, Walter Wolfgang, was ejected from the conference hall by stewards for heckling Jack Straw during his conference speech on Iraq. This became a big story and I cut the lead package for *Live at Five*. I updated the package for *Sky News at Ten* to include an apology by Labour Party Chairman Ian McCartney for the way in which the frail, eighty-two year old had been manhandled.

The next morning, on Radio Four's *Today* programme, Tony Blair also apologised to Walter Wolfgang. We had a live interview with Tony Blair at eight twenty a.m. I did lives at 10, 11am and midday and talked into and out of Defence Secretary John Reid's very funny and rather moving speech at one p.m. which closed the conference. He also apologised to Walter Wolfgang.

In the afternoon, I did a live sit-down, three-camera interview with the newly-famous Walter Wolfgang. His story had dominated coverage of the Labour conference for the previous twenty-four hours. A lifelong socialist and vice chairman of CND, he justified shouting 'nonsense' at Jack Straw when the Foreign Secretary claimed that British forces were in Iraq for just one reason, 'to help the elected Iraqi government build a secure, democratic and stable nation'. Wolfgang had been hailed as a hero by some in the Labour Party. His conference pass had initially been withdrawn but that decision had been hastily reversed and he had been in the conference hall and the centre of attention once more when John Reid apologised to him in his conference speech that lunchtime. The following year, Walter Wolfgang was elected to Labour's NEC (National Executive Committee).

The Conservative party conference in Blackpool was dominated by speeches by the candidates for party leadership. David Davis had begun as the bookies' favourite, but that soon changed. He was judged to have delivered the poorest pitch, well short of the performances of Ken Clarke, Malcolm Rifkind and even Liam Fox. But David Cameron was the star of the show, emerging from behind the podium, walking around the stage and talking without notes. He was refreshing, modern and looked like the future. The odds shifted in his favour.

I didn't get to the Tory conference that year. I was tasked with staying at Westminster and reporting on the government. While the Tories were meeting in Blackpool, Tony Blair was meeting Russian leader, Vladimir Putin, in London. They held a joint press conference. I got to ask Putin a question. I don't think he liked it too much. His piercing eyes stared into mine. I had been stared at, steely-eyed, by Margaret Thatcher in her prime but this was a different league, a death stare that felt like he was reaching in an ice-cold hand and gripping my soul in a frozen grip.

I had met him once before, on a visit to London, and he had been friendly enough while mocking the failure to find WMD in Iraq. This time he was very hostile. I also interviewed European Commission President José Manuel Barroso, which was an altogether far more comfortable experience.

While David Cameron was looking like someone who might revive the Tory brand, I was off to Paris with Tony Blair for another bilateral with Jacques Chirac. We flew out the evening before the prime minister and sent a package for *Sunrise* with a PTC from the Place de la Concorde. This time, the officials at the Élysée Palace were absolutely adamant that under no circumstances would we be allowed to park our truck and do lives inside the palace courtyard. I began arguing with them at 6.30am. Two hours later, when they weren't looking, our satellite guys simply cabled across the courtyard from the truck outside and we did our first live at 9 0'clock. Sky did a split screen at 10am with me on camera talking live as we showed shots of Tony Blair arriving and then I was live again as Blair and Chirac held an informal press conference on the steps of the Élysée Palace. ITN and the BBC had to make do with recorded footage. The officious officials never clocked what we were doing, and even cheerfully waved us off as we left!

The meeting had focused on a common European defence policy and the increasingly bitter haggling over the EU budget. We relocated to the Place de la Concorde to do more lives and sent a package which ran all afternoon and evening.

Parliament returned on October 10th. I did lives all day on the proposed new anti-terrorism laws and the election of Angela Merkel as the new chancellor of Germany. Malcolm Rifkind withdrew from the Conservative party leadership race the next day. I interviewed him and got him live into Sky News ahead of the BBC opposition.

David Cameron was on the BBC's *Question Time* programme. All week, he had been evading the question of whether or not he had taken drugs while at university. Frankly, who cared, or cares now? But he was almost visibly squirming as he refused to give a straight yes or no answer. I was still doing lives all day the next day and all evening on did he or didn't he! Apparently, it was OK to get outrageously drunk and misbehave as a member of the Bullingdon Club but not to smoke the odd spliff. Ridiculous. I thought he should have simply said, 'yes, but so did almost everyone else, and that was a very long time ago, the excesses of youth', and put the story to bed. Instead, it just went on and on. And on.

The next day, I did lives all morning and most of the afternoon on a Tony Blair speech to the TUC before I was sent to Conservative Central Office to do yet more lives for the evening news programmes on whether or not David Cameron had ever taken drugs. Monumentally tedious.

It was the same the next day. I had cut a package for *Sunrise* and did lives off the back of the package all morning. In the afternoon, we went to the Theatre Royal Drury Lane where David Cameron was presenting awards to teachers. I doorstepped him live as he arrived. Although his answers were still evasive and non-committal, neither ITN, the BBC nor anyone else was there, so we had a little scoop. More lives all evening and a package to run after I escaped at 8 o'clock at the end of a twelve-hour day.

In 2019, David Cameron finally admitted that he had smoked cannabis while he was at Eton but, by then, many other leading politicians had admitted to taking drugs when they were younger, including Michael Gove who had apparently indulged in cocaine. Yawn! Really, does anyone care? The *Daily Mail* did!

I had the early shift the next morning. My first live was at 6am with lives every hour until lunchtime and a package for the afternoon. David Cameron and David Davis had been to see Francis Maude and Sir Michael Spicer who were running the leadership election to clarify the hustings rules and other arrangements before beginning their six-week campaigns. David Cameron appeared to be comfortably ahead, but a lot could happen in six weeks.

The UK had the presidency of the EU and hosted a summit at the end of October set in the magnificent Hampton Court. I went there the day before to sort out our accreditation and get shots of the palace, interiors and exteriors, and the famous maze. Exteriors of the maze only, we had a deadline! The joke doing the rounds was that the UK was hosting the summit at the home of England's first and most famous Euro-sceptic!

The Hampton Court summit will not go down in history. Despite the usual EU communique about 'fruitful discussions', it achieved very little but was most newsworthy at the time in its response to a comment by the Iranian president that Israel should be 'wiped off the face of the earth'. I did a few lives, Adam did most of them, and I was at the Tony Blair press conference at six p.m. The prime minister was angry with Iran, with veiled threats to 'do something' about the regime in Tehran. The EU issued a statement very strongly condemning the Iranian president. So did the United States. I knew from my military contacts that the US military had war-gamed invading both Iran and North Korea at the same time and concluded that such a dual operation was feasible. This struck me as completely mad, Dr Strangelove territory.

Paddy Ashdown had been appointed UN high commissioner to Bosnia and Herzegovina in 2002 following his lobbying for military action against the Milošević regime of Yugoslavia in the 1990s. His four-year term of office was coming to an end, and I persuaded my bosses at Sky News that this was worth a story. So, at the beginning of November I flew to Sarajevo with cameraman Martin Smith. During his time in Bosnia, Paddy had greatly strengthened government institutions, brought the two ethnic armies under a single civilian command, and was nudging Bosnia and Herzegovina towards EU membership. He had become known in the press as the 'viceroy of Bosnia', but we preferred the King of Bosnia and so too, we soon discovered, did many of the Bosnians we met.

Although I had worked in Bosnia, I had never been to Sarajevo. In my mind, it was still the city under siege of the Bosnian war. We flew there via Prague as there were no direct flights. We found bullet holes in some buildings, the Holiday Inn was still a ruin and the National Library was still burnt out and very slowly being restored but the most striking thing about Sarajevo was how normal it was. Pavement cafes, markets, street art, we could have been in any European city.

We checked into the Astra Hotel, poor by international standards but luxurious by local standards. After dinner at the Inat Kroba restaurant (Bosnian pot, which is a delicious beef stew), we wandered back through the pretty Old Town. The other thing that struck me about Sarajevo was just how small it is.

Paddy Ashdown was extremely accommodating, although he too had a habit of smoking my cigarettes ("don't tell Jane"). Wheels up was at 7am and we drove in his convoy to the small town of Foča. There had been battles in and around the town between the Chetniks and the Ustaše during the Second World War, and the town had seen fierce fighting between Serbs and Muslims during the recent Yugoslav civil war. We met Serb refugees, visited a restored Muslim cemetery, two destroyed mosques and a chilling exhumation site at a coal mine where bodies had been dumped in shallow graves. We filmed Paddy meeting the town's mayor and chief of police.

We visited the Sutjeska national park for lunch with the park's director. A very large lunch, too much really. But we worked it off afterwards when Paddy decided to visit the Second World War partisan war memorial at Tjentište. Ever the Royal Marine, Paddy yomped up the hill to the memorial, leaving us trailing and panting in his wake. Even Martin, who was much fitter than me, struggled.

The hill was strategically vital during the Second World War fighting, when Tito's partisans held out against several German divisions. There had been ferocious hand to hand fighting on this hillside. The partisans had set up a large field gun with which they had pounded German positions in the valley below. The German solution was to dismantle an even larger gun, carry it up the next and slightly higher hill, reassemble it and rain shells down onto the partisans' main position.

Despite that, Tito's partisans prevailed and the war in the Balkans began to turn against the Nazis. The immediate area was also the scene of a war crime when, under direct orders from Hitler, the Germans surrounded a hospital and massacred wounded partisans and the unarmed medical staff. At a post-war trial, the German commander General Alexander Löhr was convicted of war crimes. He was executed in 1947.

Going there had little if anything to do with Paddy's work as UN high commissioner and added very little to our story about the work he had done and was still doing in the country, but he wanted to go there so we did. Paddy had fallen in love with Bosnia, he had even bought a house there which, of course, we christened the king of Bosnia's palace!

Flying home, we missed a big day at Westminster. David Blunkett had resigned from the Cabinet for the second time. There were stories about his business interests during the six months when he had not held office, although he was completely exonerated three weeks later after an investigation by the Cabinet Secretary Sir Gus O'Donnell (who was known throughout Westminster simply as God).

Next stop after Bosnia was a Gordon Brown visit to Israel. We stayed at the King David Hotel in Jerusalem, more echoes of history. No sooner had we arrived and joined Gordon Brown's convoy for the drive from Tel Aviv to Jerusalem than we turned back to the airport. The chancellor was heading back to London for that evening's vote on the anti-terrorism bill and would return to Israel on an overnight flight. I phoned this development into Sky as breaking news, and interviewed Gordon who explained why he was returning. He left, and I did lives every hour for the next five hours from Jerusalem, throwing each time to a Gordon Brown grab.

In the Commons that evening the government lost the vote to extend from fourteen to ninety days the length of time the police could hold a terrorism suspect without charge by 322-391. An extension to twenty-eight days was passed, 323-290, but it had been Tony Blair's first defeat in the Commons since becoming prime minister in 1997.

Gordon Brown duly returned the next morning and finally got to focus on Israel-Palestine, but a two-day schedule had to be crammed into a single day. We visited a girls' school in Ramallah, Gordon Brown had meetings with various Israeli politicians and attended Ariel Sharon's business conference. He was very keen to visit the Gaza Strip, so was I, but was told in no uncertain terms that it would be far too dangerous and no one could guarantee his safety. He was still up for it but was eventually persuaded not to go. When the other travelling press went to the airport to return to London with the chancellor, I headed back to Jerusalem to do lives and cut a package for the evening with our Jerusalem picture editor, Ariel.

We were done by 9pm local time, and Ariel gave me a lift back to the King David Hotel. I had been to Jerusalem before, but that didn't stop me marvelling once again, the next morning, at the Western wall, the Church of the Holy Sepulchre and the Dome of the Rock before my flight home.

Charles Clarke and Tessa Jowell went to the Barrowboy and Banker pub next to London Bridge to launch yet another government crackdown, on drunk, disorderly behaviour, I interviewed them and did live doughnuts from the pub. We recorded a complicated, in-vision graphics sequence for the *Live at Five* package, which I doughnutted from the Marquis of Granby, with the same routine again at six p.m. For a new package for 9 o'clock I did a PTC at the Red Lion in Whitehall. My third pub of the day, and not a drop taken!

My Paddy Ashdown package ran on November 21st. We had had a day to edit two versions, one long at about eight minutes and a shorter version cut down to three minutes twenty which is, in itself, quite a long piece for TV news. It would have been very easy for the programme editors to simply run the shorter version, but, to my delight, they ran it at length in the breakfast bulletins and in the evening, with the shorter version running all day in between. Verbal herograms all around the wicket. Martin had shot some great stuff.

I was invited to a breakfast meeting at Claridge's with Dame Pauline Neville-Jones, Foreign Office political director and former chair of the Joint Intelligence Committee. She was a font of wisdom and insight. She believed that many Middle East countries, in particular Saudi Arabia, were in a classic pre-revolutionary state. This was five years before the start of the so-called Arab Spring.

December 6th was Tory leadership day. We were at the Royal Academy for the results at two p.m. David Cameron got 134,000 votes, David Davis 64,000, so a victory margin of more than two to one. I did lives and packaged for *Live at Five* and *Sky News at Ten*. It seemed astonishing to me that David Cameron, at the age of just 39, with so little experience and having only been an MP for four years, was now the leader of the Conservative Party and a probable future prime minister.

The Law Lords ruled that evidence obtained from terrorist suspects by using torture was inadmissible in court. It would have been news if they had said anything different, but I did a live as the decision was announced, with lives and packages all day.

Lib Dem MPs met to discuss Charles Kennedy's health. It was an open secret at Westminster that he had a drink problem. I had been to his flat in Westminster more than once to find him fully compos mentis but with whisky fumes seeping from every pore. It seemed to me that he might indeed be an alcoholic but, if so, he was a fully functioning alcoholic. He briefed us off camera afterwards, it had been a wonderful meeting, everyone was supporting him, etc.

Charles Kennedy's health/drinking made the front page of the next day's *Times*, *Telegraph* and *Guardian*. I thought the Lib Dems lacked the expertise and ability to kill the story and that Charles' days as party leader were probably numbered.

He would be gone within a month.

My final working day of the year was December 30th. The New Year's honours list and Tony Blair's New Year message. I also cut a four-minute package on the challenges facing Blair in the first six months of 2006. In the evening, we got word that aid worker Kate Burton and her parents were about to be released in Gaza. They had been kidnapped two days earlier. They were released unharmed. I did lives every hour from the Foreign Office. Some good news to end the year.

CHAPTER 4

2006: Charles Kennedy. TB-GBs. John Prescott, the Gift that just Keeps Giving. Tories Closing the Gap. Cash-for-peerages. Getting Mobbed by Screaming Schoolgirls! Saddam Hussein Executed

Downing Street released a New Year video, billed as a day in the life of Tony Blair. In fact, it was more like a video diary full of confessions to a fly-on-the-wall camera. I found it vacuous, but it would no doubt have been of interest to at least some of our viewers so I packaged it on January 1st. It was embargoed until midnight and aired on January 2nd. I was in Downing Street all day doing lives every hour off the back of the package.

David Cameron made a speech on health, parking his tanks on Labour's lawn. His was to be a more caring, modern Conservative Party. I packaged the story for *Live at Five* with a longer version to run all evening. In Israel, Ariel Sharon was taken to hospital after suffering a massive stroke. He recovered, and would live for another eight years.

A busy first week of January got a lot more so when at five forty-five p.m. on Thursday 5th Charles Kennedy made a dramatic, though not surprising, announcement admitting that he had been treated for alcoholism for the past eighteen months, and calling a leadership election in which he would be a candidate. It was another of those 'put up or shut up' moments as he tried to appeal to the party membership over the heads of his MPs, many if not most of whom were making no secret of the fact that they wanted him to go. I packaged the story and did a live interview with Lembit Öpik, who appeared to be the only Kennedy-supporting MP willing to talk on camera.

Charles Kennedy's announcement came as ITN were preparing to break the story of his alcoholism. ITN had employed Charles Kennedy's former press secretary, Daisy McAndrew (née Sampson) as a political correspondent. Her part in the story raised eyebrows and eyes to heaven at

Westminster. She was dubbed 'the blonde assassin'. But it went far deeper than the fact that Charles Kennedy was a recovering alcoholic. Even as he emerged from his home that Friday to claim he had more than enough support to continue, his MPs were complaining that he had failed to provide clear leadership and had not made any impact for a very long time. Meanwhile, they said, the Tories under their new leader were resurgent or, as one of them put it to me, 'rampant'.

Twenty-five of the sixty-two Lib Dem MPs had already signed a letter urging him to resign. They felt the party should have done much better in the previous May's general election and now needed a new direction. I thought he should leave with as much dignity as possible. It felt like his time had come, and gone.

Charles Kennedy resigned at 3 o'clock that Saturday afternoon. I had already prepared his political obit which ran every hour once he had gone. It was a sad end to what had been a glittering political career. He had been a charismatic leader. Charles was clever, affable and very good company.

As is the way with these things, the spotlight rapidly moved on to the issue of who would succeed him as party leader. The party's Federal Executive met the following Monday to set a date for the leadership election, assuming there would be one. At that point, there was only one candidate, Sir Menzies Campbell, but there would be more. I went straight to central lobby to go live. We beat the BBC by four minutes and the bosses at Sky News were happy. That had now become the game, to break the news ahead of anyone else, and especially the BBC, even by a few minutes or even seconds. It still is.

The slogan, the masthead of Sky News became 'First for Breaking News', and quite rightly so, but any piece of trivia, any tittle-tattle, any metaphorical twitch of the net curtains became 'BREAKING NEWS'. Once, when a 'Breaking News' strap appeared, people would look up from what they were doing (in government offices, banks, and so on) and tune in. It must be something important. That is not the case any more.

Sir Menzies Campbell's first appearance at PMQs as interim Lib Dem leader did not go well. He raised the issue of the shortage of head teachers. Organisations, he declared, can find it difficult to fill a leadership vacancy, 'especially failing organisations'. He had dug a huge hole for himself, and Tony Blair cheerfully pushed him into it to loud Labour cheers.

Simon Hughes launched his leadership campaign at the Oxo tower the next day. He spoke briefly at a press conference and took four or five questions. Mine was the first. We took the press conference live, and Sky came to me immediately it was over for a long live interview with the candidate, his first.

Ruth Kelly was still struggling to explain how someone who had been cautioned for downloading child pornography had been approved for a job as a school PE teacher. He was on the sex offenders' register. Four days later, a Monday, I was still doing lives all day on Ruth Kelly's future. She would be making a statement to the House the following Thursday and would have to get it absolutely right. I cut a Ruth Kelly political obit!

That evening, Sky News aired the first Lib Dem leadership debate chaired by the talented Julie Etchingham. It was a curious affair. The patrician Sir Menzies was rather wooden, un-animated, and refused to look at the other three candidates, Simon Hughes, Chris Huhne and Mark Oaten. He kept his eyes firmly on Julie. Presumably, he had been advised to do so.

Menzies Campbell survived his second PMQs. I helped Oona King with an authored piece on reaction in Bethnal Green and Bow to their MP George Galloway's appearance in the *Big Brother* house. Cringe-worthy does not begin to describe it. Nauseating gets a bit closer. Dressed in a red leotard, he had crawled across the floor pretending to be a cat. I shudder even now at the thought of it. I asked Oona how much she regretted losing her seat to, well, that! She was unequivocal in her response, saying she never wanted to be an MP again. "It's Hell."

Ruth Kelly did enough to survive that Thursday. In her statement at midday, she had to explain why the sex offenders register and List 99 did not appear to be protecting children from potentially predatory paedophile teachers. It was felt she had done enough to reassure concerned parents. I did lives and packaged the story. Ruth Kelly had survived but was weakened. In my view, she was not very good at selling a policy, a key skill for a secretary of state, but was probably happier more in the background as an administrator or as a junior minister. She was still only 37 with four children and a very high-profile, high-powered and unpopular job. Education had become a divisive issue within the Labour Party. That evening, I interviewed Neil Kinnock, normally such a staunch Blair supporter, who was opposing the government's education White Paper.

Conservative Party Chairman Francis Maude paraded Adrian Graves, who had stood unsuccessfully for the Lib Dems in Suffolk West and had now defected to the Tories. No one was particularly interested, although our ears pricked up a little when he claimed that three Lib Dem MPs were also considering defecting to the Tories.

Two days before the Lib Dem leadership hustings in Plymouth, Simon Hughes came out as gay. This was no great surprise to anyone, but was still a story. Adam was live, I did the packages. I was also live all day at the hustings in Plymouth. Producer Jane Elston had travelled down the evening before, so by the time I arrived on the train from Paddington that morning everything was in place. I did lives before and after the candidates' speeches, which Sky News also took live. Being Lib Dems, the entire exercise was terribly civilised. My final live was with all three candidates, which worked exceptionally well. They didn't appear to disagree on very much.

US Secretary of State Condoleezza Rice was in town again the following Monday. I did lives from her hotel, Claridge's, and we took a press conference live with Condi and Afghan President Hamid Karzai. I got a question, though not the first which was reserved for one of the White House travelling press pack, and a very long and detailed answer. She was there not only to offer reassurance to the Afghans, but also to deliver veiled threats to Iran and the hostile American reaction to the Hamas electoral success in Palestine. I packaged the story for the evening, with a PTC at the Savoy. These people didn't slum it!

Into February, and a breakfast with Peter Mandelson at the European Commission. He was mischievously indiscreet about Gordon Brown, Jacques Chirac and Gerhard Schröder. My main story that day was a government defeat the previous night in a vote on the Racial Hatred Act. Labour's Chief Whip Hilary Armstrong had miscalculated badly. The government lost by just one vote after she had told Tony Blair that he didn't need to be in the Commons to vote as it was in the bag. One vote. Oops!

At PMQs, Tony Blair was getting the better of David Cameron who, in a leaflet for a by-election in Dunfermline, had described himself as a 'liberal Conservative', and said he agreed with the Lib Dems on several issues, including Iraq. Blair referred to an article in the *Telegraph* of two weeks earlier when David Cameron had described himself as 'Conservative to my core'. A week later, he was claiming to be the heir to New Labour. Now he was a liberal Conservative. No wonder, Blair concluded, that Cameron was against ID cards. Great punchline.

The Lib Dems went on to win the Dunfermline and West Fife by-election overturning a 16,000 Labour majority. This was particularly embarrassing for Gordon Brown who lived in the constituency and was MP for the neighbouring constituency of Kirkcaldy and Cowdenbeath.

I went to South Africa with Tony Blair in mid-February. Sky News flew me economy class, an eleven-hour flight. It seemed company policy had changed. Previously, we always flew business class on long flights. The flight was packed and I arrived at nine a.m. local time, seven a.m. GMT, with a very sore neck having had no sleep. Not an ideal start, but things soon improved. Producer Dan Williams, formerly of our Washington bureau, was now working in Sky's South Africa bureau in Johannesburg. We went to Pretoria to get our accreditation to cover the bilateral summit and to the Kwalata game lodge an hour away to set up in the media centre.

The next day was strange. We did lives from the Kwalata game lodge, but were getting no information from the South African government and South African TV, SABC, which was supposed to be providing pool pictures, had almost no shots at all. Number Ten press officer, Lauren Flannagan, and Ross Dixon of the British High Commission were with us and in the same boat, trying to get information, any information. Downing Street communications director, Dave Hill, told me there was a good chance of a one-to-one sit-down interview with Tony Blair the next day.

Tony Blair held a press conference, I got the first question and got him to respond to the shocking pictures which had emerged of British soldiers beating up prisoners in Iraq. Dan Williams went back to the media centre on the journalist coach to feed the Tony Blair grab to Sky News. The story was leading the news, so to get the prime minister's reaction had already more than justified the expense of covering the summit. I stayed on with cameraman Mike Donnelly as we were still hoping to get a one-to-one interview with Tony Blair. Dave Hill was blowing hot and cold. They probably didn't want me asking any more awkward questions. There were plenty to ask.

Finally, we got a long doorstep with Tony Blair and South African President Thabo Mbeki. It was exclusive, no one else had stayed behind, but they would only talk about their summit and African issues. For *Live a Five*, I did a live throwing to a Blair grab, picked up and threw to a package by my colleague Peter Spencer on Blair's tough week ahead (another one!) and then took two or three more questions. An eight-minute sequence at the top of the news, a very good way to finish the day.

Next morning, Tony Blairs BA flight was aborted on take-off. There had been a loud bang and sparks were flying as the aircraft picked up speed on the runway. It was frightening. Tony Blair didn't bat an eyelid. It had only been engine failure and everyone was relieved to disembark. It meant another twenty-four hours in South Africa. Tony Blair had wanted to visit Soweto but there hadn't been enough time. Now he could.

I did several lives from the roof of our Johannesburg bureau. Back in London they wanted more, but we had to go to Kliptown, the oldest district of Soweto, where Tony Blair was due to visit the Walter Sisulu/ANC memorial. He did a very controlled walkabout in Soweto. The security was robust, but he was very well received by the local residents. Mike got some great shots, and I did a long interview with the prime minister, who answered questions on South Africa, ID cards, Iraq and his almost plane crash, about which he was remarkably sanguine. We fed our interview from the Johannesburg bureau, were quoted on the Press Association wires which is always good, and packaged the story for *Live at Five*.

We flew back the next day, but not on Tony Blair's flight as he had left the previous evening. This time, we flew club class, but only because Sky wanted me to work the next day covering yet another Commons debate on the anti-terrorism bill. We had a few hours spare, so we visited 'the Cradle of Humankind', the apartheid museum and an African market tourist trap.

The anti-terrorism debate that Wednesday was all about re-inserting the word 'glorification' into the Bill, which is about as esoteric as politics can get. The government won comfortably enough, with a majority of thirty-eight. Tony Blair did a quick interview in Jack Straw's office at the House. I packaged the story, though God only knows what our viewers made of it. Hours of arguing over a single word.

On what began as a quiet Thursday in late February, I interviewed Jack Straw at the Foreign Office on Guantánamo and 'extraordinary rendition', covered the final Lib Dem leadership hustings at the Friends meeting house on Euston Road, an otherwise dull affair enlivened by some heckling, interviewed the candidates, and did a couple of lives in Downing Street in the evening on Angela Merkel, Silvio Berlusconi, José Manuel Barroso and others condemning David Cameron's decision to take the Conservatives out of the EPP. Not such a quiet day after all.

At a press conference with Tony Blair and Ruth Kelly in Downing Street ahead of the publication of the Education Bill, the prime minister was amused by one of my questions, describing me as a model for my colleague for the way in which I asked him about the Education Bill but also slipped in another question about Tessa Jowell in the same breath. This was live on Sky News. There had been rumours circulating in Westminster that Tessa was about to resign or be sacked. She didn't and wasn't.

We got the Lib Dem leadership result first, or rather our producer Peter Diapre did, completely slam-dunking the opposition. We were live at Lib Dem HQ. Menzies Campbell was comfortably ahead of Chris Huhne after the first vote, Simon Hughes was eliminated and his second preferences redistributed under the STV (Single Transferrable Vote) system and the Lib Dems had a new leader. I did a sit-down ten-minute interview with Sir Menzies (an ITN pool two-camera shoot to be shared with all the broadcasters) and cut the lead story for *Live at Five*.

Although a lot older than the other main party leaders, Tony Blair and David Cameron, Sir Menzies was wise enough to surround himself with young talent, including future party leaders Nick Clegg and Jo Swinson.

Culture Secretary Tessa Jowell was still being hounded by some newspapers, the usual suspects. Hugely popular, she was supported by MPs on all sides when she appeared in the House of Commons for monthly culture questions the following Monday, Tony Blair had defended her and David Cameron was being extremely courteous. The issue had concerned the business activities of her husband, David Mills, and whether there had been any conflict of interest between her personal life and her ministerial duties. The Parliamentary Standards Commissioner Sir Philip Mawer had investigated and concluded that she had no case to answer. She was off the hook, completely exonerated, and I packaged the story all day as it developed.

We were off to Bratislava and Prague for a Tony Blair visit. Cameraman Tony Fyfe and I were met at Vienna airport by a British Embassy driver, Tibor, who I had arranged to drive us to Bratislava. It's a short drive, only forty-five minutes, through very pretty snow-covered hills. It was very cold. It was the first time I had been back since the 1989 Velvet Revolution. The splendid Carlton Radisson hotel was right next to the opera house, the perfect backdrop for an 'As Live' to keep the Sky News tiger fed.

Tony Blair was late arriving at the Slovakian prime minister's official residence but held a press conference as soon as he arrived. I had to ask him about Rover cars. A House of Commons Public Accounts Committee report said that any government attempt to bail out Rover was a waste of money. The committee chairman, Conservative MP Edward Leigh, was causing mischief. I asked Tony Blair about Rover but tagged in onto a question about Slovakia, which amused him. "How do you do that? How do you get from Rover to Slovakian politics?"

After just three hours' sleep, our driver Tibor collected us at 4.30am the next morning to take us to Vienna airport for a Turboprop flight to Prague. I liked Turboprops, though they never felt completely safe. John Profumo had died at the age of ninety-one. My obit, cut months earlier, was running every hour.

One of Tony Blair's aides, who travelled with him to summits, always seemed to get the job of prime minister's bag carrier (luggage, famous red boxes, etc.). He was also called Glen. So, when we go abroad to summits etc., I'd often hear, "Glen will get your bags, Prime Minister".

And I thought and sometimes said aloud to the amusement of the travelling press pack, "Oh no he bloody won't!"

We set up at the Czech prime minister's official residence and got shots of a Tony Blair handshake with the Czech Prime Minister Jiří Paroubek and of the two men walking in the garden of the residence, high on a hill with fabulous views over Prague. At a press conference, Tony Blair paid tribute to John Profumo, talking about his charitable work after his political disgrace. We fed from a satellite truck, parked, rather bizarrely, next to a bright orange London double-decker bus which was to be used as a political battle bus in the upcoming Czech elections.

Back in London, the second reading of the Education Bill passed in the Commons the next evening. I cut a package for 5 and 6 pm and did lives between 7 and 8pm on a freezing cold Abingdon Green with several MPS including Steve McCabe, Barry Sheerman and Angela Eagle, but Sky News went to our (short-lived!) *International News* programme at eight p.m. instead of staying with the breaking news story. This was just as I was about to interview, live, Education Secretary of State Ruth Kelly and her Conservative Shadow David Willetts. I eventually interviewed Ruth Kelly live at 8.30 having persuaded the secretary of state to wait in the freezing cold for half an hour!

Before escaping that evening, I cut a package on Labour cash-for-peerages for *Sunrise*, which would be our main story the next day when Tony Blair's monthly press conference was dominated by the issue, much to his irritation. I packaged the story all day, the accusation being that Labour donors had been nominated for peerages as a reward for giving large amounts of money to the Labour Party.

The cash-for-peerages scandal would plague the Blair government for more than a year as a police investigation continued, headed by the Met's Assistant Commissioner John Yates. It led to the extraordinary spectacle of a prime minister, Tony Blair, being interviewed by the police three times, though only as a witness and not under caution.

The long and detailed police investigation eventually concluded, in July 2007, with the Crown Prosecution Service deciding not to bring any charges against anyone. Their conclusion was that although peerages may have been awarded in exchange for loans, there was no evidence that this had been agreed in advance, evidence that would be needed for a successful prosecution. So, honours had been awarded to party donors but they had not been bought.

The cash-for-peerages story had legs for the next couple of days, and we would return to it many times over the next sixteen months. I packaged the story all the next day. Lord (Charlie) Falconer made a statement in the Lords. I interviewed him, Adam interviewed David Cameron. The following day, Labour's ruling NEC met to discuss the crisis. I did lives and packages all day, and interviewed Dr Chai Patel who had lent the Labour Party one and a half million pounds at a commercial rate of interest and had been nominated for a life peerage. A week later, he withdrew his name from the list of nominees saying he had never expected any kind of reward for his loan. For the first and only time, I did a PTC in a launderette: Labour washing its dirty laundry in public, were the Lib Dems whiter than white and would the Tories come clean? Not exactly subtle!

The next day was Budget day, Gordon Brown's tenth. I was live in Downing Street, including the money shot of the chancellor holding up the famous red box. It was a mid-term budget, not exactly one to set the world alight. There was more money for schools, a few nascent green policies and higher thresholds for stamp duty and inheritance tax. PMQs that day was classic 'Punch and Judy politics'. David Cameron had prepared a few schoolboy jokes. Sir Menzies Campbell was, sadly, beginning to live up to his unkind new sobriquet 'Mogadon Ming'. I was doughnutting my package with a live top and tail from central lobby all afternoon and into the evening.

David Cameron described UKIP as 'fruitcakes, loonies and closet racists'. UKIP was threatening to use the Freedom of Information Act to force the Conservatives to reveal the names of people who had lent money to the party. UKIP leader Roger Knapmann and co-founder Nigel Farage demanded an apology. Cameron did not oblige them.

Later that day, I interviewed Gordon Brown at the Treasury on the economy not on fruitcakes and loonies, which we all found hugely entertaining, though Cameron had probably crossed a line by branding them as racists. David Cameron defended his remarks by claiming that UKIP had been infiltrated by the far right. Mostly though Gordon and I talked about babies. Sarah Brown's was due on July 24th and our second, Sebastian, was due at about the same time.

The Conservative spring conference was held in Manchester that April. We had a great two days. On the Friday, we did lives at 8,9 and 10am and David Cameron's arrival at 10.20. It was a huge media bun fight, but he only spoke directly to me ('you're live on Sky News') and only took my questions. Excellent. A live interview with George Osborne at 11 o'clock., more lives at midday and one p.m., a sit-down interview with David Cameron at 2.45 and two lives in the 4 o'clock news hour, first a live interview with William Hague then another with Michael Heseltine. A final live at 5 o'clock, then a package for the evening. I felt we had well and truly covered the first day of the Tories in Manchester.

Day two was just as busy and just as successful from our point of view. We did lives every hour all morning with lives into and out of David Cameron's conference speech, another live with Party Chairman Francis

Maude which I doughnutted at 2pm, and cut a package to run for the rest of the afternoon and evening before heading back to London.

There was a slightly daft Sky/YouGov poll on the BNP at the end of April which claimed to reveal that 55% of people said they liked the BNP's policies until they were told what those policies actually were. The 'policies' were the more mainstream ideas not the darker, racist stuff, so the poll seemed rather pointless. But, of course, it had shock value: 55%support the BNP! In my view, it also gave far too much free publicity to the BNP which had 15 councillors at the time out of total of more than 20,000. I gently mocked it in lives at 10 and 11am, and Adam did the same at midday and 1 o'clock. I packaged the story for 2pm with a fresh version to run in *Live at Five* and all evening. It only ran again once, as the programme editors finally acquiesced to our objections.

An away day in Bournemouth where Health Secretary Patricia Hewitt was addressing the Royal College of Nursing conference. She had a torrid time. She was booed, heckled, shouted down, slow hand-clapped, the works! Sky took it all live and I did a live with one of the disgruntled nurses after the performance at three 3.45 another at 4 o'clock with two angry nurses, and did live doughnuts at 5 and 6pm throwing to three minutes of the best of the action. We had expected a dull afternoon. It had been anything but.

As April gave way to May, the *Mail on Sunday* paid Tracey Temple a rumoured £200,000 to reveal all about her affair with John Prescott, a classic kiss and tell story. Horrible. I had cut a long package on Tony Blair's nine years in office which we ran on May 1st. Would his legacy be dominated by the Iraq war? And how much time did he have left? I was live off the back of the package every hour from lunchtime until eleven p.m., also answering questions on John Prescott's future prospects, which I estimated to be approximately zero.

I was asked to put together a Tony Blair political obit, just in case. This was just two days before local council elections, and the police announced that they had interviewed several senior Labour Party people about cash-for-peerages though not, at that time, Tony Blair. I worked all the next day on the Blair political obit, a substantial ten-minute piece which I thought would almost certainly never see the light of day.

As usual, we all worked all night on the local council elections, with lives and very fast turnaround packages capturing the latest results every half hour. It had been a bad night for Labour, down nearly 300 seats although, as mid-term elections go, it could have been far worse. It was a good night for the Conservatives who gained 300 council seats, while the Lib Dems were stuck, more or less unchanged.

After 10am we switched to a rolling live story as Tony Blair reshuffled his Cabinet. I did a few lives, my colleagues Adam Boulton and John Craig also did some. We had all been working all night. We got news of quite a few of the changes first after briefings from the PMOS Tom Kelly and others. I was able to confirm that Charles Clarke had been sacked as Home Secretary, the information coming from a most unusual source, one of David Davis' researchers. It emerged that he had actually been sacked the previous Sunday and was being replaced by John Reid, Tony Blair's man for all seasons or at least all Cabinet positions! Jack Straw was no longer the foreign secretary, which was a shame.

Jack Straw was replaced by Margaret Beckett, a bizarre appointment in my humble opinion but she was regarded by the prime minister as a safe pair of hands. John Prescott was stripped of his department, Ruth Kelly took over, but he retained his title of deputy prime minister with the attendant salary and perks. The excellent Alan Johnson replaced Ruth Kelly as education secretary. These were big changes, but would they be enough to keep Tony Blair in office? Had he made more enemies than friends, and would they now support a Gordon Brown leadership bid?

The following Monday, May 8th, was supposed to be some sort of crunch day for Tony Blair's leadership. It was nothing of the sort. I covered a David Cameron press conference which we took live, and not only got the first question but David Cameron kept referring back to it, 'Glen's question'. Tony Blair held a press conference at midday. I cut a package to run all afternoon, and did lives for four hours. Tony Blair attended the PLP meeting at 6pm. and cruised through it, his backing among Labour MPs still strong enough to see off the threat from Gordon Brown's supporters.

Tony Blair seemed determined to keep John Prescott as deputy prime minister despite the ridiculous sex scandal being played up for all it was worth in the *Mail* and elsewhere. Prescott had been loyal and had kept a significant section of the Labour Party loyal to Blair. A poll in *The Times* put the Conservatives ahead at 38% to Labour's 30%, which to me seemed somewhat unlikely but David Cameron's leadership was clearly having an impact.

Cash-for-peerages was keeping us busy, as was the issue of immigration which kept bubbling away beneath and occasionally above the surface. The new Home Secretary John Reid described the Immigration Directorate to the House of Commons Home Affairs select committee as 'not fit for purpose'. My package took the theme of what a mess the entire Home Office was in, a bloated government department that struggled with its workload. A year later, the Ministry of Justice was created, removing responsibility for the courts, prisons and probation services from the Home Office. Tony Blair gave a speech advocating nuclear power which I packaged, our lead story.

The Education Bill passed its third reading. I did lives in central lobby with various MPs. That same day, John Reid was forced to admit that some of the figures he had presented to the Home Affairs select committee the previous day had been incorrect. At least three foreign prisoners, a murderer, a rapist and a paedophile had been released on bail. His special advisor, Steve Bates, phoned me to tell me the Home Secretary was furious and had already sacked one civil servant with more to follow. I did lives on that in the afternoon before switching to the Education Bill vote for the evening and almost continuous lives from central lobby with a succession of MPs including the schools minister Jim Knight and ending with Shadow Education Secretary David Willetts and the Lib Dem education spokesperson Sarah Teather. The story of the new Education Bill had been well and truly told.

The next day it was a pensions White Paper. I was live in Downing Street all morning and with Tony Blair when he gave a statement and took questions after Cabinet. I got not only the first question but also the last! More lives later after a statement in the House by the Secretary of State for Work and Pensions John Hutton. Pensions were not something that overly excited me, but I realised that they were important to a lot of our viewers so I mustered up the necessary enthusiasm.

John Prescott, the gift that just kept giving, was snapped playing croquet at Dorneywood! Tony Blair was in Washington and Prescott was supposedly deputising for the prime minister. Few images could have been more damaging to the working-class man of the people, John Prescott, or more perfectly designed to alienate ordinary Labour voters. I mean, croquet! Needless to say, this kept me busy with lives and packages all day.

John Prescott and croquet! Who would have thought it! It was the only story in town the next day. I did lives and packages on this astonishing story all day and all evening. The day after, I had been doing lives all afternoon on a tax credits story, two billion pounds in over payments, when I heard that John Prescott had given up Dorneywood. It had previously, in any case, been the country residence of the chancellor of the exchequer, but Gordon Brown hadn't wanted it and it was, and remains, in the gift of the prime minister to allocate it to a senior minister.

I had been tipped off. In my first live at 9pm my phone rang twice while I was on air. First it was the office of the deputy prime minister, then the Downing Street Communications Director David Hill, who confirmed the story. I took the calls live on air, and relayed the new information to our audience as I was getting it! Of course, I should have left my phone in the newsroom or switched it off, but we didn't have a Westminster producer in the evenings. After seven p.m., as the political correspondent you were on your own. I had inadvertently brought this to light and thereafter a producer was assigned to cover the late shift. Anyway, it was an exciting evening, breaking news with the opposition trailing in our wake.

The next day, I was off to Rome for a Tony Blair summit with new Italian Prime Minister Romano Prodi. We flew out the evening before Tony Blair. Sky flew us club class which was excellent although there seemed to be little logic to these things. In February, I had flown economy class to South Africa, an eleven-hour flight. We landed at 10pm and met our Rome fixer, Maria, to discuss logistics.

At the magnificent Villa Doria Pamphili the next morning, we filmed the obligatory Blair-Prodi handshake. There was a thunderstorm. Huge hail stones. In Rome. In June! In Forest Gate in south-east London 250 police officers had been involved in a huge anti-terrorism operation that morning. One suspect had been shot and another arrested. I shouted a question to Tony Blair, no reply. It was the only story on Sky News. I did do a live at 3pm with the line that Tony Blair had been kept fully informed ahead of the police operation even though he had been on holiday. Prime ministers don't really get holidays in the way you or I might, they can't fully switch off, there is always something to be dealt with. Given that Sky News was covering the Forest Gate operation wall-to-wall, we did well to get on air live at 4 and 5pm, but that was it. An early finish, and a splendid evening out in Rome.

Normal Rome weather was restored the next day, warm and sunny. Although the foreign desk and programme editors were very keen to take lives from us, there was apparently no money to pay for a satellite truck. Our fixer Maria, who seemed to have Rome at her beck and call, did a deal with Sky Italia to get a truck to us, so we did some lives and sent a package when Tony Blair met the Pope. I sat with Tony Blair's bodyguards, Chris and Ian, on the flight home. I didn't fantasise at all about them being my own personal bodyguards. Well, not much!

I was invited to sit in on an off-camera Cabinet committee chaired by Tony Blair on anti-social behaviour, hearing from 'experts on the front line'. It felt very odd and was a very rare privilege to be in the room with Cabinet ministers including John Reid, Alan Johnson, John Hutton, Hilary Armstrong and Ruth Kelly. So this was what it felt like to be a Cabinet minister.

Next day, it was back to packaging the immigration story but the day was dominated by the news of redundancies at Sky News. Just awful, and apparently due to a massive overspend on the previous year's channel re-launch. Seventeen people lost their jobs including our Westminster colleague, Jenny Percival, and producer, Jane Elston, which was a huge surprise. My old friend David Chater had left Sky News the previous Monday. *Sky Report* at seven p.m. and the eight p.m. *International News Hour*, the centrepieces of the previous October's channel re-launch, were both axed. They had failed to establish themselves as 'appointment to view' television and had, in my opinion, simply got in the way of how we covered the news, live and fast. It was a grim day.

Al-Zarqawi was killed in an American airstrike the next day which, of course, totally dominated the news. It wouldn't end the violence and kidnappings, but it might help. Tony Blair held a press conference, and, by coincidence, the afternoon lobby briefing was taken by Jack Straw, now the leader of the Commons who had decided to reinstate the weekly briefings formerly held by the leader of the House. The spotlight was and is supposed to be the business of the Commons for the week ahead, which bills the government was planning to introduce, which debates would be held and so on but, as a recent foreign secretary, Jack knew far more than us about the activities of al-Zarqawi and the potential consequences of his removal.

I was the only reporter in the Rose Garden in Downing Street the following Monday for a pooled interview with Tony Blair on his ambition to make the government carbon neutral. Later that day, we lost our first soldier killed in Helmand province, Afghanistan, so I did lives for the rest of the day from the Ministry of Defence.

John Prescott was up before the House of Commons Standards and Privileges committee. He had failed/forgotten to include on the Register of Members' Interests a short holiday at the Colorado ranch of American billionaire, Philip Anschutz, who had invested three hundred and fifty million pounds in London's Millennium Dome. He escaped with a mild rebuke. I did lives on the story and was also tasked with cutting a package on what happens when Tony Blair is on holiday and John Prescott is nominally running the country. Of course, we included the pictures of croquet at Dorneywood just in case anyone had forgotten!

Adam Boulton and Anji Hunter got married, the 'political wedding of the year'. The guest list was like a Who's Who of New Labour including Tony Blair, Charles Clarke, David Blunkett, John Reid, Tessa Jowell, Peter Mandelson and Charlie Falconer. Other parties were represented, including Michael Howard and Sir Menzies Campbell, and a lot of friends and colleagues from Sky News. Marion was nine months pregnant, the baby was late. Neil Kinnock, as warm and friendly as ever, offered to deliver the baby there and then, General Sir Mike Jackson told him to stand back, he would 'take charge'. Marion was particularly excited to meet Mike Jackson.

Alastair Campbell chipped in. "Don't worry, I used to be a doctor."

Marion was also excited to meet Tony Blair who, hand outstretched, said, "Hi", and then, glancing down at her enormous bump. "Wow."

Sebastian was born on July 30th, eight pounds and eight ounces of beautiful baby boy. The labour had been very long and very painful. Marion had been absolutely heroic.

September, and party conference season. First up the Lib Dems in Brighton. A live with Sir Menzies Campbell when he arrived on the Saturday afternoon, then lives every hour including one with Simon Hughes, and a package on the events of the day and the conference agenda.

Next day, and lives every hour including live interviews with Lib Dem MPs including Lembit Öpik, Julia Gallsworthy and Evan Harris, Sir Menzies Campbell at a green taxes rally and a package on the events of the day. I did a long live interview with Sir Menzies on the Monday morning, followed by another with Vince Cable and lives before and after a Menzies Campbell leader's Q&A with delegates.

All of this was just the curtain raiser to the main event, speeches by the new leader Sir Menzies Campbell and his predecessor, Charles Kennedy. Charles' turn came on the Tuesday. We had spent the morning covering a rather dull debate on green taxes. Charles Kennedy's walk from his hotel, The Metropole, to the Brighton Conference Centre, a distance of two hundred metres, took twelve minutes. He was surrounded by a media scrum of around one hundred journalists and cameras. We took it live and I talked with Charles all the way, my unfortunate cameraman having to walk backwards in front of us. This particular stunt was dubbed 'Oglazavision' by our senior politics producer, Jonathan Levy, after a photo of Charles Kennedy and me appeared in the next morning's *Guardian* newspaper.

His speech was feisty, both funny and very serious. He seemed back to top form, he'd got his mojo back. I interviewed some Lib Dems afterwards, they were in raptures. The Sky News spotlight turned for a while to Bangkok where there had been a military coup, but was soon back on Brighton where we did lives and a package for the evening. After his conference speech, Nick Clegg also received a long, standing ovation, cementing his position as the rising star of the party.

At the Metropole hotel that evening, the Lib Dems held their 'Glee Club', a kind of revue show meets *Britain's Got Talent*, egged on by Paddy Ashdown. They all embarrassed themselves but had fun doing so. I found it all a bit excruciating.

Day four of the conference was all about looking ahead to Sir Menzies' first speech as Party leader. We covered some Ming walkabouts, interviewed him during a hospital visit and packaged a piece for the evening and next morning's *Sunrise*. But, if truth be told, we spent much of the day sitting in the Brighton sunshine gossiping with Lib Dems.

Sir Menzies' speech was far livelier than many people had expected. He was fulsome, to say the least, in his tribute to Charles Kennedy, describing him as 'the most successful leader in the Liberal tradition since Lloyd George'.

I vox popped the happy Lib Dem delegates and interviewed legendary cartoonist Steve Bell. He had been rather cruel all week as was his style ('go back to your constituencies and prepare for death!') and was very funny. We cut a package for the evening and headed home. The Lib Dems had had a successful conference but really didn't, in all honesty, seem any closer to government. Who knew then what 2010 was to bring?

From Brighton to Manchester for the Labour Party conference which was dominated by when rather than if the party would have a new leader and the country a new prime minister. After a summer of furious plotting by Brownites, Tony Blair had been forced just two weeks earlier to say that he would be gone within a year.

There was only one story, a kind of living, breathing, unfolding Tony Blair political obituary. I covered a Progress meeting at six p.m. with quite a cast: Peter Mandelson, David Miliband, Yvette Cooper, Alan Milburn, Harriet Harman, Tessa Jowell and Hilary Benn. Mandelson (Mandy to us, though never to his face!) attacked the unions and issued a coded warning to Gordon Brown and his supporters not to be in too much of a rush. Most of those Cabinet ministers were at the *New Statesman* party that evening, but not Tony Blair or Gordon Brown.

In his speech the next day, Gordon Brown heaped praise on Tony Blair. It was a very public reconciliation, but was completely undermined when Cherie Blair was reported to have muttered, "Well, that's a lie".

This was when Brown said, "It has been a privilege for me to work with and for the most successful ever leader and Labour prime minister."

She had been touring the conference Exhibition Centre, where Gordon Brown's speech was being shown live on television monitors. A Bloomberg agency reporter claimed she heard the prime minister's wife say, "Well, that's a lie", out loud to no one in particular, not realising that there was a journalist within earshot. This triggered a media frenzy and a five-hour mass stake out of Cherie Blair's hotel until she finally emerged to say that she hadn't said it and didn't think it either. But the damage had been done.

My lives had been covering the Gordon Brown speech, a speech by a man now assumed to be our next prime minister but, by the evening, they were all about what Cherie Blair had or had not said. The newspaper headlines wrote themselves: That's a lie! and only underneath in small print: Cherie Blair denies...

I met young Fraser Brown that day, a bonny baby! He had been born just before Sebastian. Gordon and Sarah had sent us a baby hoodie and a very sweet handwritten note.

The centre piece of the BBC party that evening was a very funny performance by the cast of *Dead Ringers*. On to *The Times* party, attended by most of the Cabinet including Gordon Brown, Alan Milburn, Alistair Darling, John Reid, Peter Hain et al. A golden opportunity to chat with ministers informally over a drink.

Tony Blair's farewell speech, his last as Party leader, was emotional, a grandstanding performance worthy of an Oscar. My day began with a live interview with Peter Mandelson. The BBC were also there, but without a live capability. Better still, he did a long live interview with me, refusing to take questions from anyone else. Shortly afterwards, Cherie Blair emerged from her hotel. I had a quick chat with her as she headed towards her car, live on camera. Back at base, they were saying they thought I was going to get into the car with her! Before the speech, I did a live interview with David Miliband, another with Ken Livingstone, and stayed outside to get Tony Blair walking to the conference hall before following him in to listen to the speech.

I did three live interviews afterwards, first with Harriet Harman and two Labour delegates, then with Lord Puttnam, Geoffrey Robinson, Geraldine James and Alastair Campbell, and finally with Hilary Armstrong and Walter Wolfgang. All shades of Labour party opinion covered. I had done seven live spots in all and each of them had been special in their own way.

After that Tony Blair performance I, and I'm sure many others, wondered whether the Labour Party had made a catastrophic mistake in forcing out such a proven election winner.

Guest speaker at the Labour conference was, once again, Bill Clinton. First though, I interviewed Bob Geldof who was also a guest again, and did lives setting the scene for the Clinton speech. It wasn't as good as his speech of four years earlier, he seemed tired. I packaged the Clinton speech for two p.m. and spent the rest of that day doing leg work, interviews and shots, for colleagues. We shared the airtime. After dinner that evening, I was tipped off that John Prescott was on stage at the Amicus unions' drinks reception and had just said he was supporting Gordon Brown for the Labour leadership. I scrambled over there to get reaction for my colleague, Jon Craig, who was doing the late evening lives. John McDonnell, potential candidate of the left who needed union support, was very relaxed about it. The Amicus general secretary, Derek Simpson, joked that Prescott had been talking about his own job, deputy prime minister, and was supporting Gordon Brown because he was the only one not after Prescott's job.

Thursday was the final day of conference and I was on doorstep duty that morning, hanging around outside the conference hotel to get an interview with anyone interesting who emerged. We got shots through a window of Gordon Brown and John Reid having breakfast together, which is always and usually wrongly interpreted as conspiring and plotting. We got an amusing live at eleven a.m. I was interviewing David Miliband when Tony Blair emerged from the hotel. I invited him to join us live on Sky News. He replied that he didn't have time, but added, "Make sure you give him a hard time". This was directed to me not his own government minister!

I watched John Prescott's last speech as deputy prime minister from the conference floor. He expressed his amazement that it was all over, that he and Tony were off, and then, of course, listed Labour's achievements in office. Later, we had a live doorstep interview with Tony Blair which Adam Boulton turned up for. It was a media scrum. Adam got the first question, then one from the BBC then the prime minister turned to me. "Glen. Oh, that's two from Sky, is that OK?" Singled out, I asked him why he wouldn't publicly endorse Gordon Brown as his successor and offered him the opportunity to do so. Only three questions, and two of them from Sky News. I hoped the bosses were watching!

From Manchester to Bournemouth for the Conservative Party conference. Labour had been the first party not to hold their autumn conference on the coast for decades. It was nice to be back at the seaside, although the third conference always finds the attending journalists a bit jaded and grumpy.

For me, the highlight of the first morning was a live interview with guest speaker, US Senator John McCain, and a long live with David Cameron and his wife Samantha walking from their hotel to the conference centre. There was David Cameron with Sam on one side and me on the other interviewing him. I got half a dozen questions and very good answers. It was live not only on Sky News but also on the BBC. It was a good example of what Levy had christened 'Oglazavision'. The director in the gallery simply remarked 'genius'. At one point, Sky News cameraman, Pete Milnes, walking backwards to get the shot of the three of us, tripped and fell over. Like the true professional he is, he got straight back up and carried on filming and we continued as if nothing had happened! Great live television.

John McCain's conference speech was disappointing. He didn't have even an ounce of Bill Clinton's charisma or oratory skill. David Cameron's speech was, of course, very well delivered and greeted with a series of standing ovations, but I felt it lacked meaningful content. He wanted a greener, more family-friendly Britain. But who didn't? His most frequently used phrase was to advocate 'social responsibility', but who was in favour of anti-social irresponsibility? But he was creating an impression, an image of youth, vigour and change. It seemed that perception really is the only reality.

After the speech, live interviews with MPs Oliver Letwin, Mike Penning and Chris Grayling. We went to a Francis Maude party chairman drinks reception, except that there was no sign of Francis Maude. He was elsewhere, sorting out a massive accreditation fiasco. Dinner that evening was in the Vesuvio Italian restaurant, which, according to the *Guardian*, was Bournemouth's finest. It wasn't, despite its fantastic location on the beach, but the food was good, the wine flowed and the company excellent. Five News political editor, Andy Bell (Spurs supporter alert!), and his team, Emma and Ben, a friendly BBC person, and assorted back-room Tories including Fiona Hill, formerly of Sky News and later to become Theresa May's chief of staff at Number Ten.

It wasn't all fun. Sometimes, we had to attend crushingly boring fringe events. I drew the short straw to attend one of them at lunchtime the next day with Oliver Letwin and John Bercow, long before he became famous/infamous as the speaker of the House of Commons. Much better was a David Cameron Q&A on climate change at the Odeon Cinema. I had a few minutes to chat with him beforehand, an invaluable opportunity with a future prime minister. Dinner that evening was with the Sky News team in the Panda Chinese restaurant. No Jimmy Saville this time, thank God!

The final day of the Conservative conference and for us the seventeenth day away at party conferences. I did live interviews with John Redwood and David Davis and a recorded interview with the American ambassador, Robert Tuttle. We got David Cameron walking shots, just a photo-op this time with no opportunity to ask questions and then that was it. Conference season over, time to go home.

Labour MP Siôn Simon created a daft and highly offensive You Tube spoof video of David Cameron's video blog in which he, 'David Cameron', offered viewers the chance to sleep with his wife Samantha. It was an incredibly stupid thing to do, and was branded as tasteless on all sides. At a lobby briefing, Jack Straw strongly condemned this stupidity and I did a live on Jack's angry reaction, strapped on Sky News as 'breaking news' which I suppose it was, though it was only a line rather than a genuine breaking news story.

The new CGS (chief of the general staff, head of the army) General Sir Richard Dannatt said the British army should pull out of Iraq where, he said, we were only exacerbating the situation. He described Tony Blair's Iraq policy as 'naive'. He had broken the taboo of the military not criticising the government in public. I did lives on the story. At the 11am lobby briefing we were told that General Dannatt had the prime minister's 'full backing' as CGS despite his remarks. This produced another breaking news strap for Sky News.

On my birthday I got mobbed by screaming schoolgirls! I was fifty-one, in my fifty-second year, supposedly the 'prime of life'. I felt more like thirty-one. I was doing a story about faith schools and how well or otherwise children from religious minorities were being treated at non-faith schools. The issue was whether or not there should be Muslim faith schools. We had filmed a piece the previous day for *Sunrise* at Hertsmere Jewish primary school in Hadlett, which had run all morning. I found a girls-only secondary school in London's East End which was seventy per cent Muslim. I hadn't arranged to film there but the head of Pashet School was very friendly and accommodating. When I did my PTC, the girls crowded around, screaming and waving at the camera, which was a lot better than just a boring PTC with some classroom backdrop.

I interviewed Geoffrey Robinson for my piece on Brown's Britain and in what ways his premiership might be different to Tony Blair's. Off-camera, we chatted and swapped Gordon Brown stories. His were far better than mine. He gave me a book, *Gordon Brown's speeches 1997-2006*, signed by Gordon. Not everyone's idea of bedtime reading, nor mine (!), but treasured nevertheless and kind of him.

I did lives at the Royal Society when Sir Nicholas Stern published his report on climate change. Pay now, he concluded, or pay far more in the future and face catastrophic floods as a result of rising sea levels with potentially millions of deaths. It was stark and very graphic. Tony Blair and Gordon Brown were there in support and to try to get concerted international action. During one of my lives, the prime minister and chancellor walked behind me across our shot and stopped to answer a couple of questions. I got the environment secretary David Miliband to do our live at midday before heading back to base to do more lives from Abingdon Green.

The Commons debated the Iraq war the next day, a joint SNP/Plaid Cymru motion demanding a public inquiry into the justification for invading Iraq. I did lives every hour all day in central lobby with live guests including Labour MPs Khalid Mahmood and Kim Howells, William Hague who was shadow foreign secretary at the time, and SNP leader Alex Salmond. The government won the vote, but only with a majority of 25.

There was a 'surveillance society' conference at the Riverside Plaza hotel. CCTV seemed to be absolutely everywhere. I had filmed in advance with cameraman Sid Bray at the Westminster CCTV control centre and interviewed the information commissioner, Richard Thomas. We did lives and packages all day, and took in some pictures filmed by our Scotland bureau at the CCTV control centre in Edinburgh. Just for fun, my daughter Maddie and I had driven the length of Holloway Road counting the cameras. We got to forty-five. Shadow Home Secretary David Davis later told me that there were even more than that and that Holloway Road had more surveillance cameras than anywhere else in Europe, possibly the world. We were more spied upon than the citizens of China or North Korea!

I discovered that every 2005 Cabinet minister had been contacted by the police about cash-for-peerages. This was a 'breaking news' strap on Sky News, and rightly so. My colleague Jon Craig was on point, the political correspondent doing the lives at the time, so I fed the new information to him. At our political unit in Westminster we were a team, and played as a team.

November 9th was another of those mad, jumping through hoops days of covering so many stories in a single day. First, it was a live on Conservative immigration policy, then a live on a Lib Dem internal document preparing for a snap general election in 2007 followed by a live interview with Sir Menzies Campbell. I interviewed John Reid and did a couple of lives as the government decided to return discretionary powers to judges having removed them three years earlier. In Downing Street, I recorded an 'As Live' on the US mid-term elections and what they meant for the Blair government. This ran off the back of a package by Sky's Washington correspondent all evening. Another live when Alan Johnson announced he would not be a candidate to be Labour's next leader but would stand for deputy leader, and finally a blog on the US mid-terms, Blair and Iraq. Quite a day.

Busy the next day too, when MI5 Director General Dame Elizabeth Manningham-Buller said there were 200 terrorist cells, 1,600 people and 30 plots under investigation in the UK, and that another major terrorist atrocity in Britain was far more likely than not. Chilling. I suspected there was a sub-plot: We need more money and more staff. I did lives all morning and headed to Downing Street where Tony Blair held a short press conference with New Zealand Prime Minister Helen Clark. Tony Blair answered our questions on the terrorism threat, saying he fully supported Dame Elizabeth. I was live in Downing Street afterwards. The BBC were nowhere to be seen, even though they had been at the press conference. This is always slightly perturbing. Did they know something we had missed? They didn't. Although my lives were about the terrorism threat, I also took a question when Lord Sainsbury resigned as junior minister for Science and Innovation and another once we knew the identity of his successor, Malcolm Wicks. I wrote a blog: 'Alarming or Alarmist?'

Tony Blair delivered a foreign policy speech at the Guildhall in which he advocated fresh talks with Iran and Syria. I did a couple of lives and packaged the story. Next day, the prime minister talked by video conference to James Baker's Iraq Study Group. We all Zoom these days, but video conferencing was far less common back then. I did lives on that all afternoon and evening and lives for *Sky News at Ten* and 11pm on the Queen's speech which we were to cover the next day.

The centrepiece of that Queen's speech was the anti-terrorism bill, a sign of the times we were living through and the government's primary obligation to keep us safe.

Sometimes, I got to interview friends for Sky News. It had happened at the Lib Dem conference when I interviewed my friend Peter Crystal a Lib Dem member, and my old university friend Lib Dem MP Bob Smith or, to give him his full title, Sir Robert Hill Smith, third Baronet of Crowmallie. Now, in mid-November, I interviewed my friend Lord Victor Adebowale on House of Lords reform. Victor sat as a crossbencher following his years of work with the homeless, including running the homelessness charity Centrepoint, and working to help the most disadvantaged as CEO of the Turning Point charity. He had advised the government on mental health issues, learning disabilities and the role of the voluntary sector. In short, he was very worthy of a peerage, unlike so many in the House of Lords. With a huge mop of dreadlocks, Victor looked as far from a member of the ageing House of Lords as you could imagine.

I had done an interview with John Reid at the Home Office on a government plan to force the parents of teenagers served with an ASBO to take parenting lessons and an escape from Ford open prison when I headed to Lancaster House where Foreign Secretary Margaret Beckett was holding a press conference with her Israeli opposite number. Ten minutes before it began, we heard that Lebanese government minister, Pierre Gemayel, the son of Lebanon's former president, had been shot dead in Beirut. I got the first question at the press conference and the first reaction from Margaret Beckett and Israel's Foreign Minister Tzipi Livni, the first Israeli reaction. Breaking news for Sky, and another 'Breaking News' strap after the lobby briefing at three forty-five p.m. with Tony Blair's first words, via the PMOS, on the Gemayel assassination.

Gemayel was only 34. His car had been forced off the road and several gunmen opened fire in broad daylight with automatic weapons. Gemayel had campaigned against the Syrian occupation of Lebanon and was the fifth anti-Syrian politician to be killed in Lebanon in less than two years. He had been seen as a possible future Lebanese prime minister. A Hezbollahbacked group calling itself The Fighters for the Unity and Liberty of Greater Syria said they had carried out the assassination.

That evening, I demolished rather too much red wine with Gordon Brown's senior advisor, Damian McBride. He was already notorious for dirty tricks, briefing salaciously not only against leading Conservative politicians but also against many senior Labour party people loyal to Tony Blair. He would later become Gordon Brown's press secretary when Brown became prime minister but would come unstuck and was sacked in April 2009 for a fabrication too far. That evening, he was convinced that Gordon Brown would not call an election if he became prime minister the following year (something that would, of course, cause much wailing and gnashing of teeth when it came to actually making that decision), that they were more concerned about a leadership bid by John Hutton than by John Reid (this seemed unlikely to be true), told me that Gordon Brown would be visiting India in January and that maybe he could get me on Brown's plane, and that he would help me set up a profile piece on Ed Balls. Neither of these came to anything. One of Damian's redeeming features was that he was an Arsenal fan, but everything he said seemed to come with an excess of spin and a degree of menace.

I covered with lives and packages the Queen's speech foreign policy debate in which Margaret Beckett outlined a timetable for the transition to democracy in Iraq and the withdrawal of British forces. We were to be out of Basra by the following spring. The next day, Alexander Litvinenko was murdered. A British-naturalised Russian defector, the former FSB officer had been poisoned three weeks earlier and had been in intensive care at UCH in London ever since. His killing bore all the hallmarks of an old-fashioned KGB assassination. I was live as soon as we heard the news of his death. The Putin government in Moscow very rapidly denied having anything to do with it.

I spent a day with David Cameron for a piece I was doing about his first year as leader of the Opposition. He gave a speech, the Scarman lecture, on poverty. We had backstage, green room access and got some very good shots from behind him as he was on stage. In his Witney constituency, a Conservative business forum lunch at a golf club. We arrived too late for lunch but in time for his quick speech and a Q&A session. We had a tour of a flour mill which involved us all wearing funny little white hats. David Cameron did a very amusing imitation of William Hague's Yorkshire drawl. We interviewed him in his car, and he recorded a promo for the piece. "Coming up, I'll be talking to Glen Oglaza about my first year as leader of the Conservative Party." Finally, a constituency surgery with a young twenty-six-year-old Down's Syndrome girl and her parents and with Joe Walcott, a local Tory councillor and grandfather of the Arsenal player Theo Walcott. It had been a hugely enjoyable day, David Cameron had the charm switched to full beam and did wide-ranging interviews which, cleverly, contained absolutely no new content. He had been incredibly accommodating.

The Iraq Study Group reported on December 6th. Headed by former US Secretary of State, James Baker, it described the situation in Iraq as 'grave and deteriorating'. I had begun the day reporting live from the Treasury on the PBR (the pre-Budget review) throwing to grabs from Gordon Brown and George Osborne before lives before and after PMQs. The Iraq Study Group recommended a phased withdrawal of US forces from Iraq and direct dialogue with Iran and Syria, something Tony Blair had been advocating for some time. Foreign Secretary Margaret Beckett made an on-camera statement at four thirty p.m. I threw her a couple of questions, even though we had been told not to by her press officers, and she answered at some length. Over-protective press officer syndrome.

The Christmas party season was upon us once again. Among others, a good gossip with David Cameron and assorted Conservative Party press officers at Conservative HQ, ditto with Tessa Jowell at the DCMS and, at DEFRA, with the tiggerish and highly energetic David Miliband and the more laid-back Ben Bradshaw. I discussed tax credits (not quite as boring as it sounds!) with John Hutton at the Department for Works and Pensions party held at 1, Carlton House Terrace and, at the Foreign Office Christmas party held at the splendour of Lancaster House, immigration, the Middle East and allergies with Margaret Beckett, who told me she was allergic to nuts, tomatoes and all dairy produce but not necessarily to Sky News reporters!

Tony Blair was interviewed by the police on cash-for-peerages on December 14th. The interview lasted two hours and began at 11am just as, at the Downing Street lobby briefing, PMOS Tom Kelly was assuring us that it wouldn't be happening that day. Tom later told us that he genuinely hadn't known. I did lives and packaged the story for *Live at Five*, updated at 8 o'clock to include an interview with Peter Mandelson done in Brussels. Tony Blair had been interviewed as a witness, not under caution, but even so a serving prime minister being interviewed by the police!

The timing was interesting and, I thought, no coincidence. It was a busy news day. A serial killer was at large in Ipswich and was believed to have already murdered five women, and Sir John Stevens published the long-awaited police report into the death of Diana, Princess of Wales, describing it as 'a tragic accident' and nothing more sinister. Moreover, Tony Blair was about to leave the country for a week, first to Brussels then the Middle East, and parliament was about to break up for Christmas, thus avoiding the possibility of any awkward questions at PMQs. All very convenient.

After Christmas, lives on a story about Hazel Blears. She had been campaigning against the closure of a maternity unit in her constituency which was problematic because, as a Cabinet minister, she was supposed to be supportive of the government's NHS policies.

On December 29th, there were strong rumours coming from Baghdad that Saddam Hussein would be executed within twenty-four hours. He had lost his appeal against the death sentence two days earlier. I did lives from the Foreign Office all afternoon and evening. When I finished work at midnight, the indications were that he would hang at dawn, three a.m. UK time.

I was supposed to be having a day off the next day but was texted very early. Saddam Hussein was, as expected, hanged at dawn. Senior politics producer Jonathan Levy phoned to ask me to go in. It was another day of hourly lives, mopping up British and EU reaction to the execution.

The final story of the year and a grim one to finish on although, in Baghdad and elsewhere in Iraq, Saddam Hussein's opponents were celebrating the death of the dictator.

CHAPTER 5

2007: Gordon Brown Prime Minister. But no General Election. Washington Again. The 'Blairwell Tour'. Sedgefield. Iraq and Afghanistan with the New Prime Minister. A New Lib Dem Leader

It was to be Tony Blair's final year as prime minister. How well would any transition of power be handled? Would there be a general election?

I did a package when the National Archive released details of Harold Wilson's resignation in 1976 under the thirty-year rule, even though it had actually been forty years. All they showed was that the resignation had been meticulously planned. There were no great revelations, nothing on the nonsense that Harold Wilson had been a Soviet agent, nor anything of much interest except to us political nerds, but of course it had resonance. A Labour prime minister standing down to be succeeded by a senior Labour minister.

John Reid delivered a speech on January 4th about the Labour party leadership, saying that New Labour did not begin and end with Tony Blair. Next morning, the *Telegraph* carried a story about cuts to the Royal Navy, which the MOD denied. My first task was a couple of lives on that before heading to an east London hospital for a Tony Blair visit. I interviewed him on health and tried to get his response to the brutal nature of Saddam Hussein's execution which had been filmed and shown around the world. I asked him three times, but all he would say was that he would have something to say about it 'next week'.

I continued doing lives at the hospital after he had left. Health Secretary Patricia Hewitt pitched up, so I interviewed her live too. In the afternoon, lives from Abingdon Green throwing to the sequence where Tony Blair repeatedly refused my invitation to comment on Saddam Hussein's execution. Verbal herograms from the bosses for my persistence.

Two days later, Ruth Kelly was in trouble for deciding to send one of her four children to a private school. The son in question was believed to be dyslexic. This was a controversial decision for a Labour minister, especially a former secretary of state for Education. At the eleven o'clock lobby briefing, we were told that the prime minister fully supported her decision, but there was still no word on when he would say something about the manner of Saddam Hussein's execution. I packaged the Ruth Kelly story for *Live at Five* and the evening bulletins. Personally, I felt her decision as a parent came first regardless of political considerations, but many in the Labour party were furious.

The second week of January was designated 'Green Britain week' but, while advocating a reduction in carbon emissions, Tony Blair said in an interview that he would not be giving up his long-haul holidays. I covered that and, later, when Downing Street announced that the prime minister would off-set his private holiday carbon emissions as well as the carbon emissions incurred by flying abroad on business.

Tony Blair once told me that he believed that if Britain shut down completely the reduction in carbon emissions would be filled in just two weeks by the expansion in China which was still building coal-fired power stations at an alarming rate.

At a press conference with the Japanese prime minister in Downing Street, Tony Blair finally condemned the cruelty of Saddam Hussein's execution, ten days after the event. I did a long live after the press conference focussing on why it had taken him so long to speak out.

In a way, Tony Blair was lucky because the story as overtaken by another monumental cock-up at the Home Office. The cases of Britons convicted abroad had not been entered on the police computer. 27,500 files were gathering dust at the Home Office. They included convicted murderers, rapists and paedophiles. I did lives on the story which, frankly, beggared belief. I knew without asking that Home Secretary John Reid would be incandescent.

John Reid made a statement after PMQs the next day when I also covered an astonishing outburst by former Home Secretary Charles Clarke. Writing in the *New Statesman*, he had trashed Blair's premiership as lofty ambition turned to dust, and said that Gordon Brown was equally culpable. It was a fantastic piece of disloyalty. Could it possibly be the pre-cursor to a leadership bid?

The government finally got its Green Britain week back on track and on the agenda but not until the Thursday when Gordon Brown took part in a live Sky News Green debate at Sky headquarters in Osterley, chaired by our political editor, Adam Boulton. I was summoned to Osterley. The senior executive producers were nervous about Gordon Brown's visit, they were not used to dealing with him. I cut the lead story for *Sky News at Ten* and did lives in the main studio at Osterley at ten p.m. and eleven p.m. Although it was our lead story as it had been our debate, a lot of people were far more interested in David Beckham's move from Real Madrid to LA Galaxy in the States on a five-year deal for bucket loads of cash, reported to be £128 million. I wished I could play football!

The news went mad for twenty-four hours on a *Big Brother* story. A contestant had racially abused a house mate, Bollywood star Shilpa Shetty. Tony Blair was asked about it at PMQs. So too was Gordon Brown who was in India on a trip I would like to have gone on although, in the end, he didn't take any travelling press.

The *Big Brother* story was the only story in town the next day. Channel 4 offered a fairly mealy-mouthed justification, Carphone Warehouse withdrew its sponsorship, the culture secretary condemned it and Max Clifford offered the opinion that the offender, Jade Goody, had been briefed in advance to cause trouble. US Secretary of State Condoleezza Rice was visiting London again. I did lives when she went to Number Ten for talks with Tony Blair, but I also had to ask him questions on *Big Brother* which I had never watched and had no intention of ever doing so.

The next day, I did live two-ways answering questions in each on several topics. GPs' pay, Gordon Brown in India, Condi Rice in London and, yes, *Big Brother*. Everyone was still obsessed, the tabloids had gone completely howling at the moon barking mad even by their own standards. Jade Goody was 'evicted' from the *Big Brother* house which was apparently decided by a public vote of the programme's viewers.

For two days towards the end of January, a story on the Catholic church attempting to block the adoption of children by gay couples. Mostly, though, I was working on the logistics of covering the World Economic Forum in Davos, Switzerland. I could really have done with a producer. The BBC was apparently planning to send thirty-seven people!

We had never covered the WEF in Davos without a producer, and it showed. We spent a tedious hour sorting out our accreditation. My first task was a sit-down interview with David Cameron. When we tried to get into the Davos Congress Centre, our passes didn't work. The accreditation, organised by Downing Street, only covered the period when Tony Blair was going to be there. Worse, we wouldn't be getting a satellite truck for at least twenty-four hours according to the duty foreign editor who had, it seemed, been completely caught out. There had been no forward planning.

I managed to blag my way in to do the David Cameron interview but we had to be escorted and were promptly escorted out again immediately afterwards. We fed the interview from an NTV truck with a friendly engineer.

We managed to get hotel rooms in Klosters, next to Davos. The foreign desk had booked us into one that was almost two hours' drive away across the Alps!

The next day was a lot better, eventually. I had to spend most of the morning phone-bashing, getting us proper accreditation, full access, a satellite truck, etc. Basically, the producer's job. We managed to find rooms at The Alexandra hotel in Davos, smaller than the rooms in Klosters but far better for actually being where the story was. We were camped at The Belvedere hotel where I did several interviews, including one with Gordon Brown which went very well.

Downing Street had announced that Tony Blair would be doing just one formal sit-down interview and it would be with the BBC's *Politics Show*. We were furious but to no avail. However, when he arrived, I got a long doorstep interview with the prime minister. At one point, the ITN reporter tried to interrupt one of my questions but, to my immense pleasure, Tony Blair told her to be quiet and took the rest of my question. Like Gordon Brown, he gave very good answers on Davos and on the incompetent state of the Home Office. We fed the interview from a Turkish satellite truck on top of a hill. The temperature was minus twenty. Sky strapped the interview as 'Breaking News' as they had also done with the Gordon Brown interview earlier. I did a live at 6.30pm (5.30 in London) but it was just the one live. We still had no satellite truck of our own and would have to pay a prohibitive fee to use someone else's.

The annual WEF meeting in Davos is a unique networking and in many ways jaw-dropping event. I have been six or seven times and am always astonished by who was there. You would be talking to someone and the chairman of Goldman Sachs would breeze past, or the Queen of Denmark, or the president or prime minister of pretty much any country you would care to name. Of course, there was an awful lot of hot air, but the mission statement of the WEF, 'committed to improving the state of the world', seemed worth the effort.

I did several live interviews on our third day there, including one with Peter Mandelson at our live point outside the Congress Centre. Sky News kept him/us waiting for more than half an hour in minus twenty and heavily falling snow. He was incredibly patient. I did a live after Tony Blair's speech and sent a package and an 'As Live' for the evening news programmes.

Like Klosters, Davos is very beautiful. On our last day I had a free hour to wander around in the Alpine snowscape. There was a media dinner on the last evening, around two hundred reporters, cameramen and photographers. We had been invited but the invitation hadn't reached us. Another by-product of not having a producer with us. Despite the obstacles, the message came from the foreign desk that they were 'very happy' with our Davos coverage back at base.

Back to Westminster and the extraordinary revelation at the lobby briefing on February 1st that Tony Blair had been interviewed a second time by the police. To interview a serving prime minister not once but twice! The interview had taken place the previous Friday, before Tony Blair flew to Davos. According to Downing Street, it had been kept quiet at the request of the police. This claim was met by us with snorts of derision. I broke the story for Sky News, well ahead of the slow-moving BBC, and did a quick live two-way in Downing Street. The BBC reporter and crew arrived just as I was finishing!

I did lives on Afghanistan and got the first question at a Tony Blair press conference with Afghan President Hamid Karzai. I also got Bushed, that is big footed by George W! I was at the High Court where judges upheld a Greenpeace claim that the government had not consulted properly on the expansion of nuclear power stations. I was about to go live. I was dropped as the American president went live from the White House. In future years, I was to get Obama-ed more times than I can remember.

I was sent to Brunel university to do a pool interview with Tony Blair for Sky, ITN and the BBC on gun crime. I got there to discover that Downing Street knew nothing about it. Clearly some wires had got crossed somewhere. I got a very short answer to a doorstep question as Tony Blair got into his car so it hadn't been a complete waste of time, but all my carefully-crafted questions went unheard.

Gun crime was also the story the next day, along with prison overcrowding. After an interview with John Reid, I did lives every hour for nine hours following our live coverage of a David Cameron speech on the importance of the family which carried distant echoes of John Major's 'Back to Basics'.

At PMQs at the end of February, Tony Blair announced a major troop withdrawal from Iraq. I had done lives on this the evening before. Both the *Guardian* and the *Sun* had also had the story the previous evening. I packaged PMQs and Tony Blair's statement to the House of Commons. Sixteen thousand troops would be coming home in the summer with more to follow later. Although this was a popular move, it begged the question: What precisely was the exit strategy?

On February 22nd we broke the story that Hazel Blears would stand as a candidate for Labour Party deputy leader, and Michael Meacher threw his hat in the ring for the party leadership. It had already been a busy day with a 'guns summit' in Downing Street during which I did lives with John Reid and another with Michelle Forbes of Mothers against Guns, followed by lives with all-singing, all-dancing live graphics. I switched to a breaking news story just after eight p.m. when UKIP was ordered by the Electoral Commission to pay back more than three hundred thousand pounds of donations before we broke the Hazel Blears story. It was one of those days when we wondered what on earth was going to happen next.

Gordon Brown seemed destined to succeed Tony Blair without a contest. Charles Clarke and Alan Milburn sent an email to all Labour Party members calling for an 'open debate' about the party's future with some very thinly-veiled criticism of Gordon Brown's style of leadership. That entirely understandable and democratic impulse to have an 'open debate' was to backfire badly on the party in 2015 when it resulted in the elevation to the leadership of the unelectable Jeremy Corbyn. At the time though, it simply looked like sour grapes. Gordon Brown's path to Downing Street seemed completely clear.

Next day, Charles Clarke and Alan Milburn launched a website which, they assured us, was absolutely not any kind of leadership challenge to Gordon Brown. We didn't entirely believe them. It was also the day of another troop withdrawal when we learnt, via a leak from a very senior source, that Britain was to pull out of Bosnia bringing home our six hundred and sixty military personnel who were still there. Turkey farmer Bernard Matthews won his case to receive compensation for the turkeys which had been slaughtered because of bird flu. We broke the story and I packaged it before heading off to Harrogate for the Lib Dems spring conference.

I had a coffee with a senior Lib Dem advisor to get the spin ahead of the conference. Our politics producer, Gary Honeyford, had earlier endured an off-camera briefing with Ed Davey. Deep joy! Gary emerged looking like he'd lost the will to live!

As anyone who's been there knows, Harrogate is a lovely town, especially in the spring. We did a long doorstep after an eve of conference rally on crime with party leader Sir Menzies Campbell, and Nick Clegg, who was impressive. The problem for the Lib Dems was that David Cameron was the new kid on the block and doing very well in the opinion polls. Part of his pitch was as a 'liberal Conservative' which was clearly aimed at potential Lib Dem voters. His tanks were parking up on Sir Menzies Campbell's lawn. Worse, a *Newsnight* poll that evening showed the public would much prefer to have Charles Kennedy as party leader.

I interviewed Nick Clegg live on the first day of the conference. I learnt from a senior Lib Dem friend that Harrogate MP Phil Willis was planning to stand down at the next election. It was a secret and I was sworn to secrecy, a confidence I didn't betray. I also bumped into my friend (Lord) Victor Adebowale who was taking a Q&A session on crime. I covered the debate on the future of Britain's Trident nuclear deterrent. Many Lib Dems were, and remain, instinctively against it but a passionate speech by Sir Menzies Campbell (really, it was!) swung the vote and the leadership won the day by 454 votes to 414. It had been close. CND badge-wearing delegates were not happy.

I did my, by now, usual PTC on stage at the podium on the evening before Sir Menzies' leader's speech. Next morning, a live with Ed Davey and more lives after Sir Menzies' speech at midday. The speech wasn't bad, it wasn't great. For all his wisdom, knowledge and political skill, Sir Menzies was not a great orator, although he had excelled himself in the Trident debate. I did a live interview with Sarah Teather and Lembit Öpik and Ben Ramm, editor of *The Liberal*. Senior Lib Dem advisor, Mark Littlewood, briefed that Sir Menzies' speech had been an overture to Gordon Brown to form a coalition, the 'progressive alliance' that Brown had advocated for some time. It was nothing of the sort and the party leadership were livid, but I had to re-cut my package to reflect the row. Not exactly the way the party leadership had wanted their conference to end.

Back in Westminster and the cash-for-peerages story was developing. It seemed there might indeed be an email from senior Downing Street advisor, Ruth Turner, expressing concern about Lord Levy. She herself had been interviewed by the police four times! An injunction against the BBC was lifted, followed by a written statement from Lord Levy's solicitor and another from Scotland Yard. This was our lead story which I kept re-packaging to reflect every twist and turn. As a coda to a busy day, I did a pooled interview with Home Secretary John Reid on gun crime and illegal immigration, excerpts from which were aired by us, ITN and the BBC.

In the House of Lords reform vote which followed a two-day debate in early March, MPs voted, perhaps mischievously perhaps not, for a fully elected upper chamber. Political dynamite. I packaged the lead story for *Sky News at Ten*. Conservative MP and former army officer, Patrick Mercer, came out with some comments about life in the army which were, wrongly in my view, interpreted as racist. Within two hours, David Cameron sacked him from his front bench position as Shadow spokesman on homeland security.

It was 'Iraq week' on Sky News in mid-March. Non-Iraq stories barely made air. I did a live on the Monday on Downing Street's reaction to senior UN weapons inspector Hans Blix saying he believed the invasion of Iraq had been illegal. Deputy Leader of the House Nigel Griffiths resigned so that he could vote against the government in the debate on renewing the Trident nuclear deterrent. I was ready to go live, but the story wasn't wanted. 'Nigel who?' and 'It's not Iraq'. It was the perfect time to disappear off to the UK Defence Academy in Shrivenham to support another theatre war game which was also, by the way, not about Iraq.

March 26th was an historic day for Northern Ireland. I did a pool interview with Tony Blair for us, ITN, the BBC and the rest of the world. In Belfast, a previously inconceivable press conference with Ian Paisley and Gerry Adams sitting side by side. These were iconic images. The Stormont Assembly would convene on May 8th with Paisley as first minister and Martin McGuinness as his deputy. Tony Blair was positively jubilant. He took a phone call from Irish Prime Minister Bertie Ahern just before I interviewed him. The interview was gushing. An historic day for peace in Northern Ireland, the culmination of ten years and more of working towards peace, and so on.

I was live for three days from the Foreign Office when the Iranians took fifteen Royal Navy sailors and Royal Marines hostage. They had been onboard HMS Cornwall when they were surrounded by the Iranians off the coast of Iran. It had become a tense diplomatic stand-off, exacerbated when the Iranians released some video of their British detainees. Having been used for Iranian propaganda purposes the hostages were all, thankfully, released a week later. On one of those days, I had done sixteen live two-ways with some good lines emerging from the Foreign Office. Rather bizarrely, I also did a six-minute live two-way with Norwegian TV.

All fifteen had been released as a gift, said the Iranians, from their (lunatic) President Mahmoud Ahmadinejad. This was obviously very good news but a question lingered over what, if anything, the regime in Tehran had been promised in return. It was a question which went unanswered.

That day, I was off to Washington to cover our American bureau. I flew upper class on Virgin Atlantic, very kindly upgraded by Virgin's director of communications, Paul Charles. Luxury! As I landed and touched base with our bureau producer Sally Arthy, the fifteen Iranian hostages arrived at Heathrow with Tony Blair insisting no deal had been done to secure their release.

The fifteen sailors and marines said they had been blindfolded, handcuffed, hooded, threatened and generally psychologically though not physically abused. My first job in Washington was, oddly, a five-minute phono for Public Service Radio explaining what had happened. By way of total contrast, I spent the afternoon in Washington Zoo with cameraman

Mike Dean. A panda in the zoo had been artificially inseminated using a panda from the zoo in San Diego. Cue very cute panda pictures and my one and only PTC with a panda!

Then it all got much more political, reporting on a George W speech on illegal immigration, lives on Iran's nuclear programme, and a piece of John McCain's presidential campaign and the other potential Republican candidates. We did lives from a McCain rally in Virginia and packaged for one p.m. (six p.m. in the UK). One of the advantages of working in Washington is that *News at Ten* airs at 5pm local time so, although you may have some very early starts, the working day usually ends at a very civilized time.

We covered an emotive trial in which three Duke university students were charged with rape. The case had racist overtures. The prosecution case had collapsed after almost a year and the three white Ivy Leaguers were acquitted. This became a cause célèbre for African Americans and their cheerleader Jesse Jackson, as did the story we covered the following day when 'shock jock' Don Imus was suspended by CBS Radio for a sexist and racist comment. He had referred to black women basketball players as 'nappy-headed hoes'. He apologised but that wasn't enough, nor should it have been.

I popped into the ITN office, in the same building as Sky's, to catch up with some chums and former colleagues. They didn't seem to do very much work! Certainly their output didn't compare to the demands of a twenty-four-hour news channel. They had just spent a week in Jamaica covering the death of cricketer Bob Woolmer. We both cut a piece on the American military training dolphins for military use. It would have made a good piece for ITN but it wasn't wanted. Sky News, on the other hand, ran our package all day.

Gordon Brown was in Washington for meetings of the World Bank and the G7 finance ministers. I did an interview with him on meeting George W Bush for the first time, the Labour leadership and so on. The next day we covered his press conference and did another interview for a package that got a very good run on Sky News. That evening, I joined Gordon and his team for drinks in Georgetown. As so often, we chatted about football and kids but also, this time, about American politics. I was singing Barack Obama's praises and saying I thought he would win the Democratic nomination. Even as the words were spilling out of my mouth, I remembered that Gordon was a big supporter of Hilary Clinton. Without a trace of humour, he asked me what Obama actually stood for. All I could come up with was 'change'. The chancellor and future prime minister was not impressed.

We had a big breaking story the next day, another American mass shooting. When will they ever learn? At Virginia Tech in Blacksburg, Virginia, an undergraduate student killed thirty-two people and wounded seventeen others using two semi-automatic pistols before killing himself. It was America's deadliest ever school/college shooting. We scrambled a team to Blacksburg while I anchored from Washington, doing lives at the top of every hour and into and out of a Bush statement and a police press conference from Blacksburg. I also packaged the story.

I finished very late and was woken by the foreign desk the next morning at 3 o'clock. Sky News wanted lives every hour from 5am (10 o'clock in London). As well as delivering those, I sent a package on Virginia gun laws which ran all evening.

Sky News now had a cast of thousands covering the story and it was time for me to go home to my proper job in Westminster. There was a vacancy coming up for a Washington correspondent and, before I left, both the deputy head of news and the head of foreign news suggested I should apply for it. The answer was 'not yet'. The timing was wrong. Maddie was very settled in school, Seb was only nine months old and Marion needed to focus on her opera singing career (although the opportunities were probably far greater for her in the States). My main priority was to get home to see them.

Seb giggled a lot and Maddie, who had just turned nine, was very excited when I unexpectedly picked her up from school. In any event, I soon learnt that Head of News John Ryley had some names in mind and mine was not among them. What's more, Westminster politics were going to become even more high profile than usual with the Blair-Brown handover and the Tories resurgent under David Cameron. I got the message that Ryley wanted my experience at Westminster and would prefer to send someone else to Washington.

Three days off, including a day of cycling with Maddie in the New Forest fulfilling a long-standing promise, then it was back to Westminster and a David Cameron speech on social responsibility. He was very blatantly targeting New Labour voters. I was live at the MOD where there were serious reservations about Prince Harry's intention to take a front line role with his regiment in Afghanistan. He would become a target, a danger to himself and those serving with him. Then it was off to Warsaw where Tony Blair was meeting the Polish prime minister and president, part of what became known as Blair's Farewell Tour, or 'The Blairwell Tour'.

Tony Blair had sent a twenty-four-page document to all Labour MPs and peers, the PLP, outlining his government's ten years of achievements. So, was he about to announce his departure date? We were at the Polish chancellery. Our Westminster news editor, Clare Parry, sent the document to me via the Polish prime minister's personal fax machine! Yes, we were still in the age of the fax machine. It took a combination of English and my very poor Polish to convince the Polish prime minister's inner office that they were about to get a twenty-four-page fax and that it was for me.

Tony Blair must have thought he was having double vision. The Polish prime minister and president were twins, the Kaczyński brothers. I wrote a blog on that. We did lives from the Belvedere Palace, including a press conference in which I asked Tony Blair if he would give me the scoop of the year so far, his departure date. "No one deserves it more than you Glen, but no." Adding, "Don't hold your breath." This was enough to keep me doing lives and packages for the rest of the day, but I made time for a bowl of borscht soup in the old town square, Starego Miasta, meticulously reconstructed after the Second World War.

Back in London and the government announced there would not be a public inquiry into 7/7 but the House of Commons Intelligence and Security committee would look again at the July 7th bombings to see if there were lessons to be learnt. I did a long, seven-minute live interview with the committee chairman, Paul Murphy.

On May 1st lives in Downing Street reflecting on Tony Blair's ten years in office. To what extent would his legacy be defined by Iraq? In the local elections the following Thursday, a bad but not awful night for Labour, just the usual mid-term election backlash against the party in power. The Conservatives made some but not yet enough inroads in the north of England though they were up 850 seats overall, while the Lib Dems were going backwards. The headline, though, was from Scotland: the SNP 47 seats, Labour 46, a sign of things to come. This, of course, kept me busy doing lives and packages on the night and all of Friday.

In Warsaw, Tony Blair had hinted that he wouldn't quit before the local elections. Now that they were done, the only question in town was when he would make the announcement. The following Monday, I did a piece on who might be in a Gordon Brown Cabinet and another on the much-respected former speaker of the House of Commons, Bernard Weatherill, who had died at the age of eighty-six.

The resignation speech came in Sedgefield on May 10th. I did lives from Trimdon the evening before and chatted to Blair advisor Matthew Doyle and Tony Blair's brilliant constituency agent John Burton to go through the logistics of the next day. Sky News sent presenters Kay Burley and Jeremy Thompson to anchor from Trimdon Labour Club and, the next morning, I was doing lives with Kay asking me questions. This was known as being 'the presenter's friend', although it was really no different to what we usually did with Kay in the studio and me out on location. Adam Boulton was live in Downing Street and presenter Julie Etchingham was on Abingdon Green with a stream of live guests. Sky News was all over the story.

We weren't supposed to be inside the Trimdon Labour Club for Blair's farewell address thanking his party workers and listing the achievements during his ten years as prime minister, but I managed to sneak in by a side door so I had a mini scoop: live phonos from inside. Our rivals were nowhere in sight.

It was, of course, an emotional speech for an emotional moment. As he was speaking to his own constituency workers, many of whom had been with him since he first became Sedgefield's MP back in 1983, it was by turns intimate and, the national message, sweeping. Among the achievements he listed: Increased spending on schools and hospitals, the minimum wage, independence for the Bank of England, economic growth, lower unemployment, lower crime, peace in Northern Ireland, tackling both poverty in Africa and climate change, gay rights, Britain at the centre of Europe, successful interventions in Sierra Leone and Kosovo. He was less expansive on Iraq and Afghanistan except to say that he believed he had done the right thing and in the fight against terrorism we must never give up. He told them and the national and global audience that Britain is, 'the greatest nation on earth'.

Afterwards, I interviewed several audience members who were both tearful and cheerful. Tearful at his departure, but cheerfully basking in the reflected glory of their Tony, their MP, their prime minister. I did a live panel with a selected group and more lives with Kay trying to capture the mood I had witnessed by being in the room. And I did live two-ways, rather oddly, with both Israeli and Japanese TV.

Tony Blair had said he would go on June 27th, still nearly seven weeks away. Plenty of political water was to pass under the bridge before then, and he planned to continue his international 'Farewell Tour'. It had been another historic day, the end of the Blair era. I felt I had once again been an eyewitness to history. I also thought that the Labour Party would miss him, this three-time election winner, once he was gone.

The next day we were off to Paris from Teeside airport via Amsterdam. We were the only crew present when Tony Blair met his old sparring partner, Jacques Chirac, but there was a huge media mob at the Élysée Palace for his farewell meeting with newly-elected French President Nicolas Sarkozy. We were allowed inside, only us. There was no sign of the BBC or ITN. Scooped! I was at Tony Blair's side. Sarkozy came bounding up to me, hand outstretched. He had absolutely no idea who I was! Blair again endorsed Gordon Brown to be his successor and we had a bit of banter on air when I asked him about the day before in Sedgefield and if he had any regrets.

"You mean have I changed my mind? It's a bit late for that."

As well as doing lives for Sky News, I also did live two-ways with France 24, the French English language TV news channel.

The spotlight was already moving from Tony Blair to Gordon Brown and so, the following Monday, I was in Southampton where Brown was visiting an eco-friendly house and delivering a speech. During one of my lives, Sky News came to me just as he was working the room behind me. Fortuitous timing.

Two days later we were in Manchester. Gordon Brown already had almost three hundred MPs nominating him to be the next leader. His only challenger, left-winger John McDonnell, was struggling to get the forty-five MPs he needed to get onto the ballot paper. He was stuck at twenty-seven.

The deputy leadership contest was much tighter. Five candidates already had the forty-five nominations they needed. Alan Johnson, Peter Hain, Harriett Harman, Hazel Blears and Jon Cruddas were all in contention. Surprisingly, Hilary Benn was struggling. He had just forty nominations and was running out of MPs to canvas. But our live two-ways were all about the leadership, the next prime minister.

Gordon Brown was at an event at 6.30pm, a Q&A with party members. It was looking as if he might very soon have enough nominations to render John McDonnell's challenge a mathematical as well as a political impossibility. An hour later I learnt that Andrew McKinlay had nominated Gordon Brown. He was the three hundred and eighth nominee. I broke the news live on Sky News, a long fifteen-minute live two-way. Gordon Brown was now the prime minister-elect.

At lunchtime the next day nominations officially closed. Gordon Brown had the backing of 313 Labour MPs, John McDonnell just 29. Hilary Benn had made it onto the ballot for deputy leader, so there would be six candidates. My 'Brown's Britain' package, which I had been tinkering with and updating for months, ran all day.

I was live all the next day when MPs voted to exempt themselves from the Freedom of Information Act. Ostensibly, this was to protect private correspondence with constituents though we suspected that this would also mean they didn't have to reveal their expenses. In the evening, I switched to David Cameron and Sir Menzies Campbell challenging Gordon Brown to a televised leaders' debate.

Tony Blair was visiting Iraq, part of his Farewell Tour. The British HQ in Basra was attacked with mortars. This was an almost daily occurrence, but did the insurgents know that the British prime minister was there at the time? Had he been the target? No one knew for certain, as I explained in lives every hour all evening. It was a Saturday. My lives the next day, an otherwise quiet Sunday, were about whether or not our Iraq policy would change under Gordon Brown. I cut a package which, unusually, ran every fifteen minutes.

The CPS wanted to prosecute Andrei Lugovoi for the murder of Alexander Litvinenko, poisoned in London the previous November. The

Foreign Office was demanding his extradition from Russia. No chance, as I explained in lives from the Foreign Office.

After a week's holiday in our favourite Tunisian haunts and two days of media training a multinational at a magnificent chateau an hour's drive from Paris, there was a scandal brewing about an alleged BAE bribe of one billion pounds to a Saudi prince to secure a 43 billion pound arms deal back in 1985. Tony Blair had blocked a Serious Fraud Office investigation. Still the prime minister, Blair was in Germany for a G8 summit. We got a good answer from him on the story, basically saying it was too long ago to have a meaningful investigation, which I packaged for *Sky News at Ten*.

To the Oval for the first Labour deputy leader hustings. Gordon Brown was there too and answered my questions on Gaza where Hamas and Fatah had been fighting each other for almost a week. I did lives on that at lunchtime and stayed for the hustings, an event which was of no interest to anyone at Sky News except, it seemed, to me! There was fresh speculation that day, just a week before Tony Blair was due to resign his premiership, that he might become the next president of the European Union.

I covered a David Cameron speech in Tooting, south London, a safe Labour seat in which he outlined his vision for Britain before heading off to Rome where Tony Blair was to meet the Pope, another date in the Blair Farewell Tour.

Tony Blair was in Brussels for an EU meeting. It was one of those hideous all-night sessions at the end of which, at 5.30am, he gave his last press conference as prime minister before flying to Rome. The EU had finally agreed on a constitutional treaty following the French and Dutch referenda rejecting the previously proposed constitutional changes. This time, there would be no referenda, except in Ireland. None of Britain's so-called 'red lines' had been crossed. So, my lives from Rome, every hour all day, focused more on the new EU constitution than on the meeting with the Pope. Because of that, it was our lead story, and my packages reflected both the EU summit draft agreement and Blair's religion.

Alastair Campbell had famously said, "We don't do God", but Tony Blair had always been completely open about his Christianity. Although he was Church of England, Cherie Blair was Catholic and their children were brought up as Catholics, with Tony Blair frequently joining them for Catholic Mass. Now, as he met the Pope, the question was whether or not he would formally convert to Catholicism. Frankly, I doubted that anyone cared much or that it was any of our business. He was days away from the end of his premiership anyway and could now 'do God' or anything else he wanted to do. The EU constitution was the important story.

The day before Tony Blair formally resigned, I cut a piece speculating on what he might do next. The EU presidency was the bookies' favourite but there was also much talk of him becoming a Middle East envoy. It ran a few times, but there were heavy floods in the north of England and Sky News went flood-tastic. Grantham Conservative MP Quentin Davies defected to Labour and launched a stinging attack on David Cameron, describing him as a PR man without any principles. He appeared on camera next to a beaming Gordon Brown.

There was that unforgettable, convention-breaking moment at the end of his last PMQs when Tony Blair received a long, standing ovation from all sides of the house. MPs are not allowed to applaud, which is why they normally wave their order papers and make those ridiculous animal noises. Then he was off to the palace to resign, followed by Gordon Brown's first audience with the Queen after which he gave a short speech outside Number Ten. It was sombre, a commitment to dedicate himself to serving the country.

Ten years of Tony Blair and now it was over. He went straight to Sedgefield to resign as an MP. He was to be the Middle East envoy for 'the Quartet' of the UN, US, EU and Russia. His new appointment was greeted with a somewhat mixed reception by the Arab countries.

The next day Gordon Brown reshuffled the Cabinet. My first task was to interview the new foreign secretary, David Miliband, at the Foreign Office and the new chancellor, Alistair Darling, at the Treasury. When the new Cabinet met for the first time, most of the new Cabinet ministers walked along Downing Street and into Number Ten and were only too happy to say a few words live on Sky News. It was a turkey shoot!

There would be no deputy prime minister. Jacqui Smith was the new Home Secretary, probably the biggest surprise of the day. Jack Straw was Lord Chancellor and Secretary of State for Justice, Alan Johnson moved to health, while John Denham and Ed Balls were to lead a divided education department responsible for higher education and schools respectively. There were plenty of new Cabinet faces, Ed Miliband, Andy Burnham and

James Purnell among them. Apart from Jacqui Smith, there were no great surprises. Des Browne at Defence was the only Cabinet minister to stay where he was.

A lot of familiar faces disappeared. John Prescott, John Reid, Patricia Hewitt, Hilary Armstrong, Charlie Falconer, Lord Goldsmith (replaced as attorney general by Patricia Scotland) and Margaret Beckett were all gone. Blairites, Hazel Blears and John Hutton, were given big jobs, Blears at Communities and Local Government, Hutton as Business Secretary. Although demoted, Tessa Jowell also had an important role as minister for the Olympics and London and would attend Cabinet.

The Blairs, meanwhile, spent a week at Chequers, a courtesy extended to them by the new prime minister. The newspapers made hay with a photo of them waiting for a train and looking slightly lost and perplexed. No more blues and twos convoys.

David Cameron followed suit the following Monday, reshuffling his Shadow Cabinet. It was only a mini-reshuffle. Frances Maude was replaced as party chairman by Caroline Spelman, Dame Pauline Neville-Jones was invited to attend the Shadow Cabinet as security advisor.

Civil servant, Michael Ellam, was the new PMOS, replacing Tom Kelly. I attended his first lobby briefing. Gordon Brown's advisor/enforcer, Damian McBride, also attended, presumably to ensure that the spin was delivered. Gordon Brown made a statement, his first as prime minister, on constitutional changes handing power back from Downing Street to Parliament and floating a few ideas, including reducing the voting age to sixteen.

His first PMQs was not a resounding success. David Cameron was much lighter on his feet. My package included an interview with Michael Howard on just how daunting PMQs can be for both the prime minister and the leader of the Opposition. Previous prime ministers, including Tony Blair, had described it as a terrifying ordeal. I also interviewed Michael Portillo and Michael Heseltine and, later, David Cameron. All were crowing over what they described as Cameron's victory, but did it really matter that much? There is no evidence that performing well at PMQs influences how people vote. William Hague was brilliant at PMQs but a fat lot of good it did him at the ballot box.

Alastair Campbell published his diary extracts in early July. Eight hundred pages! There was no hint of disloyalty to Tony Blair or to Gordon Brown. I cut a long package, Julie Etchingham interviewed Alastair live, news editor Phil Wardman voiced-over some key passages and we had shots of Alastair Campbell at his computer, a reconstruction of him writing the book. The package ran all day and all evening, the closing chapter of the Blair era.

David Miliband announced the expulsion of four Russian diplomats over Moscow's refusal to extradite Andrei Lugovoi as Gordon Brown went to Berlin for a meeting with Angela Merkel. I walked from the Brandenburg Gate to the Reichstag and on to the Chancellery, echoes of 1989. The Germans rolled out the red carpet for the new prime minister with an army band and a guard of honour. Gordon Brown looked slightly uncomfortable with all this ceremonial as Angela Merkel gently ushered him to the correct place to stand. At their joint press conference I got the first question, about Russia of course, and a comprehensive answer. After one last live, at eight forty-five p.m. local time, I wandered along the Unter den Linden in what had been the DDR, the old East Germany. There was little to remind me of how it had been before 1989. It was packed with tourists.

I had some time the next morning to be a tourist myself before the flight home. I went to Checkpoint Charlie and had a coffee at Café Adler which had been restored but was otherwise largely unchanged, unlike everything else. This west-east crossing, once so threatening and dangerous, was now a major tourist attraction. It was Disneyland Berlin. There were even two young female models in Soviet uniforms posing for tourist pictures next to old Soviet flags. The whole experience was surreal. John le Carré it was not.

After Berlin, our summer holiday in Portugal followed by a few days in Florence, one of my favourite cities. We stayed at the Brunelleschi hotel built around a sixth-century round tower, arguably the oldest building in Florence. Sitting outside a cafe one day, eighteen-month-old Sebastian had his back turned to us and was pulling funny faces at the American tourists at the next table. I apologised to them. "Not at all," came the reply. "He's a natural performer." He was, and still is. On every street corner there were opera singers with beautiful voices. I didn't dare suggest to Marion that in Florence it seemed that beautiful, talented sopranos were, well, ten a penny.

Former Conservative Cabinet minister John Redwood produced a report on economic competitiveness. It included a recommendation to abolish inheritance tax on family homes, a Tory favourite which would come back to bite Gordon Brown. Damian McBride personally brought me the report the day before it was published with a full briefing, the Labour Party spin. The BBC apparently thought they had it exclusively for their ten o'clock news but I broke the story at nine with a live at ten with extensive graphics. I went through the same routine for 11pm and left an 'As Live' version for midnight and to run overnight.

I interviewed David Cameron when he returned from his summer holiday. The theme was supposed to be the NHS, but mostly he was trying to avoid talking about Conservative plans for tax cuts. The big story that day in August was whether or not Gordon Brown would seek his own mandate by calling a general election. It was an issue that was to plague the Labour Party over the coming weeks and probably gives some Labour Party people sleepless nights to this day.

The next day David Cameron attacked Labour citing a list of hospitals the Conservatives claimed were earmarked for closure. Unfortunately for him the research was flawed, riddled with factual inaccuracies. The attack backfired.

Gordon Brown meanwhile had got off to a good start as prime minister. His so-called honeymoon period was going well and Labour was comfortably ahead in the opinion polls. He had looked suitably prime ministerial dealing with the terrorist attack on Glasgow airport at the end of June and the latest outbreak of foot and mouth disease in Surrey. Downing Street wasn't denying that there could be an early general election, all options were apparently on the table. The speculation would continue for weeks and into the Labour Party conference in Bournemouth at the end of September. It led to Gordon Brown being branded by the tabloids as a 'ditherer', and epithet which stuck.

The dilemma was obvious. While a general election would give Gordon Brown his own mandate to govern, Labour was sitting on a handsome majority of sixty-five. A lot can happen during an election campaign, a lot can go wrong. If it did, his premiership might be over before it had properly begun. By waiting, Brown would have three years to prove himself in office. While many in the Labour Party were urging him to go for it, to take advantage of his honeymoon period and the favourable opinion polls and while the Tories were still tearing themselves apart over Europe, Gordon Brown's natural caution, his famous 'prudence' some might say risk-aversion, would eventually be decisive. Basically, in this country we elect a party not a prime minister and Labour had won a clear mandate only two years earlier.

His decision was still some weeks off but the election speculation dominated politics until it eventually came.

After the debacle over the list of supposed hospital closures, David Cameron turned his attention to crime in a speech the next day. Of course, as any Opposition leader should, he was demanding a general election. I was doing lives covering the speech when the hospital closure story took a new turn. A Conservative party researcher apologised to Telford hospital which had been incorrectly included on the list. Shadow Secretary of State for Health Andrew Lansley retracted the apology. Confusion reigned! David Cameron was forced to explain as best he could. Andrew Lansley came into Sky News Westminster to do a live interview and floundered pitifully. Fiona Cunningham, who had once worked on the news desk at Sky News and would later, as Fiona Hill, become Teresa May's chief of staff at Number Ten, had ranted at me several times on the phone the previous day. Now she wasn't speaking to us at all and appeared to be sulking, which was a shame as I liked her personally. Politically, however, this was very amusing. It was hardly our fault that their Shadow Health Secretary had put both feet in his mouth and was now gnawing away at his ankles!

This was, of course, our lead story and I was doing lives every hour all day with a package for the evening news programmes. A fourteen-hour day, but it had been hilarious.

In Liverpool, an eleven-year-old boy, Rhys Jones, was shot dead by a sixteen year old. Gordon Brown described this as, "A heinous crime that has shocked the entire country". I did lives on this awful story all afternoon. At eight p.m. I had persuaded Home Secretary Jacqui Smith to come into 4 Millbank for a live interview. During her interview, we switched to a live press conference with Rhys Jones' parents in Liverpool. Jacqui agreed to stay in the studio to watch it and react afterwards. The parents spoke for a long time. It was very emotional. Jacqui Smith had tears in her eyes when we returned to her.

Afterwards, off-camera, she cried. A lot. She had two young sons of her own. It was a perfectly normal and very human reaction. Her obvious warmth and humanity were why I liked her. We got a call from the Home Office press office asking us not to use her tearful reaction again. Head of news John Ryley and head of politics Peter Lowe quickly decided, quite rightly, that we would. I agreed completely. I thought it made her look empathetic and did her no harm at all. The Home Office (and perhaps Jacqui Smith herself?) disagreed. But in my subsequent lives I did not reveal the fact that she had been in tears afterwards.

As expected, John Prescott announced at the end of August that he would be retiring as an MP at the next election (whenever that might be). Two days later, I covered the unveiling of the Nelson Mandela statue in Parliament Square, a joyful occasion, and interviewed Jack Straw on the start of a twenty-four-hour prison officers' strike which the High Court had ruled illegal.

Into September, and I was at City Hall when Boris Johnson launched his campaign to be elected London mayor. I had known Boris for about twenty years. I had first come across him in Brussels when I was working for ITN and he was the *Telegraph*'s Brussels correspondent. We heard him before we saw him, a loud boisterous public schoolboy voice booming before he entered the room. He was a vision, hair all over the place, tie halfway around his neck and hanging below his ear, waving his arms around and booming indecipherable noises. I also interviewed David Cameron about Boris' bid. Of course, in public, he was fully supportive.

Gordon Brown chaired a meeting in Downing Street, the International Health Partnership. The Norwegian prime minister was there along with ministers from France, Ethiopia and several other countries as well as the WHO. It was very long and a bit dull but also very important. The United States and Japan were not members. Shame on them. Nor were China and India.

The foot and mouth outbreak in Surrey had spread to several farms by mid-September and I did lives on the story over several days. There was a story to cover on childhood obesity, a growing problem (no pun intended) and on the chaotic farrago that was the NHS IT system. Margaret Thatcher went to visit Gordon Brown at Number Ten. I did lives after they had posed for the most unlikely of photo- ops and packaged the story of their meeting. I dare say Mrs Thatcher was only too ready to offer Gordon Brown the benefit of her wisdom and experience. Of course, the Left was furious. So were the miners. She was still a figure of hate more than twenty years on from the ill-fated Scargill-led miners' strike.

Then it was off to Brighton for the Lib Dems annual conference. We got the usual shots of the leader's arrival and interviews with Sir Menzies and Simon Hughes. Dinner for the Sky News team that evening was in the Regency fish restaurant, a favourite of mine. I mention this because the woman at the next table was the spitting image of Jacqui Smith. It was uncanny and a little unnerving.

I was doing lives every hour all day for the next few days as the Lib Dems demanded, yes, a general election. Among many others, I interviewed Charles Kennedy who seemed in good form. So too did Paddy Ashdown. At a Q&A session with delegates, Sir Menzies Campbell joked 'I'm a failure' before confusing Italy with India. It was not a good look. Despite that, when I interviewed Sir Menzies during the conference he was, as usual, calm and knowledgeable.

On the Wednesday of the conference, we struggled to get on air. OJ Simpson had been arrested again. He had allegedly robbed a Las Vegas casino at gunpoint along with three other men. The trial of OJ Simpson for murder over a decade earlier had been the story that really put Sky News on the map, the channel's coming of age. I did just two lives all day as well as lives for LBC Radio and a couple of articles for the Sky News website, something we were doing pretty much every day anyway.

The next day was leader's' speech day. Adam Boulton did the lives before and after the speech. My initial task was to get the usual leader walking to the conference centre shots and some words. For some reason, Sir Menzies sneaked out of the Grand Hotel the back way. His speech was good, almost sprightly! He pushed the right buttons and did the job he needed to do, if not inspiring at least reassuring the Lib Dems and challenging the government. I packaged the story of the day and the piece ran all evening.

Next up was the Labour Party in Bournemouth and Gordon Brown. Would he or wouldn't he? That, of course, was my topic for my eve of conference package. It hung like a dark cloud over the entire week. I did long live interviews with Peter Hain, Alan Milburn, Neil Kinnock and Douglas Alexander who was Labour's head of election campaigning and clearly wanted a general election. He had done an interview for the *Guardian* which had appeared under the possibly over-enthusiastic headline: Labour on election war footing. Publicly, though, they all remained non-committal.

Election speculation was feverish, with stories circulating about Labour fundraising, preparing election leaflets, and constituency parties being told to get ready. We anticipated that Gordon Brown would use his first speech as Party leader and prime minister to finally announce his decision one way or the other. His speech was serious, joke free, and seemed to me to be aimed at Middle England, *Daily Mail* readers. What it did not do was nail the election speculation.

Afterwards, I went to a fringe meeting with Neil Kinnock, Patricia Hewitt and Ed Miliband. Neil was very entertaining, Patricia Hewitt rather nanny-ish. I felt like I was being told off for smoking, drinking, eating, breathing! Ed was wonkish. As always, Asia Night was good fun with excellent food. Foreign Secretary David Miliband was drummed in by a troupe of Indian drummers and said a few words. The foreign secretary had a far more serious demeanour when I interviewed him live the next day on events in Myanmar (Burma) where thousands of monks had taken to the streets to protest against the regime. It was a pool interview to be shared with the BBC and ITN, as was another I did the same day with Environment Secretary Hilary Benn on the latest outbreak of foot and mouth disease.

At the *Guardian*, *Telegraph* and News International parties I gleaned some sense of the Labour leadership's thinking on calling a general election. Jack Straw, David Miliband, Caroline Flint and others were very forthcoming. Gordon Brown's foreign policy advisor, the always friendly Stewart Wood, told me he'd been arguing for an autumn election but that Gordon and others were expressing caution and wanted to wait until after the Conservative Party conference before making a decision.

Next day, I did another pooled interview with David Miliband on the worsening situation in Myanmar. Sky and the BBC ran it live and the BBC ran it again one hour later even though, by then, we had a long pool interview with Gordon Brown. Apparently, I was in the *Evening Standard*'s

Londoner's diary (not for the first time) because I had refused, but only very gently and only at first, to pay the fifteen-pound entrance fee the previous evening for 'an audience with Alastair Campbell'. An audience! Very grand! According to the *Evening Standard* there had been 'furious scenes' which was complete and utter nonsense.

Every year, Labour closes its conference with a rendition of 'Jerusalem' and the 'Red Flag' led by a professional singer. Always on the lookout for an opportunity for Marion, months earlier I had arranged for her to lead the singing. She did it perfectly, and said that Harriet Harman had been particularly nice to her beforehand and Gordon and Sarah Brown had chatted to her afterwards. As the conference closed, Adam told our viewers that the singer was 'Mrs Glen Oglaza'! I wondered what the newspaper diarists would make of that. Evidence of political bias on my part? I hoped not.

In the event, the fact that Marion Wilmann was my wife went unnoticed. There were some comments by sketch writers. Simon Hoggart wrote in the *Guardian* that the 'Red Flag', was "sung by a willowy soprano so it sounded less like a call to the barricades than Proms in the Park", Ann Treneman in *The Times* described "the opera singer dressed in a flamenco-frilled black gown", which Quentin Letts in the *Mail* described as low cut. All harmless enough.

At the Conservative conference in Blackpool, Shadow Chancellor George Osborne pulled a rabbit out of the hat when he announced that the Conservatives would raise the inheritance tax threshold to one million pounds. As a political stunt it worked. Labour was spooked. The Tories were not in any great shape for a general election despite their demands for one in public. It seemed to put the kibosh on an early election. Of course, it was a promise the Conservatives didn't keep once they were in power but as a political tactic it worked a treat.

I had suggested to Gordon Brown, in 2005, that he should consider changing the inheritance tax rules not, as George Osborne was now proposing, to raise the threshold to one million pounds but to take the primary family home out of inheritance tax altogether. His response had been that that was all well and good for 'people like you', living in a valuable house in the south of England. I had pointed out to him that these were the very people whose votes he needed to win. Labour had an issue with IHT, believing that to abolish it would impair social mobility. My view was, and remains, that this was tax originally introduced to break up large, aristocratic estates and that it was iniquitous that ordinary people were being taxed even after they had died and were not able to pass on the fruits of a lifetime of labour to their children.

While George Osborne was throwing political grenades in Blackpool, Gordon Brown was off to Baghdad with the Chief of the Defence Staff Sir Jock Stirrup. We flew on the prime minister's plane to Kuwait. Gordon Brown told me he thought Marion's singing had been, "Fantastic. Fantastic voice". From Kuwait at 2.30am, a Hercules to Baghdad airport and onto an American Blackhawk helicopter for the flight into the Green Zone.

As soon as we arrived, I was doing live phonos every thirty minutes until we got our live camera up and running. Gordon Brown met the Iraqi prime minister, Nouri al-Maliki. On the flight, Brown had told us he would have something significant to say while he was in Iraq. It came when he held a press conference to announce that 1,000 of the 5,500 British troops in Basra would be home by the end of the year. It was 'Breaking News' and almost immediately I did a long live with Adam Boulton who was live from Blackpool, where the Conservatives were accusing Gordon Brown of breaking protocol and trying to undermine their party conference. Our joint segment was long, about twenty minutes.

From Baghdad we flew by Hercules to Basra which had little to commend it, a very hot, very dusty city but also very important as Iraq's main port. I did several lives on the phone from Basra and we managed two in vision on camera despite extreme technical difficulties. This was Sky's lead story and we had been way ahead of the BBC all day despite their correspondent having the benefit of two producers travelling with him.

Feeding our material from Basra was problematic. It's hard to imagine these days when we would simply go live on our smart phones. We pooled our resources. Sky's computer wasn't working at all, ITN's was taking fifteen minutes to send just one minute of material back to London. We managed to send my PTC and the PTCs of the ITN and BBC correspondents and a few pictures. We could do no more, our time was up, and we had to fly with the prime minister on a blacked-out Hercules back to Kuwait. Sky News cameraman Martin Smith, the ITN cameraman and one of the BBC producers stayed in Kuwait and fed the best pictures back to London while the rest of us flew home on Gordon Brown's plane.

The following Saturday I was called into work on what should have been a day off in case Gordon Brown made an election announcement over the weekend or to happily speculate away if he didn't. I did lives in Downing Street as rumours grew that Brown would say something that evening. A poll for the next day's *News of the World* conducted in eighty-three marginal seats showed Conservative gains that could result in a hung parliament. That seemed to me to be decisive. The general trend of the national polls was swinging towards Cameron and the Conservatives. I was fairly certain that Gordon Brown would not risk his majority.

I cut a package on just how politically damaging a climbdown would be to Labour. The BBC's Andrew Marr was summoned to Number Ten for an interview for his Sunday morning politics programme, and that is how the prime minister announced that there would not, after all, be an election. Although we all had access to the interview, it felt horribly like a BBC exclusive. There would be no election in 2008 either.

Gordon Brown justified his decision by saying he needed to get on with governing and wanted time to set out his vision for the country. He also claimed that he had paid no heed to the opinion polls, but Labour's own polling in marginals suggested that the party's majority of sixty-five would be halved to around thirty at best, as he knew very well. The risk was too great. I did lives all evening, doughnutting my own packages which I updated every hour.

A week really is a long time in politics. Just seven days earlier the Conservatives had seemed dead in the water. Now they had momentum, the wind in their sails and Gordon Brown's reputation for strength, integrity, transparency and decisiveness was severely undermined. No prime minister would go to the country just two years after a general election victory unless he or she was absolutely certain of victory. A week earlier, Labour had been if not certain then certainly confident. But not now. The party and Gordon Brown should have nailed it one way or the other at least a week if not a month earlier. Now, the damage was done.

The right-leaning newspapers, that is all of them except the *Mirror*, the *Guardian*/*Observer* and the *Independent*, had a field say that Sunday. Bottler Brown they screamed. It might not stick, but Gordon Brown's reputation was in tatters and he had brought David Cameron and the Conservatives back from the dead, or at least out of their coma.

The next day Gordon Brown held his monthly press conference. Of course, the questions were all about his decision not to go to the country and I did lives and packages all day with David Cameron's response. It was of course the lead story. Gordon Brown also announced that British forces in Iraq would be further reduced to two 2,500 the following year. If that was an attempt to distract from the general election story it didn't work.

On the Tuesday, we had the Comprehensive Spending Review and the pre-Budget report on the same day, the clearest possible signal that the government was getting on with governing. Sky News had Kay Burley presenting from Westminster and political editor Adam Boulton presenting from a studio at Sky News HQ in Osterley, which was rather odd and the wrong way round. I packaged the story all day.

By Monday October 15th, speculation over Sir Menzies Campbell's leadership of the Lib Dems was reaching fever pitch. The party's Federal Executive was meeting that day, the Lib Dem Shadow Cabinet the next and the Parliamentary Party the day after that. These were all regular meetings but things appeared to be coming to a head, as indeed they did. I doorstepped the Federal Executive meeting as the rumours grew. Then it was confirmed that there would be a statement at Lib Dem headquarters by Simon Hughes and Vince Cable. I soon discovered it would be to announce Sir Menzies' departure and we broke the story first. Hughes and Cable announced Sir Menzies' resignation but there was no sign of the man himself. He had already departed for Edinburgh leaving behind a resignation letter. It was concise and to the point.

Questions about leadership are getting in the way of further progress by the party. Accordingly, I now submit my resignation as leader with immediate effect. I do not intend to hold a press conference or to make any further comment.

I read these to be the words of a man who was deeply pissed off. He had lasted only eighteen months and would not lead his party into a general election.

There followed an evening of mad rushing about to get a succession of leading Lib Dems live into Sky News. I cut a long package, a mix of the events of the day and a political obit, for *Sky News at Ten*, did a live at 11pm, cut a fresh package for the next morning's *Sunrise* and didn't get away until well after midnight.

Despite saying that he would not be making 'any further comment', Sir Menzies had agreed to do interviews in Edinburgh the next day, but only with political editors. Adam Boulton was there for us. In Westminster, meanwhile, the focus was already on the possible candidates for the leadership. I went to the National Liberal Club to do a PTC. Politics producer Esme Wren and cameraman Adam Murch had gone ahead and had already interviewed several leading Lib Dems. This was such an American TV news way of doing things. The producer does all the work, the correspondent just turns up for make-up and to do a PTC. See my comments from Lockerbie in 1988 in "When I stories". We cut a fine package for *Live at Five* which was widely praised and ran all evening.

Chris Huhne was first out of the blocks, announcing his leadership bid the next day. The Eastleigh MP and Lib Dem Environment spokesman had stood against Sir Menzies Campbell the previous year following Charles Kennedy's resignation. He was seen as the front runner along with Nick Clegg who had only been an MP for two years but had already made quite an impact. Clegg launched his bid two days later. I would spend much of the next two months, interviewing, doorstepping and generally dogging the footsteps of the two candidates.

When Chris Huhne launched his leadership bid in the atrium at 4 Millbank I did lives before and after his announcement and wrote a blog about the number of people the BBC had in attendance. I counted twelve, there may have been more. Sky News and ITN had three each. My comments were picked up by bloggers Guido Fawkes and Iain Dale. The BBC continued on its merrily bloated way.

In late October, Gordon Brown hosted both the Turkish and Israeli prime ministers at Number Ten, though not at the same time. I had begun the day doing lives on education, specifically A levels, before heading to Downing Street for a long live into Gordon Brown's press conference with the Turkish prime minister on Turkish politics and the Kurdish PKK. I had maintained my interest in the Kurds since spending time in Iraqi Kurdistan immediately after the first Gulf War. Later, I managed to get the first question when Gordon Brown had a press conference with Israeli Prime Minister Ehud Olmert. Later still, I sat through two hours of Metropolitan Police Assistant Commissioner John Yates giving evidence to a House of Commons Select Committee on the cash-for-honours scandal and, with Esme producing, cut a package which ran all evening. Another day of jumping through intellectual hoops from A levels to Turkish politics to the politics of Israel and the wider Middle East to cash-for-honours. As a specialist political correspondent you certainly needed a broad hinterland of knowledge and, for me in the cases of the politics of Turkey and Israel, experience.

The next day I covered a Jack Straw statement on constitutional reform and a Gordon Brown speech on liberty, but neither was wanted. Too dry? Too cerebral? Sky News was far more interested in the annual publication of MPs' expenses which my colleague Jon Craig covered creating, with his tabloid flair, a 'league of shame'.

The *Telegraph* published a poll the following morning which put the Conservatives ahead of Labour for the first time in a very long time. I did lives on that all morning before going to the Ministry of Defence to do lives on the investigation into the cause of the Nimrod crash in Kandahar the previous year. A fatal fire had broken out. All fourteen crew members on board had died, the largest single loss of life suffered by our armed forces since the Falklands conflict. There were questions about the Nimrod's serviceability. I was doing very long lives. Fortunately, I had read up and had flown in a Nimrod (for ITN in Scotland) so I knew my way around the aircraft.

The Board of Inquiry reported five weeks later condemning the age of the Nimrod fleet, the lack of maintenance and the lack of a proper fire detection system. The coroner at the inquest into the deaths went even further, saying that the Nimrod fleet had, "Never been airworthy from the first time it was released to service". And condemning what he described as a, "Cavalier approach to safety". The Nimrod wasn't finally retired until 2011 by which time it had been in service as Britain's eye in the sky and for search and rescue operations for forty-two years.

I was at a David Cameron speech on immigration at the end of October, the first time he had tackled this thorny issue since becoming Party leader two years earlier. I did lives about the speech but the big issue that day was the forthcoming visit of King Abdullah of Saudi Arabia, the first by a Saudi king for twenty years. He was to get the full red-carpet treatment, a carriage ride along the Mall and a state banquet at Buckingham Palace where he would be staying as a guest of the Queen. Despite Saudi Arabia's appalling human rights record, David Cameron took the same view as the government, that we had to engage with the Saudis. What was not said was that we needed their oil and their money, all those lucrative arms deals. Speaking for the temporarily leaderless Lib Dems, interim leader Vince Cable told us that they would boycott the visit, which no doubt had the Saudis trembling in their very expensive boots.

The Tories had another go at immigration the next day with a press release claiming that the number of foreign workers in the UK was 1.5 million. At first, Sky News accepted this at face value. I didn't, and soon discovered that the true figure was 1.1 million. The other 400,000 were Britons based abroad who'd returned home, naturalised citizens and so on. I did a live explaining this, but not until 6.30pm by which time a colleague, Joey Jones, had spent the afternoon regurgitating the press release as fact.

I went to the Royal Society of Arts, of which I'm a member, for a Lib Dem leadership hustings, Clegg versus Huhne. It was ridiculously boring. It seemed neither of them wanted to rock the boat or risk bad press by saying anything controversial, or even interesting.

The Queen's speech in early November, focused, once again, on anti-terrorism legislation. I did some lives on the speech but only after a live at the Foreign Office where David Miliband was meeting the Greek foreign minister. Greece was not the story, Pakistan was. I asked David Miliband several questions about the situation in Pakistan and he delivered the same answers as he had when I had interviewed him on the same subject the previous evening. President Pervez Musharraf must stand by his promise to put an end to the military regime by holding democratic elections the following January. The reality, though, was that Musharraf was locking up opposition leaders and blocking satellite TV, including Sky. He didn't resign as president until the following August, and only then to avoid impeachment.

The Commonwealth foreign ministers met in London. They had the power to suspend Pakistan from the Commonwealth. A press conference due at 5.30pm was pushed back and pushed back until it finally took place two hours later as the foreign ministers argued. They set conditions. If Musharraf did not fully restore the judiciary and a free press and lift the current State of Emergency, then Pakistan would be suspended. I thought this was weak and showed just why the Commonwealth, as a political force, is so often ignored. I had done lives during the delay and more after the decision.

Former Conservative MP and prisoner, Jonathan Aitken, was appointed to head a task force to advise the Conservatives on prison reform. The *Observer* had the story and I did a few lives on it on the Saturday evening before the newspaper hit the streets. Jonathan Aitken had tried to sue after an investigation by the *Guardian* and Granada's *World in Action* programme into his dealings with Saudi Arabia, saying famously that he would wield, "The simple sword of truth", to defeat, "Bent and twisted journalism". Unfortunately for him, the journalism was neither bent nor twisted, he was charged with perjury and perverting the course of justice and sentenced to eighteen months back in 1999. He had strong views on prison reform based on his own experience. Both he and the Conservative Party denied that his new role represented any kind of political comeback.

Gordon Brown was beginning to look more comfortable at PMQs. After PMQs on November 14th, I did lives as he made a statement on security and terrorism. The next day, a judge ruled that radical Islamic fundamentalist cleric, Abu Hamza, could, at last, be extradited to the United States. Abu Hamza had been the Imam of the Finsbury Park Mosque, the nearest mosque to my home in north London. He had been jailed the previous year for inciting violence and racial hatred. He had one eye and no hands due, he claimed, to injuries sustained while fighting in Afghanistan. In fact, he had lost both hands and one of his eyes while experimenting with explosives at a terrorist training camp.

In case you were wondering to whatever happened to Abu Hamza, nicknamed 'The Hook' in the tabloid press, after years of legal argument he was finally extradited to the United States in October 2012 and, in January 2015, was sentenced to life in prison without the possibility of parole.

There was another monumental Whitehall cock-up when it emerged that the details of all fifteen million child benefit claimants, names, addresses and bank details, had gone astray 'in the post'! Actually, they had been lost by a courier company. For once, it was the Treasury rather than the Home Office in the firing line. I did a package of Alistair Darling's mounting problems. Top of the pile was Northern Rock which had crashed so spectacularly and been bailed out, for the moment at least, by a liquidity support package from the Bank of England. Northern Rock was nationalised a few months later.

I covered a CBI conference, political because Gordon Brown made a speech. I did lives before and after it and before and after a Q&A session with delegates. More lives, eleven in all by lunchtime, including one with both Nick Clegg and Chris Huhne the two rivals for the Lib Dem leadership. I packaged the story for *Live at Five* and cut another package for *Sky News at Ten* after Peter Watt resigned as general secretary of the Labour Party. His resignation was pre-empted by the revelation that Labour party donor, David Abraham, had given money to the party using several third parties. Not revealing the fact that he was the donor broke the rules. Peter Watt had said he knew about the arrangement but hadn't realised they'd broken the rules governing the funding of political parties, which was naive of him. No prosecutions ensued as a result, and Peter Watt went on to do some very fine work with the NSPCC.

After a week working once again at the Royal College of Defence Studies in early December, it was off to Iraq and Afghanistan with Gordon Brown, a quick visit to both. At Heathrow's Royal suite it took almost two hours for the bags of the travelling press to be searched, which made us very grumpy. No one from Downing Street came to accelerate the process even though we were keeping the prime minister waiting on the plane sitting on the tarmac. Ridiculous.

On the flight to Kuwait, Gordon Brown chatted with us for over an hour, mostly about Northern Rock but also about the latest opinion polls as well as the current state of play in Iraq and Afghanistan. From Kuwait, a Hercules to Basra where the prime minister made a speech to the troops, praising them and confirming that Basra would be handed over to Iraqi control by Christmas. Because of the overzealous security at Heathrow, we had less time in Basra than we'd planned. We managed to send an 'As Live' and a few shots back to Sky News. The BBC team managed to send back precisely nothing!

After the Hercules flight back to Kuwait, we checked in the Marriott hotel and fed a package for Sky News at 11pm (2am in Kuwait). After a quick shower and a twenty-five-minute siesta we were off again, four hours in a Hercules to Camp Bastion in Helmand, where Gordon Brown mingled again with the troops and made a very similar speech. British soldiers were fighting in Musa Qala fifty miles away, the largest battle since the British had arrived six years earlier, driving the Taliban from the town.

After just two hours at Camp Bastion, during which we were able to feed a track, rushes and a PTC, we were back in the Hercules and back in helmets and body armour for the flight to Kabul.

The trick to flying in a Hercules over hostile territory is to sit on your helmet rather than wearing it on your head. Any hostile fire is most likely to come from the ground. The soldiers knew that and so did I. When some of the other hacks asked me what I was doing I explained it to them, but they deemed it to be too uncomfortable!

Gordon Brown went by helicopter to the presidential palace in Kabul. Sky News cameraman Martin Smith went with him but there was very little room on the chopper so the rest of us went by road in three armoured vehicles. As ever, Kabul looked poor and very dusty though the mountains were looking particularly beautiful against the deep blue sky. Sky News took the press conference with Gordon Brown and Afghan President Hamid Karzai live, I got the first question, and was the only correspondent to do a live immediately afterwards, Martin having mastered the technology. I had done two live phonos before the press conference so this was the icing on the cake. We fed our package from the BBC's satellite dish, the only dish, from where ITN and Channel 5's political editor, Andy Bell, also fed their pieces.

Another four hours on the Hercules, this time to Oman for the executive 757 flight home, eight hours of comfort after what had been an epic forty-eight hours.

Just one day off then back to work and lives covering a Police Federation conference. The cops were furious because Home Secretary Jacqui Smith appeared to be paying them an increase of 1.9% not the 2.5% pay rise agreed through arbitration. An incredible state of affairs. Another Home Office cock up? As usual I had also written a piece for the Sky News website, on our whistlestop visit to Iraq and Afghanistan.

The House of Commons Home Affairs Select committee came out against any extension of the twenty-eight days detention without charge for terrorism suspects. The Attorney General Lord Goldsmith had revealed that he would have resigned if Tony Blair had succeeded in getting it extended to ninety days. A few days later, the same committee told Jacqui Smith that she was obliged to give the police their agreed 2.5% pay rise.

On December 18th, the Lib Dems had a new leader. Nick Clegg had received 20, 988 votes, Chris Huhne 20, 477, a majority of just 511 on a turn-out of only around 60% of the party membership. For the second year running Chris Huhne had failed to win the party leadership, but around 1,300 postal votes had been caught up in the Christmas post and had missed the deadline. The majority of them were for Chris Huhne and might have handed him victory but he was gracious in defeat saying, "Nick Clegg won fair and square", and there would be no question of any recount.

The campaign had not been entirely without friction. 'Calamity Clegg' was the title of a document written by the Huhne campaign team of which Chris Huhne himself claimed to have no knowledge. Clegg registered a formal complaint about 'dirty tricks' to the party's chief whip and returning officer, Chris Rennard. The row blew over, but the epithet 'Calamity Clegg' never quite went away.

I thought it was the best result for the Lib Dems. Nick Clegg had something about him, a little of that charisma X factor thing. He was young, a fresh face to give the Lib Dems a new lease of life. I did a sit-down interview with him, his first as Party leader.

Two days later I did lives as Nick Clegg shuffled his front bench team, which the Lib Dems like to call their Shadow Cabinet. There were no great surprises. Chris Huhne got Home Affairs, Sir Menzies Campbell returned to the back benches.

Here is a little-known fact that I recently discovered. During his illustrious athletics career in which Menzies Campbell competed as a sprinter for Great Britain in the 1964 Tokyo Olympics, he held the British one hundred metres record for seven years, 1967-1974. In 1967, he ran one hundred metres in ten point two seconds. Among those he beat in that race was aspiring young American athlete OJ Simpson. Small world!

The Great Wall of China, December 2009

Peking University, Bejing. Nathan Hale on camera. December 2009

On Gordon Brown's helicopter, 2005 election campaign

David Cameron with Nigerian President Goodluck Johnson, Lagos, August 2010

Reporting from Pretoria, August 2010

Red Square October 2010

Stockholm March 2012. Nine prime ministers but we couldn't get on air!

President Obama in Downing Street March 2012

Petting a cheetah cub at the animal orphanage in Nanyuki, Kenya. He purred, but his handler kept him on a very tight leash!

Kofi Annan and Richard Branson, World Economic Forum, Davos January 2016

CHAPTER 6

2008: CRASH! The Irish Reject The Lisbon Treaty. Baby P

Nick Clegg did his first PMQs on January 9th. As leader of the third largest party he got two questions. He handled it well, keeping it simple. No jokes, no attempts to sound clever. That same day, Hilary Clinton won the New Hampshire primary but only just, marginally ahead of Barack Obama. It was all to play for.

Next day, a story that British soldiers in both Iraq and Afghanistan had been given life-saving blood transfusions by American military medics using blood that had not been tested for HIV or hepatitis. Thankfully, subsequent tests gave them the all-clear. Peter Hain confessed to the Electoral Commission that he had failed to declare more than one hundred thousand pounds of donations to his failed deputy leadership campaign. An oversight, but incredibly careless of him.

I wrote a blog and had to do a couple of lives on whether or not David Cameron had actually given up smoking. Really! I felt just ever so slightly hypocritical. ITN's *News at Ten* re-launched, back at its proper time after nine years in the wilderness first at 11pm then at 10.30. It looked good visually, presented by Trevor McDonald and Julie Etchingham, who had been poached from Sky News. It wasn't exactly must watch TV and there was no 'And Finally', but it was impressive to have lives from the Antarctic with reporter Bill Neely.

Bill, by the way, always said that his all-time favourite ITN sign off was 'Glen Oglaza, Bratislava', though it was actually 'Glen Oglaza ITN Bratislava', which doesn't scan quite so well.

By January 15th, the collapse of Northern Rock and the government's bail out had again become the lead story. Northern Rock was holding an Emergency General Meeting in Newcastle. I also cut a Peter Hain political obit, although he appeared to be toughing it out, before a sit-down two-camera interview with Chancellor Alistair Darling. I did lives at 5 and 6 pm and another at 6.15 with Shadow Chancellor's George Osborne's reaction. I would have done another at 7 o'clock but I got Pentagon-ed, a live statement from the Pentagon announcing the deployment of more American troops to Afghanistan.

The Russians arrested the head of the British Council in St Petersburg, Stephen Kinnock, son of Neil. They released him after an hour. Moscow was making a petty point rather pathetically and further souring UK-Russian relations. After lives at the Foreign Office I was diverted to British Council headquarters. We had discovered that Neil Kinnock was there. For once, and very sensibly, Neil, who was British Council chairman, was saying nothing. From there to the Russian Embassy after hints that the Russian Ambassador might speak. He didn't. Another wasted journey. Things perked up in the evening with a New Year's drinks reception at Number Ten. I chatted to Gordon Brown about babies, Kevin Keegan and football in general, and his forthcoming trip to India and China.

The next day and lives from the British Council when the CEO Martin Davidson made a statement about the situation in Russia. I also interviewed Neil Kinnock about the release of his son, who was now thankfully safe. I would have done more live two-ways but a British Airways flight from China did an emergency landing at Heathrow. It was a relatively minor incident, just a few very slight injuries, but it happened as the prime minister's plane was waiting to take off and in clear view of his aircraft. Sky News politics producer Jonathan Levy, who was travelling with the prime minister, did a live phono describing the scene and he did it as well as any reporter would have done.

Northern Rock was still a huge story and I did lives before and after an Alistair Darling statement to the House on January 21st. The markets were plummeting, not yet in freefall but heading that way. The US Federal Bank cut interest rates by 0.75% and that seemed to calm the market jitters. I interviewed Nick Clegg on a Lib Dem health policy announcement. Boy did they choose the wrong day! I did lives all afternoon after Gordon Brown said he was confident about the prospects for the UK economy, a line from the prime minister I had broken earlier.

The information commissioner demanded to see more details of MPs' expenses including those of Blair, Brown, Howard, Kennedy and Prescott.

This was as a result of a Freedom of Information request which, it emerged, had come from the BBC. And yet they were half an hour behind us breaking their own story! How on earth does that happen?

I did a piece on the anti-terrorism bill the day before it was to be debated. The government was expected to push for an extension to forty-two days for holding suspects without charge. A Sky News phone around very quickly found 33 Labour MPs who were preparing to vote against the government. Whipping them probably wouldn't help. Gordon Brown had a major rebellion on his hands.

I also did a blog on faith schools. David Cameron had told *The Times* that it was basically fine for parents to lie to get their child a place in a faith school. It was probably not quite what he'd intended to say!

Peter Hain resigned on January 24th. The Electoral Commission had referred his campaign donations to the police. Once the police were involved, he had no choice. I was the first journalist his special advisor Claire McCarthy called. It was just before noon. I shouted across the newsroom, "Hain has gone. Get Adam in the studio", while I got further details from Claire. I could have just headed to the studio myself with the breaking news but this was what we called being a team player.

Peter Hain would officially announce his resignation two hours later and said he was only resigning, "To clear my name". I did long lives off the back of my Hain political obit package. Peter Hain was Gordon Brown's first Cabinet casualty, and it was obviously politically damaging.

My colleague Jon Craig went to the Department for Work and Pensions to cover Peter Hain's resignation statement. Another colleague, Joey Jones, who was no team player, rather foolishly insisted on doing a live claiming that this was the end of Peter Hain's career. Within minutes, I had Peter Hain himself on the phone telling me that this was nonsense and that Gordon Brown had promised him a return to Cabinet once he'd cleared his name. In my next live I corrected our mistake referring to rumours circulating in Westminster without, of course, naming my selfish and foolish colleague by name. Gordon Brown was true to his word and Peter Hain returned to the Cabinet a year later.

Peter Hain was well used to being in trouble with authority. As a child in South Africa, his parents had been arrested for supporting Nelson Mandela and the ANC. They were forced to leave the country and had come to Britain in 1966. I remembered well his leadership of the Stop the Seventies Tour campaign, though I was still only a teenager. When I was eighteen he had been tried and acquitted of a bank robbery in Putney, south-west London, where I also lived. At the time, I knew his younger brother, Tom. He had been framed, rather pathetically and completely ineffectively by BOSS, the South African Bureau of State Security. By then, he was president of the Young Liberals before switching to the Labour Party.

I went to the DWP to interview the new secretary of state, James Purnell and to the DCMS (Department for Culture, Media and Sport) which was now the domain of the new Secretary of State Andy Burnham who had moved from the beleaguered Treasury to the 'Ministry of Fun'. Couldn't be bad.

David Cameron suspended Conservative MP Derek Conway who had been paying his son Freddie more than one thousand pounds a month as a parliamentary researcher even though he was a full-time student at Newcastle university. We soon lost interest in the story even though it was set against the zeitgeist of MPs' expenses, and I switched to doing lives on an early release scheme for prisoners. Prison overcrowding was still a problem. I also covered former Chief of the Defence Staff Lord Guthrie arguing against Parliament having the legal right to declare war, saying that this power should remain with the prime minister and, ultimately, with the monarch.

The police had apparently bugged Labour MP Sadiq Khan (much later to be elected London Mayor) when he visited a terrorism suspect who was also his constituent in prison. Officers claimed they hadn't realised they were bugging an MP. David Cameron and Jack Straw both held press conferences at which I got the first question and I did lives all afternoon. Justice Secretary Jack Straw said it was a police matter, but he set up an inquiry. MPs' visits are protected by legal privilege. As a former human rights lawyer, Sadiq Khan was well used to battles with Scotland Yard. Home Secretary Jacqui Smith ordered a review by the chief surveillance commissioner (I had no idea there was one!) Sir Christopher Rose. His report concluded that the detectives involved had known that Sadiq Khan was an MP but had claimed to be unaware that they were not allowed to bug his conversations. A big Scotland Yard own-goal!

The next day, I interviewed David Cameron for the second time in two days, a two-camera sit-down interview on MPs' expenses. This followed a meeting of the House of Commons Standards and Privileges committee. David Cameron assured us that all Conservative MPs would reveal all their expenses and allowances. A major political scandal was bubbling away just beneath the surface.

Former army officer and Conservative MP Patrick Mercer had asked a question about 16 Air Assault Brigade (who I knew well) at PMQs that day. About to be deployed to Afghanistan, the brigade had asked for and been refused an extra six hundred troops, an additional battalion. Gordon Brown had referred to them as 'the 16th Airborne'. Not impressive. I did lives on the story and interviewed Patrick Mercer and Shadow Foreign Secretary William Hague. The larger context was that the United States and Britain were urging other NATO countries to pull their weight in Afghanistan, yet we were preparing to send a brigade, normally numbering around five thousand troops, short by hundreds of soldiers.

Condi Rice was in Downing Street again that day, which was the day after 'Super Tuesday' in the States. John McCain seemed home and dry for the Republicans even there were concerns about his age (he was 72), while Hilary Clinton and Barack Obama remained neck and neck for the Democrats.

The next day, the Archbishop of Canterbury, Rowan Williams, gave a lecture in which he advocated the adoption of Sharia Law for some communities in Britain, 'supplementary legislations' to that of the law of the land. Cue media frenzy! Downing Street wasted no time in slapping him down. I cut a package for *Sky News at Ten*.

At PMQs in mid-February, David Cameron raised the issue of a Dutch police request for DNA samples which had lain unattended for over a year. Eleven of the suspects involved had committed crimes in the UK during the previous twelve months. The Home Office strikes again!

Next day, Sir Christopher Rose reported on the Sadiq Khan bugging scandal. Jacqui Smith made a statement to the House from the report, followed by a statement by Foreign Secretary David Miliband on what had become known as 'extraordinary rendition', in plain English the CIA torture of prisoners. It had emerged that the Americans had indeed used the UK territory of Diego Garcia to refuel these notorious CIA flights despite previous denials. Very embarrassing for the government.

The verdict from Ipswich came at 2.30pm when Stephen Wright was found guilty of murdering five women. Sky News went Ipswich-tastic for the rest of the day, there were no other stories. I went to the Chinese Embassy for a press conference. A week earlier, Steven Spielberg had resigned as artistic director to the Beijing Olympics in a blaze of publicity. The Chinese assured us that he had never been appointed to the role so he could hardly have resigned. All very Orwellian. This would have been a good story on a normal day but it wasn't Ipswich so I simply wrote a blog about it.

On a Tuesday at the end of February I did a live on the latest asylum seeker figures before covering a David Cameron speech on multiculturalism which I can characterise as, 'Hey, you lot, learn English and treat women better, oh, and Rowan Williams is completely wrong and possibly mad!' This was overtaken by breaking news. The information commissioner had ordered the release of Cabinet minutes from March 2003, the decision to invade Iraq and the legal advice of the Attorney General, Lord Goldsmith. I did lives on that. There were angry scenes that day in the Commons when Ed Davey was suspended and the Lib Dems walked out. Their Lisbon Treaty amendment had not been accepted for debate by the speaker.

There was another security breach at the Palace of Westminster the next day when protestors from 'Plane Stupid' got onto the roof of the Commons. They were protesting against airport expansion. They came down before PMQs and were arrested for trespass. They were after publicity and they got it in spades. For my package, cameraman Paul Dickie and I went up to the Upper Committee corridor, where we were not permitted to film. We had got there from central lobby, so I was trying to retrace the protestors' steps. We were apprehended by security but managed to film a clandestine PTC. There was no chance of us getting onto the roof with a camera. It had been a bit of fun and was very well-received back at Sky HQ. I even got a herogram from head of news John Ryley who was a lot less generous with his praise than his predecessors both at Sky News and at ITN.

Next day, I got a leak of a House of Commons Standards and Privileges Committee report half an hour before it was released. I did lives on that for three hours before a bigger story broke. Prince Harry had been fighting on the front line in Afghanistan since Christmas. The British press and broadcasters had known about it and had kept it quiet for ten weeks, which really took some doing. The story had broken on an American website. Sky News went Harry-tastic! There were pre-cut packages all ready to go. I did just one live after Gordon Brown issued a short statement saying how brave Harry is, how we're all proud of him, etc.

Then it was off to Liverpool for another Lib Dem spring conference but this time with a new leader.

We covered an eve of conference rally with a standing ovation, of course, for Nick Clegg. Next morning, an interview with Clegg about Margaret Thatcher who had been taken to hospital but had quickly emerged looking fine. I did lives on a Vince Cable speech. While Vince was well respected by all sides in the House of Commons for his expertise as an economist, an orator he most certainly was not.

I was standing by to do my next live when the shocking, awful news came through that ITN newscaster Carol Barnes had died. She had had a stroke a few days earlier. She was only 63. A producer in the gallery at Sky News asked me if I would like to talk on air about Carol. I didn't feel comfortable doing that and said so. Words are never enough. I should have called her husband, my friend ITN cameraman Nigel Thompson ('death wish Tommo'), but again words are never enough. I'm not going to do it here either, except to say that Carol was one of the loveliest people I have ever met and we all loved her.

These spring conferences are more of a rally, the annual conferences in the autumn are where issues are debated and policies decided. Their function, really, is as a platform for the leader's speech to the party faithful. I did long lives into and out of Nick Clegg's first speech as leader. He pressed all the right buttons and the party members went away happy. We did a final live and packaged for the evening news programmes.

After another week advising/supporting the UK Defence Academy in Shrivenham, it was back to Westminster and lives all day on a government proposal that cigarettes should not be openly displayed in shops. Adam and Anji, Jon Craig, politics producer Peter Diapre and I were having dinner with the Chancellor Alistair Darling, his wife Maggie and political advisor Catherine Macleod. I had to leave early to do a live at 10pm at the Foreign

Office which was criticising China's human rights record and another at 10.15 when the Conservatives lost an Opposition Day Debate calling for a public inquiry into the invasion of Iraq. The government majority was a modest 28, it had been comparatively close.

After lives on PMQs the next day, more lives on a vote in the House of Lords to ban bottled water. It got no further, unfortunately. I always like to say that these companies don't make water, they just produce plastic bottles.

Nicolas Sarkozy came for a state visit. He and Gordon Brown went to Arsenal's Emirates Stadium where they met our legendary manager Arsène Wenger. I did a long live, twenty minutes, sharing the airtime with French journalist Agnes Poirier. Of course, I knew far more about Arsène and the Arsenal than anyone else involved. I did more long lives into and out of a Brown-Sarkozy joint press conference. *L'entente cordiale* at the Emirates!

Bertie Ahern resigned after eleven years as the Taoiseach, the Irish prime minister. There were allegations of financial irregularities which he denied. The political vultures had been circling for some time. I very quickly boned up on that so that I sounded like an expert on Irish politics in my live two-ways. I interviewed David Trimble and went to Tony Blair's shiny new Grosvenor Square office to interview him about Ahern and his pivotal role in the Good Friday agreement. Tony Blair seemed well, relaxed, refreshed. He actually looked younger. Life after Downing Street seemed to be agreeing with him.

Of to Egypt for a week, a family holiday in mid-April. At home, the financial crisis was building and my first job back at Westminster was to cover a Bank of England fifty billion pound bailout of the banks. We were following in the wake of what was happening in the United States, most recently the collapse of Bear Stearns and the intervention of the Federal Reserve. This was just the start. The Lehman Brothers bankruptcy was still five months away.

The next day and an Alistair Darling meeting at Number Eleven with bankers and the Council of Mortgage lenders. Gordon Brown had never been a great fan of the banks, believing them to be making excess profits which they were using to line the pockets of their senior executives rather than to help small and medium-sized businesses. That day, Tory MP Bob Spink defected to UKIP. The reaction back at Sky News HQ was a massive collective yawn and a chorus of 'Bob who?' I definitely wasn't going to get that story on air. Anyway, the gathering financial storm clouds were the story of the day.

There was a daft story about Cabinet minister John Hutton failing to leave a tip in a restaurant. I wrote a quick blog on it, which was picked up by *The Times* and the *Independent*. Rather more importantly, that day I was at the Treasury doing lives when Alistair Darling had meetings with a succession of bankers. They were already beginning to look like whipped dogs.

I passed an entertaining afternoon at the Royal Albert Hall covering the Institute of Directors convention. Gordon Brown's speech was solid, David Cameron's rather lightweight. Actor Kevin Spacey spoke about business and the arts and Bob Geldof spoke, well, mostly about himself.

I was in Sheffield that May for the local council elections. In the context of a global financial crisis and profound economic uncertainty, Labour got absolutely hammered. The Tories were triumphant, especially in the north of England. The Lib Dems had also done very well and had taken Sheffield. I did lives every hour from 7 in the morning until 7 in the evening, including one with David Blunkett and another with Nick Clegg at the city's town hall where the Lib Dems were celebrating. The mood in the country was swinging decisively against the Labour Party and Gordon Brown.

I did a HEFAT course, Hostile Environment and First Aid Training, in a superb setting, sixty-eight acres of Hampshire countryside with former Royal Marines as instructors. The course lasted several days and our Sky News team did well, but it was relatively easy in warm, sunny weather and under no real pressure. It would, I felt, be very different in the dark, the cold and the rain and with some bastard trying to shoot you. But it was very valuable training for life in general and I emerged confident about my first aid skills. I was equally sure that I would not cope well with being hooded and taken hostage or with dragging a wounded colleague to safety. Thank God those skills have never been tested.

Abu Qatada, wanted in his native Jordan on terrorism charges, was released on bail under a daily twenty-two-hour curfew. This followed an Appeal Court judgement that he could not be deported to Jordan. In a website article, I suggested that this judgement was frankly ridiculous although in my TV lives I simply reported the decision dispassionately. Abu Qatada was eventually deported to Jordan in 2013.

After the disastrous showing in the local council elections, things were going from bad to worse for Labour. Opinion polls showed the Conservatives were set to win the Crewe and Nantwich by-election triggered by the death of Labour MP Gwyneth Dunwoody. David Cameron was ahead of Gordon Brown with women voters and in just about all categories, including trust and competence. Lord Levy was doing the rounds of TV political programmes to sell his memoirs and claimed that Gordon Brown must have known about loans-for-peerages, a claim angrily denied by Brown's advisor, Damian McBride. I packaged the Levy story all day.

The Conservatives went on to win the Crewe and Nantwich by-election with a swing from Labour of 17.6%. If that were to be repeated nationally, the Conservatives would win a general election with a large majority. It was the first time the Conservatives had taken a seat from Labour in a by-election since Ilford North in 1978.

There was to be an inquiry after all into the death of Baha Mousa who had died in 2003 after being detained and severely beaten by British troops in Iraq. He had died in British military custody. Seven soldiers had been charged with a war crime, only one had been convicted. I did lives on the story all day and we got General Sir Richard Dannatt, Chief of the General Staff (head of the army) live.

After three years of investigation the inquiry report in 2011 concluded that Baha Mousa had been repeatedly assaulted, subjected to 'serious gratuitous violence', and that officers of the Queen's Lancashire Regiment must have known what was going on, and accused the Ministry of Defence of 'corporate failure'. The report cleared commanding officer Colonel Jorge Mendonca of having any knowledge of the brutal beatings, but also suggested that he should have been aware of them and should have intervened.

The High Court ruled that MPs must reveal their expenses. Not surprisingly, there had been some resistance. After two days training senior executives from a multinational company at the beautiful and historic Manoir des Brumes in Normandy, I was back at Sky doing lives when Gordon Brown and Alistair Darling met oil industry leaders in Aberdeen.

At the end of May, Downing Street was denying the rather strange claim that Gordon Brown had been cold-calling voters. I did lives on that and the latest opinion polls which were catastrophic for the government.

Gordon Brown held a joint press conference with visiting Japanese Prime Minister Fukuda. Try saying that live on TV and keeping a straight face!

We were live at London's City Hall for Boris Johnson's first press conference as the newly-elected London Mayor. My producer was Richard Suchet, nephew of my former ITN colleague John. I must have been getting old. I was watching the next generation coming through.

Following results in Montana and South Dakota, Barack Obama was now certain to win the Democratic Party presidential nomination, but Hilary Clinton was still refusing to concede defeat. It now seemed that she was after the vice-presidency. I thought Obama wouldn't want the Clintons anywhere near the White House. I was wrong. Once elected president, he appointed Hilary Clinton as his Secretary of State.

Tony Blair gave evidence to the House of Commons International Development select committee in early June, his first formal public appearance since stepping down as prime minister. I covered that before doing lives in Downing Street on knife crime (up) and army pay (not up by enough). I was about to do the same at three p.m. when news broke that British diplomats had been attacked in Zimbabwe. I did four lives on this unfolding story during the next hour and three more in the following hour on the rapidly deteriorating UK-Zimbabwe relationship. We had been expecting Zimbabwe's president, Robert Mugabe, to go for some time.

Mugabe was without doubt guilty of crimes against humanity. He had turned Zimbabwe from the breadbasket of Africa to an economic basket case. By 2007, Zimbabwe had the highest inflation rate in the world, a mind boggling seven thousand six hundred per cent. By 2008 it had risen even higher and a loaf of bread cost one third of a day's average pay. Unemployment was eighty per cent and only twenty per cent of children were attending school. The WHO reported that average life expectancy was thirty-four for women and thirty-six for men. But it was the increasingly totalitarian nature of the Mugabe regime which brought the strongest international condemnation. He was locking up, torturing and in some cases murdering political opponents. He was also fixing presidential elections.

He survived as president until 2017 when he was arrested by the army and forced to resign.

On a Wednesday in mid-June politics went through the looking glass at PMQs. Labour was arguing for draconian law and order measures while the Conservatives were advocating civil liberties. My lives reflected this rather curious state of affairs. The government won the vote that evening on the extension to forty-two days permitted to hold terrorism suspects without charge but only just, by nine votes, three hundred and fifteen to three hundred and six. Despite his large House of Commons majority, Gordon Brown won only because nine DUP MPs voted with the government. When the House of Lords threw it out, as they undoubtedly would, Gordon Brown would have to rely on the DUP again. What would they demand as the price for their support? I did lives on that and my one and only live two-way for Abu Dhabi TV. I didn't explain to an Abu Dhabi audience who the DUP were! I just told the viewers that the government had narrowly won the vote and talked about the implications.

The next day, Shadow Home Secretary David Davis resigned saying he intended to force a by-election in his Haltemprice and Howden constituency and stand for re-election on the issue of his opposition to the forty-two-day decision and, as he saw it, the erosion of liberty. I thought this slightly excessive if not politically bonkers!

As he was resigning, I was in Brussels with cameraman Mike Donnelly to cover the results of the Irish referendum of the Lisbon Treaty. Ireland was the only country to hold a public vote. I was live almost constantly all morning as it became apparent that the Irish had voted No, rejecting the treaty. It was relentless and, of course, I was in my element. At lunchtime, the Irish justice minister admitted that his government had lost. I did six more lives before we took a statement from EU Commission President José Manuel Barroso. As we were waiting for official confirmation from Dublin, we did four live two-ways in the hour between 5 and 6 0'clock and four more in the next hour. Eight lives in two hours!

We grabbed dinner. This involved eating the main course, dashing down the road to do another live, and then returning to the restaurant for dessert (tiramisu since you ask!) and coffee before heading off for a final live two-way at 11pm. We sent a package for the next morning's *Sunrise* programme before returning to our hotel to collapse.

The Irish No vote was so significant because it could kill the Lisbon Treaty stone dead. I would be in Dublin the following year when the Irish held a second referendum which achieved the correct result from the EU's point of view.

The next morning was equally busy with lives every hour off the back of my package, including an interview with Nigel Farage. By lunchtime, we were no longer needed, although we cut a fresh package which ran all afternoon. It had become yesterday's story. We had had a great run.

Back in Westminster, I went to the Treasury to interview Chancellor Alistair Darling. The inflation rate was 3.3%, way above the government's target of two per cent, mainly due to increases in fuel and food prices. The Treasury press officers insisted that he would only be doing a 'clip', whatever that was, but he let me interview him so I did. For six minutes. It was a pool interview and was played out in its entirety by both Sky News and the BBC. The Treasury press office got upset because Alistair Darling's answers were very repetitive, almost verbatim. The questions however were very good! But he was robotically delivering the same sound bites in answer to every question.

They, and presumably the chancellor, thought he was only doing 'a clip'. But Alistair was a seasoned politician and he had agreed to a sit-down interview and to answer my questions. At no point had anyone said 'you'll only get one answer'. My view was that if they wanted to do a pre-arranged sound bite they could do it to their own camera. We were not the Labour Party's TV channel. And what had been the point of inviting a correspondent? I think they learnt the lesson, six minutes of the same answer question after question. It had been excruciating. The word 'clip' disappeared from the political lexicon.

Some time later I apologised to Alistair Darling and told him what had happened and where I thought the blame lay. He was completely unfazed. I suppose if you were seeing the first signs of what could and did become a global financial crisis, the least of your worries was a few minutes of embarrassment on a twenty-four-hour TV news channel.

PMQs that Wednesday was largely dominated by foreign affairs, mostly Afghanistan but also Zimbabwe, a Hamas-Israeli ceasefire and the Lisbon Treaty. David Davis officially resigned as an MP, but it seemed no one would stand against him in his self-inflicted by-election. I was, rather bizarrely, interviewed by Polish TV who wanted to know whether or not I thought Lech Wałęsa was a Western spy!

I was talking live again about Zimbabwe. The country's cricket team was banned from a tour of England due the following year and Robert Mugabe was stripped of his honorary knighthood. I was live all afternoon and evening from the Foreign Office but got replaced at 3 o'clock by Andy Burnham for Labour and at 6 o'clock by Shadow Foreign Secretary William Hague.

On the sixtieth anniversary of the NHS, Lord Darzi, a leading surgeon who Gordon Brown had appointed a government minister as part of his drive to be a government 'of all the talents', produced his widely-praised report looking ahead ten years and saying, to paraphrase, that the NHS should be clinician-led and not regulation-led.

I went to David Davis' Haltemprice and Howden constituency for his self-inflicted by-election with producer Esme Wren and cameraman Anthony Norman, known universally as 'Spiney'. Like all elections, this involved us working for most of the night which seemed rather pointless as only the Greens had put up a candidate to challenge David Davis along with the English Democrat, the National Front and several independents. Oh, and the Miss Great Britain Party, fronted by Miss Great Britain Gemma Garratt. Labour had condemned the entire exercise, 'a political stunt' and 'a farce' according to Gordon Brown while the Lib Dems supported David Davis' stance on civil liberties.

We did long lives from 10pm until 2am and interviewed David Davis several times. Free publicity for him. We also interviewed the Green Party candidate live and anti-rape campaigner Jill Saward. At 2 o'clock, with the vote apparently imminent, I did a live two-way that lasted twenty-five minutes. An epic! Of course, almost no one was watching at 2am. We also interviewed Miss GB Gemma Garratt live, we were getting very bored! I did another long live almost immediately when we finally got the results at two fifty a.m. David Davis had won by 17, 113 votes to the Greens 1, 758, receiving 72% of the votes cast. Gemma Garratt, by the way, came fifth with 521 votes. Finally, another live with the victor-of-his-own-making at 3am. Phew!

After just one hour's sleep at our hotel, we were live again at 6 the next morning and every hour until 11am when Sky's interest in the story (and mine!) finally waned. We did our lives from David Davis' home. It had been a surreal by-election. Altogether there had been 26 candidates, a record, almost all of them from the lunatic fringe.

Next day back at Westminster and lives and packages all day and evening on a rather more serious matter, the deteriorating situation in Zimbabwe where Mugabe's ZANU-PF thugs were terrorising white farmers as the country, almost inconceivably, plunged even further into economic and civil decline.

After covering stories on knife crime, a Welfare Reform Green Paper and the Equitable Life scandal in which almost one million people had lost at least part of their pensions and for which the Parliamentary Ombudsman Ann Abraham blamed ten years of 'maladministration and injustice', and another PMQs during which there were plenty of opportunities for Gordon Brown to push back at David Cameron with a light touch and a little humour as Tony Blair would have done (he either wouldn't or simply couldn't do it), we were off for a family holiday in Antigua.

We visited many of Antigua's beaches, beach after beach after beach. They say there are 365 of them. And 366 in a leap year!

While we were there, a British honeymoon couple were shot when masked gunmen burst into their hotel room. The newly-wed wife had died instantly, the husband was in intensive care. I did a live phono into *Sky News at Ten* on this awful story. We scooped the opposition simply by virtue of my being there on holiday.

The next day, news editor Phil Wardman phoned to ask, very demurely, if I would write a piece for Sky News Online. I was only too happy to do so. I dictated it from the beach at Half Moon Bay, which we had to ourselves, having gleaned (i.e. plagiarised) most of it from the *Antigua Sun* newspaper and phoned the chief of police. Later, I did two live phonos at midday and 1 o'clock (5 and 6 pm BST). Lives from a beach in Antigua! Then I got a message which had originated from Sky Head of News John Ryley that holidays were sacrosanct and I should not have any more of mine interrupted. I hadn't minded one little bit, although the story had been told by then anyway.

Radovan Karadžić was extradited to The Hague after more than ten years on the run. Of course this was huge international news, but there was a lot more excitement over the case of Josef Fritzl. His daughter, Elizabeth, told police in Austria that he had held her captive for twenty-four years in the cellar of their home. He had repeatedly raped her and she had given birth to seven children. In March the following year, Fritzl was sentenced to life.

Charles Clarke wrote another article for the *New Statesman* again attacking Gordon Brown and saying that Labour was heading for electoral disaster. The next day he was on TV calling on Brown to do 'the honourable thing' and resign. It was our lead story and I did lives every hour for five hours before switching to a Gordon Brown speech to the CBI in Glasgow for another seven lives, including talking live into and out of the speech. He ignored the Charles Clarke attack, there were far bigger fish to fry as a result of poor mortgage lending in the United States, the subprime mortgage crisis which was to lead to the financial crash.

Before heading to Bournemouth for the Lib Dems' annual conference the following Saturday, I did lives on whether or not there would be a Labour leadership challenge. This seemed extremely unlikely. Siobhain McDonagh, an assistant whip, had been the first government minister to call for a leadership contest. She got little support and was sacked from her government position. I did six lives, every hour all morning, before getting the train to Bournemouth. That day, September 13th, America's fourth largest investment bank, Lehman Brothers, filed for bankruptcy.

The collapse of Lehman Brothers was obviously a big story but no one yet quite realised its full significance. If this was a one off by an admittedly huge bank, then that might be that. But there had been an epidemic of mortgage miss-selling in the United States.

We did lives all Sunday morning at the Lib Dem conference, including lives with Nick Clegg and Vince Cable but, after lunchtime, no more was wanted from us. The news spotlight was fixed on New York and Lehman Brothers. Nick Clegg described the Labour Party as being in its 'death throes'. I doorstepped Charles Clarke at a Fabian Society fringe meeting. He was unfriendly and greeted me with a hostile outburst which made it into the pages of several national newspapers the next day.

The Monday morning was all about Vince Cable trying to explain to us what on earth he thought was going on. Lehman Brothers was gone, and the subprime mortgage crisis had claimed a second huge scalp as Merrill Lynch had been sold to the Bank of America. Now it was widely thought that the crisis could spread to the remaining American investment banks. Capitalism was in meltdown.

No government, central bank or regulator had spotted the crisis until it was too late. Their eyes were focused on the economic growth in China, high oil prices and the general state of the US economy. What they were not looking at was the domestic US subprime housing market. In Britain, inflation was low and stable. In living memory, economic problems had been driven by high inflation.

In Bournemouth, the Lib Dems were debating a proposal to cut taxes and save twenty billion pounds from public spending. They really were very worried about the threat from the Tories. Nick Clegg delivered his first speech as Party leader to the annual conference. Despite the gathering financial storm, we did lives, interviews and vox pops before and after the speech and packaged the story for the evening news programmes.

On to Manchester for the Labour Party conference. We got an interview with Foreign Secretary David Miliband more than an hour ahead of the BBC to get his reaction to a suicide bomb at a hotel in Islamabad which had killed sixty people and Thabo Mbeki being forced to resign as South African president by his own ANC party.

At a lunchtime fringe meeting the next day I asked Peter Mandelson, "Is Gordon Brown the right person to lead the Labour Party?" He met that question with a deafening silence.

When I bumped into him a couple of hours later he asked me, "Did I give you what you wanted at lunchtime?" He certainly had. In his speech to the conference, David Miliband praised Gordon Brown but only in a very muted way. He was looking and sounding very much like a prime minister in waiting, something he laughed at when I put it to him afterwards.

Gordon Brown's leader's speech was most memorable for his line that he was dealing with a global economic crisis and that, "This is no time for a novice", simultaneously swatting both David Cameron as well as David Miliband or anyone else on his own side who fancied a tilt at the leadership. His speech was interrupted several times by standing ovations, but how much if any of it would resonate beyond the conference hall?

Later, I doorstepped Charles Clarke at another fringe meeting. This time he answered my question on Gordon Brown's leadership qualities, but only to say he didn't want to talk about it! At drinks that evening with Sue

Nye, Damian McBride and David Muir, 'Team Brown', they told me they believed Gordon had done enough to re-assert his leadership of the party and of the country. Sarah Brown said baby Fraser loved the Thomas the Tank Engine birthday present I had given them a few weeks earlier.

Overnight, Ruth Kelly resigned from the Cabinet to 'spend more time with her children'. Damian McBride briefed in bar of the Radisson hotel at 3 o'clock in the morning! I got interviews between 7 and 8am with Alan Johnson, David Miliband and John Hutton supporting Gordon Brown and saying that Ruth Kelly's departure had nothing to do with his style of leadership. I got Ruth Kelly herself at 9.15. She said her resignation was in no way a criticism of Gordon Brown's leadership.

At the Conservative Party conference in Birmingham I covered Boris Johnson's speech. Boris was now the darling of the conference, a position previously held by Michael Heseltine. In his leader's speech, David Cameron promised to work together with the government to tackle the financial crisis. In reality, he and Shadow Chancellor George Osborne were to constantly criticise the measures taken by Gordon Brown and Alistair Darling, and they were almost always wrong.

In the United States, the House of Representatives voted down a proposed 700 billion dollar government rescue plan for the banks even though Democrat and Republican leaders had supposedly agreed a deal. This struck me as mindlessly destructive and monumentally unhelpful.

In early October, Sir Ian Blair resigned as Metropolitan Police commissioner. He had 'lost the support' of London mayor Boris Johnson who had basically forced him out. I reported the story live. Sir Ian had been under pressure to go since the shooting dead of Jean Charles de Menezes three years earlier, but this felt entirely political.

On October 6th, I was reporting live on the Dow Jones index in New York in freefall despite a series of bailouts by the Federal Reserve.

There was an emergency meeting at Number Ten at 5pm on October 7th. Gordon Brown, the governor of the Bank of England, Mervyn King, the chairman of the FSA (Financial Services Authority) Adair Turner and Chancellor Alistair Darling who was just back from Luxembourg where the EU finance ministers had failed to do anything or even say anything meaningful about the global financial crisis.

After the meeting, it emerged that Alistair Darling would announce a 50 billion pound bailout for the banks the next morning. The shares of some banks had plummeted by 40% in just twenty-four hours. On camera, the chancellor said there would be more details before the markets opened the next day.

This was basically the part-nationalisation of the banks. Surely that would be enough to steady the financial markets? I cut the lead story, including an interview I had done with Shadow Chancellor George Osborne.

The next morning, Alistair Darling announced a bailout of not 50 billion pounds but a total of 500 billion in three separate parcels to tackle capital, liquidity and lending. In the afternoon, interest rates were cut by 0.5% by the Bank of England and simultaneously by the US Federal Reserve and the European Central Bank, an internationally coordinated interest rate cut for the first time ever. This was clearly what Gordon Brown had meant when he had talked about 'global solutions to global problems'.

At PMQs that day, Gordon Brown had inadvertently said, "We not only saved the world…" This was seen as a gaffe and was jumped on by David Cameron, but it could be argued that this was precisely what Gordon Brown had done. He had been the first Western leader to understand that a disastrous meltdown of the global financial system could only be prevented by a massive re-capitalisation of the banks. To persuade other countries he had needed his primary skills of meticulous attention to detail and the courage to lead the way, forcefully arguing his case. He had, indeed, become the world's finance minister. By his actions he had prevented a recession from becoming a depression.

The tide had turned, the waters were beginning to recede, but it had been a very close-run thing. Apart from the impending tsunami in investment banking, the retail arms of the banks were apparently on the verge of refusing cash withdrawals and shutting down their ATM machines. We had very nearly reached the point where we would not be able to withdraw our own cash from the bank. This brought home the scale and impact of the crisis to everyone. It wasn't simply some abstract financial crisis involving incomprehensibly large sums of money. It affected every one of us.

The next day, after hourly lives in Downing Street all morning, I was off to Birmingham to interview Gordon Brown after he held a Q&A with Midlands business leaders. Sky News played the interview in its entirety, about six minutes. The British government was threatening to sue Iceland, which was defaulting on bank deposits. British local councils, which had been investing in many national and international banks to spread their risk, had almost one billion pounds invested in Icelandic banks. The country's commercial banks were hugely over-extended. Iceland's economy went into a severe economic depression and had to be bailed out by the IMF. It took Iceland years to recover.

Peter Mandelson was introduced in the House of Lords. He now had the splendid if rather Ruritanian title of Lord Mandelson of Foy in the County of Herefordshire and Darlington in the County of Durham. He was still Mandy to us! The following June, he would add First Secretary of State and Lord President of the Council to his growing list of titles. In the streets outside there were two demos that day, one to mark the anniversary of the suffragette movement with a spectacular array of Edwardian costumes, and the other to protest against climate change which involved a bit of shoving and pushing with the police. It was harmless enough, but I was there reporting it live, so the protestors got the publicity they craved.

In the evening, as expected, the Lords threw out the government proposal to extend the holding of terrorism suspects without charge to forty-two days. Home Secretary Jacqui Smith told the Commons that the government would withdraw the clause from the anti-terrorism bill and would move it to a separate bill to be kept in reserve in case it was ever needed. A face-saving device, but also another U-turn.

The next day, October 14th, Gordon Brown held an off-camera press briefing at the Foreign Press Association. He laid out his global financial rescue package, a five-point plan, but the foreign correspondents were more interested in their idea of his new hero status. A 'superhero' said one, a 'sorcerer' according to *Le Monde*, a 'saviour' according to the latest winner of the Nobel Prize for Economics. It was truly bizarre. He was asked three times: "Are you Flash Gordon or just Gordon?"

The answer was, of course, "Just Gordon", but Just Gordon chuckled throughout this surreal exchange. I did lives afterwards in Downing Street and wrote a blog about how nice the foreign press had been, not at all like us nasty British lot with all our difficult questions!

The prime minister was at a summit in Brussels the next day, so the deputies had centre stage at PMQs. William Hague danced around Harriet Harman (metaphorically, of course) throwing left jabs (also metaphorical!). In the afternoon, I covered a meeting of the Local Government Association to discuss the money local councils had locked up in failing Icelandic banks. There had been some confusion over the location of the meeting by inept or deliberately misleading press officers who really did not want us there. I did several lives, including breaking the result of the meeting, that thirteen councils were in deep trouble and seeking government help.

The Conservatives were blaming the government and Gordon Brown personally for too much de-regulation and mocking his claim, when he'd been chancellor, of putting an 'end to boom and bust'. David Cameron accused the prime minister of getting us into this mess. The Conservatives were positioning themselves to blame the Labour government for the economic crisis, ignoring the fact that it was a global crisis with its origins in the United States. Gordon Brown had hit back effectively, but the Conservatives continued the theme up to and including during the 2010 general election campaign. Gordon Brown might have become some kind of hero and economic guru to some around the world, but the Conservatives were determined to convince voters in Britain that the whole thing had been his fault.

The man behind this Conservative strategy, Shadow Chancellor George Osborne, was himself in trouble the next day over claims that he had solicited a donation for the Conservatives from Russian oligarch Oleg Deripaska when he had been a guest on the Russian's yacht in Corfu. It was the same Russian and the same yacht which had previously hosted Peter Mandelson who, we suspected, might be getting his revenge after George Osborne told too many people that Mandy had 'dripped poison' into his ear about Gordon Brown.

George Osborne, looking very flustered, denied the allegation but Nat Rothschild, supposedly a friend of both George and Dave, stood by it. It was intriguing. Someone was lying. I packaged the story all evening, updating every hour as David Cameron defended his Shadow chancellor and Rothschild repeated the allegation. Peter Mandelson was somewhere celebrating his fifty-fifth birthday. He was saying nothing but no doubt enjoying the Conservatives' discomfort.

The economy remained the story, of course. At the end of the month I covered a Q&A session at the Guildhall with Alistair Darling and the president of the European Investment Bank, interviewed Alistair Darling and George Osborne (separately, obviously!), and did more lives on both the economy and Gordon Brown's impending trip to the Gulf. We were about to visit four Gulf States in three days.

We left on November 1st with a group of senior business executives as well as the travelling press. I did a quick pooled interview with Gordon Brown in the VIP Royal Suite at Heathrow before our chartered BA flight to Riyadh during which he gave us a long briefing on the purpose of the visit. We arrived in Riyadh in the middle of the night and went straight to the Intercontinental Hotel. I had never been to Saudi Arabia before and saw nothing of it. It was hotel-airport-hotel. But across from the hotel was the Ministry of the Interior, an Orwellian monstrosity which could easily have doubled as the Ministry of Truth. I did a live phono as soon as we touched down and lives from the hotel all day and all evening. We were working with the ITN and BBC teams. None of us had a producer with us, we were pooling everything and it worked perfectly well.

I interviewed Gordon Brown again the next morning and we fed the interview in time for Andrew Marr's BBC *Politics Programme*, although it ran on Sky News slightly earlier. A quick final live two-way, then we were off to the airport where our BA crew was waiting to fly us to Doha. More lives. Gordon Brown told us he was confident that he had persuaded the Saudis to provide more funds for the IMF. It was in his role as head of the IMF Ministerial Committee that he had 'saved the world'! In Doha, he visited a terrorist rehabilitation centre and had shaken hands with former Guantánamo Bay detainees. This excited the Fleet Street hacks. While I was once again lashed to the live point at the hotel, Sky News cameraman Colin Hamilton was out and about with the prime minister providing pool pictures. He had been to the emir's palace and had also been to the royal palace in Riyadh. I was slightly envious.

Lewis Hamilton (no relation!), a big Arsenal fan by the way, won the Formula One World Championship on the last bend of the final race of the season, the Brazilian Grand Prix. After dinner with the emir, Gordon Brown did a quick congratulatory message on camera, a BBC pool. We had a quick drink in the bar with Peter Mandelson, who had also been at the dinner at the emir's palace, and Cabinet minister Ed Miliband. I had sent a package earlier which had got a good run on Sky News despite the almost wall-to-wall coverage of the US presidential election.

Early the next morning we were off by helicopter to the Ras Laffan Qatar Group's huge LNG terminal and Shell's GLP (Gas to Liquid Project), Shell's largest. After meetings with Shell executives including an old university chum (small world), we choppered to the airport and onto our chartered BA Jumbo for the short flight to Abu Dhabi. We went straight to an oil conference where Gordon Brown was speaking and from there to the astonishing seven-star and ridiculously opulent Emirates Palace Hotel from where we fed our pictures back to London.

We did a live from the sixth floor terrace outside an unbelievably luxurious suite which apparently cost £7,000 a night. Our hotel, the Meridien, was perfectly good and comfortable but felt like a Travelodge by comparison. We fed a package from there. To the British Embassy and on to the ambassador's residence where we had drinks with Ed Miliband, who was very funny and extremely indiscreet, especially about Peter Mandelson. We kept Ed company until 1.30 in the morning. He had been ordered back to London by the prime minster for a House of Commons vote. His flight was at 2.30am. He was not entirely amused.

The flight in the Jumbo to Dubai the next morning took just twenty minutes. Environmentally, this was borderline criminal but our aircraft needed to be there anyway for our flight back to London. A convoy by road in both directions would have massively reduced our carbon footprint. Our first stop, and my first live, was at Dubai's financial centre. We visited the not yet complete world's tallest building. Ten years later, I went to the top of the Burj Khalifa with Sebastian. Yes, it was spectacular but what struck me most was the view. From the top of the Empire State Building you have New York City at your feet. From the Eiffel Tower, fabulous views of Paris. From the London Eye or The Shard, some of London's most iconic buildings. From the top of the tower in Dubai, all you could see was hotels and building sites, although the view of The Palm is quite something.

Back then the skeletal Burj al-Arab as it was then called was itself a building site. Our flying visit to the Gulf ended as it had begun, with me doing a pool interview with Gordon Brown. He justified the visit and what had been achieved and congratulated the new American president, Barack Obama, on his election victory.

Back in Westminster, on November 6th the Bank of England cut the interest rate by 1.5% to just 3%. I interviewed Chancellor Alistair Darling, a six-minute interview which ran in its entirety at the top of the hour followed by a long live two-way, another six minutes, trying to explain what was going on. I did lives in the evening on a subject which was far easier to explain after a briefing from the PMOS Mike Ellam. Gordon Brown had phoned President-elect Obama to offer his congratulations and discuss the issues facing the world. Top of the agenda, of course, was the global financial crisis.

The world was shocked that November by the terrorist attack in Mumbai, shootings and bombings which went on for four days and left nearly 200 people dead and many more injured. It took those four days to flush out the nine terrorists who were all killed, the last at The Taj Hotel.

Peter Connelly was a seventeen-month-old baby who had died after suffering more than fifty injuries over an eighteen-month period. He was seen several times by Child Services in the London Borough of Haringey, my local authority. At first, we weren't allowed to use his name and he became known simply as baby P. We had witnessed the ineptitude of Haringey's social services before, in the awful case of eight-year-old Victoria Climbié seven years earlier.

David Cameron raised the case of baby P at a furious PMQs in mid-November. Gordon Brown accused him of playing politics with the horrific case. It was a slightly odd line of attack for David Cameron to take given that the Bank of England Governor Mervyn King had said in an interview that morning that he was predicting a 'deep recession', and that unemployment had just risen to 1.82 million. Maybe he was trying to blindside Gordon Brown who was far stronger than David Cameron when it came to debating the economy.

In any event, it spurred the government into action. Ed Balls announced an inquiry which was to report within a fortnight and government inspectors were sent to Haringey child services. I did lives before and after PMQs. With a two-year-old baby son myself, this was difficult. Everyone found the case of Baby P traumatic. Many of us were in tears. I packaged the story for the evening, a quick 2 minute 30 seconds pull-together for 7pm with a more crafted 3 minutes 30 for *Sky News at Ten*. It was, of course, our lead story and the front page of almost every newspaper.

Peter's mother, Tracey Connelly, her boyfriend Steven Barker and his brother Jason Owen were subsequently convicted of causing or allowing the death of a child. There were three inquiries and a national review of child services, but I know from my work with the NSPCC that these appalling atrocities continue and that most of them are never reported.

Two days later, Haringey child protection officer, Nevres Kamal, turned whistle-blower. She had raised her concerns about the state of the borough's childcare services six months before baby P had died. She said she had been victimised as a result, falsely accused of child abuse herself as the council investigated her and her nine-year-old daughter. Nevres Kamal had lost her job and had faced a police investigation. Her health had suffered. Haringey Council eventually dropped the case and paid her compensation.

While Haringey Council was persecuting Nevres Kamal and ignoring her warnings, baby P was being used as a punch bag. I did lives every hour all day and all evening. At five p.m., a judge lifted an injunction which had prevented us from showing Peter Connelly's face. Now, he was there for everyone to see, this beautiful baby boy with blond hair and huge blue eyes.

Gordon Brown was in Washington for a G20 summit. He said, "We must do everything to ensure this must never happen again." There was a pause between each of the last five words. He looked and sounded as shocked and angry as the rest of us. David Cameron blamed bureaucratic buck-passing for the death of this 'baby girl'. No one used that bit of his statement, excusing it as a slip of the tongue. At PMQs the previous Wednesday he had described the mother as seventeen years old. In fact, she was twenty-seven.

The following Monday I did lives both on the G20 summit and on Shadow Chancellor George Osborne rather foolishly talking down the pound and, again, on baby P. We still weren't allowed to name him. It had emerged that the police had wanted him rescued and taken into custody but Haringey had refused. I simply didn't understand why the head of Haringey child services, Sharon Shoesmith, hadn't yet resigned.

On December 1st, the leader of Haringey Council, George Mehan, and Liz Santry, the councillor responsible for children's services, resigned in the wake of the devastating findings of the Ofsted report commissioned by Ed Balls. Sharon Shoesmith refused to resign so she was suspended on full pay. She was sacked a week later.

We were in Leeds where the Cabinet was meeting on one of its regional awaydays. We interviewed Gordon Brown and Home Secretary Jacqui Smith and we got a long, live and exclusive interview with Foreign Secretary David Miliband. I managed to break new lines all day and was quoted on the news wires, which is always gratifying.

Conservative MP and former ITN colleague (he had worked at Channel 4 News) Damian Green was arrested for allegedly releasing leaked Home Office documents to the police. His offices at Westminster and in his constituency were searched by police officers without a warrant. I interviewed him. He said that he suspected his offices had been bugged, although no bugging devices were ever found. No prosecution ensued, although a junior Home Office civil servant was subsequently sacked after admitting that he had leaked the documents to Damian. All in all, it was a very odd affair.

Just before Christmas, I did lives all day when the Metropolitan Police Assistant Commissioner Bob Quick apologised for the Damian Green fiasco, and reported on the latest opinion polls which were still very good for the Conservatives.

On Boxing Day, the Israelis began bombing the Gaza Strip, once again. *Plus ça change*. They were still bombing, for a third day, when I returned to work on December 29th. I did lives all day and interviewed Foreign Secretary David Miliband who had to walk the tightrope all British foreign secretaries have to walk when dealing with this issue while calling on all sides to stop the violence.

The bombing continued the next day. The Israelis, never known to under-react. At least 360 people had been killed in Gaza so far. I was also supposed to do lives that day on New Year messages from David Cameron and Nick Clegg and on the honours list. Our Olympians were being honoured. But Gaza was the only story, such a sad story to end the year.

CHAPTER 7

2009: Duck Houses, Moats and Tennis Courts. D-Day Gaffes. Phone-hacking. "Too Many Tweets Make a ...". Auschwitz. Famous in Dublin!

While I was covering a David Cameron speech on tax cuts at St Stephen's club, Reuters got some awful pictures from Gaza of two dead Palestinian toddlers. No one it seemed was able to persuade the Israelis to exercise restraint. Then, as now, the Israeli government insisted their attacks were targeted, aimed at Hamas, while the rockets from Gaza were being fired indiscriminately. But both sides were killing children, and the images were heartbreaking.

Gordon Brown was planning a short regional tour which the *Guardian* was calling 'the recession tour'. I interviewed the prime minister on the train to Derby, a long pooled interview which we fed once we arrived at the Rolls Royce factory and was played in its entirety both on Sky News and the BBC. We did lives off the back of the interview, which included talking about Gaza. Israel had announced a three-day ceasefire to allow humanitarian aid to be delivered. It had ended at 3pm that day and the air strikes had resumed.

From Derby by train to Liverpool and another Cabinet meeting, supposedly taking government to the people. We got both Gordon Brown and Alistair Darling to comment on the breaking news that the Bank of England was cutting interest rates again, by 0.5% to just 1.5%, the lowest ever at the time. In Sunderland, Nissan was shedding 1,200 jobs, a quarter of the work force. I interviewed Peter Mandelson on that story, a doorstep which turned into a good, long interview.

While I was doing lives, reporter Tom Parmenter cut a package for *Live at Five* on the Cabinet meeting in Liverpool, asking local people what they thought of the idea. I think it's fair to say that the good people of Liverpool, if they knew about it at all, were not particularly impressed.

From Liverpool we were off to Birmingham where Gordon Brown was visiting a computer tech company, and finally Cardiff.

Gordon Brown held a 'jobs summit' on January 12th against the grim backdrop of job losses at JCB, Waterford, Wedgewood, Wincanton Logistics, Waterstones and others. I packaged our lead story for lunchtime and did lives from Downing Street all afternoon. The next day and more lives in Downing Street when Peter Mandelson announced a loan guarantee scheme for businesses to try to stop the rot and persuade the banks to increase lending.

The next day and a bilateral summit in Paris. I met up with cameraman Colin Hamilton and we did our lives from a TV studio on the Champs Élysée rather than the Élysée Palace. Nothing says Paris more than the Champs Élysée except, perhaps, the Eiffel Tower.

After overnighting in Paris and taking the Eurostar back to London, it was straight back to Westminster and two stories. The government had decided to go ahead with a third runway for Heathrow, which was, and remains, highly controversial. Meanwhile, the Chinese were building a new airport every five minutes! I also did a two-minute live on the US-UK 'special relationship' ahead of Barack Obama's inauguration the following Tuesday.

January 20th, Obama inauguration day. I was supposed to interview Gordon Brown at Number Ten on the new American president, but a Number Ten press officer told me he'd been called away first to take a phone call and then to a meeting, and that the pooled interview for us, ITN and the BBC was off. By great good fortune, Gordon Brown passed me in the corridor, stopped, and said he would do it. Before the interview I headed towards the wrong chair. He said, "You can have the job if you like." I replied that I wouldn't have the stamina let alone the intellect to last a single day.

The Standards and Privileges Committee reported on Peter Hain's election expenses. They had some strong words for him, but no action would be taken as he had clearly had no intention to deceive. All he had to do was to apologise to the House the following week. Our rather uncollegiate colleague Joey Jones once again did a live saying that this was the end of Hain's career in front-line politics and, once again, I took a call from Peter Hain and did a live putting the points he had made to me, that he had not been suspended from the House of Commons, had been cleared of any wrongdoing other than reporting his expenses later than required and that he would be back.

The economy continued to dominate the news and the following day I was live in Downing Street as the prime minister announced a government plan to help the struggling car industry. I talked into and out of a Peter Mandelson statement in the House of Commons and Ken Clarke's response. As I was live on air, the Information Tribunal ordered the release of the Cabinet minutes from March 2003, the decision to invade Iraq, and I had to switch subjects mid-live. My package to run all evening was on those Cabinet minutes and the crucial legal advice on going to war.

An ICM opinion poll that day had the Conservatives on 44%, Labour on 32% and the Lib Dems on 16%.

There was a strike at Totals Oil Refinery in Lincolnshire over foreign, that is EU, workers. This led to a lively exchange at the first PMQs of February over Gordon Brown's phrase at the previous autumn's Labour conference: 'British jobs for British workers'. The High Court withheld part of its judgement on the alleged torture of a Guantánamo Bay prisoner, Binyam Mohamed, after it emerged that the Americans had threatened to withdraw intelligence cooperation. I got Foreign Secretary David Miliband to comment on this live and packaged the story for the evening. Our new politics producer Hannah Thomas-Peter said "I've been run over by the news bus!" Yes, it had been another busy but not untypical day at Westminster. She would soon get used to it.

The Treasury Select Committee grilled the ex-CEOs and chairmen of HSBC and the Royal Bank of Scotland. It really was a grilling and they struggled to deal with the pointed and extremely unsympathetic questioning. I did lives on the session and again the next day when they lightly toasted more hapless bankers.

When Lord Pearson invited the odious right wing Dutch MP Geert Wilders to London I interviewed him and Labour peer Lord Ahmed. Home Secretary Jacqui Smith had banned Wilders, designating him an 'undesirable person'. Wilders flew in anyway, accompanied by a TV crew, and was detained at Heathrow and promptly deported back to the Netherlands.

Wilders appealed the decision and, in October, the UK Asylum and Immigration Tribunal overruled the Home Office ban and he visited the country. The Home Office condemned this ruling, saying it opposed all forms of extremism and that Wilders had been banned because, "His presence could have inflamed tensions between our communities and have led to inter-faith violence." Geert Wilders was getting more publicity than he could have dreamed of.

The latest monthly IPSOS/Mori poll which had the Conservatives 20 points ahead, 48% to Labour's 28%, with the Lib Dems on 17%. I reported the poll as 'Breaking News' and talked about it live every hour for several hours. Gordon Brown would certainly not be calling a general election anytime soon.

I previewed the unveiling of a Margaret Thatcher painting and interviewed the artist, Richard Stone. Rather more significantly later that day, Jack Straw announced that the government would not release the Cabinet minutes from March 2003 by using Section 53 of the Freedom of Information Act, a ministerial veto, for the first time. Technically this was correct, but the question was: What did they have to hide?

The next day, February 25th, we got the very sad news that David Cameron's six-year-old son, Ivan, had passed away. He had had a rare neurological, epileptic condition, Ohtahara syndrome. I went to St Mary's hospital Paddington where the chief executive read a short statement to camera. I did just one live immediately afterwards. PMQs was cancelled. Instead, Gordon Brown, William Hague and Vince Cable offered condolences. Nick Clegg was on paternity leave. The House of Commons was silent. Gordon Brown was particularly poignant, of course. He knew what it meant to lose a child and captured the moment perfectly. There was barely a dry eye in the House of Commons. Or in our Westminster newsroom.

Sir Fred Goodwin had resigned as RBS Chairman just before the bank revealed that its 2008 loss had been £24 billion, the worst in British corporate history. His pension, reported to be £700,000 per year was widely condemned. Treasury minister, Lord Myners, said there should be, "No reward for failure".

Both Gordon Brown and Alistair Darling demanded the return of a substantial part of Goodwin's pension, though the legal options to force him to do so seemed extremely limited. Vince Cable accused Goodwin of having 'no sense of shame' adding that if the company had gone bust, which it would have had it not been a bank and bailed out by the government, Goodwin would have got £28,000 a year starting when he reached the age of 65.

The press had a field day, dubbing him 'the world's worst banker'. Nick Cohen described him in the *Observer* as the characteristic villain of our day. And so he was. If you wanted an example of a Fat Cat banker you needed to look no further.

Two days later we were off to Brussels for an emergency EU summit. I arrived the evening before and cut a package for the next morning's *Sunrise* with cameraman Colin Hamilton. The day of the summit was the usual madness, lives and packages all day. I got the first question at Gordon Brown's press conference which we took live. The purpose of the emergency summit had been to get the French to toe the line and persuade Nicolas Sarkozy to stop making protectionist noises designed to appease French voters. The Hungarian prime minister spoke for the Eastern European countries when he warned of a new, economic Iron Curtain dividing the European Union. It is often forgotten in this country that the nations in the geographical centre of Europe look to and largely depend upon German economic and political leadership. Despite the furore over Brexit, they do not regard Britain as leading Europe. Or France for that matter.

On March 5th, the Bank of England announced another interest rate cut to an unprecedented rate of just 0.5% and £75 billion of quantative easing, otherwise known as printing money. I was in Covent Garden to interview Ed Balls about social care but the bank's announcement came just before the interview and he agreed to talk about that instead, whether or not any of these drastic measures were actually working and if Gordon Brown should apologise for insufficient regulation during his ten years as chancellor. It was a good interview, and Ed was the first Cabinet minister to publicly respond. Sky News played the interview in its entirety and I did lives in Downing Street all afternoon, including a very short statement to camera by Chancellor Alistair Darling four hours after the banks' announcement and the Ed Balls interview.

Next day it was off to lovely Harrogate again for the Lib Dems spring conference. It was a busy weekend of news so the Lib Dems hardly got on air. A Vince Cable speech was the highlight, if you could possibly call it that.

On the Monday, back in Westminster, an announcement that the RAF's fleet of Nimrod aircraft would be grounded for four weeks from the end of March, still three weeks away, to be 'made safe'. They had still not been modified since the disastrous fire of September 2006 which had killed all fourteen crew members. I did lives on the story. Surely if they were not safe they should be grounded immediately?

On the Tuesday, a police officer was shot dead in Northern Ireland. This was an even bigger story than might otherwise have been the case coming as it did in the wake of the killing of two soldiers at the weekend. The so-called 'continuity IRA' admitted responsibility.

The G20 finance ministers met in Horsham, Sussex in mid-March. At the same time, Gordon Brown was hosting the German Chancellor Angela Merkel. I did lives in Downing Street and got the first question at their joint press conference. The Germans were not too keen on any further fiscal stimulus without first seeing whether or not the already agreed measures were working. Towards the end of a twelve-hour day, I was doing lives both on Angela Merkel and the G20 finance ministers who were pledging to continue to work together to deal with the global financial crisis. It would have been news if they'd said they would not!

It was being reported that Jacqui Smith had claimed expenses for a bill that had included pornographic films viewed in the family home while she had not been there. She said it had been a mistake and she would repay the money. I did not envy her husband when she found out! But the pressure was building on Jacqui Smith and she would be gone two months later.

I was doing lives on both stories at once that day, the G20 view of the world as well as Jacqui Smith's husband apparently watching porn. On top of that there was a Gordon Brown press conference with Australian Prime Minister Kevin Rudd at which I got the first question and about which I did three hours of lives in Downing Street, which was a welcome relief from the sordid details of live chez Smith.

World leaders gathered at the Excel Centre in London for the G20 summit on April 1st and 2nd. I got a breaking news line from Treasury

Minister Stephen Timms that the government was planning sanctions against tax havens that were not 'transparent', some good lines from a lobby briefing with PMOS Mike Ellam, and I did a strange but strangely effective piece walking around as we filmed the vast media operation with our new social media producer, the wonderfully-named Miranda Richardson who no doubt got very, very tired of my constant *Blackadder* allusions! I did long lives into and out of Gordon Brown's press conference and got a front row seat and a question when Barack Obama talked to us a little later.

The headlines from the summit were that the IMF emergency fund would be trebled to 750 billion dollars, the G20 countries would work together without any protectionism (pay attention, France!), that the IMF and the World Bank would be reformed and that there would be greater international financial regulation. Gordon Brown's fingerprints were all over the G20 resolutions.

After a family holiday, a week in Sharm el-Sheikh and a weekend in Berlin, a gentle re-entry to work ahead of the Budget, including a briefing with Vince Cable which was like a seminar with your economics professor! Informed by various other pre-Budget briefings, I did lives all afternoon.

The government announced plans to reform MPs' expenses, including abolishing the second home allowance. Gordon Brown wanted a vote within a week and new rules in place by July 1st. Most MPs were a lot less keen.

A *Telegraph* poll had the Conservatives eighteen points ahead of Labour, Tories with 45%, Labour 27%, which would give them a landslide majority. The respected IFS (Institute for Fiscal Studies) suggested that the government debt figures were even worse than those presented in the Budget the day before and predicted ten years of austerity. Grim. I did lives on that and on the opinion poll in Downing Street all evening.

We were off to Afghanistan and Pakistan again at the end of April, with a stopover in Poland. Gordon Brown wanted to visit Auschwitz. I had a great team, cameraman Paul Fraser and producer Hannah Thomas-Peter, her first foreign assignment. It was a BA charter again, and again we had to go through the tortuous security in the VIP suite at Heathrow, with every piece of kit painstakingly checked. On the flight, Gordon Brown talked about 'the crucible of terror' and the need for a new approach to Afghanistan and Pakistan. You couldn't solve the problems of one without the other so long as the Taliban continued to operate across the border between the two countries with impunity. We also touched on MPs' expenses and, of course, football. We had both just watched Manchester United beat Spurs 5-2.

From Karachi we transferred to a Hercules for the two-hour flight to Camp Bastion. The body of the Hercules has just one tiny window covered with a blackout curtain. I lifted the curtain and peered through to see the most spectacular dawn over the Hindu Kush. What an experience! It was Monday morning. It sure as hell beat a Monday morning commute to work! I told the travelling press pack what they were missing. Not one of them could be bothered to move! For me, though, it was a moment I will never forget.

Camp Bastion, which was as hot and dusty as ever. We recorded an 'As Live' and a track which we would feed later from Kabul. Brown's visit was embargoed until we arrived in the Afghan capital. We had plenty of shots of Gordon Brown meeting the troops and talking with tribal elders.

After another hour in the Hercules, we drove to Kabul's presidential palace still in body armour and with an SAS driver and guard. I did live phonos at noon and one p.m. (eight thirty a.m. and nine thirty a.m. BST) before Gordon Brown's joint press conference with Afghan President Hamid Karzai which Sky News took live. I got the first question, again!

In his press conference, Gordon Brown publicy announced that he was off to Islamabad. For security reasons, this was supposed to be a secret! I did a final phono from the tarmac next to our Hercules at the airport where we had to stay behind a high wall before boarding for fear of snipers.

I did another phono when we landed in Islamabad. It seemed that President Asif Ali Zardari had cancelled a joint press conference with Gordon Brown, so Pakistan's Prime Minister Yousaf Raza Gilani took his place. Gordon Brown had a private meeting with President Zardari afterwards. We sent a new track and rushes from a very dimly-lit corner of the British High Commission Social Club! They got it back in London, were happy, and the package ran in *Live at Five* and all evening. I did a phono off the back of the package before we were back on our BA charter for the six-hour flight to Warsaw.

We arrived in the Polish capital at one a.m. on Tuesday morning. We had been on the go for more hours than I cared to remember. We checked into the Sheraton hotel for five hours much-needed and very comfortable sleep. Early the next morning, a Gordon Brown press conference with Polish Prime Minister Donald Tusk at the beautiful Łazienki Palace, the 'Palace on the Isle'. I got the first question and a long answer from Gordon Brown on the swine flu pandemic, the only story of the day. There were reported to be 100,000 cases in the UK and millions globally. We were ready to do a live via a Polish TV satellite truck but the WHO held a press conference on swine flu so, of course, Sky News switched live to that instead.

We flew to Krakow and drove in convoy to Auschwitz. I had been before, but the impact is always beyond words. I had time to walk around while Paul and Hannah were the pool crew who went with Gordon and Sarah Brown to Birkenau. Hannah was keen to go, it was her first time in this place of such unspeakable evil.

There was little interest in the prime minister's visit to Auschwitz back at Sky News headquarters. They had gone swine flu-tastic, absolutely obsessed with what was admittedly a huge story. Nevertheless, the decision was that we should stay and send a piece for *Sky News at Ten*, so we remained in Krakow while the rest of the press pack headed off to the airport for Gordon Brown's flight home.

Of course, I did my PTC beneath the Arbeit Macht Frei sign over the main gates. Hannah persuaded a helpful Polish TVN cameraman to drive the three of us with all our kit to TVN Krakow, a mad, fast drive up against a deadline. We had taken with us the BBC's track and PTC for Nick Robinson which we had agreed to feed back to London. I have to say, in all modesty, that our piece was much better. I simply had a better feel for this place.

Gordon and especially Sarah had been visibly upset. Like anyone who has been there, they were shocked by the ruthless efficiency of the genocide. The gas chambers, then to the ovens and on to the disposal of the ashes. Carried out by people who must have been completely de-humanized.

There really are no words.

Back in Westminster for a David Cameron press conference about MPs' expenses which was being debated in the House of Commons. I got WHO-ed several times as I stood by to go live. Swine flu was still the top story, but not the only story. I did lives in central lobby with Sir George

Young, Keith Vaz and Liam Byrne. The government comfortably won all the votes on MPs' expenses. The Conservatives claimed there had been a government climbdown. After the votes, the spin.

The main changes were that all expenses were to be receipted (incredibly, this had not been the case previously), MPs' staff were to be employed directly by the House of Commons authorities (no more unauthorised jobs for family members), there would be no second home allowance for MPs with constituencies within twenty miles of Westminster and all secondary income was to be declared. The biggest issue, second home allowances for MPs in further flung constituencies, was referred to Sir Christopher Kelly, the chairman of the Committee on Standards in Public Life. Hence the Tory claim of a government climbdown. But Gordon Brown could claim to have done something about MPs' expenses as he'd said he would, and he had done it quickly.

Into May, and more buffoonery from John Prescott. I had been in Lewisham where Gordon Brown was giving a speech on education. I did a live as he departed behind me, the timing could not have been better. But elsewhere, John Prescott was pulling a face, on camera, supposedly imitating Gordon Brown's smile which had become somewhat notorious. Some spin doctor or other had presumably told him he needed to smile more, but he had taken to doing it rather randomly and sometimes inappropriately. So, he would be talking about some serious subject and would suddenly smile for no apparent reason. Pulling a face, John Prescott had described it as, "The worst bloody smile in the world". Very helpful! I cut another package on Gordon Brown's leadership of his party for *Live at Five* which ran all evening.

The solids were really hitting the fan on MPs expenses. On May 8th, the *Daily Telegraph* had a leaked report into MPs' expenses which was due to be published in July. Nine pages of revelations, much of it nonsense but it was clear that some MPs, including Cabinet ministers, had been playing the system to maximise their second home allowances. John Prescott, it was reported, had claimed for some odd things including some rather ugly mock-Tudor beams for the front of his house in Hull.

I did lives on the story all day and more in the evening when we got the first edition of the next day's *Telegraph* with fresh revelations. The *Telegraph* was, of course, focusing its fire on Labour MPs. The paper suggested that Labour minister, Tony McNulty, might be facing a police inquiry. He wasn't, although the expenses scandal led to his resignation a year later. The *Telegraph* also revealed that Minister for Culture and Tourism Barbara Follett had claimed £25,000 over four years for security at her central London home. Since she had been both mugged and stalked, this was hardly surprising. The *Telegraph*'s beef appeared to be that she was very wealthy and could have paid for the additional security herself.

The MPs' expenses story kept us very busy for the next few days. The *Sunday Telegraph* had a front-page splash on Sinn Féin MPs' expenses, although they appeared to have done nothing wrong. Inside, more on Labour MPs but surprise, surprise, nothing on Conservative MPs. Not yet. An opinion poll in *The Sunday Times* had the Conservatives sixteen points ahead of Labour. Another, in the *Mail on Sunday*, had Labour polling at just twenty-three per cent, the lowest the paper claimed since modern polling had begun in 1943. As well as seemingly endless lives, on that Sunday afternoon it was every half hour, I interviewed Sir Alistair Graham, ex-chairman of the committee on Standards and Public Life, doorstepped Cabinet minister Hazel Blears who had been singled out by the *Telegraph*, and interviewed Labour MP Sir Stuart Bell who gave me the breaking news line that MPs would, the following day, approve an independent audit into all future expenses.

Conservative front benchers Michael Gove, Chris Grayling, Francis Maude, and Andrew Lansley all featured in Monday's *Daily Telegraph*, as did Alan Duncan, apparently for gardening expenses. On the Tuesday, the *Telegraph* had revelations about some frankly ridiculous claims by Conservative MPs, including for the cleaning of a swimming pool, a new portico (David Davis) and, best of all, Douglas Hogg claiming for the cleaning of a moat! His duck house was to become notorious. This kept me busy doing lives and packages all day and evening again. The Lib Dems had not yet been mentioned and appeared to be in the clear, at least for the time being.

On that Tuesday I interviewed Harriett Harman and Nick Clegg and packaged the story of the latest expenses revelations. In the evening, Hazel Blears handed back £13,000 very publicly on camera. I got away at midnight, a fourteen-hour day, but what a story!

Wednesday, and others were following Hazel Blears' example, including junior minister Phil Hope who handed back £41,700 while maintaining that he had kept to the parliamentary rules. He had actually claimed far less than many MPs. I packaged the story, taking in a lively PMQs, for *Live at Five* and all evening.

There was an EDM (Early Day Motion) to unseat Michael Martin as House of Commons speaker. Although he was regarded by many MPs as an ineffective speaker, I thought few MPs would have the courage to sign it. He was gone less than a week later.

The expenses scandal was, by now, rocking both major parties. Labour's Elliott Morley was suspended from the Labour Party after the *Telegraph* accused him of continuing to claim expenses for a mortgage that had already been paid off. Two years later he was convicted of false accounting and sentenced to sixteen months in prison.

Married Conservative MPs, Andrew MacKay and Julie Kirkbride, (another former colleague who had once worked at ITN's Westminster unit) were also in trouble. The *Telegraph* reported that they were both claiming expenses for what were, in effect, two second homes, one in Westminster the other in Kirkbride's Bromsgrove constituency. Since MacKay didn't own a property in his Bracknell constituency, they declared neither home as their primary residence. The *Telegraph* accused them of 'double dipping'. In the previous year they had claimed £45,000 between them. They had to pay it back. MacKay resigned as an aide to David Cameron, Julie Kirkbride continued to work as an MP before stepping down the following year.

On Monday May 18th, the House of Commons speaker, Michael Martin, made a vacuous statement in which he said nothing about his future. MPs who wanted him gone were furious and planned to table a motion of no confidence. I did lives and a package for *Live at Five*. Many MPs, too many to ignore, believed he had handled the expenses scandal incompetently from start to finish. After weeks of dogged resistance, Michael Martin resigned the next day. He made a statement, if you could call it that. It lasted all of thirty-three seconds. It was obviously a huge day at Westminster, so we had Kay Burley and Jeremy Thompson presenting from Abingdon Green. I put together a four-minute package for *Live at Five* which I updated to include a Gordon Brown press conference at five thirty p.m. on reforming MPs' expenses.

Michael Martin was the first speaker to be sacked since 1695. Seven had been beheaded in the Middle Ages and just beyond, including two on the same day in 1510. So, as I reported at the time, Michael Martin might consider himself lucky not to have lived in earlier times!

Then, something completely different. Actress Joanna Lumley, the daughter of a Gurkha regiment officer, was leading a campaign to get better treatment, including decent pensions, for the Gurkhas. She won; the government saw sense. I was live almost continuously from midday for an hour. Joanna Lumley was box office! She and the celebrating Gurkhas held an impromptu press conference in Old Palace Yard which we took live and which I completely hijacked despite the presence of many other reporters, including three from the BBC. It was, in effect, a one-to-one interview. The executive producer at Sky Centre in Osterley, John Dowden, sent a message: 'Oglaza masterclass'!

The reaction of Jonathan Levy, now head of politics at Sky Westminster, was that he had been at lunch and hadn't seen it. "Weren't there any other reporters there?" Yes, mate, there were!

On to Downing Street where Joanna Lumley and her Gurkhas were to have tea with Gordon and Sarah Brown. I did lives before this a live one-to-one with Joanna Lumley in Downing Street. This time, strangely, there were no other reporters present, only a lot of cameras. Joanna Lumley described Gordon Brown as, "A brave man who has taken a brave decision". I was happy for the Gurkhas, who had been poorly treated for far too long and, of course, it had been the correct decision.

As we were with the jubilant Gurkhas, to everyone's surprise the much-respected North Norwich Labour MP Ian Gibson became the latest MP to offer to stand down. He was, reportedly, claiming expenses for a flat in which his daughter was living rent free. He was prevented by a Labour Party disciplinary panel from standing for Labour at the next election. He resigned and the Conservatives took the seat in the subsequent by-election.

At the end of May, I was live for twelve hours all day for two days when Julie Kirkbride announced she would not be standing at the next general election. The Conservative MP for South West Norfolk, Christopher Fraser, did the same, citing not any expenses anomalies but his wife's poor health. Within minutes, another one was gone. Labour MP for Luton South, Margaret Moran, had been claiming expenses for her partner's house in Southampton, one hundred miles from Luton. She had also, it emerged, claimed her second home allowance for her homes in both London and Luton and claimed expenses to renovate both. Margaret Moran denied any wrongdoing, but three years later she was convicted to a two-year supervision and treatment order after evidence from psychiatrists that she was not well enough to plead in person. Her fraudulent claims had amounted to more than £53,000, the highest of any MP.

As well as exposing the MPs' expenses scandal, the *Sunday Telegraph* was firing broadsides at Alistair Darling. I was live all day. The Lib Dems called for his resignation. *The Sunday Times* claimed that Gordon Brown wanted Ed Balls to be his chancellor. It had been another fourteen-hour day of lives and packages emanating from this speculation which, as it turned out, had been idle.

Next day, June 1st, and another package on Alistair Darling's trials and tribulations including grabs from Gordon Brown and Peter Mandelson, both very supportive, and Vince Cable, decidedly less so. In the evening, I went to a David Miliband Fabian lecture on Europe and interviewed him afterwards. He neatly sidestepped a question about Gordon Brown's leadership. We learnt that there was indeed to be a Cabinet reshuffle and that it could come by the end of the week. We already had news of some junior ministerial appointments, including promotions for twin sisters Angela and Maria Eagle.

The Labour plotters were scheming away. On that Wednesday, Hazel Blears announced that she would be resigning from the Cabinet. It looked very much like she was about to be sacked anyway. Cue pandemonium, mutterings and more about Gordon Brown's leadership, and this on the day before European and local council elections.

On the day of those elections, James Purnell announced he would be resigning as Work and Pensions secretary and called on Gordon Brown to step down as prime minister. Unlike Hazel Blears or Jacqui Smith, who would also be gone by Friday, he was not about to be moved, he was a rising star. It was another damaging blow to Gordon Brown's authority. I packaged the story after searching in the House of Commons committee corridor for plotting, disloyal backbenchers. They weren't hard to find.

I was working on a package for *Sky News at Ten* but, at 9.55pm, James Purnell delivered his bombshell. An absolutely manic three hours followed in which I interviewed many of the players including George Osborne and Eric Pickles for the Conservatives, Jim Knight, Tessa Jowell and many others. Labour MPs, Graham Allen and Barry Sheerman, publicly called on Gordon Brown to go, but the Cabinet circled the wagons. I was live at eleven forty-five p.m. as David Miliband put out his statement of support for Gordon Brown. The Foreign Secretary was widely seen as the man most likely to become Party leader and prime minister if Gordon Brown was forced to resign, so his statement of support appeared to be decisive. But I still had to keep going until 2am by which time even the most workaholic or insomniac MP had finally gone home.

As the Cabinet reshuffle unfolded the next day, Friday, we were off to Normandy for the 65th anniversary of D-Day. Darling, Mandelson and David Miliband remained in post, Alan Johnson was the new Home Secretary, Yvette Cooper replaced James Purnell. Alan Sugar was made a peer and appointed 'Enterprise Tsar'.

At Dover, cameramen Ed Baylis and Tony Fyfe, producer Arnie Woll and I boarded the ferry for the six-hour crossing to Normandy. We were joined by an additional team scrambled by Sky News to reinforce us, reporter Ursula Errington and cameraman Gary Blayer. We drove from Caen to Bayeux to meet up with producer Nick Ludlam, who was masterminding Sky's coverage of the event and did a quick recce of the cathedral where the main service was to be held the next day.

I did long lives before and after the Remembrance service at Bayeux Cathedral on the event itself, but mostly on just how much trouble Gordon Brown might be in with his own party. We travelled in the prime minister's convoy to the Château de Bellefontaine, a hotel, to meet D-Day veterans. After a prolonged argument with Downing Street press officers concerned about the prime minister's schedule, I secured an interview with Gordon Brown for us, ITN and the BBC. Just one question each before we headed to Colleville-sur-Mer and the American cemetery above Omaha Beach.

We got an excellent position very near the stage. Gordon Brown gave a good speech, although he called Omaha 'Obama beach' at one point, while Barack Obama referred to the RAF as 'the British Royal Air Corps'!

We left cameraman Ed Baylis there to send track and rushes and my PTC to be edited in London to lead the six o'clock news while we headed off with Gordon Brown to Arromanches, Gold Beach, which had been taken on D-Day by the British and where you could still see the remains of the temporary and vital Mulberry Harbour.

We were live from the ceremony in Arromanches. Gordon Brown was booed by some of the crowd. I initially assumed this was political but, when I asked them, they explained that they were expressing their disappointment. They had wanted to see the Queen and thought she should have attended.

Not surprisingly, Labour got slaughtered in the council elections. The European election results were equally dreadful for Labour. The government was being blamed for both the state of the economy and the MPs' expenses scandal.

Back in London, the morning after returning from Normandy, and the fallout from Labour's dreadful showing in the elections. They had received just 15% of the vote in the European election and had come third behind UKIP! The Conservatives took more votes than Labour in Wales for the first time. Because Labour voters had stayed at home, the BNP took two seats, in Manchester and Yorkshire and Humberside, and now had two MEPs. I had started the day at 5am and did lives every half hour until lunchtime on both the European and local council election results and looking ahead to that evening's meeting of the PLP when Gordon Brown would have to confront his would-be assassins. Adam Boulton did the lunchtime live, but I was back live in Downing Street for 2pm because our colleague Joey Jones had been told by 'a source' that the Cabinet was meeting to discuss the PLP meeting. It wasn't.

The PLP meeting itself came to nothing. The rebels had little support, for now. Gordon Brown survived, for now. Labour MPs feared the irresistible political pressure to call an early election if they deposed Gordon Brown and elected a new prime minister, an election they would almost certainly have lost.

A few days later, I interviewed Gordon Brown when he visited a school in Stepney, a pooled interview on his leadership, of course, and on Shahid Malik who, along with Sadiq Khan had been the first Muslim to be elected as an MP and who Brown had now appointed to a ministerial role. I had been asked to put a question to him about the footballer Ronaldo who had just been sold by Manchester United to Real Madrid for £80 million. He was only too happy to answer. Sky News played the interview in its entirety, but only used the Ronaldo grab in all later bulletins.

Gordon Brown announced an inquiry into the Iraq war, the Chilcot Inquiry. It would not report until after the next election. I believe that's called kicking it into the long grass. In fact, Sir John Chilcot took more than seven years to report. When he did his findings were unequivocal. He concluded that, in 2003, Saddam Hussein had not posed an immediate threat, the search for a peaceful solution had been abandoned too quickly, the intelligence on weapons of mass destruction had been presented with unjustified certainty, and that the legal basis for going to war was 'far from satisfactory'.

On June 18th, MPs' expenses were finally made public. Large sections of the official release were redacted, blacked-out for 'security' and 'data protection'. It was ridiculous, a worthless document, positively Orwellian. If the *Telegraph* had not leaked the information, we would never have known about flipping second homes, claiming for non-existent mortgages and the many other crimes and misdemeanours. I did lives and packages on this story from midday up to and including midnight.

I worked all day a few days later on the election of the new speaker of the House of Commons. There were ten candidates, including Ann Widdecombe. John Bercow, Sir George Young and Margaret Beckett were the front runners in what was, basically, a popularity contest. I was recutting my package as the results were announced. In the first ballot, John Bercow was ahead of Sir George Young with Margaret Beckett trailing in third place. Six candidates went through to the second ballot in which Ann Widdecombe came sixth. John Bercow beat George Young in the run-off between the two. MPs had elected him speaker even though many in his own Conservative Party disliked him. Around half of the Conservative MPs didn't applaud the result, as is traditional. Very churlish of them. The whole process was over by 8.30pm, mercifully early.

I interviewed the Israeli defence minister, Ehud Barak, and Gordon Brown held a press conference with the Rwandan president. Only one pool question was allowed, so I asked the president of Rwanda a question on behalf of the BBC World Service and Gordon Brown about war crimes and the ten pence rate of tax. Frank Field was tabling an amendment in the House of Commons that afternoon which could have derailed the entire Finance Bill. The BBC ran the lot by not Sky News. It was the day of Michael Jackson's funeral and Sky News had gone Jackson-tastic!

On July 9th the *Guardian* claimed that *News of the World* reporters had used private investigators to hack into the mobile phones on hundreds, maybe thousands, of people including pop and film stars and politicians, among them John Prescott. My package included interviews with David Cameron, Charles Clarke and, later, John Prescott, Alastair Campbell and Chris Huhne. *News of the World* editor, Andy Coulson, had resigned two years earlier over the phone-hacking scandal. He was now the Conservative Party's director of communications and the Labour knives were out. There was an Urgent Motion in the House of Commons. Even Gordon Brown, at a G8 summit in Italy, voiced his opinion. Yates of the Yard read a statement saying there was no new evidence so he had nothing new to investigate. I was updating my package every hour with a definitive version for *Sky News at Ten*.

Two days later, Andy Coulson would give evidence to the Culture, Media and Sport select committee. I did lives before and after his 'evidence'. He said nothing new for an hour and a half in a very warm, stuffy room, the Wilson room. He denied any knowledge of phone-hacking. His roller coaster career was to continue. He became David Cameron's director of communications in Downing Street after the 2010 election but, four years later, he was convicted of conspiracy to intercept voicemails and sentenced to eighteen months.

The Cabinet held another awayday on July 23rd, this time in Cardiff. It was the day of the Norwich North by-election following Ian Gibson's resignation. I was offered interviews with any number of Cabinet ministers including Peter Mandelson, Alan Johnson and Alistair Darling, but had to turn them all down while the polls were still open. It was a very hot day at Glamorgan's cricket ground. I did lives all morning but couldn't say much while people were still voting in Norwich. The Cabinet met at two p.m. I did lives on the shortage of British military helicopters in Afghanistan while they met and, afterwards, got an exclusive grab from Gordon Brown on swine flu, which was permitted under electoral law. More lives on the helicopter shortage at 5 and 6 o'clock before heading back to London.

The Conservatives took Norwich North with a majority of 7,400 overturning Ian Gibson's 5,000 majority. The Labour vote was 70% lower than it had been in 2005, thousands of Labour voters had not turned out. They were angry, apparently, at the way in which their popular MP Ian Gibson had been disciplined by the Labour Party. It was another Labour own-goal, a self-inflicted wound, a needless by-election which had handed yet more momentum to David Cameron. I did lives on the result and its significance until very late in the evening, with a break in the afternoon to attend a David Miliband press conference with the Syrian foreign minister. I got David Miliband to talk about Norwich North and swine flu, but he wouldn't talk about the Labour leadership.

TV presenter, Esther Rantzen, decided to stand as an independent candidate in Luton South. She turned up as I was doing vox pops with voters so I did an interview with her before her press conference in the Market Hall at Luton's Arndale Centre. Very glamorous! We sent a package for *Live at Five* which included Esther whooping enthusiastically behind me as I finished my PTC. The bosses back at Sky News loved it.

In the election in 2010, she came fourth behind the Labour victor, the Conservatives and the Lib Dems, but ahead of the BNP, UKIP and the Green Party.

More fun the next day when David Cameron swore on the radio. "The public are pissed off with politicians." No problem there. But "Too many tweets makes you a twat", was not so clever. He had no idea what he had just said. Someone from his press team had to explain the meaning of the vernacular! My package on that story also included Peter Mandelson saying Gordon Brown might agree to a televised debate with David Cameron during the following year's general election campaign, something for which Sky News was pushing very hard.

At the end of July, Sir John Chilcot outlined the remit of his Iraq inquiry, and then I was off on holiday to Cuba, again, for two weeks.

I could write a book about Cuba, but I won't. At least not yet. My first task back at Westminster at the end of August involved doing lives every hour from Downing Street on the release from prison in Scotland of the Lockerbie bomber, Libyan Abdelbaset al-Megrahi, on compassionate grounds. He had been diagnosed with terminal prostate cancer. Since I had been in Lockerbie all those years ago, in December 1988, I was able to reflect on the bombing and the anger of many that he was being released. I did lives on the same story all the next day as the row over Megrahi's early release intensified. Those objecting included both British and American politicians as well as many of the families of those who had been murdered.

There followed the revolting spectacle of Megrahi arriving home in Tripoli to national celebrations. Hundreds of Libyans gathered at Tripoli airport to welcome him back, waving flags and throwing flower petals. Megrahi was accompanied by Saif Gaddafi, son of the Libyan dictator. It was truly nauseating.

Gordon Brown was meeting Israeli Prime Minister Benjamin Netanyahu. At their joint press conference, which we took live, I got the first question which was on Lockerbie, of course. Gordon Brown wouldn't say whether or not he agreed with the Scottish justice minister's decision to release Megrahi, but he expressed his anger and revulsion at the welcome he had received in Tripoli. I did lives and packages reflecting the appalled reaction to Megrahi's reception in the Libyan capital.

Falkirk West Labour MP and former army officer, Eric Joyce, resigned as a junior defence minister disillusioned with the war in Afghanistan and what he saw as the government's lack of support for the military. This was about more than just helicopters. I was live almost non-stop for an hour after the story broke at 7 o'clock and then had a package followed by a live every hour until midnight. I also wrote a blog on mad Colonel Gaddafi calling on the UN to abolish Switzerland!

My colleague Jon Craig dubbed Eric Joyce 'air miles Eric' which was funny but, I thought, a little unkind as his constituency was so far from Westminster that flying was the only sensible option. However, he was the top-claiming MP in 2005-06, and more than 60% of the claim was for staff and office costs. He made a pledge to reduce his costs, was only the eleventh highest spender the following year but, a year after that, he was again the most expensive MP.

Earlier in the year, TV presenter Jeremy Clarkson had described Gordon Brown as a 'one-eyed Scottish idiot'. Scottish MPs and disability groups had been furious and called for him to be sacked. Clarkson had had to apologise. Now he had insulted Gordon Brown again in remarks to a TV studio audience which had not been broadcast but had been widely reported.

The oafishness of Clarkson's remark beggars belief. When he was sixteen, a rugby injury left Gordon Brown blind in his left eye. He had spent months in a hospital bed in a darkened room not knowing if he would go completely blind. Just imagine how terrifying that must have been for a teenage boy. It was a fear that would continue to haunt him. Now, in the autumn of 2009, he had to go to London's Moorfields hospital for what Downing Street described as a routine check-up. It was anything but. He had a torn retina in his right eye. Surgeons saved his eyesight.

While we are on the subject, there are other aspects to Gordon Brown's blindness in his left eye. We knew to stand or sit slightly to his right when we interviewed him. His notes for speeches, meetings etc. were written in large bold felt tip so that he could read them. This, by the way, made them a lot easier for us to surreptitiously read! Because he lacks peripheral vision and can only see out of his right eye, his awkwardness at a podium or on camera was due to his having to resist any tendency to look sideways, out of his good eye.

At the TUC in Liverpool, General Secretary Brendan Barber and the prime minister gave speeches clearly sketching out the battle lines for the forthcoming election. I packaged the story and did lives every hour until midnight. Gordon Brown addressed the TUC the next day and used the word 'cuts' for the first time. I did lives in the evening pointing out that there would be a severe economic cost as we began to recover from the global financial crisis whoever was elected in 2010.

Baroness Patricia Scotland, the attorney general, foolishly but unwittingly had employed an illegal immigrant as her housekeeper. I did just one live on that. There were far stronger stories to cover. Gordon Brown was in Brussels that day. One of us should have gone with him, but for once Sky News made the wrong decision and didn't send anyone. That left the field clear for the BBC who got Gordon Brown to talk about Baroness Scotland, some leaked Treasury documents, and President Obama's decision to abolish the missile shield in Poland and the Czech Republic. We had access to the material, but it wasn't the same as doing it ourselves.

I got an exclusive interview with Patricia Scotland the next day. She'd been fined £5,000 for employing an illegal housekeeper but had kept her job as attorney general. It had been a genuine mistake. I went to her office in Central London to doorstep her and she gave me a very good, long interview. There were no other journalists there. The *Evening Standard* front page carried excerpts from the interview once we had aired it with a credit 'she told Sky News', which is always satisfying.

There was a daft story doing the rounds that President Obama had 'snubbed' Gordon Brown because they hadn't held a bilateral meeting at a G20 summit. This was clearly nonsense. They had talked a lot, co-chaired meetings, and were clearly working very closely together on the big issues of the global economy, climate change, terrorism and nuclear proliferation (i.e. Iran). Gordon Brown did a round of interviews to make the point. There were rumours that junior Business Minister Shriti Vadera was to quit her government job. Some, including my Sky News colleague Joey Jones, were reporting this as a damaging blow to Gordon Brown. I doubted it, and it turned out that he had asked her to concentrate on the G20, working from the Cabinet Office. If anything, this was a promotion. Interesting, but obviously not as exciting as a ministerial resignation.

I did lives on the story all afternoon, and another when Baroness Scotland's housekeeper was arrested and bailed. Patricia Scotland's PPS, Stephen Hesford, had resigned the day before in protest over her remaining in government. But the story of Patricia Scotland's housekeeper felt like yesterday's story, and it was. The housekeeper, Loloahi Tapui, had used a forged passport and was later jailed for eight months and deported to her native Tonga. At her trial, she admitted that the *Daily Mail* had paid her ninety-five thousand pounds. An inquiry confirmed that Baroness Scotland did not know that Tapui was an illegal immigrant, so she kept her job as attorney general.

On the eve of the Labour Party conference in Brighton, Sky hosted a dinner. We were lobbying for a TV leaders' debate during the 2010 general election. Margaret Beckett told us it was, "Inevitable because Peter says it will happen". So, Mandelson was definitely onside. At a Sky Arts party afterwards, Gordon Brown's closest aide, Sue Nye, told me there would be a TV debate but Sky might not host it. Apparently, David Frost was constantly on the phone, lobbying.

I doorstepped Foreign Secretary David Miliband outside his hotel the next morning on the news that Iran had tested a missile with a range of 2,000 kilometres. He said he needed to get fully briefed, did so, and re-emerged to do a live interview. Alistair Darling's speech was dull but exuded competence. Peter Mandelson delivered a by turns serious and very funny speech, vintage stuff which brought to life what had been, on its first day, a rather lacklustre conference. It felt remarkably like the speech of a leader-in-waiting. I went to a fringe meeting on Afghanistan with General Sir Mike Jackson, and interviewed Defence Secretary Bob Ainsworth on the contradiction of a troop surge without a clear exit strategy.

At a 'diversity' event, formerly called Asia Night, there was not only superb curry but also belly dancers. They stopped just before Harriet Harman arrived. Keith Vaz had joked, "Quick, she's coming. Hide them or she'll shut us down"! In the BBC *Ten O'clock News*, their political editor Nick Robinson reported that Gordon Brown would agree to a TV debate and that he would say so in his speech the next day. I had to spend an hour phone-bashing to establish that this was absolutely not the case.

I still had time to get to the *Guardian* party where I spoke to Gordon Brown advisor Stewart Wood about the next day's speech and a TV debate. He said they were, "Still arguing about it". Peter Mandelson told me it was still undecided.

If it happened, we would have a televised debate between the party leaders in an election campaign for the first time. It would be an historic moment in both politics and broadcasting. Sky News, and particularly Head of News John Ryley, was pushing for it as strongly as possible. The rest, of course, is history as we would see the following April.

I found myself chatting over a drink in the bar of the Grand Hotel with Sinn Féin's Martin McGuinness. I almost had to pinch myself. This was the same Grand Hotel the IRA had blown up back in 1984. How times had changed.

At the *Telegraph* party, I chatted to Shriti Vadera about her new role organising the G20. She had been amused by the inaccurate reports of her ministerial resignation the previous week. I was also introduced to Nancy Dell'Olio, who had become famous as the partner of the former England football manager Sven-Göran Eriksson. It turned out she was a Labour Party supporter.

Why so many dining and drinking events at party conference? Because that was where you got the gossip and found out what was really going on as people were less discreet and more open. PR people would call it a 'networking event'. But you needed stamina to manage both the very late nights and the early mornings, as well as a high alcohol tolerance level.

I was due to go to Dublin immediately after the Labour Party conference for the re-run of the Irish referendum on the Lisbon Treaty. Martin McGuinness had told me he thought it would be a very close Yes. He added that people in Ireland were dissatisfied with the government in Dublin, largely because unemployment was high, so it could be very close. I talked to the Irish ambassador the next morning who predicted the same outcome, a close Yes, though obviously without McGuinness' criticism of his government.

I did lives before Gordon Brown's speech from our glass bubble overlooking the conference stage and watched it from the conference floor. Sarah Brown delivered a fine introduction and the speech was passionate at first with a rather dull middle section which was nevertheless full of substance and looked to the future. There was a very well written rhetorical flourish at the end ('never stop believing') which he didn't deliver particularly well. But the Labour delegates were happy and fired up to fight an election campaign.

The *Sun*'s headline for the next morning was "Labour's lost it". The newspaper declared itself for the Conservatives. It had been attacking Gordon Brown for months, but the timing seemed odd. Yes, it was designed to damage the Labour conference, but I thought it might be more effective to declare for one party or the other during the election campaign, which is what the *Sun* and others normally did. I got reaction from Jack Straw, Keith Vaz and others while Adam did the late evening lives on the story. The Labour Party press officers described the *Sun* with the very strongest of Anglo-Saxon expletives.

The *Sun*'s story dominated our story the next morning. There were rumours that Peter Mandelson had called the *Sun* 'a bunch of c***s' at the News International party the previous evening. The hacks were after him. I found him and he told me that he had called them 'silly chumps' adding, "Glen, my mother would never allow me to use language like that"! Adam did an interview with Gordon Brown which got a bit grumpy if not actually bad tempered. The Labour Party was not in a happy place.

I was up very early the next morning to do lives on the last day of the conference. I covered a dull speech by Bob Ainsworth and an excellent one by David Miliband. He strayed away from foreign affairs towards the end, focusing on domestic policy. This, of course, was widely interpreted as part of his bid to establish himself as a future party leader. I did two lives in the midday news, first to discuss the Miliband speech then to mark the end of the conference. The singing was led by two amateurs, Labour Party employees. It was Division Four compared to Marion's Premier League performance.

From Brighton, straight to Heathrow to fly to Dublin for the Irish Lisbon Treaty referendum, take two. We stayed at the marvellous Hampton Hotel, though I would have preferred the historic Shelbourne Hotel on St Steven's Green where the Irish Constitution had been drafted in 1922 and where I had stayed before. I was in bed by 11pm, it had been a long 18 hour working day.

Next morning we filmed at some polling stations, where unusually we were allowed to film both inside as well as outside. It seemed every lamp post in the city was festooned with Yes or No posters. There were Yes posters on almost every bus. Dublin had gone referendum-tastic! We vox popped some voters and did lives in the evening and a package for *Sky News at Ten*. In between, we checked out the layout at Dublin Castle and sorted our accreditation. Dinner was in an Italian restaurant, Tuscana, recommended. Outside a bar, the friendly bouncer recognised me. "You're that Glen Oglaza from the Sky News." We strolled by the Liffey and stopped in a pub for just a couple of pints of Guinness, 'vitamin G' according to a taxi driver.

Referendum day, and the result had never really been in doubt although the margin of victory was far greater than had been expected. A majority of two to one, 67% in favour of accepting the Lisbon Treaty. I learnt two Irish words Ta and Nil, yes and no. We did a couple of early morning lives but we weren't wanted again until midday, so producer Harriett Tolputt and I sorted out logistics and adjourned for coffee with the Irish newspapers.

We did lives at the top of every hour from midday, as well as extra lives at 2.50pm after a press conference by the Irish Taoiseash Brian Cowen and at 4.50 after David Cameron reacted to the referendum results. We packaged for *Live at Five*.

We were famous in Dublin, where people watched the news avidly, and especially Sky News. When I had arrived at the airport, the passport officer had welcomed me by name even before I'd handed him my passport. Everywhere we went, even without a camera, we heard people saying, "There's that Sky News"! If one of our main presenters had been in Dublin, he or she might well have been mobbed in the street! That Saturday afternoon, the retired police superintendent who curated the Garda museum next to Dublin Castle and right beside our live point and from where dozens of British and International correspondents were broadcasting, came in and opened up the museum specifically for me to sign the visitors' book! This was utterly incredible and ridiculously flattering. Fame at last!

Once my swollen head had shrunk back to its normal size, we doughnutted my package at 6 and 7 o'clock with long lives. And that was it. The package would run for the rest of the evening but no more lives were required. We were finished and de-rigged by 7.45. Time to enjoy Dublin's nightlife. This involved a Lebanese restaurant followed by Guinness in several pubs where I was recognised. People wanted to talk to me about the Lisbon Treaty. A disco, which was very naff and funny, a couple of nightclubs, and a taxi back to the hotel at 3.30am with the crew and two attractive young ladies they had met. I left them to it and crawled off to bed. I had been on the go for nearly twenty-four hours.

I had learnt long ago that not everyone at Sky News was as diligent as I was in catching the news on their days off, especially at weekends. So I was a little disappointed but not at all surprised when, on the Monday morning after the Dublin weekend, one or two of them asked me, 'how was your weekend?' and, 'what did you get up to at the weekend?' Back to earth with a bump!

I didn't go to the Conservative conference in Manchester, I was holding the fort in Westminster, but I did a couple of lives after David Cameron's speech on the Thursday. The day before, they had announced that General Sir Richard Dannatt was to be the party's advisor on defence just two months after retiring as the CGS, when he had been so critical of the government. I went to the Tower of London where Sir Richard was being 'installed' as the one hundred and fifty-ninth constable of the Tower, a splendid ceremony despite the heavy rain.

Sir Thomas Legg released his audit of MPs expenses on October 12th. Gordon Brown had to repay £12,000 because Sir Thomas had declared retrospective limits on cleaning and gardening backdated for five years, which seemed to me to have unfairly moved the goalposts. Gordon Brown said he would pay and so should everyone else to draw a line under the affair. I packaged the story and updated it to include a meeting of the PLP that evening at which Labour MPs expressed their anger at Legg's setting backdated limits when they had not been the rules at the time, and at Gordon Brown for acquiescing so easily. They felt it was unfair and they may have been right, but they received absolutely no public sympathy. Brown's response was the correct one to assuage the outrage in the country. Take the financial hit and move on.

I asked the prime minister about it in a pooled interview the next day when he was visiting a community centre in north London. He made it clear that it was his view that it was the responsibility of all Members of Parliament to try to win back the trust of the people.

The next day producer Esme Wren, cameraman Andy Lamb and I were in Redditch in the wake of Jacqui Smith's half-hearted apology to the House of Commons two days earlier. It was an easy shoot, everything we needed was within two hundred yards of the town's market square. We interviewed a campaigner who wanted Jacqui Smith to resign as the town's MP, the chair of the local Labour Party who was supportive, and the editor of the *Redditch Standard*. A few vox pops and a PTC and we had our package. Andy and I cut a two-minute-forty-five piece which we live-doughnutted for *Live at Five* and 6pm.

While Esme headed back to London that evening, I was on the train to Preston where Gordon Brown was visiting the next day. He toured Leyland trucks. I got a decent interview on bankers' bonuses (Goldman Sachs, J P Morgan and others were at it again, paying their senior executives very generous bonuses), and on the Conservative MP for Spelthorne David Wilshire who had paid thousands of pounds of parliamentary allowances into his own private company. The next day he announced that he would not be seeking re-election. Right winger Wilshire was a bête noire for Labour so many in the party were celebrating his downfall, but Gordon Brown was carefully circumspect.

The next day, back in Westminster, I interviewed the odious Dutch far-right politician Geert Wilders, leader of the Dutch Freedom Party. He had won his appeal against the Home Office ban and had come to Britain where he had a lot of Special Branch protection. A judge had ruled that there was no evidence that he posed a threat to public order or community relations and that it was more important to allow free speech than to impose a ban without any evidence. Wilders' views on Islam were particularly obnoxious. He quoted from the preface to George Orwell's *Animal Farm* at his press conference. If liberty means anything at all it means the right to tell people what they don't want to hear. I wondered what Orwell would have made of that.

That afternoon we had a breaking story from the High Court where a judge had ruled that American Intelligence documents in the (torture) case of Binyam Mohamed should be made public. Foreign Secretary David Miliband was furious and the government was planning to appeal the decision. David Miliband came into our Westminster studio to do a recorded interview. I persuaded him to do it live, but the producer in the gallery at Sky News Centre didn't want to take him. Esme and I had to complain to the news desk and above, while the foreign secretary was sitting in the hot seat as his words were on a Sky News 'Breaking News' strap. Absurd! After a few minutes delay we won the argument and he did a long live interview. I did lives on the High Court judgement for *Live at Five* and 6 o'clock and packaged it for *Sky News at Ten*.

The rest of October included covering a speech by Gordon Brown on climate change fifty days ahead of the big climate change conference in Copenhagen. On October 20th, I had to wait for three hours in the Thatcher room at Number Ten before Afghan President Hamid Karzai finally held a press conference in Kabul. Karzai agreed, after much persuasion including several phone calls from Gordon Brown, to re-run the Afghan presidential election on November 7th, less than three weeks away, a logistical nightmare. One point three million out of the six million votes cast were suspicious. There had clearly been fraud. Karzai finally appeared flanked by UN Representative Senator John Kerry and the American, British and French ambassadors. Visual evidence of international pressure being brought to bear. I got a long, eight-minute, pooled interview with Gordon Brown afterwards which was aired live on Sky News and the BBC.

In the Moncrieff bar in the Palace of Westminster the press gallery welcomed the new speaker, John Bercow, who gave a witty and appropriately short speech. The next evening, dressed in my tux much to the amusement of my colleagues, I was off to the Tower of London again, this time for a dinner in honour of ex-Australian Prime Minister John Howard. I took my Australian friend, ex-ITN producer Rebecca Denholm. Given Howard's politics, the guests were a mix of Tory MPs including Michael Howard (no relation), David Davis, Edward Leigh and John Redwood, plus assorted right-wing headbangers and a smattering of right-leaning journalists many of whom seemed about twelve years old! But the setting, the New Armoury, was spectacular, we had a private tour of the Crown Jewels, the food was superb and the wine and champagne flowed very generously. John Howard made a speech, right wing of course, but surprisingly charming.

I did lives on the court case of Tessa Jowell's husband, solicitor David Mills, who had been investigated by the Italian authorities for money laundering and tax fraud while working for Silvio Berlusconi. He lost his appeal in a court in Milan and might have faced jail, but I discovered what he and his lawyers already knew: That if he kept appealing until the following spring, the case would lapse and be dropped under Italy's Statute of Limitations. He had found himself caught up in the weird and wonderful world of Silvio Berlusconi and Italian politics.

In early November, Home Secretary Alan Johnson sacked the chairman of the Drugs Advisory Council Professor David Nutt. He had frequently disagreed with government ministers, in particular over the classification of illegal drugs. The trigger was a speech in which he had said that alcohol and tobacco were more harmful than LSD or cannabis, and that the, "Hunting down of low-level cannabis users" was, "obscene and absurd". He viewed the recent re-upgrading of cannabis from a class C drug back to class B as politically-motivated and not scientifically justified. This was in direct contradiction of government policy and, so the argument went, had crossed the line from science to politics. This had led to a huge row, to the resignations of several other government scientific advisors, and kept me busy doing lives every hour. Inevitably and unjustifiably the tabloids dubbed him 'The Nutty Professor'.

On the day the Czechs finally signed up to the Lisbon Treaty, David Cameron was facing a rebellion by Eurosceptic Conservative MPs. He addressed his party's MPs and peers in committee room fourteen. I tweeted from outside as they cheered and banged their desks, the traditional signal of approval. I broke the news from that meeting of Cameron's proposal of a UK Sovereignty Bill. At a press conference afterwards at St Stephen's club, David Cameron outlined some frankly unrealistic proposals, including demanding fresh UK opt-outs which would have to be agreed by all the other twenty-seven EU member states so were never going to happen, and a muddled argument over which should be the final court of appeal, the UK Supreme Court or the European Court. Although David Cameron had largely muted the internal party opposition and bought himself some time, the seeds of the 2016 Brexit referendum were being sown.

The next day, France's Europe minister, Pierre Lellouche, added fuel to the flames by dubbing the Conservative Party's policy on Europe as 'pathetic' and 'autistic'. Shadow Foreign Secretary William Hague had to deliver a diplomatic response!

I was live at the RCDS the next day covering a Gordon Brown speech on Afghanistan. I had broken the news the day before that he would be doing the speech but that there would be no dramatic announcement, simply a continuation of existing government policy. This despite the fact that five British soldiers had been murdered by an Afghan policeman as they were drinking tea together. The soldiers had been mentoring and training the Afghan police. This was one of the greatest problems for British forces in Afghanistan. The Taliban had infiltrated the Afghan police, and the army too. In his speech, Gordon Brown reaffirmed the Afghanistan mission but warned Hamid Karzai to clean up his act and stamp out corruption or forfeit international help. The warning was very strongly worded.

The *Sun* had a story the following Monday. The mother of one of the soldiers killed in Afghanistan, Grenadier Guardsman Jamie Janes, was angry because Gordon Brown's handwritten letter of condolence was badly written, contained spelling mistakes and had been addressed to Janine James when her name was actually Jacqui Janes. It was obviously a mistake, but it was not a mistake a prime minister should have made. Someone should have checked. Gordon Brown phoned her to apologise and issued an apologetic statement. I did lives all afternoon from Downing Street and a package for *Live at Five*.

That evening, I moderated a discussion on the twentieth anniversary on the fall of the Berlin Wall at the Frontline Club. It was November 9th. The event was sold out. The panel, Ann Leslie, Peter Miller and Nick Thorpe and I answered questions from our very well-informed audience. I bought Peter and Nick's excellent books.

The Jacqui Janes story dominated the next day. The *Sun* had released a recording of the phone call Gordon Brown had made to her to apologise. He had spent a quarter of an hour on the phone to her but she was still angry because he hadn't apologised in the right way! At least according to the *Sun*. At a press conference in Downing Street, Gordon Brown was emotional. He knew what it meant to lose a child. I interviewed the *Sun*'s political editor, the otherwise very sharp Tom Newton-Dunn, who had just spent the BBC's politics show calling Immigration Minister Phil Woolas 'Andy'! An easy enough mistake to make but not as easy as James/Janes.

I packaged the story for *Live at Five* with a re-cut for six p.m. after an ITN pool interview with Jacqui Janes. Apparently at John Ryley's insistence, the package was to run unchanged all evening. Head of news John Ryley, a man rarely given to handing out praise, phoned me later at home to say well done. I had apparently covered a difficult story with great judgement. This was good to hear.

Phone calls and emails to the *Sun* and Sky News were overwhelmingly sympathetic to and supportive of Gordon Brown and highly critical of the *Sun*. The general consensus appeared to be that most people felt the *Sun* was exploiting a grieving mother.

A few days later the *Sun* had to make the same apology itself after it too misspelt Janes and wrote Jones on its website!

Sky News was changing from Standard Definition to High Definition, HD. Along with every other on-screen Sky News person, I had to go to Sky News Centre in Osterley to be HD-tested. Apparently, I was fine, although the stylist thought I should get my eyebrows plucked! Crime correspondent Martin Brunt was jokingly demanding "free Botox for the over-forties"!

The White House was furious after cables from the US ambassador in Kabul were leaked. In these, he had urged President Obama not to send any more troops to Afghanistan. I was in Downing Street to try to doorstep NATO Secretary General Anders Rasmussen after his meeting with Gordon Brown. I hadn't expected much, but he had needed little prompting to come over to our live position directly opposite Number Ten and answer half a dozen of my questions. This was live and exclusive, no other reporters or crews were present. The interview was greeted back at Sky News Centre with some relief. The BBC had an interview booked with him for later that day, but there had been a cock-up on our forward planning desk and we hadn't booked an interview with him at all. Well, we had one now! "Gold stars Glen," said Westminster news editor Clare Parry. "As many as you want."

Liz Truss survived a de-selection meeting. Some members of her local Conservative association were unhappy because of claims that she had had an affair with Conservative MP Mark Field. She would still be the candidate for the safe Conservative seat of South West Norfolk. She defeated the motion to de-select her easily enough, by one hundred and thirty-two votes to thirty-seven, seeing off the so-called 'Turnip Taliban'.

Next up, the next day, was to cover a story about body armour. A soldier who had been killed in Afghanistan two days earlier had previously blogged that he was waiting for new body armour. For once the MOD responded swiftly, saying that the new body armour was no more effective than the one he had, just slightly more comfortable (or less uncomfortable, and I speak from bitter experience!), and would not have saved his life.

David Cameron appeared on Mumsnet. I did the pool interview with him afterwards, it was used by the BBC and ITN but not by Sky News! There was a huge row after a blatant handball by Thierry Henry leading to the winning goal as France knocked Ireland out of the World Cup. Our Arsenal hero had been playing basketball in the Irish penalty area and, somehow, the referee hadn't noticed. It was glaringly obvious. The Irish FA was demanding a replay as was the Irish justice minister when he spoke to Sky News. The Taoiseach Brian Cowen was actually to raise the matter with French President Nicolas Sarkozy!

In late November the latest MORI opinion poll had the Conservatives just six points ahead of Labour, the narrowest lead for two years. In a general election, this would result in a hung parliament.

Tony Blair was not to be EU President, no great surprise. The EPP (European People's Party) wanted someone from the centre-right, someone dull and lacking in charisma to be a chairman rather than a leader. They got their wish, the former Belgian Prime Minister Herman Van Rumpuy, a bureaucrat for whom the phrase 'charisma bypass' might have been coined. Labour peer Baroness Ashton was to be the EU high representative for Foreign Affairs, in effect the EU foreign minister.

Gordon Brown held a press conference in Downing Street with Pakistan's prime minister, who rejected Brown's assertion that Osama bin Laden was almost certainly hiding somewhere in Pakistan. He was, as we were to discover less than eighteen months later.

On Abingdon Green I had to cover the BNP's Nick Griffin reading out the names of those who had fallen in Afghanistan. This as an odious spectacle. What was it that Dr Johnson had said about the last refuge of the scoundrel? That same day, Chancellor Alistair Darling announced that bankers' bonuses were to be heavily taxed, though I had no doubt their accountants would find some way of circumventing any such measures. I interviewed Boris Johnson, who said the bankers had brought this on themselves.

I chaired a panel of Michael Howard, Sir Menzies Campbell and Malcolm Wicks at Westminster Hall for *The House* magazine's annual conference entitled 'Parliament and politics in 2010'. It was a lively, forty-minute session which could easily have gone on for a lot longer. That evening, early Christmas drinks in David Cameron's office, with David Miliband at the Foreign Office and at the Treasury with Alistair Darling.

The expenses for MPs' second-home allowance for the year 2008/09 were officially published. There were some bizarre items. Who on earth claims for three garlic crushers as one Tory MP did? I bought three garlic crushers to use as props in my PTC for my package. I couldn't resist!

The next day I watched a very bad-tempered House of Commons Defence Select committee, James 'three garlic crushers' Arbuthnot arguing with Quentin 'Belltower' Davies. He had reportedly claimed £20,000 for the maintenance of a belltower at his eighteenth century mansion!

Defence Secretary Bob Ainsworth announced some cuts in defence spending to fund an extra twenty-two Chinook helicopters for use in Afghanistan.

At his Christmas drinks reception that evening, Ed Balls, who I liked a lot, gave a short, bizarre speech which included wife-swapping, a homophobic anecdote, and how he imagined Schools Minister Vernon Coaker naked, upside down and wrapped around a pole dancing pole. Deeply disturbing!

Sir Thomas Legg reported on MPs' expenses. He had written to two hundred MPs demanding they pay back some of the money they had claimed. Eighty had replied refusing to do so, saying they had been unfairly treated. Maybe they had, but it was time to swallow their pride, cough up and move on. Conservative MP Bernard Jenkin was ordered to return £63,000 in expenses that he had used to pay rent to his sister-in-law. This was later reduced on appeal to £36,000. Labour Junior Minister Siôn Simon had to repay £20,000 he had paid in rent to his sister. A pattern of behaviour appeared to be emerging.

On December 21st I did lives from the climate change conference at the QE2 building in Westminster. That day, the leaders of the three main parties, Brown, Cameron and Clegg, finally formally agreed to TV debates as part of the following year's election campaign. There would be three debates. Lots were drawn. ITV got the first, Sky News the second, with the BBC getting the third and final debate. This didn't seem fair. Sky News had been arguing and negotiating for months for the debates to happen. Now, ITN wanted their debate to be exclusive, while Sky News and the BBC had agreed to allow live access to all broadcasters. But it had been a fantastic achievement to get agreement. It would transform the general election campaign. I packaged the story for *Sky News at Ten*, including a grab with our own Head of News John Ryley, who had done so much to make it happen.

Just before Christmas it was announced that Gordon Brown would be called to give evidence to the Chilcot inquiry into the Iraq war of 2003 but not until after the general election, and that Tony Blair could be called as early as January. The Metropolitan Police passed case files on two more MPs' expenses to the Crown Prosecution Service. Chilcot and MPs' expenses once again kept me busy doing lives all day.

On December 30th, British hostage Peter Moore was released after two and a half years in captivity in Iraq. He had been taken in 2007 by Shia militants. Foreign Secretary David Miliband praised Mr Moore's great strength and resilience, Gordon Brown said he was 'hugely relieved' by the 'wonderful news' of Peter Moore's release. It was a positive story, a positive note, on which to end the year.

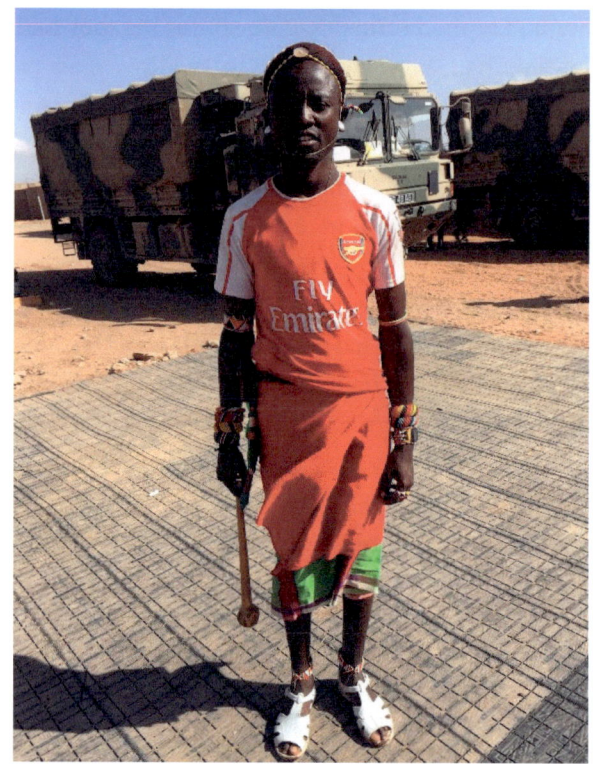
Arsenal fan, Kenya. We are everywhere! March 2016

Working in Oman. Martin Chidlow on camera. October 2018

Holodomor memorial Kiev February 2019. The starving girl clutching an ear of corn

Holodomor memorial Kiev: Her hollow eye sockets.

CHAPTER 8

2010: Coalition Government. Leaders' TV Debates. Cleggmania. The Chilcot Iraq Inquiry. "Some Bigoted Woman". MPs Prosecuted for Fraud. The Miliband Brothers. Fartgate! Beijing and Seoul

General election year.

The campaign looked like being bitter, it might or might not be very close, we were in for an exciting few months ahead.

Let battle commence!

On my first day back at work after the holidays, Monday January 4th, the opening skirmishes. The Conservatives launched a poster campaign and various Shadow Cabinet ministers visited marginal constituencies. Alistair Darling issued a document which claimed to expose a thirty-four billion pound gap in Tory tax and spend plans. Since the economy was going to be the top issue of the election, it was already clear what the key messages of Labour and the Lib Dems would be, to ask voters to put their trust in the tried and tested experience of Gordon Brown and Alistair Darling, and Vince Cable for the Lib Dems, and not to believe the unrealistic promises of David Cameron and George Osborne, who they portrayed as clueless lightweights. The Conservatives had talked about 'an age of austerity' at their previous autumn conference. Now, they were backpedalling furiously.

David Cameron tied himself up in knots over his proposed tax cuts for married couples, a promise he had made the previous month. Now, it had been downgraded to an aspiration, after which the Conservatives issued a press release saying it was a tax pledge after all. The Lib Dems accused the Tories of 'fantasy politics' in pledging extra money for the NHS without saying where the money would come from. All of which kept me doing lives, our lead story, from two p.m. until midnight. And that was just day one.

Immediately after PMQs that Wednesday, another Labour Party bombshell. Geoff Hoon and Patricia Hewitt had emailed all Labour MPs calling for a secret ballot on the Labour leadership and describing the party as 'deeply divided'. A double stabbing in the back for Gordon Brown.

I did lives on this astonishing act of treachery. I got the text of the email first, thanks to Jeremy Corbyn, a little scoop. Hoon-Hewitt appeared to have very little PLP support, but Cabinet ministers were slow to respond. Eventually Alan Johnson, Ed Miliband and, crucially, Jack Straw and Alistair Darling came out in support of Gordon Brown. Finally, David Miliband put out a lukewarm statement supporting the campaign for a Labour victory but failing to mention Gordon Brown by name. I packaged for the evening. Our Sky News colleague Niall Paterson had got a very good, long interview with Geoff Hoon after the story broke. More Labour Party self-harming. They may or may not have been 'deeply divided' but they were doing a very good job of making themselves appear so.

What were Hoon and Hewitt playing at? Gordon Brown might be a damaged brand, but why damage it further? Labour MP Eric Joyce blogged that two Cabinet ministers had been supposed to resign but had bottled it. The BBC's Nick Robinson named six: Jack Straw, Harriett Harman, Douglas Alexander, Bob Ainsworth, Tim Murphy and... David Miliband. Some of those named seemed extremely unlikely, but Hoon and Hewitt must have believed they would get some support. Or were they simply incompetent?

The next day, David Miliband and Jack Straw were far stronger in their support for Gordon Brown, with Straw accusing the BBC's Nick Robinson of 'sub-standard journalism'. I did a long live with Peter Mandelson who had been meeting business leaders at the Department for Business and did lives at 5 and 6pm. Gordon Brown was also at that meeting but had decided not to get involved in the Labour plot, if you could possibly call it that, to topple him.

The following couple of weeks were largely dominated by the Iraq inquiry and those giving evidence to it. Alastair Campbell gave testimony for four hours. We innovated a new way of covering this. While Alastair was giving evidence, we had a split-screen with him on the left and my tweets, a continuous running commentary, alongside. This was mostly serious but also allowed for a bit of fun, for example when he said he had always had a very good relationship with the press I tweeted: *That's not quite how we remember it!* The bosses loved it and it was a technique we would employ throughout the Iraq inquiry.

Tony Blair's Downing Street Chief of Staff Jonathan Powell gave evidence for three hours during which he insisted that Blair had not made any kind of deal with George Bush when they had held talks at George W's Crawford ranch, and that Attorney General Lord Peter Goldsmith had not been bullied into giving favourable legal advice. While Powell was a key member of Blair's inner circle who had been instrumental in securing the Northern Ireland Good Friday Agreement, it soon became clear that Geoff Hoon was not exactly in the loop. In two three-hour sessions, he gave the impression of not knowing much at all about what had been going on or about Blair's thinking.

I also tweeted live on a split-screen when Jack Straw gave evidence. He had been foreign secretary at the time. We were getting to the meat of the inquiry. He said the Americans had favoured illegal regime change in Iraq but that he and the British had argued against it. The decision to go to war had 'haunted' him. He was initially against the invasion of Iraq but had eventually come to the conclusion that there was no option as he believed Saddam Hussein did possess WMD. He said he had tried his best to get a second UN resolution specifically sanctioning military action. It was an intense three hours of evidence during which he also blamed the French and the American Neocons although for very different reasons. The French had been obstructive, the Neocons far too keen to go to war.

The inquiry, announced by Gordon Brown in June 2009, was initially to be held in private but that changed after outraged condemnation in the media and in the House of Commons. So now, we were able to witness this procession of ministers and diplomats having their decisions put under the microscope.

Foreign Office lawyers, Sir Michael Wood and Elizabeth Wilmshurst, had given advice that a second UN resolution was necessary and claimed that Attorney General Lord Goldsmith had changed his initial advice and given the Cabinet its legal justification for the invasion. The attorney general's former legal secretary, David Brummell, told the inquiry that Lord Goldsmith had been discouraged from advising against invading Iraq. The lawyers were firm in their belief that going to war without a second UN resolution would not be legal. I tweeted live on our split-screen as they gave evidence. We were getting an unprecedented insight into how the decision to go to war had been taken. Newly de-classified documents were laying bare the entire process and government decision making and the legal advice were being meticulously inspected. The Foreign Office lawyers said their advice was simply ignored.

Lord Goldsmith himself denied, in his evidence to the inquiry, that he had been under political pressure to change his legal advice although he did admit changing his legal opinion from it being a 'reasonable case' to argue for the legality of military action to it being 'lawful' in order to provide clarity, especially to the military and the civil service who were demanding a definitive answer.

Former International Development Secretary Claire Short gave her evidence and, as expected, laid into Tony Blair, accusing him of lying to her and misleading Parliament in the build up to the invasion of Iraq. She had resigned believing the war to be illegal without a second UN resolution and fearing, she said, a humanitarian catastrophe. She claimed that Lord Goldsmith's legal advice was not circulated to the Cabinet and that Tony Blair cut her off whenever she tried to raise the issue of Iraq. She claimed that Tony Blair had persuaded her not to resign on the same day as Robin Cook by assuring her that the UN would lead the reconstruction of Iraq once Saddam Hussein was gone and by telling her that George Bush would support the creation of an independent Palestinian state.

"There was no emergency. No one had attacked anyone. There wasn't any new WMD. We could have taken the time and got it right."

This was all too easy to say in retrospect and we had heard a lot from Claire Short in the weeks following the invasion in 2003, but to hear her excoriating criticism pulled together in one evidence session was powerful. She was slaughtered in the newspapers but a heroine to the anti-war coalition.

Spare a thought for the poor stenographer at the Chilcot Iraq inquiry. I blogged on some of her funnier mishaps. She referred to Jack Straw as the former 'furniture secretary' and kept typing 'the Eric inquiry'!

After Claire Short, by way of total contrast, John Reid told the inquiry that he believed on the evidence available at the time that the decision to invade Iraq was absolutely correct. He said he hadn't wanted to hear the legal arguments in detail, he had wanted clarity. "I wanted to know: Is what we're about to do lawful, or is it illegal?" Contradicting Claire Short, he said that he and every Cabinet minister was given every opportunity to ask questions, give their opinion and disagree with Tony Blair. The advantage of tweeting live on a split-screen as he was speaking was that I was able to refer back to Claire Short's evidence and highlight the contradictions.

Of course, the centrepiece of this period of evidence to the Iraq inquiry was the appearance of Tony Blair himself, which came after Lord Goldsmith and the lawyers but before Claire Short's visceral attack. I tweeted live on our split-screen. Tony Blair seemed tense at first but soon got into his stride and repeated his by now very familiar arguments, above all that he had made a judgement based on the evidence available and took full responsibility for that judgement. He gave no ground and blamed the French and the Russians for blocking a second UN resolution while maintaining that the existing UN resolutions justified and made legal the invasion of Iraq. Saddam Hussein was extremely dangerous and there had been 'no doubt' that he did have WMD capability which he had been hiding from the UN weapons inspectors.

The most poignant moment came at the end when he was asked if he had any regrets. He said he did not. I thought he could have said he regretted the loss of life, sympathised with the bereaved families and perhaps added that many more people would have died had Saddam Hussein remained in power. He chose not to, presumably a deliberate, pre-meditated choice.

On February 8th we learnt that three Labour MPs, Elliott Morley, David Chaytor and Jim Devine, were to be prosecuted over their expenses claims. David Cameron made a speech in which he accused Gordon Brown of failing to deal with the expenses scandal in the Labour Party as part of a general salvo against Brown's abilities as a leader. The Conservatives were trying to position the MPs' expenses scandal as a Labour Party issue and an example of government incompetence. I interviewed Harriett Harman and Nick Clegg and packaged the story for *Live at Five*. That same day, Jack Straw gave evidence to the Chilcot inquiry for a second time.

We got an advance copy of an interview Gordon Brown did with Piers Morgan two days before it was broadcast. He was very open about the death of baby Jennifer Jane. It was very moving. I did lives around excerpts from the interview and packaged the story for the evening news. It was a very soft interview and should have given Gordon Brown's image a boost. I was on my way home at eleven p.m. when the Pentagon announced Operation Moshtarak, a new and concerted effort to drive the Taliban out of Helmand Province in Afghanistan. The announcement was supposed to have come the following day. I turned around and did lives at midnight and one a.m. which ran as an 'As Live' for the rest of the night.

David Cameron did a web broadcast in which he was basically saying that his Conservative Party now represented the values of New Labour, 'a strong economy and a fairer society'. I suggested in my lives that he was presenting himself to the voters as the heir to Blair.

After an interview with George Osborne the next day I was left with the distinct impression that he would prefer David Cameron not to say too much, smile a lot, and remind the voters that they didn't actually like Gordon Brown, and to win the election by default without talking too much about Conservative plans which, of course, included significant if not Draconian spending cuts.

The Cabinet had another awayday in mid-February, this time in Durham. We did lives all afternoon as well as covering other events, a visit to a school etc. I had set off with producer Esme Wren from King's Cross at seven thirty a.m. and we were back at King's Cross thirteen hours later having travelled back with Ed Balls' special advisor, Balshen Izzet, and two treasury spads. Wine was taken and we adjourned on arrival to the St Pancras champagne bar. As well as work we discussed relationships and marriage, a discussion which confirmed to me what I already knew, that I really don't understand women at all!

The next day and the 'battle of the economists'. Sixty-seven economists had signed a letter in the *FT* supporting the Labour Party, trumping the twenty who had written to *The Sunday Times* supporting the Conservatives. Gordon Brown was giving a speech as a Progressive Governance conference. I did lives before and after the speech, interviewed Peter Mandelson on the mothballing of the Corus steelworks on Teesside, and did a pooled interview with George Osborne to get his reaction to the economists' letter to the *FT*. I also did lives after James Purnell announced he would not be standing at the general election. A varied and busy day.

Andrew Rawnsley wrote a book in which he accused Gordon Brown of being a bully. This provoked a furious denial/rebuttal by Downing Street. I interviewed David Cameron, Nick Clegg and Peter Mandelson on the story as well as the founder of the National Bullying Helpline, Christine Pratt, who claimed that her charity had received distressed phone calls from staff working in Gordon Brown's office. Peter Mandelson had gone on the offensive, accusing the Tories of 'dirty tricks'.

There had been accusations of a conflict of interest between the charity and a company run by Christine Pratt's husband. I packaged the story and broke two new lines that day. First, that all four patrons of the National Bullying Helpline, including Ann Widdecombe, had resigned not least because the revelation about staff in Gordon Brown's office, even in the unlikely event of it being true, breached confidentiality. The Charity Commission investigated the charity's accounts and Christine Pratt later resigned. My second breaking news story was that Gordon Brown was to give evidence to the Chilcot inquiry on March 5th.

The next day, I interviewed Peter Mandelson after he spoke at a very dull Regional Development Agency conference. He was very strong on the bullying story. Before we moved on to talk about regional funding and Northern Ireland, he told me, on camera, that he had an email claiming that John Major had thrown his dinner at a civil servant when he was prime minister. One of the claims against Gordon Brown was that he was in the habit of hurling his mobile phone at staff members when he was angry. I did a live using part of the Mandelson interview, but not the claim about John Major. I called John Major's office who strongly denied the story. Peter Mandelson's spad called to say Mandy didn't want it used. I was tempted, but if Mandelson didn't stand by the story, we couldn't use it. Peter Mandelson phoned me to say, "Major's people have gone ballistic." He said he'd thought he was just talking to me, even though we had been recording an interview and the camera had been clearly pointing at him! The real problem, he said, was that although he had the email he couldn't prove it was true. So, a non-story.

On Sky News that evening, Alistair Darling said that 'the forces of Hell' had been unleashed against him by Gordon Brown's aides, meaning Damian McBride and Charlie Whelan. Why on earth did he say that on television? Inexplicable.

The next day was Wednesday, PMQs. David Cameron failed to find the net despite the 'forces of Hell' open goal. I cut the lead package for *Live at Five* and all evening, with Esme producing.

In early March, the rules of engagement for the leaders' TV debates were finally agreed by the political parties and executives from Sky News, ITN and the BBC. They had agreed to seventy-six rules! I interviewed Nick Clegg, ITN did Gordon Brown, the BBC did David Cameron, three pooled interviews which I packaged for *Live at Five*. I did my PTC at the Mothers' Union office in Westminster where the negotiations had taken place. We did a small re-cut for *Sky News at Ten* to include the SNP's Angus Robertson who had wanted to be included in the leaders' debate. The SNP wasn't a national UK party so there was no reason why they should be. Besides, they had just 6 MPs. The Lib Dems had 62.

When Gordon Brown gave evidence to the Chilcot inquiry on March 5th I was the 'presenter's friend', doing lives with presenter Kay Burley on Abingdon Green as his four hours of testimony unfolded. The prime minister told the inquiry that Tony Blair's decision to go to war in Iraq had been, "The right decision for the right reasons". Brown said he had been fully involved in the run up to the invasion of Iraq, spoke of the gravity of the decision, and praised the military. Unlike Tony Blair, he also used the opportunity to express his sadness at the loss of life, both military and especially civilian. He also claimed that, as chancellor, he had never turned down any request for additional equipment by the Ministry of Defence. This was later disputed by military commanders including the then Chief of the Defence Staff Admiral Lord Boyce, who claimed that they had been 'starved of funds'.

Gordon Brown revealed that he had not seen private correspondence between President Bush and Tony Blair and hadn't expected to, and said he was unaware of Attorney General Lord Goldsmith's initial doubts about the legality of the war adding that, constitutionally, the Cabinet had only needed to be informed of the attorney general's final conclusion. Many in the Labour Party had believed that Gordon Brown had secretly opposed the war. Even if that had been the case, he could hardly distance himself from decisions taken when he was chancellor. However, he also took the opportunity to take a swipe at US Defence Secretary Donald Rumsfeld and the America Neocons, and the total lack of a post-war reconstruction plan for Iraq.

In one section, on the cost of the war and how he had funded it, he bombarded the inquiry with numbers and statistics. It was pure Gordon and felt like he was delivering a Budget statement. The bottom line was that the total cost of the war had been eight billion pounds.

David Miliband gave evidence to the inquiry the following Monday. I tweeted live on our split-screen as he gave his testimony. He managed to avoid saying anything remotely controversial. The entire exercise felt like an academic foreign affairs seminar.

The next day, I was in Belfast. Producer Harriett Tolputt and I arrived in the evening and ate in what had become known as the 'Cathedral Quarter'. How Belfast had changed. We could have been in any European city. The story the next day was the Northern Ireland Assembly passing the Police and Criminal Justice Bill. We did lives every hour from seven a.m. until seven p.m. For reasons best known to themselves, the Ulster Unionist Party voted against the bill. It was a mystery to everyone else too, including David Cameron and Hilary Clinton who had urged them to support the legislation which was a vital component of the ongoing peace process in Northern Ireland. Both Martin McGuinness of Sinn Féin and the DUP's Peter Robinson, who was Northern Ireland's first minister at the time, laid into the UUP who appeared to be sulking because they were no longer the largest Unionist party and were feeling left out of Northern Ireland coalition politics. Politically, this was particularly embarrassing for David Cameron who had entered into an electoral pact with the UUP, a pact that could prove vital if there was a hung parliament after the UK general election.

Back in Westminster, I had to go to a joint SNP/Plaid Cymru press conference at which they whinged about being omitted from the leaders' TV debate. They were actually happy enough with Sky News because we had consulted them, but they were deeply pissed off with both ITN and the BBC because they had not. I cut a package later that day with producer Stephanie de Groote on the election timetable once Alistair Darling had confirmed that the Budget would be on March 24th. This involved me doing four PTCs, at Number Ten, Number Eleven, Buckingham Palace and Westminster Bridge, the PTCs popping out of an election calendar.

Graphics-tastic! Producers are expected to come up with these occasionally bonkers ideas, but this one worked and the package looked good.

As early as March 15th, Gordon Brown was saying that if there was a hung parliament he would fight on and try to form a government. He was speaking on Radio Four's *Woman's Hour*. I did lives on the ramifications of this all day and interviewed Alistair Darling on the same subject the next day.

April 6th was the Big Day, Gordon Brown officially called the election. We had known the day before and I had done lives all day and evening. Gordon Brown went to the palace after which he made a short speech on the doorstep of Number Ten surrounded by his Cabinet colleagues. "I am one of a team, not a team of one." Before metaphorically firing the starting gun. "Let's go to it."

There was a carnival atmosphere on Abingdon Green. The broadcasters had erected tents, marquees and scaffolding platforms. It was the hottest day of the year so far. I was writing blogs, recorded an election promo for the Sky News website, and did live two-ways with LBC Radio. I didn't get on air on television until the evening, when I was live almost every fifteen minutes from 8 until 11pm. Westminster was in a state of frenzied over-excitement.

'Dave' and 'Boris' (Cameron and Johnson) visited some Chelsea Pensioners. Good pictures which I packaged. The story doing the rounds was that Boris was trying to upstage his leader.

At the end of that first week of the campaign I was doing lives on the row over the Conservatives' proposals for tax cuts for married couples and an opinion poll conducted in 96 marginals which showed the Conservatives ahead, but only slightly.

I covered the launch of the Labour manifesto on March 12th. It looked like safety first, there was nothing radical. The party released a dreadful little film to go with it. The Conservatives launched their manifesto the next day, unusually a hardback book. I did lives as they did so. The latest polls had them just 6% ahead of Labour. Half the Shadow Cabinet spoke at the launch at Battersea Power Station. It was widely noted that Chris Grayling was kept well away from any cameras or microphones! Later, UKIP launched its manifesto. I interviewed Lord Pearson's wife, Caroline, a Party leader's wife who was standing as a candidate herself. She seemed very nervous.

The Lib Dems launched their election manifesto the next day. There were no great surprises but the launch was well staged and well delivered. Earlier, I had interviewed Peter Mandelson, Ed Balls and Andy Burnham after a Labour Party election press conference, and David Miliband revealing two fairly low-level Tory defectors.

The first television leaders' debate, on April 15th, exceeded all expectations. Many people had expected it to be dull, but the three leaders got stuck in, challenging each other directly and mocking each other with gusto. Nick Clegg was the star. He looked very relaxed, easy enough if you're the leader of the third party. He delivered his answers directly to camera, to the TV audience, the voters. He addressed audience members by their first name, a tactic quickly adopted by Gordon Brown and David Cameron, but less convincingly. He lumped Brown and Cameron together as 'those two', branding them as the same, the old, tired two-party system. The catchphrase of the night was 'I agree with Nick', used several times by David Cameron and even more so by Gordon Brown.

David Cameron looked nervous at first but soon mastered the medium of the TV debate with his usual fluency, explaining policy in simple language. Speaking fluent human. Gordon Brown, by contrast, looked tired. His answers were packed with policy detail, probably largely indigestible to a mass TV audience. He scored two good hits: "This is not *Question Time* it is answer time, David", and, "You can't airbrush your policies like your airbrush your posters". Although David Cameron and Nick Clegg looked far more youthful, Gordon Brown had the advantage of simply looking and sounding far more prime ministerial.

Nick Clegg undoubtedly won the debate and by some margin. 'I agree with Nick' was the headline in several newspapers. The polls showed him way ahead of the other two. "Cleggmania" screamed one headline. I did lives all the next day. A YouGov poll had the Lib Dems in second place. Conservatives 33%, Lib Dems 30%, Labour 28%. Suddenly, it was neck and neck. We thought the TV debates would be transformational but this was nothing sort of sensational.

The newspapers went Clegg-tastic for a few days and so did the opinion polls. The debate had taken place on a Thursday evening and for the next three days I found myself doing lives on the aftermath. The Lib Dems were enjoying a huge bounce in the opinion polls. They were first in one, second in two others. How would the bigger two parties fight back? Something unprecedented might be happening if, and it was a very big if, the Lib Dems could somehow keep the momentum going. But this was only the first of the three TV debates. Surely Labour and the Conservatives would have learnt some lessons and were already preparing to do better next time?

The Tories hit back with 'vote Clegg, get Brown'. David Cameron and Ken Clarke issued dire warnings about the prospect of a hung parliament. 'The Bond markets won't wait, Sterling will wobble'. Did they really believe that people would allow the Bond markets to dictate how they would vote?

The second TV debate, in Bristol, was hosted by Sky News and was a lot closer. Both Brown and Cameron raised their game. Nick Clegg performed well again, and the momentum still appeared to be with the Lib Dems, but far less so. The *Mail* and the *Telegraph* joined the Tories in an all-out assault on Nick Clegg. The *Mail* had a ridiculous claim about a 'Nazi slur' against Britain, while the *Telegraph* was inaccurately reporting ridiculous and totally unfounded allegations about payments into Nick Clegg's bank account. While after the first TV debate, the papers had said that Clegg was more popular than Winston Churchill, now they were saying, I kid you not, that he was less popular that Genghis Khan!

I wrote a piece on what a fantasy Labour/Lib Dem Cabinet might look like, and speculated that if the Lib Dems could persuade enough people that this was an election they might actually win, then it was not beyond the bounds of possibility that they could at least win enough seats to form a coalition in a hung parliament. At the time, the almost universal assumption was that any such coalition would be with Labour. Just for fun, I wrote a piece on what a Conservative/Lib Dem Cabinet might look like. As if!

The following Monday I was live all morning first before and after a David Cameron press conference and then before and after a press conference with Ed Balls and Douglas Alexander at Labour Party HQ. Both sides were firing broadsides at the Lib Dems. Vote Clegg get Brown, and Vote Clegg get Cameron! But what, I asked, about Vote Clegg get Clegg! One of my lives was specifically about how the civil service was preparing for a hung parliament and a coalition government. This was now looking the most likely outcome with ten days to go. But a lot could happen in ten days of an election campaign.

And so it did, catastrophically for Gordon Brown, just two days later. The prime minister was campaigning in Rochdale. He chatted to a voter, Gillian Duffy, who it turned out was a lifelong Labour-supporting grandmother. She wanted to talk to him about immigration, especially from Eastern Europe, which was still a very difficult topic for many Labour people who thought that even to address the issue of immigration was racist. But it certainly was an issue. Two million Eastern Europeans had arrived in Britain since EU enlargement in 2004, the cost of EU free movement. Gordon Brown had agreed to wear a Sky News lapel mic during his walkabout. He was still wearing it when he got back into his car. He had simply forgotten to give it back.

I wasn't in Rochdale that day. I had been at an Institute of Directors conference at the Royal Albert Hall where I had got the first live interviews with both Vince Cable and George Osborne. But all other activity ceased once we heard what the prime minister had said when he got into his car with his advisor Justin Forsyth. When Justin asked who that was, Gordon Brown replied, "Some bigoted woman". Realising he was still wearing a microphone, he clumsily took it off and threw it out of the car window. All of this might have passed unnoticed had not our eagle-eared colleague Niall Paterson assiduously played it back in the edit van in Rochdale.

It was a disaster for Labour and mushroomed out of control. Gordon Brown had to abandon his schedule and go to Gillian Duffy's home to apologise in person. Later, as a guest at a local radio station, he sat head in hands as the clip was played to him, an iconic image of the 2010 election campaign. I estimated at the time that this unfortunate gaffe might cost Labour as many as twenty seats. Kay Burley mischievously asked, on air, "Can we have our mic back please, Prime Minister?" The lazy newspapers dubbed it 'Bigotsgate'.

There was a curious moment that afternoon back in our Westminster newsroom. Peter Mandelson was doing the rounds of the TV studios, defending Gordon Brown and saying he had simply misheard or misunderstood what Gillian Duffy had said. Our colleague Joey Jones suddenly appeared out of nowhere, and marched straight into the studio to do a live on a 'Breaking News' line, that when Peter Mandelson's advisor had told him about the Rochdale incident Mandelson's initial reaction had been, "Where was Justin?" This was hardly breaking news, but, more importantly, Adam was supposed to be doing the lives that afternoon. It was bizarre behaviour. None of us was amused. This was most certainly not the behaviour of a team player.

The third and final leaders' TV debate was hosted by the BBC in Birmingham. It was very lively. Gordon Brown did OK but looked a little marginalised as David Cameron attacked Nick Clegg, who more than held his own. I did a ten-minute live two-way with Norwegian TV. I had no idea why they were so interested. Next morning, I was live at six, seven and eight a.m. discussing the debate before heading to Harrow where Tony Blair had entered the campaign, visiting a clinic. His advisor Matthew Doyle was playing silly buggers, the upshot of which was that there would be only one TV interview, and it would be done by ITN. It was a poor interview. I did some lives from Harrow and cut a package. Blair was such a natural campaigner in a way that Gordon Brown could never hope to be.

Monday May 3rd, three days to go, and I did lives every hour on the latest opinion polls and into and out of a Nick Clegg speech in Lewisham. All three main party leaders spoke at a church conference in Westminster Hall. They all went down well with that audience, Gordon Brown, the son of a church minister, best of all. A well-known anti-nuclear protestor heckled Gordon Brown and got within two feet of the prime minister. There was no harm done, but the close protection officers had not been close enough. It was a serious security breach.

On the Wednesday, the eve of the election, I did lives every hour from Westminster as the parties girded their loins for the final push and on the latest opinion polls, which remained close. I bumped into George Osborne, with whom I was due to spend election night in his Tatton constituency. He was the Conservatives' main election strategist and thought they were heading for a seven seat overall majority. I thought it was still wide open.

Election night at George Osborne's constituency count with producer Fiona Robinson. Our main mission was to get Osborne in front of our live camera as often as required. Although I was barely getting on air it was fascinating to sit with George Osborne and his team as the results came in from around the country. The exit poll at 10 o'clock had the Conservatives on 305, Labour on 255 and the Lib Dems on 59. We were all highly sceptical, especially of the Lib Dem figure. Had they actually lost seats? Where was the Lib Dem surge? What had happened to Cleggmania? But the exit poll was remarkably accurate. The final result was Conservatives 307, Labour 258, and the Lib Dems just 57.

The Conservatives were well short of the 326 seats needed for an overall majority. The Conservatives' attempt to blame the dire state of the economy on Labour profligacy rather than the global financial crisis and to tap into the disillusion of so many voters who, after the expenses scandal, were inclined to regard most MPs as crooks and liars had worked, but not by enough. Labour and the Lib Dems were nowhere near an overall majority between them. Impasse?

We were scratching our heads, it was puzzling. Had the Lib Dems been the victims of a classic third-party squeeze? Had the attacks from both sides (Vote Clegg get Brown, Vote Clegg get Cameron) actually been effective? Had Clegg peaked too soon? Had people simply reverted to type when it came to casting their votes? If the Conservatives had come in at under 300, the Lib Dems could have done a deal with Labour. It looked like they would have to deal with David Cameron, or the Conservatives could try to form a minority government which no doubt would very swiftly be followed by another general election. George Osborne's election strategist's mind was working through the ramifications of this problematic result with his team.

Labour's Jacqui Smith, Charles Clarke, Tony McNulty and Mike O'Brien were all gone. So too were leading Lib Dems Evan Harris and Susan Kramer. Nick Griffin was soundly beaten in Barking.

No one knew what to do or what would happen next. No one, that is, except for David Cameron and his strategic brain George Osborne. Cameron wasted no time in making the Lib Dems a "big, open and comprehensive" offer. Nick Clegg said the Conservatives had won the most seats and therefore should be allowed the first crack at forming a government. Gordon Brown, who was still at Number Ten for now, said he agreed with Nick (again!) but that if the Lib Dems couldn't come to an agreement with the Tories they should talk to Labour. Days of torturous negotiations followed.

I hadn't had a particularly tiring election. I had made a few forays into the country but had spent most of the time at Westminster at the headquarters of the three main parties and pulling together the main election news of the day. I had not been out on the campaign trail for day after day following a gruelling schedule. So I found myself in pole position to cover the coalition negotiations.

It quickly became clear that the Lib Dems had two red lines. They wanted a referendum on proportional representation (which they got, and lost) and they wanted to cement Britain's place at the top table of the European Union, which put them in a position diametrically opposed to the increasingly influential Eurosceptics in the Conservative Party.

The crucial meetings took place at the Cabinet Office on Whitehall, just around the corner from Downing Street.

On the Sunday, the Lib Dem and Conservative delegates met for more than six hours. I did lives almost constantly from outside the Cabinet Office from 6am. I managed to break just one news line, that David Cameron was to meet his Conservative MPs in small groups starting at 5pm. I did lives before and after William Hague made a statement saying that the talks were ongoing, had been "constructive" and "positive" and would resume, and doorstepped the Lib Dem negotiators, David Laws and co, as they departed. Nick Clegg had a meeting with Gordon Brown followed by one with David Cameron.

Things came to a head the following Monday. Conservative-Lib Dem talks resumed at 10am. but not for long. Lib Dem MPs were due to meet at lunchtime and were expected to rubber stamp a deal. I was live from Lib Dem HQ as they met and then six times in two hours from the Conservatives at St Stephen's club. The Lib Dems wanted 'clarification' from the Conservatives on three key issues, including electoral reform, and said they wanted to talk again to the Labour Party. Gordon Brown appeared in Downing Street to say he would step down once Labour had elected a new leader. Although this felt inevitable, it turned everything on its head as Nick Clegg had insisted he would not keep Gordon Brown in power. So the Lib Dems resumed talks with Labour.

It was beginning to dawn on the Labour Party that the Lib Dems had no intention of forming a coalition with them. They were being used to exert pressure on the Tories. Many in the Labour Party, including Gordon Brown, could not quite believe this and regarded it as an act of betrayal. How could the Lib Dems, supposedly a centre-left progressive party, prop up a Conservative government? Many Lib Dems were equally perplexed. They had a tribal loathing of the Tories. But the reality was that the Conservatives had won the most seats, Labour and the Lib Dems could not form a majority government between them, and the Lib Dems were seizing their chance of being in power rather than opposition for the first time in almost a century. What was less clear was how the Lib Dems would square their pre-election opposition to deep spending cuts and sign up to George Osborne's policy of austerity.

William Hague, meanwhile, was in effect, negotiating in public that Monday offering a referendum on AV (the Alternative Vote system) and saying that they would not accept another unelected Labour prime minister. Gordon Brown's announcement that he would be standing down came at five p.m. He was sacrificing himself in a last desperate attempt to keep Labour in power. He had no choice.

I moved to the offices of the Work Foundation in Matthew Parker Street, Westminster, where the Lib Dems Federal Executive Committee was meeting to do lives at six and seven p.m. 'Fair votes' protestors, who had been holding demonstrations in Parliament Square, had moved to this location. From there to Lib Dem HQ for more lives, including a 'Breaking News' line at eight fifty p.m. that Lib Dem MPs were to meet an hour later. So, on to the Grand Committee Room, Westminster Hall, for that meeting where I doorstepped Nick Clegg and others live, including Simon Hughes and Paddy Ashdown, who was decidedly not at all pleased with the way the negotiations were going. I did lives until just after twelve thirty a.m. when the meeting broke up without any conclusion. There were to be more meetings the next day. This process was becoming excruciating.

The next day, Tuesday 11th of May, it was finally all over. Gordon Brown resigned and left Downing Street, David Cameron became prime minister in a coalition government with Nick Clegg as deputy prime minister.

There was a growing sense throughout that day that a change of government might finally be imminent, even though the Lib Dems had begun the day in talks with Labour's negotiating team. I was doing very long lives in Downing Street, including live interviews with Ed Miliband and Ed Balls who both described the talks as constructive, positive, etc. But their body language told a different story. They didn't have enough seats, or, it seemed to me, the will to cling on to power. Many in the Labour Party were already saying that a period of opposition and renewal under a new leader might be the better option.

I did lives all afternoon from Downing Street while Adam Boulton was around the corner at the Cabinet Office, where talks between the Conservatives and Lib Dems had resumed at 2 o'clock with Vince Cable saying they were "very close" to an agreement. I did lives from Downing Street from 2 until 5.15pm, by which time it was clear that Gordon Brown could be about to go. I knew that those in the room with Gordon Brown included Peter Mandelson, Ed Balls, Ed Miliband, Andrew Adonis and Brown's close advisors, Sue Nye and Stewart Wood. When Sky News cameraman Paul Dickie spotted the Downing Street photographer going in, I knew this must be it.

I had a choice. I could stay put and wait for the prime minister to depart or I could swap places with Adam. I have always been a team player with a deep and sometimes misguided sense of loyalty. I thought our political editor should probably be in Downing Street, so I phoned our Westminster newsroom and told them so. Adam and I swapped places at 5.30.

When Adam arrived, the assembled press, dozens of them, began the playground chant of, 'Fight! fight!'

The previous day, Adam had had an altercation with Alastair Campbell live on air in which Alastair had made some outrageous allegations about Adam's political allegiance and Adam had angrily replied, "Don't tell me what I think!" Alistair kept baiting Adam who was apoplectic, screaming at him right in his face. Presenter Jeremy Thompson had placed himself between them genuinely fearing they might come to blows. This moment of pantomime relieved the pressure in Downing Street. By now, the hacks all had the feeling that something momentous was about to happen, the sense of anticipation was palpable.

I did lives from the talks at the Cabinet Office at 6, 6.30, 6.45 and 7 o'clock and twice at 7.30 with brief statements from William Hague and Danny Alexander, both simply saying they would be reporting back to their respective leaders.

Gordon Brown resigned at 7.30. He made a short, dignified statement before walking along Downing Street with Sarah and their sons John and Fraser beside him and then going to the palace to inform the Queen. We learnt later that Peter Mandelson had advised him to go while it was still daylight rather than be seen to be skulking away under cover of the night.

My day was far from over. Once Gordon Brown had departed, I went to the Local Government Association building where both the Lib Dem parliamentary party and their Federal Executive met to approve the formation of the coalition, which they did almost unanimously. I did lives every hour until I broke the news of the Lib Dems' decision. I did a long live after a Nick Clegg statement on camera at 12.30 am which included live interviews with Chris Huhne, Simon Hughes and Norman Baker.

And suddenly that was it, the 2010 election was finally over. We had the first coalition government since the Second World War. History had been made. And we could get our lives back, catch up on some sleep and stop living on Mars bars and Lucozade!

Of course, in reality it was far from over. The next day, after posing on the doorstep of Number Ten, David Cameron and Nick Clegg held a press conference in the Downing Street Rose Garden which was embarrassingly chummy. They looked like close buddies from very similar backgrounds (Eton and Oxford, Westminster and Cambridge). As so often, Channel 5's political editor Andy Bell asked the best question.

The final act of this very peculiar election was playing out. David Cameron announced the names of some of the members of his new, coalition Cabinet. Nick Clegg, who would henceforth have to live with the label of being a 'yellow Tory' would be deputy prime minister. The Lib Dems would get five Cabinet ministers. Theresa May was the new Home Secretary.

I had my annual appraisal at work. How I hated those things. But it was very positive.

David Miliband wasted no time in declaring his candidacy to be the next Labour leader. He did so after meetings that day of the PLP and the Shadow Cabinet. The SHADOW Cabinet. That must have felt very strange after thirteen years in power. I did lives before and after Miliband's declaration and we took him live. He said that the forming of the coalition government meant that only Labour now represented the progressive centre-left. For the first time in a very long time I finished work that evening by 8 o'clock, while it was still light.

I did lives in Downing Street all the next afternoon when the new Cabinet met for the first time and the Privy Council went to the palace for an audience with the Queen. Most commentators were predicting that the coalition would only last a few months, a year at most. It was some achievement that they held it together for a full five years, but at a catastrophic cost to the Liberal Democrats. I also did a live for Fox News, trying to explain to their audience how British elections work and what coalition government meant. I suspect they were none the wiser.

I actually had three days off, a long weekend, before returning to Westminster the following Monday for an off-camera briefing with the IFS (Institute for Fiscal Studies). The economy was in a desperate state, which had been one of Nick Clegg's main justifications for going into coalition with the Conservatives. He said the country needed stable government. George Osborne announced the date of his first Budget. I did a couple of lives and a package for *Live at Five* which ran all evening.

The next day I packaged the first sitting of the new House of Commons. I interviewed Harriett Harman who said her advice to new MPs was to ignore all advice! She announced that nominations for the Labour leadership would officially open the following week, with the result expected on September 25th. I also interviewed Colonel Bob Stewart, Rory Stewart, Caroline Lucas and John Woodcock. Nick Clegg sat next to David Cameron, a strange image. John Bercow was re-elected speaker. There was no division despite a smattering of shouts of 'No' from the Conservative benches. The Labour PLP met in the evening, and my package also included an interview with the new Leader of the Lords, Lord Strathclyde, and the ceremonial from the House of Lords.

There was a big turnout for drinks that evening for newly-elected MPs. They were mostly Conservatives, of course, but at least some of them appeared to be Cameron-style liberal Conservatives. Time would tell.

The next day, Nick Clegg gave his first speech as deputy prime minister at Islington College, Holloway Road, very conveniently just down the road from where I lived. I was live as he arrived behind me, perfect timing, and did lives after the speech which was billed as a big speech on reform, changing the voting system, enhancing human rights and dismissing any notion of ID cards. He claimed this represented the biggest set of reforms since the Reform Act of 1832. But what, I wondered, about votes for women and the 1928 Representation of the People Act? Later, on Abingdon Green, I did lives on the Clegg speech and on Ed Balls entering the contest to be the next Labour leader.

We got some details on the coalition's programme for government the next day at a press conference with David Cameron, Nick Clegg, George Osborne, Vince Cable and, for some reason, Theresa May. I did lives all morning on that and on Diane Abbott's announcement that she would be a candidate for Labour leader. Diane Abbott!

She was a strange one. Almost every MP, and there were six hundred and fifty of them, would say hello, stop for a chat, or at least nod to acknowledge my existence. All of them, except Diane Abbott. She would stick her nose in the air, as if at some bad smell, and march straight past. I passed her one day on a day off, at Muswell Hill garden centre, and got the same treatment. It was bizarre. When you bumped into MPs on a day off, often both with wives/husbands and sometimes children, you always stopped to pass the time of day. It was basic good manners. Just a short time earlier I had bumped into Douglas Alexander with a child on his shoulders and of course we stopped to chat about the state of the Labour Party and of the nation. Maybe Diane Abbott felt she had been caught out once too often by journalists, or maybe she shared the extreme Left's ingrained distrust of my profession.

Alistair Darling tabled an urgent question on Tory plans for six billion pounds of spending cuts. It was dealt with very effectively by Chief Secretary to the Treasury David Laws. How strange it was to see a Lib Dem Cabinet minister so strenuously defending what was very obviously a Conservative Party policy. I did a couple of lives on that and more the same afternoon on the Queen's speech debates on foreign policy and education. Academies, so called 'free schools', and the Lib Dem policy of the Pupil Premium.

David Laws didn't last long as a Cabinet minister, less than three weeks. He was replaced by Danny Alexander. He resigned from the government because the *Telegraph* reported that he had improperly claimed thousands of pounds in expenses. It emerged that he was renting rooms at a property owned by a man the *Telegraph* described as his 'secret lover'. David Laws came out as gay before the *Telegraph* outed him. Because he and his long-term partner were not in a civil partnership, he was deemed to have broken the rules. This seemed monstrous and very unfair. Eventually, he was found to have only unintentionally broken the rules and returned as minister of State for Schools with attendance at Cabinet two years later.

On the day Danny Alexander replaced David Laws as Chief Secretary to the Treasury, Israeli commandos attacked aid ships heading to Gaza. Nine people were killed. There was international outrage. The new Foreign Secretary, William Hague, did a pooled interview condemning the Israeli action. I did lives on both Danny Alexander's appointment and the condemnation of Israel.

David Cameron's first PMQs on June 2nd was completely overshadowed by a shocking story from Cumbria where taxi driver Derrick Bird had shot dead twelve people, including his own brother, and injured another twenty-five in random shootings before turning his gun on himself. There were awful echoes of Hungerford and Dunblane. I did lives from the Home Office, including a live interview with Home Secretary Theresa May.

The next day was dominated by the Cumbrian shootings, with many eyewitness accounts, and by plans to review once again our gun laws. David Cameron made a statement on the shootings during a press conference with Canadian Prime Minister Stephen Harper. He would be visiting Cumbria the next day. I interviewed John Woodcock and Rory Stewart who were both MPs for constituencies in Cumbria.

I did lives on June 9th on the Labour leadership runners and riders. John McDonnell dropped out, transferring his support to Diane Abbott. The Miliband brothers, Ed Balls and Andy Burnham would be on the ballot paper. So too Diane Abbott who just scraped enough nominations including those of David Miliband and Ed Balls who had been pressed into 'lending' her their support in order for there to be a female candidate. This struck me as absurd. Where were the credible Labour women like Harriett Harman, Yvette Cooper or even Caroline Flint? Diane Abbott as prime minister! It was mind boggling.

The Office of Fair Trading announced it was to investigate investment banks, and not before time in my opinion. I did lives on that and on Conservative minister David Willetts hinting that university tuition fees might have to increase, which would put the Lib Dems in a very difficult position since they had signed a pre-election pledge to oppose any increase in tuition fees.

This was, of course, the issue which was to have such disastrous consequences for the Lib Dems. It was all very well signing a pledge as an opposition party with little if any expectation of being in government. Scrapping or even reducing tuition fees at a time of such drastic fiscal restraint was unrealistic. Vince Cable knew that, so did the Labour Party, and the universities themselves were telling us that their funding was in crisis and unsustainable.

Tuition fees wasn't even particularly high on the Lib Dem agenda, and certainly well below electoral reform, increasing the tax-free personal allowance, a Pupil Premium of additional funding to help poorer children, climate change and Europe. But Lib Dem MPs, including Nick Clegg, had publicly signed the pledge card. It was a broken promise that would undermine public trust in the party.

The Lib Dems were holed below the water line. The issue exacerbated the feelings of betrayal that the Lib Dems had entered into the coalition in the first place. They were attacked from all sides, accused of being weak and unprincipled. It would culminate in the almost total destruction of the Liberal Democrats in the next general election, in 2015, when they were reduced from 57 MPs to just 8.

Nearly forty years after the event and at a cost of £200 million, the Bloody Sunday inquiry presented its report the next day, all five thousand pages of it. Lord Saville's inquiry, established by Tony Blair in 1998, tackled head-on the accusation that there had been a cover up following that awful day in January 1972. In the House of Commons, David Cameron acknowledged the inquiry's findings, that British soldiers had fired first and that they had shot fleeing, unarmed civilians. He apologised on behalf of the British government. Saville concluded that the Paras had been out of control, had shot innocent civilians without warning and had then lied in attempting to hide the truth.

I was doing lives speculating on what we could expect in George Osborne's first Budget when the news broke that Lib Dem Cabinet minister Chris Huhne was leaving his wife for another woman, someone who, incidentally, used to work at Sky News. I included that fact in my lives, though I was at pains to point out that this was a private, personal matter with no political implications.

The following Monday, I was doing lives and packages on the government's promised cap on immigration (which, of course, they never achieved) when Culture Secretary Jeremy Hunt compared the good behaviour of England fans at the World Cup with the behaviour of fans at Hillsborough in 1989. Very, very foolish. Although he apologised almost immediately, no amount of apologising was sufficient.

I covered a speech at King's College London by the new Secretary of State for Justice Ken Clarke in which he said he wanted fewer prisoners and more effective rehabilitation. With cameraman Adam Cole, I went to the Kennington rehabilitation centre. I found some of the people there truly inspiring. They seemed determined to get their lives back on track. We packaged the story for *Live at Five* but had to update it when it turned into a Tory row. Conservative MP Phillip Davies said he disagreed with Ken Clarke, pointing out that the Conservatives had voted for more not fewer prisons. Former Home Secretary and Party leader, Michael Howard, stuck his oar in, saying he was 'not convinced' by Ken Clarke's approach. Prison overcrowding remained a problem as it had been for many years.

In Northumberland police were searching for Raoul Moat who had killed one person and injured two others in a two-day shooting rampage. After almost a week they found him near Rothbury. There was a six-hour stand-off with armed police. It was front page news and Sky's lead story for days. It caught my interest for two reasons. First, because the story was unfolding in my old stomping ground from my Metro Radio days and I knew intimately the area where the police were searching, and secondly because our old friend Paul Gascoigne got involved. Bizarrely and disturbingly, Gazza turned up at the stand-off in his dressing gown and carrying some chicken and lager. He was at his most vulnerable at the time, fighting drug addiction and alcoholism. He was convinced that Moat was a friend of his although the two men had never met. He later admitted he had snorted a lot of cocaine and had drunk a lot of whisky. It was tragic to see Gazza in such a state.

After a week supporting the RCDS, at the end of July I was reporting on just why Ed Miliband was standing for the Labour Party leadership against his older brother David. Opinion in our Westminster newsroom was divided. I was firmly in the camp that believed it to be an act of betrayal. Many of us with younger siblings had thought the same, not least because

Ed's career had more or less shadowed David's but now he wanted to leapfrog his brother at the final hurdle, for the top job. I also thought David would make a better Party leader and potential prime minister. The other school of thought, harder-headed and argued most strongly by Jonathan Levy, was that all is fair in love and war and politics, and that Ed had every right to throw his hat in the ring. This saga of the two brothers would start to resemble a Greek tragedy, and was to reach its denouement in September.

I was back to our gimmick of splitting the TV screen and live tweeting as we covered Generals Sir Richard Dannatt and Sir Mike Jackson giving their evidence to the Chilcot Iraq inquiry, and I did the same when John Prescott gave his largely incoherent testimony two days later.

God (Gus O'Donnell), the head of the civil service, confirmed something we already knew, that he would retire before the next election. As Cabinet secretary he was on his third prime minister after Blair and Brown. It meant that if we didn't know something we could no longer say 'go and ask God'.

David Cameron's father Ian had a stroke while he was on holiday in France. It sounded very serious. Adam was taking a week off so our newly-appoimted deputy political editor Joey Jones was stumbling his way through the lives in Downing Street while I packaged the story. Joey was, without a doubt, the Sky News political correspondent with the least on-screen presence, but ours was not to question why etc. We got the news from Downing Street at 3.30 that David Cameron's father had passed away. The prime minister flew to France. It was a Wednesday, so Nick Clegg took PMQs with Jack Straw representing Labour. There was enormous sympathy for David Cameron. What a roller coaster of emotions he had been through. The death of his son Ivan, winning the general election, the birth of his daughter Florence and now the death of his father. I couldn't even begin to imagine what he must have been going through.

The Lib Dems met that autumn in Liverpool. Clegg's leader's speech was persuasive as he justified going into coalition with the Conservatives to the Lib Dem delegates. The British pulled out of Sangin Province where the Americans were taking over. Afghanistan seemed insoluble.

After more than four months, voting for the Labour leadership finally closed on September 22nd. The result would be announced the following Saturday at the Labour Party conference in Manchester. I was busily phoning the campaign teams of David and Ed Miliband, Ed Balls and Andy Burnham, all of whom I knew. We wanted to get the result first before it was officially announced. I did Sky News lives and two-ways with LBC Radio. David Miliband was by far the favourite.

I was in the conference hall in Manchester the next day for a moment of history, the election of a new Labour Party leader and potential prime minister. I did live interviews with David Miliband and Andy Burnham as they arrived. I didn't get the result early from any of the four main candidates, but I did get it from someone else who had been in the room before the candidates trooped onto the stage for the official announcement. As Harriet Harman read out the results from the early rounds, and as Diane Abbott, Andy Burnham and Ed Balls were eliminated, I got a text. It simply said: *Ed won*. Over on the BBC, Nick Robinson had already called it for David Miliband and they were running a strap, 'David Miliband wins Labour leadership'. I had a quick conflab with our head of politics Jonathan Levy. I had just one source and it wasn't from someone I knew well and knew I could trust, although I believed it to be true. So we erred on the side of caution and waited for Harriet Harman to officially announce the result that Ed had indeed won in the final run off against his brother, by a whisker. David had won among Labour MPs and MEPs and most Constituency Labour Parties, but the unions had swung it for Ed.

The unions had, at first, backed Ed Balls but had switched to supporting Ed Miliband who, they calculated, had a better chance of stopping David Miliband who they regarded as a Blairite. They had also managed to engineer a long campaign. David Miliband would have won a short one. The unions had needed the time to organise.

In the corridors away from the main conference hall, I had members of David Miliband's team literally crying on my shoulder. Where had it gone wrong? Had it been hubris? Could they have worked harder to woo the unions? In the main conference hotel bar that evening, the unedifying spectacle of Charlie Whelan and other members on the Unite union swilling back their beer and bragging about how they had 'stuffed' the Blairites.

I got various reactions after the vote from Harriet Harman, Andy Burnham, Tony Woodley of Unite and others and did some lives. There was a huge media scrum around Ed Miliband. Was it the best possible result for the Labour Party? I thought not. Ed was a nice person and very clever, but he did not look like a prime minister-in-waiting. His older brother did.

David Miliband's wife, Louise, was later quoted as saying she regarded Ed Miliband's action in thwarting his brother as an act of 'unforgiveable treachery'. I thought the key word was 'unforgiveable'. It was all positively Shakespearean.

I liked Ed. I liked Ed Balls and Andy Burnham too. But, without any party allegiance, I thought it a great shame that David Miliband would not be getting his opportunity to one day become prime minister.

The next morning, we were outside the Midland Hotel early. Ed Miliband was due to go on Andrew Marr's BBC Sunday morning programme. Our mission was to get him first. I was at the front of the hotel, producer Gary Honeyford spotted him emerging from the back. We got a very good walking interview with him, the first interview with the new Labour leader, a scoop. Plaudits all round and the interview got played over and over again on Sky News that morning to spike the BBC's guns. I packaged around this interview for midday, with fresh packages which ran every fifteen minutes that Sunday afternoon.

The next morning was doorstep morning again and this time we got live interviews with both Ed Miliband and David Miliband, separately of course. David Miliband gave a brilliant short speech ahead of a Q&A on foreign affairs, with praise for his brother, an appeal for party unity and, perhaps, some extracts from the leader's speech he would have delivered had he won, a glimpse of what might have been, the leader the party could have had. He received a long and emotional standing ovation before he started and when he finished.

I did a few more interviews, Jack Straw among them, and went to diversity night that evening. David Miliband attended, of course, as Foreign Secretary. I only managed to get a very quick word with him, the place was jam-packed with commiserating supporters, although I knew many of them were to the left of David Miliband and had voted first for Ed Balls with Ed Miliband as their second choice once he was eliminated. Some of them also told me they had voted for Andy Burnham before giving Ed Miliband their second choice votes and here, if nowhere else, there were also plenty of Diane Abbott supporters.

Ed Miliband delivered his first speech as the new Party leader the next day. His delivery wasn't great and not a patch on his brother's the day before, but he would grow into the role. Of course, his people were talking it up, spinning away furiously. I got a grab with David Miliband in which he praised his brother's speech but would say nothing about his own future.

I went to the News International party that evening. A lot of members of the Shadow Cabinet were there and I chatted to a few, Alistair Darling, Ed Balls and Yvette Cooper among them. The Shadow Cabinet was closing ranks around the new leader. It was time to move on, look to the future etc.

The next day, the story wasn't really in Manchester. We were waiting for a statement from David Miliband who had left the conference the previous evening and was back in London, although we knew what he was going to say. We did a few walking shots of Ed Miliband. The Manchester weather had returned, it was cold and raining. His brother David said he would continue as an MP, recharge his batteries, give Ed some space.

From Foreign Secretary and widely-anticipated Party leader to the backbenches. Politics can be a cruel business. I knew he wouldn't stay there long.

I should have gone to the Unite party at the Midland Hotel that evening, the last night of the conference, but I was a bit tired. I had worked ten days in a row with early starts and very late nights. Besides, I didn't think I'd be able to stomach the gloating.

After the weekend off to recharge my own batteries, it was off to Birmingham for the Conservative annual conference. They were in power so what they said mattered, but it felt anti-climatic after the drama in Manchester. Boris Johnson gave a speech in which he was very funny and very rude about the French. George Osborne used his speech to explain and justify his spending cuts. This was a well organised, regimented conference. There were few voices of dissent, though I searched for them, and none of the scheming and plotting, triumph and failure we had witnessed in Manchester the week before.

I got the only live interview with Martin McGuinness the next morning to get his reaction to a bombing in Londonderry the previous night. He was attending his first Conservative conference which he said felt very strange. I did some lives, including a couple on the Conservatives' plans for child benefit which had not gone down well with the Tory newspapers. Most of the Cabinet came to the News International party that evening, including David Cameron and his wife Samantha.

David Cameron's first speech to the party conference as prime minister was a little lacklustre. He didn't need to campaign any more so the tone was calm and measured and the content uncontroversial. I wrote a blog on the changing face of the Conservative Party, fewer blue rinses, more youthful.

On the Friday, back at Westminster, Ed Miliband announced his Shadow Cabinet. Alan Johnson was to be Shadow Chancellor, Ed Balls would shadow the Home Secretary and Yvette Cooper was Shadow Foreign Secretary. These were interesting choices and looked very credible. In the evening, all evening, I did lives on the astonishing story of the Chilean miners who had been trapped underground for sixty days but were expected to be rescued the following Monday.

I did a pooled interview with Major General Gordon Messenger on the failed American Special Forces attempt to rescue Scottish aid worker Linda Norgrove who had been kidnapped by the Taliban. Tragically, she had been killed during the rescue attempt. Her death had some slight added poignancy for me as we shared our Aberdeen university alma mater, although she was a lot younger than me and had graduated more than ten years after I had.

The next day, Wednesday, I interviewed Vince Cable on the Royal Mail privatisation. This had no chance of getting on air as the miners in Chile were being rescued, live on TV. Quite rightly, Sky News went Chile-tastic with wall-to-wall coverage.

On my birthday in October, Chile's President Sebastián Piñera was visiting David Cameron in Downing Street. I filled a lot of *Live at Five* with this, mostly about the incredible rescue of the Chilean miners who had been trapped underground for weeks. I did long lives at 5.00, 5.15 and 5.40 and managed to get a long live interview with President Piñera at 5.50pm. I had single-handedly filled much of that news hour!

The next day, the SDSR (Strategic Defence and Security Review) revealed significant cuts. Twenty-five thousand civilian jobs, seven thousand army, five thousand navy and five thousand RAF posts were to go. The famous Harrier Jump Jets were to be scrapped. This seemed very odd, the Harriers were so versatile. There would be no new Nimrod reconnaissance aircraft. But we were to build two new state-of-the-art aircraft carriers.

The Comprehensive Spending Review the next day was one of those big, set-piece events in Westminster dominated for Sky News by presentation and presenter-led. George Osborne's statement came after PMQs. I tweeted live on both on our split-screen. Osborne announced draconian cuts, as many as half a million public sector jobs might go, £80 billion was to be saved over the next four years. He was taking a huge gamble on economic recovery and growth.

Then it was off to Nottingham where David Cameron and Nick Clegg were doing a 'prime minister and deputy prime minister direct' event. I took twelve-year-old Maddie, although it wasn't one of those take your kid to work days. But it was half term and she got to briefly meet the prime minister. I only did one live two-way, Maddie was the sound recordist, that is the sound recordist let her hold the mic. Sky News was doing an Afghanistan day, so little else was getting on air. Sky News correspondents Alex Crawford and Stuart Ramsay were, once again, sending excellent reports from Afghanistan. Maddie had enjoyed meeting Cameron and Clegg and seeing how live TV worked.

The following Monday, I did lives from a Theresa May speech on terrorism at RUSI after which I was invited to lunch at the Chinese Embassy. I couldn't go. I had to sit through two hours of Danny Alexander, the Lib Dem chief secretary to the Treasury, giving evidence to the House of Commons Treasury Select Committee. Danny Alexander for two long, long hours! He was trying to justify the draconian cuts in the CSR two weeks earlier, and claimed the Lib Dems had protected essential public services for the most vulnerable in society. It wasn't so much dull as completely soporific.

We had our own little 'gate' at Westminster, 'Fartgate'. A certain ginger-haired senior Lib Dem was about to do a live in our small live studio at Millbank when flatulence got the better of him. It was a proper, unmistakeable fart with one buttock raised! That particular studio is tiny, just a chair, a camera, a microphone and a small speaker. Andy Burnham, who was next in, waved his hand in front of his nose and simply said, "Bloody hell"! The camera had been recording at the time so we had the images of Fartgate, but were absolutely forbidden by our management, on pain of death or at least dismissal, from releasing them anywhere. Several picture editors were trying to work out how they could get them in the public domain without being found out but eventually gave up and Danny Alexander's blushes were spared!

Andy Coulson, who was still the Downing Street director of communications, had been interviewed by the police about phone-hacking. It was one of those days of doing lives and packages every hour for fourteen hours, our lead story.

Next stop was China and South Korea. David Cameron was attending the G20 summit in Seoul with a visit to Beijing on the way. The long flight to Beijing was relatively painless. The prime minister gave us a full briefing on the plane. When we arrived in Beijing he was greeted by a red carpet and a full guard of honour.

I did a live phono as soon as we arrived even though it was the middle of the night back in the UK. We drove in David Cameron's convoy to, er, Tesco! This was strange as the Tesco seemed familiar but the shelves were almost entirely filled with rice and an astonishing variety of noodles. From there, we went to a magical six-hundred-year-old temple where the British Council was training social entrepreneurs. This was one of the few areas of old Beijing to have survived the city's redevelopment, narrow back streets away from the high rise buildings and hideous urban motorways of modern Beijing.

I had been to Beijing before, in the early 1980s. Back them, almost everyone wore a pyjama suit and rode bicycles. We too rode bicycles and many of them almost fell off theirs as they did a double take. Westerners on bicycles! Now, it was almost all multi-lane urban motorways, expensive cars and designer clothes.

The roads were closed for our convoy as we moved around the Chinese capital and lined with Chinese police shoulder to shoulder standing to attention. Thousands of them.

I did lives every hour from our hotel and then from our Beijing bureau in the very early hours of the morning UK time, and every half hour for the *Sunrise* programme. My final live was for the top of *Live at Five* and I left two as lives for 6 o'clock and *Sky News at Ten*. By this time I was a bit tired! After a ten-hour flight, I had been doing lives from 1am up to 5pm GMT. Of course, I was absolutely loving it. Our indispensable Chinese fixer, Sunny Ma, gave me a lift to the hotel at 2am local time for some well-earned sleep.

We headed off in convoy the next morning to visit the Great Wall of China. It did not disappoint. It was absolutely fantastic. I did a PTC, got a few words with David Cameron, and took a lot of photos. We visited a primary school where children in traditional costumes played music and sang for the British prime minister. Very sweet.

At Peking University, David Cameron delivered a mildly provocative speech in which he urged the Chinese to embrace political as well as economic freedom. I did lives before and after the speech which *Sunrise* took live. The *Sunrise* producer couldn't believe the university was called Peking University, surely it should be Beijing University, so I did my lives in front of a large sign, 'Peking University' to dispel any doubts. I did lives for three hours. The other correspondents were off to Tiananmen Square and the Great Hall of the People, basically for a bit of tourism, but I was lashed to the live point with our excellent and very hard-working cameraman Nathan Hale, who was such a joy to work with. Never any dramas. Sadly perhaps, I was far happier doing live two-ways and packaging the story than wandering around being a tourist.

We flew with the prime minister to Seoul and drove in convoy to the Intercontinental Hotel, part of the G20 conference complex. Producer Gary Honeyford and I worked exceptionally well together despite having very different temperaments. Gary's Irish blood pressure was suffering from the complexity of the G20 logistics, agreeing TV pools, and having rows with the BBC, whereas I was very laid back most of the time, until roused. But it worked. I would calm him down when he needed it, he would gee me up when I needed to spring into action which frequently involved telling the BBC team that no, they could not go first at every event.

We sent a package for *Live at Five*. We were nine hours ahead of London. I crawled into bed some time after 2am again. The next morning and a sit-down interview with David Cameron at the British Embassy. In London the previous night, students (and anarchists) from a demo against tuition fees had stormed Millbank Tower. So I asked him three questions on that, one on a Welfare White Paper which was about to be published, one on the G20 summit and one on human rights in China. I think you could call that a fairly wide-ranging interview. Sky News aired the lot. I did lives throwing to a Cameron grab on the G20 summit every hour. I also wrote a blog on the work of Save the Children who were urging the G20 leaders to do more to help the world's poorest.

The next day was the main day of the summit. We did live phonos and sent a track and a PTC for a package to be edited together in London before David Cameron's press conference at 4.30pm local time, early morning back in the UK. No one was able to conquer the technology to play it out live, but news agency APTN played it back to London and for the rest of the world as soon as it finished. We sent a fresh track and PTC, and Sky News in London had both the David Cameron and Barack Obama press conferences. We headed to the airport in the prime minister's convoy, sirens wailing. It really is the only way to travel!

The flight home was long, twelve hours. We had a quiz with George Osborne as quiz master. David Cameron came back for a chat, and I managed to get some half sleep stretched out across four seats. Most of the Fleet Street hacks stayed up drinking which was disturbingly noisy but also very funny. Stories were told, songs were sung.

The day after we got home, Aung San Suu Kyi was finally released from house arrest in Myanmar. Finally.

I was off to Normandy for two days' corporate media training at the fabulous Château de Romainville. The Château lacked the magic of the Manoir des Brumes but was still very splendid. Built in Anglo-Norman style, it had served as a French military hospital in the First World War and was put to the same use by the Germans in the second. The food, all Normandy-sourced, was spectacular and the wine cellar was available, stocked with Margaux!

Back at Westminster at the end of November for a Theresa May announcement on an immigration cap which I thought they had set far too low and was unrealistic, and so it proved. It also added to the narrative that immigration was somehow a bad thing when, in my view, the reverse was true, although there had to be some controls. I did lives all morning from Downing Street on that story and on North Korea which had launched a salvo of artillery shells at the South, provoking some dangerous and irresponsible speculation about the prospect of a war. At midday, I also had to include the announcement of the date of the wedding of Prince William and Kate Middleton. It was to be the following April and there would be a national holiday.

Howard Flight, no longer a Conservative MP but about to be elevated to the House of Lords, put his size tens in it again at the end of November. I had been covering a David Cameron speech on happiness and well-being (really!) and doing lives as students demonstrated yet again against tuition fees when we got word of Flight's outburst. He wanted child benefit abolished to, "Discourage the middle-class from breeding". But added that, "For those on benefits there is every incentive". You could not make it up! I got reaction from David Cameron, who was suitably appalled, and gave it to Adam who was doing the lives.

On December 1st there was a slight flurry of excitement when Wikileaks revealed that Bank of England Governor Mervyn King had criticised David Cameron and George Osborne before the election. It was hardly earth-shattering. He had described them as inexperienced and obsessed with winning the election. Tell us something we didn't already know!

England failed to win its bid to host the 2018 World Cup. It would be held in Russia. Twitter went ballistic with accusations of FIFA corruption. A corrupt organisation had given the World Cup to a corrupt state! It later emerged that, despite David Cameron, Prince William and David Beckham giving a very good presentation and despite England having had the best technical and commercial bid, we had received just two votes, and one of those had been our own. So, years of work and millions of pounds had translated into just one vote.

Vince Cable opened the House of Commons debate on students' tuition fees, leading for the government as students marched outside accusing the Lib Dems of betrayal. The government won the debate by 21 votes. I had predicted a majority of 25 so I was pretty close. Home Secretary Theresa May reported back on the policing of the student tuition fees demonstrations. I did lives on that and on the House of Lords debating student tuition fees, and we took an Ed Miliband press conference live.

Education Secretary Michael Gove did a U-turn on school sports funding. I did a couple of lives on that and more from Downing Street when a Trade Union delegation led by Brendan Barber had a meeting with David

Cameron, the first such meeting with a Conservative prime minister in decades.

Vince Cable was the victim of a *Telegraph* sting and I reported it live. Talking to an undercover *Daily Telegraph* reporter posing as a Lib Dem supporter, Vince had described the coalition Cabinet as being 'at war', saying he might use his 'nuclear weapon' and resign from the Cabinet, bringing down the coalition government. It felt like daft, vain chest-beating. I was live later that day in Downing Street when the Cabinet met. Oh to have been a fly on that wall!

George Osborne came out with a homophobic comment at Treasury questions just before Christmas. When gay Labour MP Chris Bryant suggested he should be more sensitive about the effect of government spending cuts and, in the Christmas spirit, to try to act more like Prince Charming, Osborne replied, "At least I'm not the Pantomime Dame"! There was some laughter among MPs, but there were far more gasps of horror.

On a quiet news day, in December, head of news John Ryley asked our producers, Clare Parry and Gary Honeyford, to phone all 57 Lib Dem MPs to ask them if they still supported the coalition. Of course, all 39 who replied said they did. Turkeys do not vote for Christmas.

CHAPTER 9

2011: Cuts, Cuts and More Cuts. AV Referendum. The Arab Spring. Fukushima. Bin Laden. A Day Trip to Benghazi. More Phone-hacking. South Africa and Nigeria. Moscow Again

On January 4th the VAT rate went up to 20%. I did lives without revealing that I personally regarded the increase as iniquitous. Ed Miliband had been leader for one hundred days. How was he doing? I answered as objectively as I could, not brilliantly but not terribly either, he was still growing into the job. He was certainly improving at PMQs.

Barnsley Central Labour MP Eric Illsley was to be charged with three counts of false accounting. He was sentenced to twelve months in February. That same day, I was also doing lives on bankers' bonuses yet again. The pantomime villains of 2011 were still the fat cat bankers and those MPs who had over-claimed their expenses. The guilty MPs, and there were too many of them, had seriously damaged our democracy. So many people were now saying they're all the same, all bent, all in it just for themselves. This wasn't true, I knew many honest, hard-working MPs whose motivation was genuinely to make the country better but they were drowning in the waves of public disillusion.

I did lives on a David Cameron speech ahead of a new NHS bill, and when the Iraq inquiry resumed. This became a lot more interesting when the inquiry saw a written statement by Attorney General Lord Goldsmith advising Tony Blair that an invasion of Iraq would be illegal without a second UN resolution just three days before Blair had told MPs the exact opposite in January 2003. Tony Blair gave evidence to the inquiry for the second time three days later. They didn't lay a glove on him despite the Goldsmith revelation. Andy Coulson resigned as Number Ten director of communications the same day, which took Blair off the air, no doubt to his relief. Coulson was a much bigger story. I got this as a breaking news line from a Downing Street insider.

The economy was tanking again. Figures released at the end of January revealed that GDP had shrunk in the last quarter of 2010 by 0.5%. It had been expected to grow by a similar amount. Had growth stalled or was this just a glitch? The government blamed the bad weather in December. I wrote a blog about Tory MP Dr Liam Fox who had responded to an 'is there a doctor on board' announcement on a flight from Turkey. It had turned out to be nothing serious.

Unrest was growing in Egypt following the fall of the government in Tunisia. February 1st saw the 'March of a Million' in Cairo's Tahrir Square and in other Egyptian cities. This had echoes of 1989 and the domino effect after the fall of the Berlin Wall. Despite the army being on the streets, it felt like President Hosni Mubarak was finally on his way out. It wasn't yet being called the Arab Spring.

Liverpool signed Andy Carroll from Newcastle United for £35 million which was a record but only for a few minutes, just until Chelsea signed Fernando Torres from Liverpool for £50 million. This was good for Liverpool, good for Chelsea, but not so much for Newcastle who had just sold their best player. I was asked to do a live on the increasingly ludicrous sums being paid for footballers but the request was quickly rescinded. This wasn't politics it was sport, and the sports news team at Sky News were understandably protective of their patch.

On February 2nd, Jack Straw was the final witness at the Iraq inquiry. It was his third appearance. PMQs that day was dominated by Egypt. There was none of the usual Punch and Judy politics. In Cairo, Mubarak-supporting thugs had provoked violence at otherwise peaceful demonstrations. It was very ugly. I tweeted live on a split TV screen on all three stories that day, the Iraq inquiry, PMQs and the violence in Cairo.

I had been doing early shifts, starting at 5am, with Sophy Ridge shadowing before taking over the dreaded early shift. She would go on to do an excellent job and I would go back to working more civilised hours. Our politics executive producer Jonathan Levy gave me a very fine batch-numbered bottle of Aberlour malt for working nearly two months of early shifts 'without complaining once', which was very kind of him.

Sir Gus O'Donnell produced his report on Lockerbie and the release of al-Megrahi which concluded that the British government had not put pressure on or lobbied the Scottish government but had facilitated the Libyan government's dealings with Holyrood to get Megrahi released early on compassionate grounds. I did lives and packaged the lead story for *Sky News at Ten*.

Ed Balls had his first Treasury questions against George Osborne the next day. I watched the theatre from the press gallery, as I often did for PMQs. George Osborne suddenly announced a bank levy, forcing the banks to cough up an extra £800 million over the next twelve months. We had our lead story, which I packaged for *Sky News at Ten*, on how the government was finally trying to bring the banks to heel.

At PMQs the next day, David Cameron was getting very red-faced and hot under the collar. Ed Miliband had the best line. "The prime minister should not get so angry. It will cloud his judgement." Pause. "He's not the first prime minister I've said that to!" Cue uproar in the House. I wonder if Gordon Brown was amused? Or not?

Ed Balls was particularly adept at annoying the new prime minister. He knew David Cameron had a temper and it was great spectator sport as Cameron, red-faced, would tell Balls to "Shut up" or to "Stop waving your stupid hand".

The next day was dominated by two stories. I did lives on both. MPs voted to deny prisoners the vote, overwhelmingly by 243 votes to just 22 with Cabinet ministers and the Shadow Cabinet abstaining. The motion was jointly introduced by Conservative David Davis and Labour's Jack Straw, which was a first! I interviewed both afterwards and John Hirst, a prisoner who had successfully taken his case to the European Court of Human Rights, and packaged the story for *Sky News at Ten*. In Egypt, Mubarak was showing signs of stepping down. I was live when he announced at 4 o'clock that he would be making a statement on television that evening. There was no other news until he did so, forty-five minutes later than expected. He said he had no intention of resigning. It was astonishing.

The next day he was gone. After nearly three weeks of protests, there were jubilant scenes. Egyptians were dancing in the streets. I would love to have been back in Cairo rather than reporting this historic moment from London, but their excitement glowed through the TV screen.

Before going to New York, I did a story about Larry the new Downing Street cat. We spent over an hour at Number Ten. Larry would not sit on my lap or let me hold him long enough to do a PTC. Nor would he let the BBC or ITN correspondents anywhere near him. So much for my affinity with animals! I got a couple of scratches which I tweeted to general amusement back at our Westminster newsroom. Eventually, I got a reasonable PTC. This cat did not like TV cameras! I cut a jolly package which ran all evening and provided *Sky News at Ten* with a classic 'And Finally'.

Maddie, aged 12, was obsessed with Lady Gaga. I had already taken her to see Gaga four times in London, including at Twickenham Stadium. We spent five days in New York, her first time. At the Lady Gaga concert at Madison Square Garden, she was probably the youngest person there, I was certainly the oldest. New York had become so clean and safe, 'Disney New York' to some New Yorkers. Personally, I had found it too violent and threatening in the past. The night before the concert it had snowed heavily. Central Park was a veritable winter wonderland.

At Sky News Westminster they anointed me 'Dad of the year' for taking my daughter all the way to New York to see her favourite pop star.

"My Dad never did that for me," they'd say.

"Nor did mine," I'd reply.

Back at work at the end of February and lives at the Foreign Office on Libya, where protests against Colonel Gaddafi's regime had deteriorated into a civil war. The Foreign Office was being criticised for being too slow to respond to what was becoming the Arab Spring. Rebels held the cities of Benghazi, Tobruk and Misrata. Gaddafi still controlled Tripoli. In Libya, Sky News correspondent Alex Crawford and her team, Martin Smith and Tim Miller, were doing incredible and very brave work and were deservedly showered with awards afterwards.

In early March, I was live at the London School of Economics when Sir Howard Davis resigned as director over donations from Libya. Labour held Barnsley Central in the by-election triggered by the departure of Eric Illsley. Dan Jarvis held the seat for Labour with an increased majority. The Lib Dems came an embarrassing sixth, behind the Conservatives, UKIP and even the BNP and an independent. Their candidate, Dominic Carman, son of the famous barrister George Carman QC, received barely a thousand votes. They had been second in 2010. UKIP took second place this time. It felt like a barometer pointing to what was to come, unbelievable as that seemed at the time.

William Hague had to make a statement to the House explaining a botched diplomatic/SAS operation in Eastern Libya which Sir Menzies Campbell described as, "Ill-conceived, poorly-planned and embarrassingly executed". Fortunately for them, they were captured by rebels and flown home. Not the regiment's finest hour. I learnt a few weeks later from an SAS insider that a specialist military team, including some Hungarians who were apparently leaders in the field, had been searching for WMD to see if Gaddafi still had chemical weapons. By way of light relief and trivia, Number Ten's new director of communications Craig Oliver had arrived late in Downing Street that day and missed the prime minister's convoy to Derby, much to our amusement if not his.

I was live at a press conference with Foreign Secretary William Hague and Palestinian President Mahmoud Abbas, on Libya of course. I did more lives later when we had eyewitnesses claiming that Gaddafi's forces had unleashed a tank bombardment on the town of Zawiya. This was the random killing of innocent civilians. In my lives I said this was a potential game-changer, but was it? The international response was weak, at least initially.

In Japan, the Fukushima nuclear reactor, damaged in a tsunami, was leaking radiation. There had been several fires and three explosions as the reactors overheated and widespread radioactive contamination. It was the worst nuclear disaster since Chernobyl in 1986. The whole world was terrified. At the House of Commons Energy Select Committee, Lib Dem Cabinet minister Chris Huhne gave evidence on what, if any, lessons could be learnt by the UK. The questions for us, as political correspondents, were to try to explain if our nuclear power stations were safe. Or not.

Later that day, I broke the text of a UK-Lebanon sponsored UN resolution to impose a no-fly zone over Libya. Was it too little too late? Gaddafi's forces were advancing on Benghazi. The BBC were nearly half an hour behind us with the story. Five days later I was live in Downing Street every hour when the no-fly zone was imposed.

After supporting the Higher Command Staff Course at the UK Defence Academy in Shrivenham once again, which this time included a visit by the Duke of Edinburgh looking remarkably sprightly at the age of eighty-nine and commando night, the Royal Marines' party which invariably got very messy and descended into total mayhem, I was off to Pakistan with the prime minister.

En route to Pakistan we visited the Gioia del Colle Italian air force base where David Cameron spent two hours with RAF Tornado and Typhoon fighter pilots. Our Sky News colleague Joey Jones had got into a bit of a mess after reporting something someone had told him off the record. When David Cameron chatted to us on the flight to Italy, he said, "This is off the record. Joey Jones isn't here, is he?" This was said without a trace of humour. The prime minister was clearly very annoyed.

We landed in Islamabad at 6.30am (2.30am in the UK) and drove in convoy to the diplomatic compound. David Cameron and Pakistan's Prime Minister Yousaf Raza Gillani held a joint press conference. I got the first question. In his opening statement, Gillani had said that in relations with Britain, "The sky's the limit".

Cue David Cameron. "You just said the sky's the limit, and the first question is from the man from Sky."

I did lives after David Cameron made a speech at a technical university and did a one-to-one interview with him at the British ambassador's residence. Waiting for our flight home, Chief of the Defence Staff General Sir David Richards chatted to the assembled hacks. He was terribly indiscreet. He said he'd been watching Sky News and thought my colleague Sam Kiley, who was risking life and limb on the road to Benghazi, was passing on military advice to the rebels, for example, to form a defensive line rather than simply fleeing in panic. He should have stopped there (actually he should never have started), but he took questions. On Libya, he said, "We should call victory while we're ahead", having averted a potential massacre in Benghazi.

The hacks were scribbling away furiously. I asked him about Libyan WMD. He said there was a WMD dump in the desert which was under constant surveillance. "The advice is not to hit it unless you have to." He also categorically denied that there were any British special forces in Libya. Surely this was untrue?

Afterwards, Downing Street press officer, Ben Saoul, declared it all 'off the record' without really understanding what that means. The assembled hacks resolved to use it only 'to inform their journalism' and would only use any of it if they got it confirmed by other sources. I urged them not to use the comments about Sam Kiley at all, it could possibly put his life in danger. I thought the rest should be passed on to defence or other correspondents. Patrick Wintour of the *Guardian*, who was the lobby chairman, agreed.

So, we had another row with Downing Street about being 'off the record'. On the flight home, David Cameron expressed his deep displeasure that the *Telegraph* was splashing the next day on a throwaway line, a joke during a Q&A about Kashmir, when he had said that Britain's colonial past was responsible for "all the world's ills".

The main highlights of the trip were a British pledge to provide another £650 million for education in Pakistan, which provoked questions about Madrasas and the need for more money to be spent on schools and teachers at home, and the enhanced sharing of anti-terrorism technology. But would Pakistani intelligence leak it to the Taliban? Sir John Sawers, head of the Secret Intelligence Service, MI6, was also on the trip. He didn't talk to us at all. I cannot for the life of me imagine why not!

After a chat with head of politics Jonathan Levy, we decided to give the general's comments to fellow correspondent Niall Paterson, though not the General's remarks about Sam Kiley. The source would have been too obvious had I reported them myself.

The campaign for the AV referendum was launched in mid-April. I did interviews with David Cameron, John Reid, Ed Miliband and Vince Cable but not Nick Clegg, who was out campaigning. We got him later but he adamantly would not campaign alongside Ed Miliband even though they were on the same side, in this at least. The No campaign's main argument seemed to be that an Alternative Vote system was too complicated. They weren't even trying to argue that first past the post is fairer and more representative of how people actually vote, just that it added a needless layer of complexity. I thought, and said on air at the time, that they appeared to regard the voters as too thick to understand the AV system.

Other lives that same day included covering the tuition fees row, David Cameron threatening a veto were Gordon Brown to stand as a candidate to lead the IMF, and on Libya where the British army was to send a team of officers to advise the rebels (an improvement on being advised by our colleague Sam Kiley!).

David Cameron criticised judges for making up privacy law on the hoof. There had been several 'super injunctions' recently, preventing the newspapers from printing salacious stories about footballer Ryan Giggs, actor Hugh Bonneville and others. Parliament, not judges, makes the laws was the thrust of his argument, as I explained in my live two-ways. Defence Secretary Liam Fox and CDS General Sir David Richards went to Washington for talks on Libya. I received a briefing so I could do lives on what they would be saying to the Americans.

Libya was still dominating the news, but so too was Syria where Assad was attempting to crush the Arab Spring uprising by force. His tanks and soldiers were slaughtering civilians. I did lives when Foreign Secretary William Hague made a statement in the House condemning the regime's violence in Syria. Oh, and there were daft Royal wedding stories, previewing 'the big day'. Believe it or not, I had to do a live and write a blog on what the prime minister would be wearing. A morning suit, if anyone cared. And Andrew Marr was finally outed, though only initially on Twitter, for having an affair with Alice Miles of *The Times*. From the carnage in Libya and Syria to a Royal wedding to Westminster tittle-tattle, April was a strange month.

US Special Forces finally found and killed Osama bin Laden. He hadn't been hiding in a cave after all, but was in Abbottabad near Islamabad, a town that was home to Pakistan's military academy. It seemed almost inconceivable that Pakistani intelligence hadn't known he was there. I did lives in Downing Street after breaking the line that COBRA was meeting in the wake of the successful American operation.

There were no exit polls when the polls closed on the AV referendum. A YouGov opinion poll found far too many people who didn't fully understand what they were voting for, or against. The referendum was held on the same day as local council elections. I was in Leicester for a parliamentary by-election to interview Labour's Jonathan Ashworth who won the Leicester South seat with an increased majority after Peter Soulsby had resigned to stand as a candidate for Mayor of Leicester. In Scotland, there was an SNP majority for the first time, paving the way for an independence referendum.

The Lib Dems were massacred, losing half their councils including Liverpool, Sheffield, Bristol and Newcastle and suffering a total meltdown in Manchester and elsewhere. Nick Clegg once said that Angela Merkel had warned him that the junior partner in coalition governments always did badly at the next election. It was happening, and far worse was to follow in 2015. The Conservatives had actually gained 60 council seats, while the Lib Dems had lost 842, almost all of them to Labour. After a day of lives mulling over these election results including a live interview with Lib Dem Simon Hughes, I broke the news that Pauline Neville-Jones was standing down as minister of state for Security and Counter Terrorism at her own request. Nick Clegg gave a speech on 'muscular Liberalism'.

In Downing Street, I interviewed Formula One racing drivers, Lewis Hamilton and Jenson Button, after they had had a meeting with the prime minister. It was a UN road safety day. Although the BBC had actually set up the interviews they stood to one side as I interviewed the two drivers. Excellent!

I was live at the High Court when the government sought a contempt of court order against the coverage by the *Sun* and the *Mirror* of innocent landlord Christopher Jeffries following the murder of Joanna Yates in Bristol. Jeffries was being persecuted by the media, and not only by the *Sun* and the *Mirror*. It was a short hearing and the order was granted. I was live with the decision well ahead of the BBC who hadn't seemed to be in the game lately. The main political story that day was the suspension of David Laws from the House of Commons for seven days. It was thought he might return to the Cabinet but not for a while. I wrote a sympathetic blog, 'Imagine you're David Laws'. I thought he had been treated shabbily and without compassion. He had not benefited financially but had simply wanted to keep his sexuality private.

On a busy day in mid-May I sat through nearly two hours of Nick Clegg giving evidence to the House of Commons Constitution Committee, which was not uninteresting but not strong enough to make the news. I was supposed to do a live on David Laws but Joey Jones 'broke' the line that Laws was being investigated by the police. He wasn't. I finally got my teeth into a good story after Ken Clarke, in a radio interview, differentiated between 'serious' rapes and others (apparently not serious!). He spent the rest of the day correcting himself.

On the day that the *Sun*'s appeal against the contempt order on privacy was being heard in the High Court, John Whittingdale tabled an emergency question after Lib Dem MP John Hemmings named Ryan Giggs in the House of Commons. That married Ryan Giggs had been having an affair was the worst kept secret in the world. We took legal advice on whether or not we could also name him without the cover of Parliamentary privilege. We might possibly be in contempt, but could argue qualified privilege. His name was already out there thanks to John Hemmings. We decided to go for it, and I broke the story.

President Obama came for a two-day visit. The first day, when he was doing mostly ceremonial duties wearing his Head of State hat, was overshadowed (excuse the pun) by another cloud of volcanic ash from Iceland. All Scottish airports and several in the north of England were closed, but it wasn't anywhere near as serious as the previous year.

On his second day, Barack Obama was wearing his Head of Government hat and doing the politics. I was live in Downing Street, some of them very long lives as his convoy drove up to the door of Number Ten. The armour plating on Cadillac One, also known as 'The Beast', the presidential car, was something to behold. It looked like it could resist a tank round. A Number Ten press officer stepped out into Downing Street. There would be two British questions at the Cameron-Obama press conference later that day and the three broadcasters had to draw lots. We won, so did the BBC. ITN lost. Just before the press conference at Lancaster House, Downing Street Director of Communications Craig Oliver, a former journalist at both ITN and the BBC, told me that they would be getting the two questions. His spurious argument was that the questions should be asked by political editors and the BBC and ITN had sent theirs. I thought this was outrageous. We, Sky News, would decide who we sent to a press conference, not Craig Oliver thank you very much! Head of politics Jonathan Levy was as furious as I was and was on the phone trying to get Oliver's decision reversed, and later sent a formal letter of complaint.

Still, even without asking a question, it was great to be there, in the garden at Lancaster House, in the front row just a few feet from Obama. Later, I was in Westminster Hall when Barack Obama addressed both Houses of Parliament, following in the footsteps of the Pope and Nelson Mandela. He delivered a fine speech, basically saying nice things about the British. He received several standing ovations. The MPs and peers were like fans with a rock star, which in political terms is what he was.

After Obama's visit to London, I was off to Deauville in the prime minister's aircraft for a G8 summit. Ratko Mladić was arrested in Serbia. At last! Sixteen years after Srebrenica and Sarajevo. I did a pool interview with David Cameron on the arrest of Mladić and lives for the rest of the evening. Adam did the early lives the next morning off the back of a package I had sent the night before for *Sunrise*. I took over the live spot for five hours before a David Cameron press conference, including talking about Russia. Moscow had now also decided that Gaddafi must go. David Cameron gave me the first question at the press conference, so honour (and normal service!) was restored after the nonsense over the Cameron-Obama press conference in London. I asked a double-header about Libya and Sharon Shoesmith who had won a High Court appeal that she had been unfairly dismissed as Head of Child Services in Haringey. Technically correct presumably, but really: Had she no shame?

On the last day of May, after a quiet start, I worked on three stories. I got a tip off that Chris Huhne's expenses were to be investigated by the Electoral Commission and broke the story. I did a quick live on FIFA corruption before returning to Ratko Mladić who had been extradited from Belgrade to The Hague to face a war crimes trial. It had taken the Serbian government just five days since his arrest to get shot of him. I packaged our lead story.

June began with a speech by the CGS, the head of the army, General Sir Peter Wall at RUSI. He remembered that I had media trained him many years earlier, and he remembered the lessons from that media training! He called for an increase on defence spending once the economy recovered. He also said that Afghanistan could not be won militarily, there had to be a political solution. This had now become the accepted view which even Washington seemed to accept. I did a couple of lives before being squeezed out by FIFA which had re-elected Sepp Blatter as its President unopposed. It was utter nonsense. The 'FIFA Congress' looked ridiculous, bloated and North Korean. I switched in the evening to covering care for the elderly and the company Southern Cross, the country's largest operator of care homes, which was in deep financial trouble.

The following weekend I had a day trip to Benghazi! It was a facility with Foreign Secretary William Hague and International Development Secretary Andrew Mitchell, just me and cameraman Richie Mockler, with a reporter from *The Times* and another from the *Telegraph*, a small group. The mission was to get a television exclusive interview with the Foreign Secretary in Libya. We flew from RAF Northolt on the Queen's flight. William sat in the Queen's chair, much to his amusement and ours. When we arrived there was mayhem. We were greeted and surrounded by dozens of Libyan rebel 'security', sporting bandoliers of cartridges, dressed in black and all wearing sunglasses. They all thought they were Rambo! Over-zealous, just a little. Fortunately, we travelled in a convoy of four Toyota Land Cruisers driven by former British soldiers who were actually providing our security.

The carloads of Rambos kept getting in the way! When we arrived for a visit to a hospital, we were eight cars behind William Hague's car. It was impossible even for Richie, a former Royal Marine, to get the arrival shot. We made sure we were in pole position when he went to meet the Libyan rebel leadership, the National Transitional Council. William Hague was mobbed by well-wishers in Freedom Square. Our phones weren't working, nor was our sat phone. We went to the EBU (European Broadcasting Union) live point, in a hotel, to feed our material. Sky News isn't a member of the EBU but of its rival organisation, ENEX. Fortunately, I knew the EBU coordinator, Olivier, from my days at ITN, so we fed pictures from his satellite dish and he found us a working sat phone so I could do live phonos into Sky News as we travelled around Benghazi.

After William Hague held a press conference, we negotiated doing our one-to-one interview. It had been set up as a sit-down interview in a hotel room. It could have been anywhere, so I took us outside with a mosque as a backdrop. Our security team was twitchy and thought the location was too exposed, but William was completely relaxed about it.

We had no time to feed our interview, we were rushed back to the airport for the flight home. We would have to do it the old fashioned way and hand carry it back. On the way home when we stopped to refuel in Malta, as we had done on the way out, I did a live phono and sent a track, only phone quality, with a Benghazi sign-off. From the toilet of an aircraft parked up for refuelling in Malta!

We landed back in Northolt just after midnight. The foreign desk was very happy. My package had been running and would continue to run as our lead story all night, despite the poor phone quality of my voice track.

The Hague in Benghazi interview ran all the next day. It had been a long, sometimes frustrating but exhilarating day. I really missed covering news from difficult foreign places where it was a struggle to get anything on air. I missed the mud on my boots. It amused me when people asked me what I'd done at the weekend and I replied that I'd been on a day trip to Benghazi!

After the exciting madness of Benghazi it was back to regular Westminster politics. I did lives the following Monday on the IMF supporting George Osborne's deficit-reduction measures, and the growth forecast for the year being reduced from 2% to 1.5%, as well as previewing a David Cameron speech the next day on the NHS.

Cameron's speech started late so I chatted to Adam live on air in our Westminster studio after getting some lines from the speech at the lobby briefing. In the afternoon, I did lives after a White House statement on Libya, Syria and Yemen. I watched an excellent BBC documentary that evening on children living below the poverty line. Clever, articulate children with appalling parents. After all those years of a Labour government and Gordon Brown's commitment to tackling child poverty, a commitment that continues to this day, the problem was actually getting worse.

Foreign Secretary William Hague held a press conference with the South African foreign minister at Lancaster House. I was there to ask about Libya and Syria, but also about Tony Blair who had said that the EU needed greater integration and an elected president. Who, we wondered, could he possibly have in mind?

The strike by teachers and civil servants on June 30th kept me busy doing lives all day as it had done for several previous days as talks to avert the strike faltered, although I'd managed to get away for a long weekend in Barcelona.

After a week supporting the RCDS strategy exercise in early July, the news desk phoned me at 5.30 on a Saturday morning. "Are you OK for your live at six?" I had no idea I was supposed to be working that day! These things sometimes happen. I scrambled in and was live at 6.30 and at the top of every hour for the rest of the morning on a familiar story, phone-hacking by the *News of the World* when Andy Coulson was the editor.

Two days later we played Hunt the Gordon! Brown had told the *Guardian* that both the *Sun* and *The Sunday Times* had hacked his bank records and the medical records of his son Fraser, who had cystic fibrosis. He was understandably upset and very angry. But that day he was like the Scarlet Pimpernel, there was no sign of him anywhere.

David Cameron expressed his sympathy for Gordon Brown the next day in Cardiff, where the Cabinet was meeting on one of its awaydays. I did lives and a short interview with the prime minister in which he said his heart went out to Gordon Brown and that there would be a fresh police investigation and a judge-led inquiry to get to the bottom of the whole phone-hacking affair. We were visiting the Royal Mint in Llantrisant, about twenty miles from Cardiff. Before the Cabinet met, David Cameron gave a short speech about Wales where he said more private sector investment was needed with less reliance on the public sector. His announcement of a judge-led phone-hacking inquiry was new and had made my day trip to Cardiff worth the effort. He announced it formally in the House of Commons the next day.

We were off next to a far more exotic location, Africa. Specifically, South Africa and Nigeria. Cameraman Phil Hooper and I travelled on the prime minister's Virgin charter. David Cameron came back for a long chat about UK-South Africa relations, and I managed to get a few hours' restless sleep on the ten-hour flight.

Dawn in Johannesburg and I did two live phonos before we drove in convoy to the historic Union Buildings in Pretoria for a press conference with David Cameron and South African President Jacob Zuma. Cameron and Zuma, the prime minister and the president, had to hang around while the British Business Delegation, Vodafone, Diaggio, Waitrose and the increasingly infamous Barclay's Group Chief Executive Bob Diamond among them, posed for photographs!

In Johannesburg, Cameron visited a football academy (sponsored by Spurs!) and the apartheid museum at Liliesleaf farm, once an ANC safe house, to meet Archbishop Desmond Tutu. It was Nelson Mandela's ninety-third birthday. I did lives from the Johannesburg stock exchange where David Cameron sat on a panel for a Q&A. We sent a track, rushes and a PTC to be edited back in London.

The trip was overshadowed by the domestic phone-hacking scandal. John Yates of the Yard resigned and we got the terrible news that *News of the World* whistle-blower Sean Hoare had been found dead at his home in Watford. On the six-hour flight to Lagos I did a live phono to break the news that this Africa trip would be truncated. David Cameron would fly back to make a statement to the House. From Nigeria, the plan had been to visit Rwanda and South Sudan, the world's newest country. From a personal point of view, this was disappointing.

We arrived in Lagos in the dark and drove in convoy to our hotel. There was little to see. After a short sleep, I did lives early the next morning. Nigeria was on BST so there was no time difference, which was good news for our return home. We drove in convoy to Lagos Business School where David Cameron made a speech on Africa which was very well received. Sky News couldn't take it live because the sound quality, from Nigerian TV, was so poor. At the presidential palace, David Cameron held a joint press conference with Nigeria's president, the splendidly named Goodluck Jonathan. I got the first question, but Sky News was laser-focused on the phone-hacking scandal.

As well as John Yates, the Metropolitan Police Commissioner Paul Stephenson had also resigned. This was a big enough story in itself, but the Culture, Media and Sport House of Commons select committee was hearing evidence from Rupert and James Murdoch, followed by former *News of the World* editor Rebekah Brooks, who had resigned as chief executive of News International a few days earlier. These were electrifying moments, surpassed only by the evidence to the Leveson Inquiry the following year. Meanwhile, senior Metropolitan police officers were being grilled by the Home Affairs select committee.

We drove fast in our convoy to the airport. Lagos flashed by, dirt poor markets, fishing villages. We took off early. I chatted with International Development Secretary Andrew Mitchell. David Cameron was busy writing the statement he would deliver to the Commons the next day. It had been a good if drastically shortened trip. David Cameron insisted that Africa is very important to the UK and it was vital that we fulfilled our commitments to Africa, but there was only one story and it was happening in Westminster. This had been very distracting and he no doubt felt that he should perhaps have stayed in London. We were certainly getting back as quickly as possible.

On the flight home, we were briefed about an exchange of emails between Yates of the Yard and David Cameron's chief of staff, Ed Llewellyn. They had been described by both Yates himself and by Cabinet secretary Sir Gus O'Donnell as perfectly proper, but as soon as we landed, our Westminster producer Gary Honeyford was on the phone. Sky News was very excited about the emails and wanted a live phono from me immediately (that's immediately as in five minutes ago!). I did it for the top of *Sky News at Ten* from the Royal Suite at Heathrow. What they really wanted to know was whether or not David Cameron had seen the testimony of the Murdochs. I answered that and talked about the emails and the statement the prime minister would be making in the House the next day.

I was doing lives on the increasingly convoluted phone-hacking scandal. Colin Myler and Tom Crone of the *News of the World* were claiming that James Murdoch had known about phone-hacking, which was not what he had told the CMS select committee. Suddenly, there was only one story. A lunatic gunman had murdered students at a summer camp on an island near Oslo. I was on standby to go live, twice, but was dropped for two live press conferences, first with Norwegian Prime Minister Jens Stoltenberg and later with Oslo's police chief.

More details emerged the next day on the Norway massacre which Sky News was covering wall-to-wall. More than sixty students had been shot dead at a Workers Youth League Summer camp on the island of Utøya. We saw the first images of the killer, Anders Breivik. He didn't look like al-Qaeda, more like a neo-Nazi. And so it turned out when the thirty-two-year-old right-wing extremist was finally arrested on the island. Eight more people had been killed and two hundred injured when he had earlier detonated a car bomb outside the prime minister's office in Oslo.

The only other story that day was the shocking and very sad news that singer Amy Winehouse had died. She was only 27, the same age as Jimi Hendrix, Janis Joplin, Jim Morrison of The Doors and Kurt Cobain of Nirvana had been when they had died.

David Cameron was accused of sexism when he told Labour front bencher Angela Eagle to 'calm down dear' during a Commons row over NHS reform. Shadow Chancellor Ed Balls began gesticulating at the prime minister, which he liked to do to wind him up, and demanded an apology. Downing Street dismissed it as 'a humorous remark', but it will probably form part of David Cameron's legacy, along with losing the Brexit referendum and promptly resigning.

David Cameron was also to get exposed by a newspaper, for cycling to work followed by a chauffeured car carrying his suit, shoes and papers. He was trying to look 'green'. It was even more embarrassing than when he told an audience that he supported West Ham. He was supposedly an Aston Villa fan. He tried to explain this away by saying he had got confused because both teams wore the same colour shirts! He was, like Tony Blair before him, trying to be 'normal' and bloke-ish, a lover of football. Gordon Brown's love of football was genuine, but The Arctic Monkeys? Really? They really shouldn't do it. People instinctively know when politicians are faking it.

In mid-August, there were riots and looting in London, Birmingham, Liverpool, Nottingham and Bristol. David Cameron had cut short his holiday to chair a COBRA meeting. The House of Commons was recalled for an emergency debate, which I covered live. I was still doing lives on the same story days later when both David Cameron and Ed Miliband gave speeches on the riots and Theresa May chaired a ministerial meeting at the Home Office.

August was proving to be unusually busy in Westminster. On a not untypical day, August 17th, I did lives on the recent riots and proposals for tougher sentencing, then on breaking news that the CPS had asked Essex police to further investigate Lib Dem Cabinet minister Chris Huhne. Back in May, his estranged wife Vicky Pryce claimed that he had pressured her into taking his driving licence penalty points. He had denied allegations of perverting the course of justice. After that, more lives on stricter prison sentencing, magistrates having so far dealt with more than a thousand cases following the riots, and then switching to A level results expected the next day.

It did not end well for Chris Huhne who had to endure two years of unfavourable media coverage while the affair played out. In February 2012 both Huhne and Pryce were charged and he resigned from the Cabinet. The legal arguments dragged on until February 2013 when Chris Huhne pleaded guilty and resigned his parliamentary seat. A month later, they were both sentenced to eight months in prison. The Lib Dems held on to his Eastleigh seat in the subsequent by-election but the Conservatives took it in the Lib Dem wipe out of 2015.

The next day, David Cameron, Angela Merkel and Nicolas Sarkozy issued a joint statement on Syria announcing tougher EU sanctions and saying that Assad had to go. At the time, as I said in my lives, Assad's days seemed numbered, but he somehow stayed in power.

Private Investigator Glenn Mulcaire, who had been sentenced to six months back in 2007 for illegal phone-hacking on behalf of the *News of the World*, was suing his former employer. I did lives on that and broke the line that he was suing News International for his legal fees which they were no longer paying. In the phone-hacking trial which ended after eight months, Mulcaire was sentenced to another six months, suspended for a year. Andy Coulson was sentenced to eighteen months. Rebekah Brooks was acquitted of all charges. She had been on holiday and unaware of the most scandalous of the phone-hacking cases when the *News of the World* had hacked the voicemail of missing thirteen-year-old schoolgirl, Milly Dowler, who was later found murdered. A piece of low life scum called Levi Bellfield had killed her and two other girls. He was given two whole life orders, so he will never be released. He will die in prison. Good.

In early September, I did lives on why military action against Syria was considered logistically impossible, and on documents found in the office of the former Libyan Intelligence chief Moussa Koussa in Tripoli which compromised both MI6 and the CIA, suggesting that both had colluded in 'rendering' terrorist suspects to third countries, in this case Libya.

Alistair Darling's memoir, *Back from the Brink*, was published, which we had expected to be dull. It wasn't. He claimed that the Brown government had been dysfunctional, there was an atmosphere of 'chaos and crisis'. I was asked in my lives why he hadn't resigned. He'd answered that question in his book, saying he had stayed on as Chancellor out of loyalty and because he hadn't wanted to damage the Labour Party.

A few days after the discovery of the Moussa Koussa documents in Tripoli, I was reporting that they would be referred to the Gibson inquiry. The former Intelligence Services Commissioner Sir Peter Gibson was investigating the allegation that MI6 was complicit in 'extraordinary rendition' and, therefore, in the torture of prisoners.

After three years of investigation, Sir William Gage's inquiry reported on the death in British custody in Iraq of Baha Mousa in 2003. As reported earlier in this book, the inquiry concluded that he had been hooded and beaten, starved of food and water and kept in painful stress positions. "A large number" of British soldiers had assaulted Baha Mousa, many others including some officers must have known about it. His death was described as an "appalling episode of serious gratuitous violence" and the MOD was condemned for "corporate failure".

We flew to Moscow on a charter flight from London's City Airport on a Sunday evening, a painless four-hour flight. David Cameron and Foreign Secretary William Hague briefed us on the plane. We landed at midnight and went straight to the magnificent Kempinski Hotel on the bank of the Moskva River opposite the Kremlin. I was going to go outside for a smoke when I realised that every table in the hotel's enormous reception area held an ashtray and then noticed that people were smoking. It seemed the nanny state smoking police hadn't yet reached Moscow!

I didn't have a producer with me on this trip. After a long and tedious meeting about pool TV arrangements and the logistics of covering the visit, it was off to bed at 2.30am, but only for four hours. The next morning, we travelled in David Cameron's convoy to Moscow's State University where the prime minister gave a speech in which he dealt head on with the elephant in the room, the murder in London of Russian FSB defector Alexander Litvinenko back in 2006. We went in convoy to Red Square where the prime minister laid a wreath at the tomb of the unknown soldier, then onto the Kremlin for a signing ceremony with Russian President Dmitry Medvedev, who was basically keeping the seat warm for Putin. I did a PTC in Red Square with David Cameron and William Hague behind me and another in the Kremlin with its magical churches and their incredible variety of bells.

It felt strange to be back in Moscow, even for such a flying visit. The city was clearly more prosperous though still very corrupt. Gangsterism remained largely unchecked, and there was bugger all actual political pluralism.

I peeled off to do two lives from our Moscow bureau, driven by our driver Genady through dreadful traffic and recorded a track and sent rushes to be edited in London. I could have done another live but had to get back to the Kempinski for Cameron's departure, so our Moscow correspondent

Amanda Walker took over. We drove in the prime minister's convoy to the airport where he got a big send off with a guard of honour and a military band. As in Beijing the year before, it felt more like the visit of a head of state rather than a prime minister.

It was September, party conference season. First, though, a couple of stories to cover. Unemployment had risen and the TUC was calling a day of action for late November. David Cameron and Nicolas Sarkozy went to Tripoli. We were told the day before but sworn to secrecy. There would be no press on the trip except for a pool camera and a Press Association reporter. They were welcomed as heroes both in Tripoli and later in Benghazi.

The Lib Dems met in Birmingham. I did a package for *Live at Five* and lives before and after a Nick Clegg speech to a Lib Dem rally on the Saturday evening, the eve of conference.

Sunday was busy, covering speeches by Vince Cable and Danny Alexander as the TUC mounted a demonstration outside. The Lib Dems were now a party of government and worthy of a TUC demo. In the evening, between hourly lives, a dinner with Adam, Chris Huhne and others, including Tim Farron, a future party leader though few imagined it at the time. My package and an 'As Live' ran at midnight and probably beyond, but I was asleep by then with a heavy cold.

I covered Chris Huhne's speech. For once, some important news from a Lib Dem conference. As the Cabinet minister responsible, he was planning to crack down on the big six energy companies. I did lives all afternoon, but only until 8 o'clock. Dinner with our Sky News team. When we returned to The Hyatt, they all wimped off to bed, some of them had very early starts the next morning. I didn't, I had already cut the package from the conference for the next morning's *Sunrise*, and you can't attend the Lib Dem conference without going to the Glee Club, which was suitably funny and truly awful but the younger Lib Dems enjoyed themselves. Drink probably helped. A lot of it. As usual, Paddy Ashdown was cheerleader-in-chief. I amused myself by treating it as a study in social anthropology! But I chatted to a lot of Lib Dems who are, on the whole, very nice people and very good-humoured. I didn't head off to bed until 3am.

On the final day of the conference, I did live interviews with Vince Cable, Chief Whip Alastair Carmichael and two very young Lib Dem delegates. Our executive producer Esme Wren asked me to head back to London to do lives all evening from Westminster while everyone else packed up our mountain of kit and travelled home..

Labour met in Liverpool. The feed from their conference went down for nearly ten minutes right in the middle of Ed Miliband's leader's speech. I was holding the fort in Westminster and had to go straight into the studio and fill, fill, fill! It was easy, I had plenty to say about the state of the Labour Party. I had also seen an advance copy of the speech so could paraphrase what he was saying while we couldn't see or hear him saying it.

Theresa May left her weekly appointments diary in a Glasgow concert hall. Someone handed it in. Apparently this was not a security risk but only, in my view, because it had not fallen into the wrong hands. The Tories met in Manchester. The theme was 'modern compassionate Conservatism', but their dilemma was how much credit they should allow the Lib Dems to take for the more compassionate elements of the coalition government's policies. They were still very conscious of being labelled the 'Nasty Party'. There was a rumour that the government was planning to increase the motorway speed limit to eighty miles per hour. I asked the Roads Minister Mike Penning who told me it wasn't true, they were still consulting. I interviewed Transport Secretary Phil Hammond who admitted that a higher speed limit might indeed result in more fatalities, but only "marginally and manageably"!

We took George Osborne's speech live, Boris Johnson delivered his comic conference turn, and Theresa May made the rather bizarre claim that an illegal immigrant couldn't be deported because he had a cat! In fact, he had a British girlfriend, his common law wife, and, yes, their cat was part of their 'family'. Cue the launch of #catgate on Twitter which meant great merriment, a lot of pictures of cats and much embarrassment for Mrs May. We split the screen for David Cameron's speech, with him speaking on the left and my tweets on the right, a running commentary as he was speaking.

I did a piece on the death of the party conference. Where once they had been the forum for thrashing out and voting on policies, with disagreements vociferously aired, they had become simply advertising opportunities, tightly-controlled and with very little room for dissent. What mattered most was to give the impression that the party, whichever party, was united.

Defence Secretary Liam Fox was in trouble over claims that he had given a lobbyist, Adam Werritty, inappropriate access to the MOD and had taken him on overseas trips. Dr Fox made a statement after Defence Questions on October 10th denying any inappropriate behaviour. Two days later, the net was tightening during a lively PMQs. It was remarkable that David Cameron hadn't already sacked him. Perhaps he would be too much of a threat from the backbenches. There was a hiatus in the story the next day, although Ed Miliband and Ed Balls unveiled Labour's economic plan for growth and used the opportunity to stick the boot in. My lives were ostensibly about the economic plan but mostly about how Liam Fox was clinging on.

The next day he was gone. I did lives every hour from 6am both on Liam Fox and another story. Cabinet Office Minister Oliver Letwin was snapped by *Daily Mirror* photographer, Steve Back, dumping sensitive government documents in a public bin in St James' Park. Not clever. After midday, there was only one story. I was still doing lives every hour and at three forty-five broke the news that Dr Fox's resignation was imminent. He resigned at four p.m. There followed a couple of hours of post-resignation madness. Phil Hammond moved from Transport to Defence. I cut a Liam Fox political obit for *Sky News at Ten*. It had been another of those fourteen-hour days.

The Liam Fox political obit was a little premature. He returned to the Cabinet in 2016 when Theresa May appointed him secretary of state for International Trade. Three years later, he was sacked in a Cabinet reshuffle by the new prime minister Boris Johnson and replaced by Liz Truss.

On October 20th, I was doing lives on David Cameron and Europe along the lines of just how much trouble he was in ahead of a debate on a possible EU referendum and the growing strength of the Conservative Eurosceptics when we got very strong rumours that Gaddafi had been captured in Libya, and then that he had been killed in Sirte. Gruesome video images emerged of the final moments of Muammar Gaddafi, wounded and bloodied, being roughed up by Libyan rebels before they killed him and dragged his body through the streets.

At the end of October I was reporting on GCHQ's role in combatting the increasing menace of cybercrime, and on the economy. One billion pounds of Regional Growth Fund money had finally been released by the

Treasury ahead of the next day's growth figures, which were expected to show an increase of 0.3%. I was live in Downing Street the following day when those growth figures were released. At 0.5% growth in GDP for the third quarter of the year they were better than had been anticipated. I also wrote a blog on the upcoming G20 summit in Cannes, 'Cannes or Can't'.

The head of the UK Border Agency, Brodie Clark, was suspended in early November. Checks had been reduced to 'level two'. Had terrorist suspects been allowed into the country? And had there been ministerial approval for the reduction in the alert level? I also interviewed Culture Secretary Jeremy Hunt on the Olympics and got to hold the Olympic torch, apparently one of eight thousand in the torch relay. Jeremy managed not to drop it! I also did lives that day when George Papandreou finally stepped down as Greek Prime Minister to make way for a coalition government of national unity. Alarm bells were ringing in Italy, could Berlusconi be the next to go?

Theresa May looked particularly uncomfortable, even by her standards, at the Home Affairs select committee when she was asked whether or not there had been ministerial approval for the UK Border Agency reducing the threat level. Immigration Minister Damian Green was keeping a very low profile. Brodie Clark officially resigned and threatened to sue the government for constructive dismissal.

We did some lives on the story, but Sky News was far more interested in a court case from the United States where Dr Conrad Murray had been found guilty of the involuntary manslaughter of Michael Jackson.

I did lives every hour all day when thirty business leaders, chairmen and CEOs, wrote to the *Telegraph* asking the Chancellor George Osborne to reduce the top fifty pence tax rate back to forty pence. No chance! More lives on a William Hague speech on security and the invaluable work that MI6 and GCHQ were doing to keep us all safe, and on an Ed Miliband speech at the Social Market Foundation. I got the first question at the subsequent Q&A session, a double-header on the top two stories that day in mid-November, plans by Virgin to buy Northern Rock for seven hundred and fifty million pounds and Sepp Blatter's latest faux pas, this time on racism in football. Ed wouldn't be drawn on whether or not Blatter should resign, but many of us thought he should have been sacked long before.

I was live when the actor/comedian Steve Coogan gave evidence to the Leveson inquiry. He made some very good points exceptionally well. The McCanns also gave evidence to the inquiry and claimed that some newspapers had behaved appallingly and had actually impeded the search for their daughter Madeleine. Unforgiveable if true.

On the day of George Osborne's autumn statement, I went for breakfast at Claridge's with Steve Forbes of *Forbes* business magazine, the seriously rich American entrepreneur and, more interestingly, candidate for the Republican presidential nomination in both 1996 and 2000. He hadn't got through the primaries. I found him very clever and amusing but wrong about most things, not only the flat tax concept he so passionately advocated, although he certainly had a point when he had said that the American Declaration of Independence was only one thousand, three hundred words long, the Bible has seven hundred and seventy-three thousand words but the US tax code was seven million words long and still growing. Personally, I like to use another American example, Lincoln's Gettysburg address, when urging people to be succinct. Just two hundred and seventy-one words.

Forbes was backing Rick Perry, but accepted that Mitt Romney was most likely to win the Republican nomination for 2012, correct, and that Barack Obama would lose, wrong. Then again, he would say that wouldn't he? There was a bit of pointy-headed talk on the economy, the 'US Bonds shortened yield curve' whatever that might be, and he thought George Osborne was being "statist" in helping businesses directly, bypassing the banks. He thought Germany should be doing more and criticised Angela Merkel for being too wary of inflation. Hardly surprising, I suggested, given Germany's experience in the 1930s. He had certainly provided me with plenty of food for thought, as well as an excellent breakfast.

Two million public sector workers went on strike the next day, November 30th. The issue was public sector pensions. More than half the schools in England were closed, thousands of hospital operations were cancelled. There were marches and rallies across the country. I covered PMQs that day, and the government statement on the strike by Paymaster General Francis Maude which followed.

The strike was our lead story, but I switched in the evening to do lives on the expulsion of all Iranian diplomats from Britain and the closure of the

Iranian Embassy following the trashing of the British Embassy by a mob in Tehran.

In early December, I covered a speech by David Cameron on Life Sciences, but our questions were all about the euro. Germany and France, Merkel and Sarkozy, had agreed a new set of criteria for the euro following the Eurozone crisis of the previous year. This would require a new treaty, potentially very big trouble for David Cameron. I was teased on Twitter for being seen eating a cheese roll in the background when one of my colleagues was doing a live. Well, it was lunchtime!

Two days later, I was still doing lives on the increasing pressure on David Cameron to hold an EU referendum, as well as lives on NHS reforms and PMQs, after which I had to sit through two hours of George Osborne giving evidence to the House of Commons Treasury select committee. Treasury select committees hurt my poor non-economist brain at the best of times, but I had already been working for more than ten hours and was losing the will to live!

The Brussels summit at the end of the week failed to reach agreement. David Cameron used the British veto at 4am to block any deal because the other states refused to give the UK an opt out, which our government regarded as necessary to protect our vital financial services industry. I was live all day and packaged the story for *Live at Five*.

When David Cameron made the usual post-summit statement to the House the following Monday, Nick Clegg was not in his usual seat next to the prime minister, provoking cries of 'Where is Clegg?' and 'Où est Clegg?' from the Labour benches. I think they meant 'Où se trouve Clegg' but no matter, they were enjoying themselves. I did a pooled interview with Nick Clegg an hour later in which he said that, although he disagreed with David Cameron over Europe, the coalition government would survive until 2015. He messed up his first answer, a factual error, but when I pointed this out to him he told me off for interrupting, so I left him to it. He seemed under pressure and was uncharacteristically brusque, harried and was dashing between meetings. At the end of the interview, he clumsily took off his lapel mic and rushed off, not a good look. The interview was played out in its entirety by both Sky News and the BBC, including the unfortunate beginning and the rather unprofessional end.

The same story dominated the next day, the euro, Nick Clegg and coalition cohesion. When the Cabinet met, I was doing lives in a very cold Downing Street.

We did a secret Santa in the office. I got a Lady Gaga wall calendar, very appropriate, and gave it to Maddie. I had seen a hideous Borat-style lime green mankini which I had thought would be a perfect, funny secret Santa gift. What I hadn't realised that the person I gave it to was gay. I'm always the last to know such things. A typical conversation:

Me: "Have you heard that so and so is going out with so and so?"

Everyone else: "Oh, for god's sake Glen, they split up three months ago."

As is usually the way with secret Santas, people soon worked out who gave what to whom, and for the next few weeks the recipient of the lime green mankini kept giving me very strange looks!

The secret Santa sleuths don't always get it right. I had given one of my colleagues, a keen golfer, a book on golf and a particularly fine bottle of wine. He thought they were from someone else and repeatedly thanked him profusely! The secret Santa rules meant I couldn't say a thing.

Europe was continuing to dominate British politics. I did lives when several countries showed signs of 'wobbling' and coming over to the British point of view, and a press conference with William Hague and the German Foreign Minister Guido Westerwelle. We took the press conference live and I got the first question. The North Korean dictator Kim Jong-il had just died and been succeeded by his son, Kim Jong-un. It was easy to remember their names. The older one had been ill and had been succeeded by the Young'un! North Korea was in mourning, with state television pumping out wall-to-wall pictures of people weeping. I asked them about North Korea and, of course, about the euro. Westerwelle was very conciliatory and made an impassioned case for the EU and the euro, saying for others it's about a single moment or a single currency but for Germany it was, "The answer to the darkest chapter in our history". And he illustrated this with some stories from his own teenage years. It was emotional. I did lives every hour after that, also taking in a George Osborne statement in the Commons on bank reform and his intention to separate retail banking from investment 'casino' banking. He also refused to pay any more into the IMF unless it was specifically for global restructuring and not to prop up the euro.

Just before Christmas, it emerged that the Conservative MP for Cannock Chase Aidan Burley had been foolish and tasteless enough to go to a stag party in a Nazi SS uniform. Guests had been giving Nazi salutes. So far so very bad. But to make matters worse, he did so in France, where such behaviour is illegal. David Cameron had sacked him from his position as a PPS (Parliamentary Private Secretary). The groom was being prosecuted in France and his French lawyer said it was unfair that Burley was not also facing charges. I did lives on this pitiful story all day with more lives and a package all evening.

Aidan Burley courted controversy again the following year when he tweeted that the opening ceremony of the London Olympics was 'lefty multicultural crap'. This led to a barrage of criticism, especially from Londoners proud of the multiculturalism of our great city. He'd only been elected an MP in 2010, and stood down before the 2015 general election.

Ed Miliband's Christmas drinks at the Zeitgeist Jolly Gardener's gastro pub in Lambeth was a jolly affair (pun intended!), but the Home Office Christmas drinks in the Westminster Arms was fairly dire, lots of dull men in suits and awful cheap wine. I missed the Irish Embassy party, I was working, which is probably just as well!

It had been quite a year. The Arab Spring, Libya/Gaddafi, phone-hacking and the closure of the *News of the World*, UK riots, Berlusconi finally forced to step down, more economic meltdown. We had lost Steve Jobs, Václav Havel, Amy Winehouse and too many others. And the population of the world hit seven billion.

CHAPTER 10

2012: Leveson. The Olympics. Nine Prime Ministers but Capello-ed. Omnishambles Budget. Coalition Cohesion? Assange. Plebgate. 'I'm sorry'

Diane Abbott had an excellent start to the year when she tweeted that White people love playing divide and rule, provoking a row and accusations of racism. A Sky News colleague was interviewing her in Hackney, her constituency, when Labour leader, Ed Miliband, phoned her and told her she had to apologise. She did, but it was one of those non-apologies, she claimed that some people had 'misinterpreted' what she had said. So she didn't apologise for what she had said, only for any offence caused. She claimed her remarks had been taken 'out of context'. This has become a common form of defence for politicians, used later by, among others, Boris Johnson, Jeremy Corbyn and Priti Patel. Basically, they're saying more fool you for being offended, I'm sorry you're so stupid.

I did lives on the story with a break at 4pm. when I got Obama-ed and Sky News switched to a live statement from the White House, and for three hours in the early evening before I switched to the story of the Unite union rejecting the government's deal on pensions. We had Unite General Secretary Len McCluskey live at 6 o'clock.

David Cameron criticised nursing standards. Interviewed on the radio, the final question was who would play him in a film and what would the film be called? Meryl Streep was being praised for her sublime performance as Mrs Thatcher in the film *The Iron Lady*. He avoided answering, but Twitter went into meltdown with #Cameronmovies. Among the best were With Clegg and I, Bring me the Head of Miriam Gonzáles Durántez, East of Eton, Shallow Gove, 007 Licenced to Cut, All Quiet on the Recovery Front, Up the Euro, Carry on Brussels, No Euro Please we're British and Referendumb and Dumber! There were many, many more.

I did lives on David Cameron offending the nursing profession but, fortunately for him, Ed Miliband intervened. Bob Holness, the presenter of TV show called *Blockbusters* had died at the age of eighty-three. Just the day after all that Diane Abbott nonsense, Ed tweeted Blackbusters by mistake. Oops. And Twitter was at it again, with people suggesting TV shows for Ed Miliband. They included I'm Sorry I Haven't a Clue, Celebrity Big Brother, and Come Diane with Me!

I went to a press conference with Nick Clegg and fellow Liberal Europeans which was interesting enough but slightly esoteric and didn't make the news, so I switched to doing lives on a Scottish independence referendum with more lives the next day when the Secretary of State for Scotland, Michael Moore, declared that the referendum proposed by the SNP would be illegal but the government would be willing to transfer powers to Holyrood if the referendum was held soon with a straight Yes/No choice. SNP leader Alex Salmond wanted a third choice on the ballot paper, ceding more powers to the Scottish parliament while remaining in the Union. This would probably have split the Unionist vote enough to hand the SNP victory. He also wanted the referendum held in 2014, the seven hundredth anniversary of the battle of Bannockburn. He got that wish though not, of course, the result he'd hoped for.

David Cameron held a joint press conference with the new Italian prime minister, Mario Monti. Sky News carried it live. There was only time, they said, for one question and it fell to me. I asked David Cameron about the IMF and the Falklands (Argentina was making very silly sabre-rattling noises) and gave Monti the opportunity to talk about the Costa Concordia disaster. A few days earlier, the Italian cruise ship had run aground in shallow waters, struck a rock and sunk. Thirty-two people had died, nearly three hundred passengers had been rescued. The disaster and the rescue operation had dominated the media, including Sky News, for several days. There were questions about why the cruise ship had steered so catastrophically off course. All Mario Monti could say, at that early stage, was that there would be a full investigation. Just over a year later, five people were convicted of manslaughter and negligence.

I covered the Home Affairs select committee when it condemned the previous summer's Border Agency fiasco, and did hours of lives on the government's unrealistic immigration target before switching to Chris

Huhne. Essex police were sending emails written by Vicky Pryce to the CPS which now had to decide whether or not to prosecute.

The government suffered a massive defeat in the House of Lords in a vote on the Welfare Reform Bill. What was remarkable was the number of Tory grandees who had rebelled. They included Lords Howe, Lawson, Mackay, Carrington, Brittan and Wakeham. It was like a roll call of the Thatcher years. I did lives in the build-up to and after the vote.

I was live with the Director of Public Prosecutions Keir Starmer for the dramatic announcement of his decision: Both Chris Huhne and his ex-wife Vicky Pryce were to be charged with attempting to pervert the course of justice. You know you're getting old when the DPP is younger than you! Mind you, if that wasn't bad enough, the prime minister was even younger. Chris Huhne was not at the Department of Energy and Climate Change so we went to his house for his resignation statement. Although he was quitting the Cabinet, he said he would fight the court case and would remain an MP.

At Admiralty House, I broke the news before Nick Clegg officially announced it that Ed Davey would replace Chris Huhne as Secretary of State for Energy and Climate Change. We moved to the Cabinet Office for a photo-op, a Nick Clegg-Ed Davey handshake, and around the corner to the DECC for another choreographed live, Ed Davey saying a few words as he arrived at his new ministry.

I had started the day doing lives from six a.m. from the Royal College of General Practitioners strongly condemning the Health Bill before going to Keir Starmer's announcement sealing the political fate of Chris Huhne. My final live was twelve hours later. It had been a freezing cold day of frenetic activity. The Lib Dem press team had done a very good job in what had been very difficult circumstances.

It was a lot colder in Stockholm. I was there a few days later with cameraman Phil Hooper for a Nordic-Baltic summit. We had two rooms at the splendid Grand Hotel, opposite the Royal Palace. One was a suite, initially allocated to me but I gave it to Phil. I'm all heart! Actually, there was a good reason for this as he had a lot of kit and the suite had a balcony, perfect for doing lives.

There were nine prime ministers attending the summit. Sweden, Norway, Finland, Iceland, Denmark, Latvia, Lithuania, Estonia and the UK. David Cameron was the Grand Fromage! Sky News wanted lives from us that evening, but Fabio Capello resigned as England manager at seven thirty p.m. There were no other stories, not even Syria, as Sky News went Capello-tastic. We weren't needed so we had dinner with some of the Number Ten press team at an Italian-Swedish fusion restaurant, Undici. The food wasn't bad, the company was excellent but the bill was horrendous! Afterwards, we went to a bar where David Cameron's director of strategy, Steve Hilton, was holding court. We didn't stay long!

The venue for the summit was Stockholm's Photography Museum. I know it was Stockholm not Copenhagen, but the day felt like a series of scenes from *Borgen*. David Cameron did a sound bite on Fabio Capello saying he was a good coach but was wrong about John Terry, England's former captain, who had been sacked by the Football Association following allegations of racist abuse.

Fabio Capello ruined my day! I got dropped from doing lives several times as Sky News went Capello-tastic again. It was minus ten centigrade but felt a lot colder. I was about to go live, the third aborted attempt when Harry Redknapp appeared outside his home in Poole to tell the waiting cameras that he hadn't even thought about the England job, he had a job to do at Spurs etc. Yeah, sure Harry! I was dropped again an hour later when Sky News did a live with Alan Sugar instead, talking about the football.

The press conference with nine prime ministers really was like a scene from *Borgen*, with the role of Birgitte Nyborg being played by Danish Prime Minister Helle Thorning-Schmidt (married to Stephen Kinnock) and a spin doctor, who of course we called 'Kaspar', actually telling me where to stand to ask my question.

I was about to go live after the nine prime ministers' press conference. I was dropped with just seconds to go. The presenter back in London was actually reading out the link to me: "David Cameron is in Stockholm for a meeting of... no, we're going to go live instead to..." and they went to... Max Clifford! Harry Redknapp I could completely understand, even Alan Sugar, but Max Clifford? Really!

Or, as I expressed it down the line to London when the studio director apologised, "Max Clifford? Max fucking Clifford? Are you fucking kidding me?"

To be fair, it wasn't the football story. Clifford was beginning his evidence to the Leveson Inquiry and we were taking it live. I had covered a summit and not got on air once, although Sky News had used the Cameron grab on Capello. On a normal day we would have been doing lives from Stockholm every hour, but I got Capello-ed and then Leveson-ed. I wrote a blog, 'Five times a day' lamenting my experience. I can think of no other time when not two or three or even four but nine prime minsters had sat like ducks in a row for a press conference.

Back in Westminster, I had to sit through a four-hour health debate in the House of Lords. The outcome was boringly predictable. Lib Dem peers backed the coalition government and the bill was passed. The evening was much livelier, reporting on the release on bail of Abu Qatada. Despite reassurances from his native Jordan, the decision was taken because it was believed he might be tortured if he was deported. The UK was a signatory to the UN Convention Against Torture. Abu Qatada was electronically monitored, and was only allowed to leave his home twice a day for a maximum of one hour each time. A bit like the rest of us during the Covid lockdown of 2020!

I had to sit through another House of Lords debate, a five-hour borathon on the Welfare Reform Bill. It was Valentine's Day, nothing for me! The *Mad Men* actor Jon Hamm came in to be interviewed. Many of the women in our Westminster newsroom seemed to turn to jelly. It was bizarre and very funny. He's handsome enough but he's not very tall. I did a live on the cost of the trees in the atrium at Portcullis House which were being rented (rented!) for thirty-two thousand pounds a year. Ridiculous. More lives on the UK's credit rating, which was slipping, while still listening to the Lords welfare debate.

I did lives before and after a David Cameron speech in Edinburgh in which he presented strong arguments for the Union and against Scottish independence. The prime minister was off to Paris the next day for a bilateral summit which Sky News decided should be covered by our team in Brussels rather than by a political correspondent. Nevertheless, I did several lives on the Paris summit from London. Nick Clegg, William Hague, Phil Hammond and Ed Davey were also at the summit. Adam was even grumpier than I was that we weren't there. I wrote a blog on the 'Entente Amicable' I also did a couple of lives on the withdrawal of iris recognition machines at UK immigration. A waste of £5 million.

In late February, David Cameron hosted another 'health summit' in Downing Street. The Health Secretary Andrew Lansley was beasted by protestors as he passed through the Downing Street gates, nothing physical just giving him a piece of their minds. I covered defence questions that day, and an urgent question on the appointment of a university 'tsar' to oversee university admissions. Angry Tories were screaming 'social engineering', the policy was defended by Vince Cable. William Hague spoke in a debate on Iran and Britain's further deteriorating relations with Tehran.

Representatives from fifty countries gathered at Lancaster House for a special conference on Somalia. I did lives all morning and interviewed International Development Secretary Andrew Mitchell at lunchtime. David Cameron held a press conference with UN Secretary General Ban Ki-moon and Somalia's interim prime minister which we covered live and at which, yes, I got the first question. Then as now, Somalia was a hopeless basket-case. Later, I got a question at a press conference with US Secretary of State Hilary Clinton and a very good answer on both Somalia and Syria. I was really there to ask about Chris Tappin, a British businessman who was being extradited to the United States for illegally selling weapon parts to Iran. She answered at length. There were leaving drinks for Sky News politics producer James Johnson. It was packed and noisy. He was not only very good at his job but also very popular and would be missed.

The following week, Chris Tappin's wife, Elaine, gave evidence to the House of Commons Home Affairs committee to express her dismay at her husband's extradition and I interviewed her live afterwards. I persuaded their son Neill to come into our studio at Westminster to do a live. Chris Tappin's extradition to Texas had followed years of appeals and legal argument. A few days later, he appeared in court in El Paso wearing an orange jumpsuit, handcuffed and in shackles. Nearly a year later, in January 2013, Tappin was sentenced to thirty-three months in prison, but was allowed to serve the second half of his sentence in the UK.

At the end of February, Unite General Secretary Len McCluskey was proposing strikes and civil disobedience to disrupt the London Olympics. He was roundly condemned on all sides. James Murdoch left the field of battle. He resigned as executive chairman of News International and would be running the family's TV business from New York.

David Cameron admitted that he had ridden a horse owned by Rebekah Brooks, not good optics. The posh, horsey, country set in the Cotswolds out of touch while initiating sweeping welfare cuts. His director of strategy, Steve Hilton, was off to California for what was described at the time as a one-year sabbatical. The eccentric Hilton and California seemed like a good fit, as I said in my lives. He went on to found a Silicon Valley tech start-up company.

The first PMQs of March was sombre. Six British soldiers had been killed when their Warrior armoured vehicle hit a powerful IED (improvised explosive device). It was the worst single loss of British lives in the conflict since the Nimrod crash in 2006. The same day the government cut its funding of Remploy, the agency which finds jobs for disabled people, insisting that the one thousand seven hundred jobs involved would not be cut but the money would be deployed to help find work for the disabled. Labour MPs were furious when the minister responsible, Maria Miller, produced a WMS (written ministerial statement) rather than going to the Commons to explain. I interviewed her and Liam Byrne for Labour and threw to grabs from both of them in my lives that evening.

The six soldiers killed in Kandahar province were named the next day when more details of the incident emerged. They were from the 3rd Battalion of the Yorkshire Regiment and the 1st Battalion the Duke of Lancaster's. They had been in a two-Warrior patrol group south of Lashkargah. As well as reporting on that and the expressions of sympathy from politicians from the prime minister down, I was also doing lives on a government plan to allow train operating companies to run the rail infrastructure, the tracks etc., which the unions said would lead to severe job losses. That evening, it was off to Gateshead for the Lib Dems spring conference.

The next morning, Friday, we'd been asked to do lives all afternoon, which was only the eve of the conference but we were surprisingly in demand. Sky News wanted lives every hour starting at midday. We cracked on every hour until 6 o'clock, after which we covered the eve of conference rally at 6.45.

It was a far busier weekend than I had expected, which was good. We were live more often than every hour all day and evening on the Saturday, lives from me at the top of each hour and assorted Lib Dem interviewees at half past the hour. We sent an 'As Live' for midnight previewing Nick Clegg's speech the following day. Sunday morning was equally busy for us, with lives every hour from 7 o'clock and an extra live at 10.30 after the leadership was defeated in a vote on health policy. The delegates were restless, many of them still unhappy about going into coalition with the Conservatives. Nick Clegg used his speech to try to reassure them, talking about the Lib Dem policies being enacted by the coalition government and the opportunities of being a party of government rather than existing in endless opposition.

Before we left Newcastle that Sunday afternoon, producer Gary Honeyford and I went to the top of the Baltic Flour Mill, now an arts centre, for the view and took a quick walk through the Quayside market. The transformation of the banks of the Tyne since I had worked in Newcastle more than twenty-five years earlier was a wonder to behold. Twenty-five years! Where had it gone?

David Cameron was off to Washington and I did lives on that and when Rebekah Brooks was arrested again along with her husband Charlie, a close friend of David Cameron's since their school days at Eton. It was economics again early the next morning when the *FT* and *The Times* had a story, which had obviously been briefed to them, that George Osborne was considering issuing one-hundred-year government bonds. This was not within my comfort zone, and I was relieved when the Sky News business unit took over the story. At least they knew what it meant! I switched to covering PMQs. With David Cameron on his way to Washington, Nick Clegg stood in with Harriett Harman batting for Labour. Clegg did well, to loud Tory cheers. I wondered how that would play with Lib Dem voters, and whether or not he would even hold onto his own seat at the next election. He did hold onto Sheffield Hallam in the Lib Dem annihilation of 2015 but only just, and only with Conservative support despite a huge swing to Labour.

On the Friday, lives on speculation that George Osborne might, after all, scrap the fifty pence top rate of tax in the following week's Budget, and more when Dr Rowan Williams announced he would be standing down as Archbishop of Canterbury at the end of the year. The government was no doubt relieved to be rid of such a troublesome priest! I returned to talking through the Budget speculation for *Live at Five* at the end of another twelve-hour day. It had been a busy ten-day run. I was ready for a weekend off.

There was speculation that the government might part-privatise the country's motorways and other main roads through a PFI scheme. I was doing lives on that the following Monday when the shocking news came in off a shooting incident at a Jewish school in France, near Toulouse. When Sky News returned to the roads controversy, it was covered by a regional reporter standing beside the M6, which was a far better way of telling the story. I had a long chat with Dr David Owen, former Foreign Secretary and co-founder of the SDP, on the state of the nation when he came in to do a live interview. This is, no doubt, a minority view but I regarded him as a member of that small group of politicians who were the best prime ministers the country never had.

I had an interesting encounter with a senior civil servant when David Cameron went to the Department or Business. He told me that when Gordon Brown had been prime minister and visited the department he had ignored the cameras, gone straight into meeting people and had asked often difficult questions. Compare and contrast, he suggested, with prime minister Cameron who was, at that moment, heading straight for the cameras. Ever the PR man!

I wrote a blog on the lack of a Budget purdah. The Budget proposals seemed to be leaking like the proverbial sieve. The next day, I was doing lives on the suggestion that George Osborne might introduce some form of hypothecated taxation and on his plan to launch a National Loan Guarantee Scheme. The Queen addressed both Houses of Parliament, one of the events marking her Diamond Jubilee.

What emerged was the infamous Omnishambles Budget which resulted in several dramatic U-turns. There was the caravan tax, the church tax (to impose VAT on improvements to church buildings), and the granny tax, freezing personal tax allowances on pensions. All provoked fury and had to be reversed. But best of all, and the one that caught the public imagination and the most attention of the media, was the so-called pasty tax, the proposal to charge the full twenty per cent VAT on hot takeaway food. At least one newspaper labelled it 'Pastygate', of course. George Osborne was asked when he had last eaten a pasty and said he had no idea, which was interpreted as his being out of touch with the everyday lives of ordinary people. As all of these proposals unravelled, I was explaining to our viewers that, "This is what a screeching, hand-brake government U-turn looks like". The pasties were saved!

On a day off, Ken Livingstone's battle bus turned up in Holloway Road where I was shopping. He was a candidate for London Mayor. He got out and started soap-boxing just six feet away from me. There was no escaping politics.

The Sunday Times mounted a sting operation to expose that large party donations could buy you access to the prime minister. It was the only story in town. I packaged it for *Live at Five*. The package was so well received, thanks largely to a fine PTC shot by cameraman Paul Dickie, that no changes were required and it ran all evening.

I did a live the next day on the Falklands and the latest ridiculous Argentinian rhetoric before going to a press conference with William Hague and the Bosnian foreign minister. William spoke about the Falklands and about Syria. The vile Assad was visiting the city of Homs where he said that he would comply with UN Secretary General Kofi Annan's six-point peace plan. But, of course, actions speak louder than words.

Sky News hosted a London mayoral debate. Ken Livingstone looked old and grumpy, Boris Johnson was clearly restraining himself and resisting going too over the top or doing comedy, the Lib Dem candidate, Brian Paddick, was dull.

On May 1st the House of Common Culture, Media and Sport committee reported on their nine-month investigation into phone-hacking, concluding that Colin Myler and Tom Crone of the *News of the World* had "misled" them. Tom Watson and the Labour committee members issued a minority report in which they condemned Rupert Murdoch as unfit to run a media company. I also did lives for the second day running on the long queues forming at Heathrow airport. The Border Agency was excelling itself again.

As expected, François Hollande was elected French president, the voters having rejected Nicolas Sarkozy and austerity. I covered the story live, but from London not Paris.

Rebekah Brooks gave evidence to the Leveson Inquiry on May 11th. I was in Downing Street all morning. Among her revelations were texts with David Cameron, three tête-à-tête dinners with Tony Blair, Gordon Brown's fury when the *Sun* turned against him in the middle of the 2009 Labour conference, an email supposedly incriminating Jeremy Hunt, not bullying the government over Megan's Law, and her claim that she had got Sharon Shoesmith of Harringay children's services sacked in the wake of the death of toddler Peter Connelly. The one I thought tabloids would have most fun with, and they did, was the revelation that David Cameron signed off his texts LOL, thinking it meant Lots of Love until someone in Downing Street pointed out to him that it actually means Laugh Out Loud.

I did lives when the RCN claimed that sixty thousand NHS jobs were under threat and on cuts to disability benefits, and reported on a successful Royal Navy attack on a Somali pirate base. I did lives around a Theresa May speech to the Police Federation conference in Bournemouth, and when Jack Straw gave evidence to Leveson. I covered a David Cameron speech on the economy and the euro currency crisis and went straight to Labour Party HQ to do a pooled interview with Ed Miliband to get his reaction, which Sky News played out in its entirety a few minutes later.

The European Court of Human Rights ruled on votes for prisoners broadly supporting the position of the Italian government and, by proxy, that of the British government, but opposing a 'blanket ban'. As clear as mud! Either prisoners had the right to vote or they didn't. Which was it?

There was plenty more Leveson evidence to cover, including Ken Clarke and Vince Cable, none of it particularly earth-shattering. Jeremy Hunt's spad, Adam Smith, was followed by the CMS department's permanent secretary, Jonathan Stevens, who basically dumped on the spad and expressed his loyalty to his minister. Sir Humphrey strikes back! I kept that observation for one of the online pieces I was writing every day.

I was doing lives on Tony Blair giving evidence to Leveson, a master class, when I switched to the government U-turn on the pasty tax, announced in the Budget two months earlier. It was another of those midday to midnight days as I had also done lives in Downing Street when Mervyn King and Adair Turner met David Cameron, George Osborne, Nick Clegg and Danny Alexander, the quartet running government economic policy.

I did lives every hour when the BMA voted for a day of industrial action, and previewed Jeremy Hunt's appearance at the Leveson Inquiry the following day. When Jeremy Hunt gave his evidence and all eyes were on Leveson, the government chose the moment to announce a U-turn on the cap on charity donations announced in the Budget. It was the third Budget U-turn in a week. Omnishambles! I covered that in the afternoon, with lives and a package every hour all evening. The package included a PTC in Downing Street where they were hanging bunting to celebrate the Queen's Diamond Jubilee, visually an absolute gift. It was our lead story.

Prince Philip was taken to hospital that day with a bladder infection as a "precaution". That evening, I watched the Queen's Jubilee concert from Buckingham Palace. Madness stole the show by singing 'Our House' from the roof of the palace. I would love to have been there. My invitation must have somehow got lost in the post!

The next day was the final day of the four-day Diamond Jubilee celebrations. Once again, thousands of people lined the Mall. There was a service of thanksgiving at St Pauls cathedral (where I had once sung the Messiah as a school chorister, though only in the chorus!), and a lunch at Westminster Hall. I am not usually one for Royal events, but can be a sucker for pomp and circumstance, and I had a clear view of the Sovereign's Entrance at the Houses of Parliament as the Queen arrived. We watched the Battle of Britain memorial flight and the Red Arrows fly past from the sixth-floor balcony at 4 Millbank. The Queen broadcast a short message of thanks at six p.m. For us at Westminster, normal service would be resumed the following day.

The next day was largely spent not doing lives! I had begun with a Foreign Office briefing on the Falklands and an interview with Foreign Office minister Jeremy Browne. I was in the studio ready to comment on an Ed Miliband speech but was stood down. I interviewed Mohamed Nasheed, president of the Maldives, on the forthcoming Rio Earth Summit and on his regime which had come to power in a coup four months earlier, although he denied it was a coup. I stood by to do lives on the Eurozone but David Cameron and Angela Merkel held a press conference in Berlin, something Downing Street had assured us was not going to happen and the reason we hadn't gone to the German capital. I finally got to do a live on the Eurozone at 3 o'clock and, an hour later, in Downing Street when it was announced that no government ministers would be attending the Euro 2012 football tournament in Ukraine in protest at the continuing imprisonment of Yulia Tymoshenko. We rushed to the Foreign Office to interview William Hague on Syria, where there had been another massacre by Assad's forces, and my live was dropped just as they were coming to me. They went live instead to our correspondent Amanda Walker who was in Donetsk, Ukraine, the correct decision. The Hague interview was good though and was taken live by both Sky News and the BBC and, apparently, by LBC and Radio Five Live. It had been a busy day, covering six different stories.

Forced marriages was top of the political agenda when, as expected, David Cameron announced that the law would be changed and a new criminal offence created. Parents who forced their children into a marriage could go to prison. I did lives on the story all day and a package for *Live at Five* which ran all evening.

On Monday June 11th, George Osborne and Gordon Brown gave their evidence to the Leveson Inquiry. Gordon Brown essentially accused Rupert Murdoch of lying under oath, while George Osborne had to explain his role in the appointment of Andy Coulson as Downing Street director of communications. I also covered a Theresa May proposal to tighten up immigration rules and give these precedence over Article 8 of the European Convention on Human Rights, which was bound and probably designed to provoke another row with the ECHR. It smacked of populism. All other stories were eclipsed that day when it emerged that David Cameron had left a pub to drive back to Chequers before realising that he had left his eight-year-old daughter Nancy behind! This caused much amusement.

I covered John Major giving evidence to Leveson and did lives on a government plan to crack down on Internet libel and abuse. As we all know, it didn't work. As I write, Premier League footballers are being racially abused on Twitter with no consequences for the offenders. The next day, I did lives from 6am ahead of Nick Clegg giving evidence to Leveson.

David Cameron was at the Leveson Inquiry the next day. Government ministers were out and about to demonstrate how busy the government was despite the prime minister being up in front of the beak! I interviewed Ken Clarke, Theresa May and Ian Duncan Smith. David Cameron gave evidence for five hours with a one-hour break for lunch. It was intense, but we learnt nothing new. David Cameron was almost as good as Tony Blair at handling such situations.

I did my first newspaper review on Nick Ferrari's breakfast show on LBC, which was fun but involved a horribly early start. I love doing radio, the intimacy of the relationship with the listener is so much closer than that with the television viewer. The good news was that they sent a car for me with all the papers so I could read on the way to the studio and decide which stories to talk about. I would do the LBC morning paper review several more times after I eventually left Sky News the following year and always enjoyed it.

David Cameron had attacked comedian Jimmy Carr's perfectly legal tax avoidance scheme as 'immoral' and 'dodgy'. Sky News wanted a package for the evening, our lead story. I interviewed Ed Miliband and Labour MP John Mann, who took great delight in pointing out the tax avoidance schemes of big Tory Party donors. There were plenty of TV pictures of Jimmy Carr including, fabulously, a sketch poking fun at bankers paying just one per cent of their income in tax which was, apparently, precisely what Carr had been paying. Visually, the piece made a refreshing change from the House of Commons green benches and endless politician talking heads.

David Cameron hosted Aung San Suu Kyi in Downing Street and I found myself just six feet away from a living legend. At Westminster Hall she was afforded the rare privilege (think Obama, Mandela, HM the Queen) of addressing both Houses of Parliament. It was an inspiring speech and not too long, just twenty-five minutes, nicely balanced between the past, the present and the future. There was clearly a long way to go to achieve democracy in Burma/Myanmar. Whatever may or may not have happened since, Aung San Suu Kyi's status at the time was little short of sainthood.

Ed Miliband made a speech on immigration the next day. Labour had decided to stop avoiding the issue though its position was, of course, far less bellicose than that of the Conservatives. I did lives every hour from 6am, with a package and a live for *Live at Five* and 6pms. Another of those non-stop twelve-hour days.

At Treasury Questions, Chancellor George Osborne told the House that the three pence increase in fuel duty, announced in the Budget and due to come into effect on August 1st, would be postponed until the end of the year. Not quite another Budget U-turn, but certainly applying the brakes. I broke the story and did lives every hour from 3 o'clock until midnight with a live interview with Shadow Chancellor Ed Balls in *Live at Five*.

That next day we had a huge story, a financial scandal, when Barclays was fined a record £290 million for fixing the LIBOR rate. Chief Executive Bob Diamond said he would be waiving his bonus. Waiving his bonus! I thought he and others should be on their way to prison. It was extremely bad for the City of London and therefore for the British economy. The question was: how many other banks had been doing the same? Twenty other banks were being investigated for similar corruption. It seemed the regulation of the banking sector had been far too weak and now the chickens were coming home to roost.

That evening, I went to Portcullis House for Sinn Féin's summer reception. The Queen had visited Northern Ireland the previous day and had shaken hands with Northern Ireland Deputy First Minister and former IRA Commander Martin McGuinness. It was an historic handshake and would become an iconic image, symbolising peace in Northern Ireland. I had met Martin McGuinness many times before. That evening, we shook hands and I said "I'm shaking the hand that shook the hand." He laughed and said he'd been getting that all day.

I did lives on the two stories that dominated the political news the following Monday, the Barclays bank LIBOR fixing scandal and the EU. The Barclays chairman had resigned, but Chief Executive Bob Diamond was still refusing to go. On Europe, David Cameron said there might be an EU referendum, but not yet. Liam Fox gave a speech advocating leaving the EU. The Conservatives were tearing themselves apart over Europe again. This was difficult for David Cameron, great for Labour and almost impossible for the Lib Dems, so pro-European and in coalition government with the Conservatives.

I listened to David Cameron's statement to the House on Europe, and I was due to do a live on it at 5 o'clcock. At no notice, at 4.30, I was in the studio to do a live on a George Osborne statement on the banks, but Speaker Bercow kept allowing questions to David Cameron on Europe and I had to do a bridging live talking about both issues for twenty minutes, including a two-minute commercial break! My lovely colleague Sophy Ridge said it had been, "Like a Shakespearean monologue"! A monologue certainly, though anything but Shakespearean.

Bob Diamond finally resigned the next day. I did lives all evening from the Bank of England as Sky News went Diamond-tastic. He gave evidence to the House of Commons Treasury select committee the next day. He didn't reveal much, but came across as unaware of what was going on in his own organisation. Incompetence, or a calculated performance? We doorstepped him as he left, a huge media scrum. He grinned, but said nothing. I did my

PTC in the Wilson Room, in the chair from which he had given his evidence. A bit cheeky, but no one objected and Sky News loved it.

David Cameron and Nick Clegg were in Birmingham to reaffirm their commitment to the coalition government. Their troops, both Conservative and Lib Dem, were markedly less enthusiastic.

G4S Chief Executive Nick Buckle appeared before the House of Commons Home Affairs select committee. He was like a lamb to the slaughter. Drinks that evening as Sky News reporter/presenter Sarah Hewson was about to go on maternity leave. I always referred to her as 'Sarah Hews-on Sky News' her married name was Sarah Hughes, and 'Sarah Hughes, Sky News' scanned so much better! Our erstwhile politics producer Tom Raynor, who had left us to be Sky News Middle East producer was also there, back in London before heading to Afghanistan with David Cameron and Sophy Ridge, her first foreign assignment.

The fighting intensified in Syria, and I did a long pooled interview with Foreign Secretary William Hague after Russia and China vetoed the latest UN Security Council resolution, vetoes which William Hague described as "inexcusable and indefensible". Earlier, I had interviewed Labour leader Ed Miliband after a speech on G4S and what was shaping up to be a security shambles for the London Olympics, just a week away.

In the evening, Ed Miliband's summer drinks reception. I learnt two things from Stewart Wood, who had run Ed Miliband's leadership campaign. Firstly, that the leadership campaign had been so long not because of some fiendishly Machiavellian manoeuvring by the NEC or the unions but because Lord Sainsbury, a David Miliband supporter, wouldn't pay for a special conference, around £250,000, to elect a new leader. Talk about ironic. Most in the Labour leadership had actually wanted a short campaign and a quick decision to avoid giving the Tories a clear run lasting months. Secondly, while some were urging Ed Balls to stand down, Ed Miliband had wanted him in the contest so that he could paint him as the Brownite candidate and his brother David as the Blairite allowing him, Ed, to come through the middle.

I did lives every hour the next morning when Ed Miliband delivered a speech on immigration, exactly the same speech he had given a month earlier! In Aurora, Colorado, just east of Denver, a mass murderer called James Eagan Holmes burst into a cinema during a midnight screening of the latest Batman film, *The Dark Knight Rises*, throwing grenades and firing various guns into the audience. Twelve people were killed and seventy injured in the deadliest mass shooting in Colorado since the Columbine high school massacre of 1999. Not surprisingly, Sky News went Denver-tastic with wall-to-wall coverage.

With all the focus on Denver, I wrote an online article, 'Boris for Prime Minster, the fantasy of the Tory right'. Not a fantasy any more!

Ed Miliband said he would find it 'difficult' to work in a post-2015 coalition with Nick Clegg. Of course. His mission was to work for a Labour victory not another hung parliament. Given what happened in 2015 and subsequently, a Lab-Lib Dem coalition would have been a far better outcome for him and the Labour Party, and would have avoided the Brexit referendum.

The next morning, Treasury minister David Gauke criticised cash-in-hand payments to cleaners, builders etc., the so-called 'black economy'. He wanted it stopped. No chance! I did a couple of lives on that. Producer Vickie Bird told me some astounding gossip about two of our colleagues who had been having an affair for some time. As usual, I was about three months behind the gossip curve! In the evening, I had a drink with a couple of Sky News reporters in the Marquis of Granby, our favourite Westminster watering hole. They were both in full whinging mode on how bad morale had become at Sky News headquarters in Osterley. In our semi-autonomous Westminster bubble we were fairly immune to what went on in Osterley. I was suddenly called back to work for some breaking news, that the government was to seek a High Court injunction to prevent the PCS union, whose members included Border Agency staff, from striking two days later. I went straight into the studio to do a live. After a flurry of phone calls, I got statements from the PCS and the Home Office and did lives for the rest of the evening until midnight.

The next day, after twenty-four hours of brinkmanship, the PCS called off the strike. I did lives from the Home Office and also wrote a piece, 'Thatcher and the Falklands', for our Margaret Thatcher online obit for whenever that might be needed.

On the eve of the London Olympics, Republican presidential candidate Mitt Romney was visiting. I packaged the story, including a PTC in Downing Street as he emerged to talk to the press. Before leaving the States,

Romney had criticised London's preparations for the games. Now, he was backpeddling furiously. My package ran every hour from *Live at Five* until midnight with a live two-way off the back.

Like most of the country, I watched the fabulous Olympics opening ceremony the next day. The Red Arrows flew over my home in Highgate, from where I could also hear the spectacular fireworks at the end, the sound travelling like rumbling thunder from East London. I was at home because I was about to go on holiday to Cyprus with Maddie and Seb.

Back in the saddle at work in mid-August and lives in Downing Street on Adam Jones, a thirteen-year-old boy who had been abducted by his Qatari father three years earlier. He had written to David Cameron saying he was terrified and being kept under house arrest, and begging to be brought home to his British mother Rebecca. David Cameron had replied, and the Foreign Office was on the case. I did several lives on the story, and more when Defence Secretary Philip Hammond said that the experience of G4S and the Olympic Games security had taught him that the private sector does not have all the answers, especially for the MOD. Cue the sound of a large penny dropping!

I did a live when Boris Johnson, in a newspaper interview, urged David Cameron to "stop pussyfooting about" over a new airport and other infrastructure projects. As Mayor of London, Boris was advocating a new London airport next to the Thames estuary. The Duke of Edinburgh was taken to hospital in Aberdeen, a bladder infection again and once more 'as a precaution'. Sky News rolled on the story for nearly three hours. With no TV to do, I wrote an online piece about Ecuador deciding whether or not to offer Julian Assange asylum in the Ecuadorian Embassy in London. I escaped that evening at ten fifteen p.m. but was called back to do a live at eleven p.m. It seemed that under the Diplomatic and Consular Premises Act of 1987, the police could enter the Ecuadorian Embassy to arrest Assange. I left a long 'As Live' for the midnight news and was home in time to watch it.

When Ecuador officially decided to give asylum to Assange the next day, I broke the news on Twitter and then on TV, and got the first reaction from the Foreign Office. On a quiet Thursday in mid-August, this was a big story. I interviewed Foreign Secretary William Hague on Assange at five p.m., an interview which Sky News ran in its entirety a few minutes later.

I did lives every hour the next morning on government plans to sell off school playing fields. What a dreadful idea that was. After lunchtime, the story disappeared. It was a very busy day with stories from Syria, where Assad continued slaughtering civilians, and Russia where the Pussy Riot protestors were sentenced to two years in prison. Moors murderer Ian Brady said he would reveal the burial place of the last of his victims, whose body had not been found. And there was Assange. A busy day.

The rest of August was almost equally busy. I did hours of lives on whether or not our Olympian medallists should be honoured in the New Year's honours list. I saw no reason why not, but some attention-seekers were objecting. George Galloway, in his weekly podcast rant, defended Julian Assange by arguing that the rapes for which he was wanted in Sweden were not actually rapes at all. This enraged Rape Crisis and other relevant charities and became our lead story. I did lives all afternoon and evening, with a fresh package and a live for 9 o'clock and *Sky News at Ten*.

It emerged that Asil Nadir had been a major Conservative Party donor in the late 1980s. Nadir, the boss of the Polly Peck textile company, had fled to Northern Cyprus and stayed there for twenty years to escape British justice. He had returned in 2010 to face the music and was sentenced on this day in late August 2012 to ten years in prison for fraud and theft. I did lives on the story all evening, with a final live at 11 pm on a phone call between David Cameron and Barack Obama in which they agreed that if Assad so much as threatened to use chemical weapons, the West would respond. He did, we didn't.

That evening, two T-Shirts and a bottle of Belize beer arrived for me, sent by the Belize Olympics team some of whom I had interviewed weeks before. I gave the T-Shirts to producer Clare and fellow correspondent Sophy. One of our Westminster team, VT Editor and MCR (master control room) supremo Chris Scott announced that the next day was his birthday, so he got the beer!

I did hour after hour of lives the next day on GCSE results. Grades were down for the first time since they'd been introduced in 1988. Head teachers were accusing Education Secretary Michael Gove of political manipulation, something he denied. After several requests, he finally did a live interview with us. I was live from the Department for Education. It was another of those very long days with lives every hour from lunchtime until midnight. This was August, the so called 'silly season', it was supposed to be relatively quiet!

August ended with two stories. The Serious Fraud Office was to investigate Barclays bank, which had appointed a new group chief executive, and exams regulator Ofqual defended the GCSE results. Both stories kept me busy over two days. I also interviewed Lord (Tim) Bell, PR guru and architect of Mrs Thatcher's three election victories, on David Cameron's performance so far as prime minister, the forthcoming Cabinet reshuffle and coalition cohesion. How much longer could the coalition government survive?

Cabinet reshuffles always lead to frenzied speculation at Westminster. David Cameron's reshuffle on September 4th was the first since the coalition government had been formed over two years earlier. A reshuffle was overdue, the Cabinet needed freshening up. I had done lives all the previous day speculating on what changes the prime minister would make. We had got most of it right. David Cameron disliked reshuffles, believing that ministers needed time to be effective, so it was no surprise that the most senior positions remained unchanged.

The most significant changes included the promotion of Chris Grayling to Lord Chancellor and Secretary of State for Justice. No one saw that coming! His predecessor Ken Clarke was appointed minister without portfolio. Jeremy Hunt was the new Health Secretary, replacing Andrew Lansley. Justine Greening moved, apparently with some reluctance, to Dfid. She had been Secretary of State for transport, tasked with resolving the issue of a third runway at Heathrow. Andrew Mitchell, who had been very popular at Dfid, became chief whip. Maria Miller was the new Secretary of State at Culture, Media and Sport, while Owen Paterson got Defra. Grant Shapps became Conservative Party chairman, replacing Baroness Warsi who was no longer a member of the Cabinet but allowed to attend as senior minister of state. A survivor. Ian Duncan Smith had apparently simply refused to move from the Department for Work and Pensions.

The Lib Dems were unchanged, but David Laws was back, promoted to Minister of State for Education and the Cabinet Office, with the right to attend Cabinet.

There were plenty of changes in the lower, sub-Cabinet ministerial ranks, notably Michael Fallon and Matt Hancock both moving to the

Department for Business. The Tories were parking their tanks on Vince Cable's lawn!

As well as doing lives on Sky News, I was doing long ten-minute explainers for LBC Radio, which was fun. Or my idea of fun anyway.

In early September, I covered Richard Branson giving evidence to the House of Commons transport select committee. He had lost the West Coast line franchise and was deeply pissed off about it. I had met Richard several times, but Maddie had asked me to get his autograph, so I did. Earlier the same day, Queen guitarist Brian May had been in to talk about his campaign to stop badger culling, so I got his autograph for her too!

David Cameron made a statement on the 1989 Hillsborough stadium disaster. He delivered it extremely well, but the content was shocking. There had been a huge, orchestrated police cover-up. One hundred and sixty-four documents had been altered to remove criticism of the South Yorkshire police who were attempting to blame the fans. Most chilling of all was the revelation that if the police and emergency services had responded quicker, at least forty-one of the ninety-six lives lost could have been saved.

The House of Commons was very emotional. Having been at Hillsborough all those years earlier, I was choking up, tears welling. Afterwards, I had to sit through a transport select committee report on the West Coast line, which seemed so utterly trivial, almost meaningless in comparison. I did lives on Hillsborough all evening. The next day, the families of the ninety-six began their campaign for truth and justice and for prosecutions.

Vince Cable rejected the Beecroft report, a story I had touched upon several times over the previous few months. Adrian Beecroft had been asked by the government to review employment law. Most controversially, he had suggested that employers should have the right to no-fault dismissal, or 'fire at will'. Vince Cable was crystal clear: "At a time when workers are proving to be flexible in difficult economic conditions, it would almost certainly be counter-productive to increase fear of dismissal". I did several lives on the story, but it later faded into the background as Sky News went Kate-tastic. There was a huge row when a magazine published some paparazzi pictures of Kate Middleton. I was reduced to writing an online piece on why Nick Clegg's opposition to boundary changes might leave the way clear for a Labour victory at the next general election. Of course, it didn't.

I interviewed former Education Secretary Kenneth Baker and did lives all evening on a proposal to replace GCSEs with an 'English baccalaureate' by 2017. That didn't happen either.

Sky News was going through severe cutbacks. There would be redundancies. I was very concerned. I fitted the profile of age and salary, perhaps my face no longer fitted. I had seen it happen to others often enough, both at ITN and Sky News.

Two WPCs, Fiona Bone and Nicola Hughes, were killed in a gun and grenade ambush while responding to a call to a suspected burglary in Greater Manchester. I did lives on this shocking story all evening, including an on-camera expression of sympathy and condemnation by David Cameron, "A despicable act of pure evil", and similar statements from Ed Miliband and others. The question I was being asked was whether or not all police officers should be armed. I suggested not as neither the police nor MPs were advocating such a move. But the country was shocked. Their murderer, Dale Cregan, was sentenced to whole life in prison the following June.

'I'm sorry.' September 19th was I'm sorry day. As a curtain raiser to the Lib Dems annual conference in Brighton, Nick Clegg used a PPB to issue a mea culpa, apologising for the tuition fees U-turn fiasco. I thought this very odd, why remind people? But apparently it was a constant issue on the doorstep. I did lives all evening. By the next day, Nick Clegg's 'I'm sorry' had become a meme set to music and was proving very popular on You Tube. All profits were, we were told, going to Sheffield's children's hospital.

Although the Lib Dems had clearly made a terrible error of judgement in pledging not to raise tuition fees, they were also the victims of political dissembling. Both Labour and the Conservatives had made it clear during the coalition talks immediately after the 2010 election that they wanted university tuition fees to rise. Indeed, it was Tony Blair's government which had introduced them in 1998 and increased them in 2004. But it was the broken promise, so publicly made, which did the damage. It was a matter of trust.

To the Lib Dems annual conference in Brighton with producer Gary Honeyford and cameraman James Green. After an early morning train from Victoria, I went straight to our live position for lives every hour, including Nick Clegg's arrival and a David Laws speech in the afternoon. In between the hourly lives and talking to Lib Dem delegates, I also packaged the story, such as it was, for *Live at Five* with a live two-way off the back of my package and did the same routine at 6 and 7 pm before Nick Clegg spoke to a Lib Dem rally. No mention of 'I'm sorry'! We cut a new package for 9 o'clock with lives at 10 and 11pm. An exhausting day.

We were live again the next morning from 6am and every thirty minutes all morning. It was a Sunday and there was little other news. We had a break while Adam did the afternoon lives. Two of my lives in the evening were squeezed out after John Terry announced his retirement from international football.

Plebgate was the latest 'gate' story. Cabinet minister Andrew Mitchell was alleged to have called a policeman guarding the entrance to Downing Street a 'pleb', something he denied. But later that Sunday evening, the *Sun* got hold of a transcript of the police officer's report to his superiors, claiming that Andrew Mitchell had called him a pleb. I did a live at 11pm which ran as an 'As Live' all night.

Sunrise wanted a package from Eastbourne, a Conservative target seat. I interviewed Eastbourne's Lib Dem MP Stephen Lloyd and drove there with cameraman James Green. We interviewed a local councillor, two sixth form boys at a school on tuition fees and Nick Clegg's 'I'm sorry', and did some vox pops and a PTC. The sea on the way to Eastbourne was rough, so we took a few shots for a line about stormy times ahead for the Lib Dems. Terrible cliché I know, but the package desperately needed some pictures.

Back in Brighton, we did lives that evening on embargoed excerpts from Nick Clegg's leader's speech to be delivered the next day, which was largely spent waiting for the speech. When it came it was rather lacklustre, an attempt to raise the morale of his battered troops. Lib Dem internal polling made very gloomy reading, the party's future prospects were not looking at all rosy.

An early start the next morning, and more lives on Julian Assange. He had now been holed up at the Ecuadorian Embassy for one hundred days and had sent a message by satellite to the UN in New York where Foreign

Secretary William Hague was meeting Ecuador's foreign minister, Ricardo Patiño, a meeting which I suspected was almost certainly pointless.

While Labour met in Manchester I was holding the fort in Westminster. It was quiet, so I wrote an A-Z of this year's party conferences for the Sky News website which everyone seemed to find amusing and, hopefully, instructive. I also wrote a piece about Ed Miliband's 'humble origins' in Primrose Hill ahead of his conference speech. He was going to bang on about Haverstock school yet again. I tweeted his speech, a classic One Nation speech, which, impressively, was over an hour long without any notes or autocue.

The Department for Transport reversed its decision over the West Coast line franchise. Richard Branson had been exonerated. I did just two lives, not so much a U-turn as a total derailment! Another omnishambles fiasco. But there were too many other stories. Five-year-old April Jones was still missing in Wales. Her mother appealed for information and David Cameron also made a public appeal. We learnt that April suffered from cerebral palsy. She had been missing for four days and had not been off the front pages. Sky News was being presented from the search area, with full presentation and six reporters working on the story. A huge search by police officers and volunteers was to continue for the next six months, the largest and longest missing person search in British history. The police had already arrested a local man, Mark Bridger, who was subsequently sentenced to life for abduction and murder. Little April's body was never found.

As well as the search for April Jones, it was also the day of the funeral of WPC Nicola Hughes who had been murdered in Manchester. Even Richard Branson, standing by to do a live interview for Sky News by satellite from New York, was dropped.

The Conservatives were meeting in Birmingham. I tweeted George Osborne's speech, which was more Tory chief strategist than Chancellor of the Exchequer. He didn't get a standing ovation, just polite applause as the delegates headed for the exit. It seemed apparent that many ministers were keeping their heads down and were nowhere to be seen, except for Ken Clarke and Boris Johnson, whose speech was as ebullient and effervescent as usual.

The mood of the conference was deflated. Everyone there seemed to think the Conservatives would lose the next election, everyone that is except Boris even though a loss would boost his chances of getting his hands on the leadership. He was treated like a rock star, even though he said nothing substantial or of any consequence. He might as well have been chanting 'oggy oggy oggy'. His adoring fans would undoubtedly have responded with 'oi oi oi'! Ann Widdecombe spoke at a packed anti-gay marriage rally to great enthusiasm. And the party was still tearing itself apart over Europe.

David Cameron had to negotiate his way through this mess in his leader's speech. He spoke directly to the country, over the heads of his party's conference delegates, on the theme of Britain being an 'aspiration nation'. But the pressure from the Eurosceptics was relentless and would prove irresistible. Just three months later, he promised and IN/OUT EU referendum if he were to win the 2015 general election.

That October, the revelations about Jimmy Saville were becoming more stomach-turning by the day. He had died a year earlier. I and many others thought it a great travesty that he wasn't still alive to face the music and be, metaphorically at least, whipped through the streets.

I phoned arch-Eurosceptic Tory MP Bernard Jenkin. I said, "Hi, it's Glen." He must have misheard me and thought I'd said 'Graham', something which happens occasionally. He thought I was Graham Brady, chairman of the 1922 committee of Conservative backbenchers. Presumably he had been waiting for a call from Graham. The knives were out for Andrew Mitchell over plebgate. Jenkin outlined his devious plan. Summon Mitchell to the Executive of the 1922 committee and then argue his case to David Cameron, after which he would be 'our chief whip'! He also said that he'd heard that Conservative MP Patrick Mercer had heard that there was more to come out about Andrew Mitchell, but he didn't know what. I hung up. I had no idea what to do with this information. I called him back, as myself, and arranged for him to do an interview. His tone was very, very different when talking to a journalist!

The vultures were circling. Nearly four weeks after the plebgate story broke, Andrew Mitchell had still not resigned as government chief whip. I did lives and packages every hour for twelve hours on an otherwise quiet Saturday. For *Sky News at Ten* I did live at the top of the hour on a *Sunday Times* story that retired generals were using their military contacts to help arms companies, which seemed to me a somewhat tenuous 'exclusive', with my Andrew Mitchell package running ten minutes later. I thought I deserved a productivity bonus!

Andrew Mitchell finally resigned six days later, reluctantly allowed to go by David Cameron. It had been a textbook example of how not to deal with a negative story.

On a more cheerful note, double Olympic medal winner, Christine Ohuruogu came in with her medals. They were large and surprisingly heavy. Maddie was still after autographs and Christine was happy to oblige.

It was the day before my fifty-seventh birthday (fifty-seven! OMG!). The *Evening Standard* reported my age as forty-seven! Excellent. My colleagues produced a birthday cake and a card and gathered around to sing happy birthday, which was incredibly sweet of them.

It was time for a break and a few days in Barcelona to reflect on the past few months and think about the future. Celtic was playing Barca in the Champions League and the Plaça de Catalunya had been completely taken over by a sea of green and white, thousands of very drunk but very good-natured and funny Celtic fans. There were tickets available for the game, being sold from an official kiosk on Las Ramblas, but not to British passport holders. I switched the charm to full beam to no avail.

We learnt that Conservative MP Nadine Dorries was going to the celebrity jungle, a TV show, *I'm a Celebrity, get me out of Here* in which contestants are publicly ritually humiliated! She had not asked permission and several Tory MPs were furious. Maybe they were envious? I did a couple of lives before going, as usual, to the 11am Downing Street lobby briefing. We had got some words off camera from David Cameron. The BBC still didn't have his reaction. I did a live ahead of a Theresa May statement on child abuse cases in North Wales and broke the line that the investigation into the police handling of those cases would be conducted by 'an independent figure' rather than another police force. I also did a PTC for *Live at Five* on the US presidential election, Obama's victory over Mitt Romney, part of a special sequence from our correspondents in Beijing, Moscow, the Middle East, Delhi and London, my contribution. The sequence worked well, was informative and looked good.

BBC Director General George Entwistle was under increasing pressure to resign after *Newsnight* falsely implicated Lord McAlpine in the north Wales child abuse scandal. I was live every hour from five p.m. and scrambled to BBC Broadcasting House for his resignation statement and chairman of the BBC Trust, Lord (Chris) Patten banging on about how George Entwistle had been so 'honourable'. Jeremy Paxman publicly supported Entwistle and launched a scathing attack on the BBC management, calling them "cowards and incompetents", "bloated time-servers" and worse. This astonishing outburst kept me doing lives until midnight with more lives the next day as questions were being asked about the position of Chris Patten, and George Entwistle's pay off, reported to be £450,000. CMS select committee chairman John Whittingdale had done ITN and BBC interviews outside Broadcasting House and was on his way home. Sky News had somehow missed him. I called him and he agreed to turn around and come into our Westminster studio for a live interview.

I did lives on the election of Police and Crime Commissioners and on the local elections, and more on Amazon, Google, Starbucks et al not paying their full UK taxes. John Lewis boss, Andy Street, said they were damaging British businesses which do pay their taxes and undermining the UK tax system. *Plus ça change.*

That afternoon, Esme briefed us on Sky's 'five-year plan'. Coming soon, I thought, the Great Leap Forward! The management actually admitted there was a 'culture of bullying' at Sky News. A 'people's survey' of staff revealed that morale among Sky News staff (at Osterley HQ, though not a Westminster) was way below the average for the rest of Sky. This came as no great surprise.

I was in Southampton for the Hampshire Police and crime commissioner election. It looked like being one of the more interesting elections. Former army lieutenant colonel and Conservative MP Michael Mates was the favourite. I had met him many times when he had run Michael Heseltine's Tory leadership campaign. He was also the father of my erstwhile ITN colleague James Mates. But he had a problem. Local Conservative councillor Simon Hayes had failed to win the Conservative nomination and was standing as an independent.

The turnout was shockingly low, less than 15%. I did a live at 2pm when we got the result of the first round. Mates was ahead, but only by 5,000 votes. It wouldn't be enough, as he himself admitted when I showed him the result as he arrived at the count. He hadn't seen it and looked crestfallen, and then a little angry. As far as the Conservatives were concerned, Hayes had only run to spoil Mates' chances having failed to be selected as the Tory candidate himself. Sky News took the result live at 4.30 and I did a quick live two-way before packaging the story for *Live at Five*. After the second choice votes of the other candidates had been transferred, Simon Hayes won by a considerable margin, 25,000 votes.

SAS sergeant Danny Nightingale had served in Northern Ireland, Bosnia, Lebanon, Turkey, Iraq, Afghanistan, Syria and Libya. Earlier in the month a court martial had sentenced him to eighteen months after police had found a Glock pistol and more than three hundred rounds of ammunition in his house. There had been a campaign, supported by several MPS, to have his conviction overturned. I did lives on the story. A week later, the court martial appeal court suspended his sentence.

I did lives on women bishops. The Church of England synod had rejected the ordination of female bishops despite a majority of lay members voting for the proposition. The majority had fallen short of the two-thirds needed. I switched to covering a House of Lords debate on the Justice and Security Act which was designed to provide oversight of MI5, MI6 and GCHQ but also, controversially, proposed 'closed material procedures', in other words secret courts, denying the fundamental right to a fair trial in public. It was a Kafkaesque proposal. Even more surreal was the story I switched to at 11pm: Nadine Dorries had been the first to be voted out of the *I'm a Celebrity* jungle. Viewers of that bizarre programme had, it seemed, failed to warm to her.

I did lives the next day on prisoner voting. The ECHR had said that the British government should revisit the issue so there was now a draft bill which would be scrutinized by a joint Commons-Lords committee, which was bound to take some time. This appeared to have much the same effect as a Royal Commission, a mechanism for kicking the issue into the long grass. I got dropped twice to make way for better stories. First, when it was announced that Tony Hall was to be the new BBC director general and then when it was decided that Premier League football referee, Mark Clattenburg, would not be charged with racism after Chelsea had formally complained to the Football Association about his alleged use of 'inappropriate language' towards their player Mikel John Obi during a game against Manchester United a month earlier.

I covered the Croydon North by-election at the end of November. Head of politics, Esme Wren, phoned me just after 9am. There had been no forward planning, but the morning editorial meeting had decided Sky News should have a package for *Live at Five*. On the train to Croydon I phoned the Conservative, Labour, Lib Dem and UKIP campaigns and interviewed their candidates when I arrived with cameraman Tony Fyffe. We didn't have a producer. Lee Jasper arrived on an open top Respect Party bus even though it was cold and pouring with rain! But it all worked, we fed a piece for *Live at Five* and were back in our Westminster newsroom in time to watch it run at 6 o'clock and all evening.

Nadine Dorries, back from 'the jungle', was summoned to a meeting the next morning with Conservative chief whip, the patrician Sir George Young who, I'm sure, was not a viewer of that particular programme. She was on probation and the party whip remained suspended.

The day before Lord Justice Leveson published his report at the end of November, I previewed what we expected to be his conclusions in lives from 6 am, with an extra live at 8.45 because Hugh Grant was late for his live interview. I switched from 9 o'clock to doing lives every hour until 5pm on government plans to allow building on more of our precious greenbelt. I also wrote an online piece about former Lib Dem MP and child sex abuser Cyril Smith. The Labour MP for Smith's former seat of Rochdale, Simon Danczuk, called for an inquiry into the abuse. The CPS said Smith should have been charged more than forty years earlier. It was revealed by a former Special Branch officer that both the police and MI5 knew about the allegations against the paedophile rapist. Smith had died in 2010. Like Jimmy Saville, he wasn't alive to answer for his revolting crimes.

The sordid, hideous details of Smith's offences emerged slowly over the next five years. So too did the evidence of a cover-up to protect Smith's paedophile ring. There had been one hundred and forty-four complaints against Smith. All attempts to prosecute him had been blocked.

Leveson reported the next day. It was a two-thousand-page report into the 'culture, practises and ethics of the press' with, thankfully, a forty-eight-page executive summary! He wanted the Press Complaints Commission abolished and replaced with a new independent regulator underpinned by statutory legislation. He also made recommendations which would change the Data Protection Act and the powers of the information commissioner. I was doing lives for Sky News and LBC Radio. David Cameron made a statement in the House. He welcomed many of Lord Leveson's recommendations, but said he was against changing legislation both in principle and for practical reasons. He had "serious concerns and misgivings" about such changes to the law. Labour's Ed Miliband called for the report to be implemented in full. Nick Clegg concurred. Unable to agree with his coalition partner, he made his own statement on behalf of the Lib Dems urging that the law be changed.

Part two of the inquiry was not to be published until after criminal prosecutions of the guilty phone-hackers, but the Conservative manifesto for the 2017 general election said this second part of the inquiry would be dropped. Culture Secretary Matt Hancock confirmed this in a House of Commons statement in March 2018.

Unpicking the Leveson report and the reactions to it kept us busy for several days. Two days later, a Saturday, I started work at 9.30. My colleague Peter Spencer did the daytime lives while I worked on a package for *Live at Five* which ran, with a live two-way off the back, every hour up to midnight. Another long day. The next day, I was off the Leveson hook and doing lives and a package previewing George Osborne's Autumn Statement, due the following Wednesday.

There was a small additional flurry of Leveson aftermath the following Tuesday, three lives in Downing Street, before a pooled interview with Nick Clegg on the Succession Act. Either a first-born man or woman could succeed to the throne in future, and he or she would be allowed to marry a Catholic. The country was slowly being dragged into the twenty-first century. Kate Middleton, the Duchess of Cambridge and future queen barring accidents or revolution, was pregnant. The newspapers were almost cover-to-cover. Apparently, we should all be very excited and happy for the golden, royal couple. Sky News, of course, went Kate-tastic.

George Osborne's Autumn Statement followed PMQs the next day. He slashed the welfare budget and extended his austerity measures. He admitted that he had failed to meet his own public spending targets. He scrapped the three pence increase in fuel duty announced in the omnishambles Budget and due to come into effect later in the month. The economy would shrink by 0.1% for 2012 and grow by just 1.2% in 2013, the weakest post-recession recovery since before the Second World War.

Tax relief on pensions was reduced, corporation tax cut by 1% to 21%, local government budgets were severely cut. There was some extra money for 'infrastructure projects', including the HS2 rail link and for science and education. The personal tax allowance was increased by £1,335 to £9,440 per year, a Lib Dem policy.

No sooner had he sat down than the ratings agency Fitch warned that the UK could lose its AAA rating. Sky News went into full pointy-headed economics mode and started looking more like Bloomberg TV, with the screen full of graphics about growth forecasts, the budget deficit, the structural deficit, national debt, government borrowing, bond trading, bond yields etc., etc., etc. I did a couple of lives and couple for LBC Radio, but first I needed to find out who these ratings agencies were and why they mattered!

The next day I got Branson-ed and Umunna-ed! I was about to go live to talk about the West Coast rail line when Sky News suddenly managed to get Richard Branson live, then on tax and the Autumn Statement when Shadow Business Secretary Chuka Umunna popped up instead.

December was already shaping up to be a busy month at Westminster and it didn't disappoint. Prime Minister David Cameron was our guest at a press gallery lunch on December 12th. My own guest, Fiona Cunningham (nee Hill), stood me up! She was too busy working with her boss, Home Secretary Theresa May, on the Data Communications Bill, which was to become known as 'the Snooper's Charter'.

David Cameron expressed his sympathy to the family of Jacintha Saldanha, a nurse who had worked at King Edward VII's hospital in Westminster where the Duchess of Cambridge was being treated for severe morning sickness. Just over a week earlier, an Australian radio station had called pretending to be the Queen and the Prince of Wales asking after the Duchess' health. Jacintha took the call, fell for the prank, and put the caller through to the nurse who was looking after the Duchess. Most of us had laughed at the prank. We weren't laughing any more. Jacintha had committed suicide. No one had blamed her, it clearly hadn't been her fault.

I was sent to doorstep Keith Vaz, who was supporting Jacintha's family, at St Stephen's entrance. Two freezing cold hours later he swept past without saying a word. At the time, the *Daily Mail* (of course) had accused him of seeking the limelight. It was only much later that we learnt that Vaz's father had committed suicide, which had motivated him to try to help.

David Cameron made a statement after PMQs in mid-December on the inquiry into the death of Pat Finucane. The Belfast human rights lawyer, who had represented IRA members including Bobby Sands and other Maze prison hunger strikers, had been murdered by loyalist paramilitaries the UDA in 1989 with the collusion of the British security services. David Cameron had admitted to the collusion the previous year but had refused to accede to calls for a public inquiry. Instead, a review was set up chaired by Sir Desmond Lorenz de Silva. Although Sir Desmond criticised a 'wilful and abject failure by successive governments', Pat Finucane's family dismissed his report as a whitewash.

The *Daily Telegraph* reported that the new CMS Secretary of State Maria Miller had claimed more than £90,000 in parliamentary expenses for the mortgage and other costs for a house in south London where her parents lived. She claimed her parents lived with her as 'dependents', and David Cameron declared himself satisfied with her explanation.

The Maria Miller saga dragged on for sixteen months until she finally resigned from the Cabinet in April 2014.

I did lives on the story in the afternoon and early evening, with more lives on Libyan dissident, Sami al-Saadi who, with his wife and four children, had been secretly flown from Hong Kong to Tripoli where he had been tortured by Gaddafi's henchmen. The 'extraordinary rendition' had been a joint British-Libyan operation. Now, the government had agreed to pay Sami al-Saadi two point two million pounds in compensation, but without admitting any liability. Evidence of the UK's role had come to light the previous year when Gaddafi fell and documents were discovered in the office of his former spy chief Moussa Koussa. As for the British refusal to accept liability for its part in his abduction Sami al-Saadi simply said, "I think the payment speaks for itself".

The Foreign Office Christmas drinks reception was at Lancaster House. It was attended mostly by ambassadors, there were very few journalists. It was far too upmarket for us lot! William and Ffion Hague were meeting and greeting, and William delivered a short and typically witty speech.

I did lives all day when it was announced that the Queen would attend Cabinet the next day. It would be her first time, and she would be the first monarch since George III in 1781 to attend Cabinet. I was on the early shift the next morning and did lives every half hour from six a.m., but it was deemed to be a Royal rather than a political story, so our Royal correspondent (or Crown correspondent as they were once called or, colloquially, 'crested reptiles') took over. I would have liked to have seen her again, especially as she walked from Number Ten to the Foreign Office with William Hague after the meeting within touching distance of our live position. But there were other fish to fry.

Ken Clarke led the second reading debate on the Justice and Security Bill and #plebgate reared up again. CCTV footage was released of Andrew Mitchell talking to the police officers at the Downing Street gates, but you couldn't hear what he was saying and lip readers couldn't discern the word 'plebs'. I phoned him. He was not happy that we were once again covering the story, and once again protested his innocence. I did lives on the story and a radio package on the Queen at Cabinet.

That evening's Christmas drinks reception was at Number Ten. It was surprisingly uncrowded, so I had plenty of 'face time' with the prime minister and chatted with assorted Downing Street aides.

I did more on plebgate the next day, lives from the Downing Street gates and from the studio. We had fresh words from the afternoon Downing Street lobby briefing, David Cameron fully supporting Andrew Mitchell, etc.

It was almost Christmas, but on Sunday December 23rd I did eighteen live two-ways. Eighteen! And all of them on plebgate. Andrew Mitchell had written a long piece for *The Sunday Times*. I was live at the top of and at half past every hour. Somehow, I also managed to cut a seven-minute politics year-ender. Phew!

CHAPTER 11

2013: The Leveson Report. Cameron Promises a Brexit Referendum. Chris Huhne. Same-sex Marriage. Leaving Sky News

Nursing a hangover like everyone else, I began January 1st with an online piece outlining the perils and potential banana skins awaiting the government in the year ahead. There was a row over the introduction of control orders, which had been replaced by TPims, terrorism prosecution and investigation measures. They were being blamed for the abscondment of terrorism suspect Ibrahim Magag on Boxing Day. Unlike control orders, under TPims suspects could not be forced to relocate to more isolated parts of the country. Magag had simply disappeared in north London. I did lives on the story and returned to it a week later when Home Secretary Theresa May came under fire in the Commons and her Labour Shadow Yvette Cooper asked if, by abandoning control orders, she had "personally made it easier" for terrorism suspects to abscond.

Ed Miliband gave a speech in which he used the phrase 'one nation' thirty-two times. I counted them! My main story that day was to report on a pensions White Paper introducing a flat rate pension from 2017. I did lives every hour on that for ten hours, from midday until nine p.m. Much more interesting was a story I broke at ten p.m. The UK was to send two RAF transport C17s to help the French counter-terrorism operation in Mali, where the government was fighting al-Qaeda.

Since then, the British commitment to Mali has increased, part of a multinational operation to combat ISIS, but success is elusive. Mali is a huge country and locating the ISIS fighters is, as a senior British Army officer recently put it to me, "Like finding a grain of sand in the desert".

In Algeria, al-Qaeda terrorists seized a gas installation part owned by BP. Dozens of Westerners had been taken hostage. I did lives every hour all evening. We were asked by the Foreign Office not to reveal the number of

Britons working at the Tigantourine gas facility near Amenas because it was believed that at least two or three British workers had eluded capture, were hiding and had not been found. The al-Qaeda terrorists were hunting door-to-door for foreign workers, dragging some from their beds in the accommodation blocks and shooting others as they tried to run away. Of course I, along with the BBC and ITN, agreed to the request.

The next day, Algerian special forces attacked the gas facility, for the hostages an extremely dangerous move. COBRA met twice that day. I did lives every half hour from the Cabinet office and, later, from Downing Street when David Cameron warned us, on camera, to prepare for some bad news. It seemed the Algerian operation was not going well. The prime minister was due to go to Amsterdam the next day to deliver his Europe speech. It was postponed, he was staying in Downing Street to oversee the crisis. I continued doing lives until midnight. The Algerians had ignored calls from Cameron and others to exercise restraint. It seemed that to them killing the al-Qaeda terrorists was more important than rescuing the hostages.

When Algerian soldiers stormed the Tigantourine installation, a vital facility which provided 10% of Algeria's gas supply, at least 39 foreign hostages were killed along with 29 of the 32 terrorists. The other three were captured. 685 Algerian workers and 107 foreigners were freed.

David Cameron finally promised an in/out EU referendum if the Conservatives were elected in 2015, saying, "It's time for the British people to have their say".

In a heated exchanged at PMQs, Ed Miliband accused him of 'running scared' of UKIP, whose opinion poll ratings had been rising, and said Cameron was going to "put Britain through years of uncertainty and take a huge gamble with the economy".

David Cameron said he would fight "heart and soul" for the UK to remain in the EU. The Tory Eurosceptics couldn't believe their luck. No doubt Dominic Cummings was lurking in the shadows somewhere rubbing his hands and preparing for the battle ahead.

David Cameron promised to negotiate a better deal for Britain and to reform the European Union. My own view, which of course I couldn't express on air at the time, was that he was indeed running scared of UKIP and the Eurosceptics in his own party and that promising this referendum was an act of very poor judgement and hubris. Successful in the referendum on Scottish independence, he believed he would win this one too.

February arrived with a story on gay marriage. MPs were to get a free vote. For me, eight hours of hourly lives and I had to re-cut another senior reporter's package because the programme editor hadn't liked the package's structure. I always hated doing that, it seemed such an insult to a colleague.

One of the very few times I was in trouble when I worked at ITN was when I re-voiced a package written by a very senior correspondent, far more senior than me. It had been a last-minute job, so I had no time other than to read out what was in front of me. ITN editor Dave Mannion told me he did not like the writing. When I pointed out to him who had written it, he apologised.

I was on the same story the next day when local Conservative Party chairmen delivered a letter expressing their opposition to gay marriage. What is the collective term for this group of Conservative Party chairmen? An anachronism of? Anyway another day and evening of lives and packages on the same story.

On February 4th, Chris Huhne changed his plea to guilty, resigned as an MP and would now be prosecuted for attempting to pervert the course of justice.

I was on early shift the day MPs voted to allow same-sex marriages. I did lives at 6, 6.30 and 7 o'clock from our Westminster studio, then every hour for the rest of the morning from Downing Street as the Cabinet met. MPs voted overwhelming in favour of equal marriage rights for gays, a majority of 255, but only after a heated debate. More than half the Conservative MPs either abstained or voted against the bill, which was at the heart of David Cameron's attempt to modernise the party. Nick Clegg described the vote as, "A landmark for equality in Britain". The Catholic church continued to actively campaign against same-sex marriage.

While MPs were debating in the House of Commons chamber, the Argentine foreign minister was meeting an all-party group of MPs in one of the House of Commons committee rooms. I slipped away to do a quick live from the committee corridor, but what I really wanted was an interview in light of Argentina's recent bellicose noises about the Falklands. We had been told that he wouldn't be doing any press. I tried. I even travelled with him in the lift down to the ground floor, but he simply would not play ball and refused to talk to me either on or off camera. On the day of the gay marriage vote, he probably wouldn't have got on air anyway, except with a declaration of war!

The next day, Michael Gove performed a U-turn on GCSEs and the proposed English baccalaureate. GCSEs were here to stay. I did lives on that, and on the Bank of England governor Mark Carney giving evidence to the House of Commons Treasury select committee when a scandal broke. Findus had been accused of using up to 100% horse meat in its frozen lasagne. I did lives on that story every hour all evening.

It was time to leave Sky News. 2013 seemed a reasonable time to move on. The next general election wasn't due until 2015, and seemed likely to result in another coalition or possibly a Tory win. No one foresaw the obliteration of the Liberal Democrats from 57 MPs to just 8. Angela Merkel had warned Nick Clegg that junior coalition partners always got the blame, but no one expected the scale of the disaster that was to befall the Liberal Democrats. Nor had anyone foreseen David Cameron's rash (to say the least) decision to promise a referendum on EU membership to see off UKIP and placate the Eurosceptics in his own party. And very few, if any, expected him to lose that referendum.

My bosses insisted that they did not want me to leave, but we spent the next month negotiating a payoff. The haggling began the very next day. I ended up getting not quite everything I'd asked for, but enough. I was already mentally elsewhere, focussed on where my journey might take me next.

They say you either work to live or live to work. I mostly lived to work. There were long-suffering friends, dinner parties when I'd be away in Birmingham, Berlin or Baghdad, concert tickets or tickets for the football usually had to be cancelled or given away. There had been incredibly patient girlfriends and an increasingly impatient wife. God only knows how they put up with me, until they didn't any more.

Meanwhile, nothing had been formally agreed and I threw myself into work with my usual gusto. Ed Miliband made a speech on the economy in which he supported Vince Cable's idea of a 'Mansion Tax' on houses sold for more than two million pounds. This scuppered us by the way. Our house was valued at two point one million pounds and was on the market. It certainly wasn't a mansion! In our part of north London, two million pounds simply bought you a large family home. Thanks Vince!

Home Secretary Theresa May was tightening up a judge's recommendation on deporting foreign criminals and wanted new legislation qualifying the right of foreign criminal suspects to a family life, flying in the face of Article 8 of the ECHR. I also did lives that evening on horse meat, again, ahead of a DEFRA meeting the following day.

I was live before, during and after the DEFRA 'summit' on horse meat, ten hours of lives every hour. Shadow Environment minister Barry Gardiner demanded to know why David Cameron hadn't pursued prosecutions for what the prime minister himself had described as a 'shocking crime'. Eventually, in May, a Dutch meat wholesaler was arrested for selling three hundred tonnes of horse meat as beef. More meat wholesalers were prosecuted three years later.

I did lives previewing the Eastleigh by-election triggered by Chris Huhne's resignation. David Cameron was campaigning in the constituency, not for the first time. I also did lives that day on new rules on domestic energy tariffs, George Galloway storming out of a debate at the Oxford Union, and an online analysis piece on the economy. Apart from my mangers, Jonathan Levy, Esme Wren and the HR department, no one knew I was also digging my escape tunnel.

My online piece about the economy, focussing on the January public sector borrowing figures, was prescient. Two days later the ratings agency Moody's downgraded the UK's AAA rating. I did lives all afternoon and evening on that and on the Eastleigh by-election, two days away.

Against all expectations, the Lib Dems held Eastleigh with 13,342 votes, down 14%. UKIP received 11,571 votes, one thousand more than the Conservatives who had dropped to third place in a seat they had been expected to win. It was a disastrous result for David Cameron. Without the Lib Dem postal votes, UKIP would have had their first elected MP. If the vote on the right hadn't been so split, the Lib Dems would have lost, presumably to the Tories. Labour were also-rans with just 4, 088 votes.

March was to be my last month at Sky News. D-Day was March 4th when I had a meeting with Jonathan Levy and HR at which we agreed my pay off. I would leave at the end of the month. So I had less than four more weeks of Sky News. I felt a mixture of excitement and a little trepidation.

After sixteen years, leaving Sky News was going to feel very strange. I told political editor Adam Boulton who sympathised and offered to write me a 'glowing reference' if I needed one.

Meanwhile, the work continued for a little while longer. I did lives when Chris Huhne's wife Vicky Pryce was found guilty of attempting to pervert the course of justice and wrote a Chris Huhne political obit for when he was sentenced four days later. I also did lives that evening, every hour, on a David Cameron speech on the economy. He said he was sticking to Plan A. He was channelling his inner Margaret Thatcher. TINA, There Is No Alternative.

Talking of which, Lady Thatcher died on April 8th. That month also saw the Boston marathon terrorist attack, and Sky News had become Pistorius-tastic. In South Africa, paralympian Oscar Pistorius had been accused of murdering his girlfriend Reeva Steenkamp. He claimed he had mistaken her for an intruder. When he went to trial the following year, Sky News was all over it, treating it with the same level of coverage they had given to the OJ Simpson trial all those years earlier, the story that had first put Sky News on the map.

Non-Sky friends and friendly MPs I had told about my leaving Sky News were unanimous. It was 'exciting' and 'a great opportunity'. I went to see the excellent play *This House* at the National Theatre with Bethnal Green and Bow MP Rushanara Ali, who also thought leaving Sky News would "open up a world of opportunities".

I did lives from Milton Keynes, a David Cameron Direct event. I got a couple of questions, on the economy and Tory divisions over Europe. Back at Millbank, I told our lovely news editor Clare Parry and my colleague Jon Craig that I was leaving before I put out a note to all Sky News staff: *I'm off*. Within minutes I got more than a hundred kind replies. I was really touched by some very sweet messages. *What will we do without you?* being a favourite.

I did my last ever early shift on March 12th, lives on a Cabinet meeting standing in the freezing cold in Downing Street. That was one aspect of the job that I probably wouldn't miss! I received dozens more well-wishing messages from colleagues at Sky News HQ at Osterley. Colleagues I spoke with at Westminster all had the same message, sad to see me go but also excited for me. The reality of leaving Sky News after sixteen years was beginning to dawn on me and it felt very, very odd.

This continued for several days, hundreds of very touching emails from well-wishing colleagues and MPs, word had got out. And a lot of phone calls and face to face chats. I had no idea I'd been so appreciated.

My last weekend working for Sky News. On the Saturday, I did lives from the Tory spring forum at London's Connaught rooms, a one-day event. In the evening I switched to Eric Joyce and his latest 'brawl' in a Commons bar, a storm in a teacup really, and the way it was being reported in the newspapers. On the Sunday, more lives on Leveson, thirteen in all. I had worked two busy weekend twelve-hour days for the last time. I had enjoyed it, of course, but I wouldn't miss the long hours.

George Osborne delivered his fourth Budget. I did lives all evening. The personal tax allowance was increased again, this time to £10,000 per annum. National insurance contributions were cut for employers. Government spending was to be cut by a further £2.5 billion. The economy was expected to grow but only very slowly, government borrowing would increase but only modestly, but government debt as a share of GDP was set to rise from 75.9% in 2013 to 85.6% in 2016.

It was an immense pleasure and privilege to have access to and stride around the Palace of Westminster, though not for much longer. I thought I should probably have a show reel. VT editor Chris Scott kindly cut it with me in between lives on the Budget and a preview of a Nick Clegg speech on immigration to be delivered the following day.

David Cameron gave a speech on immigration a few days later which I covered live. I attended the afternoon lobby briefing, my last experience of the Downing Street Follies, though I didn't know it at the time. I bumped into Conservative MPs Michael Howard and Nicola Blackwood, who now both sit in the House of Lords and said they couldn't understand why I was leaving Sky News. I had had lunch that day with one of my favourite MPs in the Members Dining Room. It was a privilege to be there, almost certainly for the last time.

I went to Downing Street to do a strange PTC for a film that two of Sky's cameramen, Pete Northall and Adam Murch, were making, their own personal project. I was supposed to be reporting in the nineteenth century, and they dressed me in a tall top hat and a frock coat. In the middle of this bizarre spectacle, David Cameron emerged from Number Ten and looked suitably bemused! It occurred to me that this might be the last time the prime minister would see me in Downing Street.

I was doing lives on Portsmouth South Lib Dem MP Mike Hancock who was to be investigated by the city council for 'improper behaviour' towards a female constituent. He was a councillor as well as an MP. He had already been cleared by the police and by an internal Lib Dem inquiry but, in June 2014 he settled out of court with the woman, known only by the pseudonym 'Annie'.

I was doing lives every hour all day on the Hancock story when Adam phoned with something of a political bombshell, strong rumours that David Miliband was to resign as a MP to take up a big role for a charity in New York. This had an air of inevitability about it. He had repeatedly said he wanted to end the "brothers' soap opera". It turned out that the *Mirror* had the story as an exclusive, their source being two unnamed Labour MPs. I called Jim Murphy and Douglas Alexander, my two prime suspects, Alastair Campbell and anyone else I could think of to stand up the story. I did lives every hour all evening, and enjoyed waxing lyrical about the popular, talented David Miliband who many in the Labour Party still thought should be their prime-minister-in-waiting.

He was off to run International Rescue in New York. Alastair Campbell's nickname for David Miliband when they had worked together in Downing Street had been 'Brains'. *Thunderbirds* aficionados were very amused that Brains was going to run International Rescue.

The next day was my final day at Sky New. From the moment I posted my news on Twitter, I was inundated with the kindest imaginable comments of praise and good wishes. MPs Ed Balls, Louise Mensch and Keith Vaz were particularly effusive among many, many others. I would be greatly missed, I was a great loss and so on. Even the normally acerbic Guido Fawkes published some very kind words: "goodbyes are flooding in for one of the nicest blokes in politics, seasoned hack Glen Oglaza who is leaving Sky today". Apparently I was "one of the most popular and best-liked people in Westminster".

My lovely Sky News colleagues at Westminster produced champagne, a cake and a 'sorry you're leaving' card which I will always cherish. I made a short speech, they laughed in all the right places, followed by a lot of goodbye hugs. It was very touching. I was having an out of body experience. This couldn't actually be MY departure, could it? But my overwhelming sense was one of relief. Several of us went downstairs to the Atrium bar for a couple of very jolly hours over a few beers. They were very supportive. I should be positive, the future was bright. I was the last to leave the newsroom that evening. I lingered. I would never return to that desk, my place of work, again.

I woke the next morning feeling immensely positive. There were many, many more tweets, and emails with rather vague job offers (please get in touch, etc.) and ideas about what I should do next. First, though, I needed some time to assimilate my new reality.

First on the agenda was a week's holiday with Sebastian in Tunisia, one of our favourite holiday destinations. Maddie was 15 and far too cool to go on holiday with a parent! The Tunisians had built too many five star hotels and couldn't fill them, so they were relatively cheap. Ours, the Amir Palace, was magnificent. Many of them were to stand empty after the terrorist attack in June 2015 which devastated Tunisia's tourism industry. One day on the beach we built an ever more elaborate structure which began as a castle but developed into a Mayan temple complex, an oasis, a jungle and a complex network of tunnels. Seb loved it, and for me it was the perfect post-Sky News antidote.

It was also the anniversary of the death of Tunisia's first president, Habib Bourgiba, a national holiday, so we went to Monastir to visit his mausoleum. Seb amused everyone with his drawings. At the age of 6 he was a talented little artist.

My 'leaving do' on April 18th was in the Atrium at 4 Millbank. Adam made a nice speech, I made mine. Among the gifts were an iPad and a painting by my friend, cameraman Paul Dickie, a talented artist, which contained a hidden message, AH DOCTOR, referring to a story we had covered in Aberdeen when we had both been working for ITN, the memorial service for the victims of the Piper Alpha disaster. No journalists were allowed in, but the sweet elderly ladies on the door who mistook me for a Church of Scotland minister said, "Ah Doctor, the other ministers are over there". And in I went! Paul had been calling me 'Dr Oglaza' in a Scottish accent ever since.

Several people gave me their own personal good luck cards, which was very sweet of them. Several reporters, news editors and programme editors added to the fun and the camera crews were well represented. I had only invited five MPs. They all turned up and I wish I'd invited more. Most of the spads and the lobby journalists I had invited made it. But this was really an event for the lovely team at Sky News Westminster. I had great support from the people who really mattered to me, my talented Westminster gang and from a few old faces who had worked with us over the years. Again, it felt surreal. Was this really MY leaving party?

I had a coffee at St James' church in Piccadilly with David Miliband who said it had taken him two years to find the right job so I shouldn't rush into anything and should find something I felt passionately about, and maybe do some writing or lecturing until the right thing came along. We talked about the IRC in New York. He very flatteringly said, "You represented honesty and integrity in political reporting", and that I had, "A great TV manner". The compliments were mutual. I still couldn't quite understand why he wasn't the leader of his party and potential prime minister.

I found his advice very sound and decided to take the summer off to think about my next move. He was very frank about his own situation since failing to win the Labour leadership, treading water while seeking a way out. What about the EU, he asked? Brussels needed a good shake-up and wasn't too far away from the children.

The next day, I went to a press gallery lunch with Jon Craig as his guest. I had to be a guest now. My former lobby colleagues were extremely welcoming. Nigel Farage was the after-lunch speaker and was very amusing, but I needed to cut the Westminster umbilical cord.

I went to see a head-hunter, the one who had found my friend and Sky News colleague Harriett Tolputt her job as head of press at Oxfam. He said I would be a "trophy catch". I thought that sounded like money! Mostly, though, he wanted to talk about politics, he was a Lib Dem. And no, I did not ever want to work for a political lobbying firm.

Any excuse for a holiday, I took myself off to Tenerife for a week in May. I spent the rest of that late spring and early summer doing media training. I found it rewarding to see the improvement in people's performances. During the last exercise of the day, I liked to tell them, "You could not have done that at nine a.m. this morning". And it paid the bills. I was also very moralistic about who I trained, so it also felt rewarding to be helping a good cause, campaign, charity or ethical company.

I had taken to hanging around outside Highgate cafes reading the papers and gossiping with friends, which is how I'd first met Ray Davies of The Kinks, one of my boyhood music idols and the one of the very best songwriters of his or any generation. His first question was usually, "Have you been in the field?" And I would have to explain that I wasn't doing that any more, at least for now. Ray is also an Arsenal fan!

I was still occasionally media training at Château de Romainville in Normandy. One of my partners in crime was Tim Friend, who had also worked both at ITN and Sky News. Now, he was an Al Jazeera correspondent and spent a lot of his time travelling around Europe. He was about to go to Croatia. He highly recommended working at Al Jazeera, but I wasn't sure that I wanted to step straight back onto the twenty-four-hour news treadmill. Not sure at all.

I did the early morning paper reviews on LBC a few times and had another week supporting the annual RCDS strategy exercise, but mostly that summer I was spending a lot more time with Maddie and Seb and loving every minute of it. I took them on safari to Kenya and Tanzania. They didn't much enjoy the rough camping. The first time I had been on safari, in Kenya, I found it mind-blowing. Here was life on earth largely without humans, just animals in their natural habitat without human interference. Maddie simply observed, "I don't really like animals that much"! And there was no Wifi!

We sometimes had elephants, baboons and even water buffalos strolling very close to our various camps. One night we heard a lion roar. It was a distant roar, but six-year-old Seb was concerned. "Daddy, are the animals going to eat us?" I was tempted to reply that they always ate cubs or children first and wouldn't want tough old meat like mine, but of course what I actually said was no, and anyway I would protect him. He was satisfied with that and went back to sleep. They were far happier when we got to Zanzibar and a hotel on the beach.

As we left Nairobi airport, the arrivals hall burst into flames, a huge fire. The airport closed and we had narrowly escaped being stranded.

Friends teased me that I had started it with a discarded cigarette end, but it was in arrivals not departures!

The day after we got back I did a live two-way for LBC. Two eighteen-year-old British volunteer teachers from north London, Katie Gee and Kirstie Trup, had had sulphuric acid thrown in their faces in Stone Town, Zanzibar. Truly shocking. As I had just returned from there and knew the street where it had happened, I was asked about how safe Zanzibar was. It appeared to have been a random attack, seemingly motiveless and completely out of character for the island.

I was also doing frequent live two-ways for STV, Scottish Television, from Westminster covering politics downstairs from the Sky News studios at 4 Millbank, which felt very odd. It was good to be keeping my hand in but, even months after leaving Sky News, the reality of that fact had still not completely sunk in.

In May, off duty soldier Lee Rigby was murdered in broad daylight in Woolwich, south-east London, near the Royal Artillery Barracks where he was stationed. It was a frenzied attack by two men wielding knives and a machete. I knew members of his regiment, the Royal Regiment of Fusiliers. His killers claimed they were avenging the killing of Muslims by British soldiers in Iraq and Afghanistan. They were condemned by British Muslim leaders and universally vilified; the country was shocked. They were sentenced in February 2014 to serve at least forty-five years.

At the end of August, the government lost a vote on taking action against Syria, a motion which had already been watered down. It had been close, 285-272, just 13 votes in it, but the ghost of March 2003 hung over the chamber during the debate as MP after MP claimed that they had been lied to and the invasion of Iraq had been a mistake if not illegal. That evening, there was a shocking report of a napalm attack on a school in northern Syria. Assad faced no consequences. What message was the House of Commons vote sending to the Syrian dictator? Or to our allies?

Later that year, in August, a chemical gas attack killed more than fourteen hundred people in Damascus, many of them children.

Far more shocking to me personally that August was the news that cameraman Mick Deane had been killed in Cairo. He had been shot by a sniper as he was filming anti-government demonstrations. One of the very best cameramen in the world, Mick was a font of wisdom and sound advice, a mentor to many and one of the warmest and funniest people I had ever met. And, like all great news cameramen, he was also a brilliant journalist with excellent editorial judgement. The news from Cairo left me and everyone else who knew him numb with shock.

I had a long and rather liquid lunch with former Sky News colleagues Jon Craig, Paul Dickie, Gary Honeyford, Niall Paterson and Colin Clements, a good gossip and catch up. The afternoon slipped by. It felt like a final farewell to Sky News, a final departure event.

In early September, there was another Syria debate during House of Commons foreign questions (questions to the Foreign Secretary) and John Kerry was at the Senate Foreign Relations committee. I tweeted live on both. I was still something of a workaholic and political obsessive. I really needed to let it go! But there were constant reminders. That evening, Channel 4 aired a documentary, *Siege in the Sahara*, about the al-Qaeda seizure of the Tigantourine gas installation in Algeria back in January.

I went to friend's barbecue in Dartmouth Park, north London, in the next street to Ed Miliband's house. I was still obsessed! But I was finding other things to do to fill the Sky News void. I started learning Spanish, going to the gym, did a weekly pub quiz with friends at The Bull in Highgate and got to go to see the mighty Arsenal at the Emirates more often than I had ever been able to. I was slowly adjusting to having a more 'normal' life where work wasn't the be all and end all.

I had, and still have, a close affinity with Kenya so I was even more shocked than most by the terrorist attack on The Westgate shopping centre in Nairobi that September. Sixty-eight people were killed, including four terrorists, and more than two hundred injured. The killers had used guns and grenades and had held many shoppers hostage. It took four days to end the attack. I knew that shopping centre, I had shopped there myself.

At the phone-hacking trial at the Old Bailey at the end of October, we learnt that Rebekah Brookes and Andy Coulson had been enjoying 'physical intimacy' for six years! She denied that it was a six-year secret affair, which is how it was being reported, but had been on and off between 1998 and 2004. Had David Cameron known? Several friends texted me to say: *I told you so.*

In November I was off to Episkopi, Cyprus, to support a British army exercise. This was the first of several such jobs in Cyprus. I had been there before both for work (ITN) and on holiday, but the view from the British sovereign base looked very different, its vital strategic position in the eastern Mediterranean. The accommodation was certainly very different, sharing a room with a bunk bed! But we had a great team and the thing I liked most about army food, school puddings. Apple crumble and custard! Sticky toffee pudding!

In early December, STV asked me to do a live on George Osborne's Autumn Statement. I declined. I didn't know enough about it and, although I could have read into the story, I would feel a fraud doing it. I no longer had my finger on the Westminster pulse and, anyway, it really was time to cut the Westminster umbilical cord. That day, Nelson Mandela finally passed away. Of course, Sky and the other news channels went open-ended as the tributes poured in from around the world. Mandela really had been THE political giant of our time. As President Obama put it at the memorial service five days later, "He made me want to be a better man. He speaks to what's best inside us." RIP.

I was invited again to the Irish Embassy Christmas drinks reception, always a grand affair, but I didn't go. I didn't feel it was legitimate to do so as I was no longer a political correspondent. Silly really.

I did, however, go to a press gallery lunch with Boris Johnson as a guest of my friend David Wooding of the *Sun*. Boris did his comedy turn, and it was great to catch up with some of my former Parliamentary lobby colleagues.

Among my Christmas cards were two, from Adam Boulton and our lovely politics news editor Clare Parry, saying how very much they missed me, which was very sweet of them. The feeling was mutual.

I took Maddie to New York for a few days and to experience New Year's Eve in Times Square. She was obsessed with Lady Gaga and had been long before most people, so I took her for dinner on New Year's Eve to Joanna's Trattoria on Upper West Side owned by Gaga's (Joanna's) parents, Joe and Cynthia. She was beyond excited, and even more so when I asked Joe to come and say hello. "Hey Maddie, Happy Noo Year's" he said in his New York accent. It was a fabulous way to end what had been a turbulent year.

CODA: LIFE AFTER SKY

2014 – 2021:Folgore. UKIP win in Europe! WEF, Davos. INSEAD. Lib Dem Wipeout. Parsberg 'Hearts and Minds'. Corbyn. BATUK. Brexit. Theresa May PM. Jürgen, Tim and the Major. Trump! Defence Diplomacy in Oman. Karaoke in Bydgoszcz. Kiev. The Dog Botherer of Tbilisi. Mazir-i-Sharif. Boris Johnson Prime Minister! Warships in the Med. A Plague of Locusts. Under Quarantine in Stavanger. Covid. Lockdown.

Andy Reeds had risen through the ranks, including time with 2 Para, and had spent eight years in the SAS. Having risen to the rank of major his last job in the army was to organise media interview training, having taken over from Major Ken Molyneux-Carter. He did a very clever if risky thing, left the army and effectively privatised his own job. In partnership with RAF reservist David Bennett, he set up a company, Crown Media, which has grown over the years, its focus shifting to providing simulated media for the British military and NATO. The company now has on its roster a talented pool of journalists and cameramen/editors.

I had worked with Andy when he was still in the army and continue to do so to this day. Over the following years, Crown has become the source of many stories and little foreign and domestic adventures in, among other places, Kenya, Afghanistan, Oman, Cyprus, France, Germany, Spain, Poland, Italy, Georgia and Norway.

I had been to the Normandy barracks, Sennelager before. Now, in January 2014, I was back. This, like many other exercises, was designed to test a headquarters staff, there were no exercising troops. The issue was Afghanistan drawdown, i.e. withdrawal. As I write, seven years later, it has finally happened. The Americans simply abandoned Bagram airbase, leaving the Afghan military and security forces to deal with the Taliban as best they could. The outcome with those awful scenes from Kabul was horribly predictable even if it happened far faster than anyone had imagined.

In my downtime, I was busy reading. Iain Dale had kindly invited me to be a judge in the political book of the year awards, along with Jacqui Smith and Steve Norris. It was an impressive shortlist; I had a lot of reading to do.

In early February, I was in Pisa with Andy Reeds and our splendidly named cameraman Atilla 'Til' Mustafa attempting to media train the Folgore (lightning), the Italian parachute regiment who were famous for having fought valiantly at El Alamein. The centrepiece of their parade ground was a statue commemorating their role in that battle. It was a privilege to be there. They strutted and preened as only Italian officers can! Andy said they were the only part of the Italian army that was any good, but couldn't resist adding that this was because they had been trained by the British, that is his Paras.

The Folgore boss, Brigadier Lorenzo D'Addazio was an Anglophile with an English wife and a daughter at Exeter University, and keen to get his senior officers trained. The only problem was that they kept disappearing from our training room to the coffee bar downstairs. When we went to find the officer who was supposed to be standing by to be our next 'interviewee', they'd insist we took an espresso and stop to chat.

I had never been to Pisa. It did not disappoint. The leaning tower is an absolute miracle, it really should not be standing. The food was, of course, spectacular. Local wild boar, home-made tiramisu and local red wine. We went to Lucca and took Seb's former nanny Sylvia, who was now back at home, to Viareggio for dinner. I would return to Lucca that July with Seb to stay at Sylvia's family's glorious Tuscan villa, Villa Aladino.

Later in February and three more times later in the year I was back at the UK Defence Academy in Shrivenham training members of the Higher Command and Staff Course, the 'baby generals' as we called them, already senior officers some of whom were destined to go to the very top. It was the custom back then to get a kind letter of appreciation and gratitude from generals and others of similar rank commanding the Staff College. I've kept mine and they are still treasured, not least the one from Commadore (as he then was) Sir Tim Laurence, husband of Princess Anne, the Princess Royal. It is a custom that, sadly, seems to have died out.

Shrivenham could get very complicated. On one exercise, we were running three theatre war games simultaneously! I acted as 'news' presenter and news editor across all three, which could be very confusing as each diverted in a totally different direction from the same starting position. Fortunately, I had a very good journalist working on each, Mary Green, Steve Clarke and Kitty Logan, which eased the pressure on my poor, over-taxed brain.

In early March Russia annexed Crimea without a shot being fired. In my view, this was inevitable, the Crimean Peninsula was home to Russian's Black Sea fleet. But the question troubling the world was whether or not Russia would also try to annex the Eastern part of Ukraine which, unfortunately for the Ukrainians, was not a member of NATO or the EU.

We chose the political book of the year in early spring over a breakfast meeting. I was late, and the other judges had already had a discussion so I was invited to contribute my tuppence worth. I said a few words about each book and why I had chosen *The Pike*, a biography of Gabriele d'Annunzio by Lucy Hughes-Hallett as the winner. The others concurred. They had arrived at the same conclusion.

I was doing a lot of media training, mostly in London but also at Media City in Salford, and in Edinburgh, Bristol and elsewhere. And I guested on several Arsenal podcasts, which was fun.

Someone very well-placed suggested I apply for the job of Al Jazeera Washington correspondent which had just become vacant. But for me that ship had sailed, I was enjoying my life in London, my children and the work I was doing.

In May, UKIP won the European elections, becoming the biggest UK party winning 24 of the 73 seats and 27% of the vote, the first time neither Labour nor the Conservatives won the popular vote at an election since 1906. In Scotland, the SNP achieved almost a clean sweep. The Lib Dems lost ten of the eleven seats they were defending and won just 7% of the popular vote, a sign of things to come. I was doing the early morning newspaper review on LBC, but of course we just talked about this unprecedented election result.

I was also doing occasional lives for Deutsche Welle, the English language German 24-hour news channel. I had and have no idea who watched it. In mid-September I did a live for the Germans reporting the results of the Scottish independence referendum. It had been a resounding victory for No on a turnout of 85%, but 1.6 million Scots had voted Yes. It was a can of worms. There was the West Lothian Question, the issue of 'Devo Max', and questions about Wales, Northern Ireland and English regional devolution. I did a live the same evening on the same subject for STV.

I couldn't resist tweeting Ed Miliband's speech to the Labour Party conference that September, the last annual conference before the 2015 general election. I thought it was tepid and hardly the speech of a prime-minister-in-waiting. Unflattering comparisons were being made with Tony Blair's barnstormer of 1996. At a dinner party at a friend's house in Greenwich, someone asked me about Labour's chances of winning in 2015. I was preparing a thoughtful, nuanced response when my friend Rory, who was a little the worse for drink, cut right across me and declared, "Ed Miliband will NEVER be prime minister!" It wasn't quite how I would have answered the question, but he was right.

In November, Mark Reckless held his Rochester and Strood seat despite having defected from the Tories to UKIP and UKIP had their second MP, after Douglas Carswell who had also defected from the Conservatives, and their first elected as a UKIP candidate. He was to go on to change parties three more times, not only reckless but also, it seems, restless. While his majority of more than 3,000 seemed comfortable it was also vulnerable. The misery continued for the Lib Dems whose candidate received just three 349 votes, 0.9% of the vote!

By the end of the year, 2014, I was still occasionally tweeting the yah-boos of PMQs, but the politics addiction was slowly wearing off. I was still doing early morning newspaper reviews for LBC and enjoying it, and I was delivering a lot more media training. Most journalists think they can do media training but only a few are actually any good at it. Teaching is an entirely different discipline.

I had covered the World Economic Forum annual meeting in January in Davos for both ITN and Sky News. Now, in 2015, I was to get a different perspective on this unique event, an insider's view. Steve Clarke, who I had worked with at the RCDS and elsewhere, had been a senior manager at Reuters which had the contract to cover the WEF. He had been asked to produce the VNRs, video news releases, of the annual meeting which would be sent to television newsrooms all over the world and he put together a great little team, the two of us and cameramen/editors Steve Gravenor and Dom Archer.

Our first task, after going out to get some GVs of Davos looking beautiful in the snow set against a deep blue sky, was to cover the opening ceremony, an Andrea Bocelli concert. Then it was down to business. Al Gore, Tony Blair, who was a big star at the WEF and with the international media, and the Italian, Turkish and Chinese prime ministers. Day two, and Angela Merkel, Christine Lagarde, Tim Berners-Lee and Gordon Brown in his United Nations role as special envoy for global education. Some prime ministers cash in after they leave office, Gordon was doing his bit to help educate the world's poorest children. He was as friendly to me as always. I bumped into George Osborne and his aide (and later wife) Thea Rogers. He was doing a round of interviews, including Sky News. Next day was meeting US Secretary of State John Kerry and French President François Hollande, and listening to Bill and Melinda Gates and many others. We were feeding comprehensive and very newsy VNRs, our material was being used all over the world.

We amused ourselves in the evenings by watching Richard Quest's bizarre performances from the wings of CNN's rooftop live position.

Our final evening, our work done, revolved around eating and drinking. Among those propping up the bar at the Belvedere Hotel were John Kerry, Richard Branson and Christine Lagarde. The WEF media team 'thank you' dinner, a feast of fondue and far too much Swiss white wine, was followed by the superb and packed Reuters' party in the Europa piano bar. Everyone had worked hard and was demob happy. We finished at a club downstairs from the piano bar (very handy!), the Cabana Club, which was like a very LOUD student disco. Or maybe I was just showing my age. When we staggered off at 3.30am it was still going strong. Boring, staid Davos in boring, staid Switzerland. Who would have thought it?

The WEF annual meeting in Davos would become an annual gig, a week every January, although the 2020 Covid pandemic forced us to cover it remotely, by Zoom. Of course, this is much, much cheaper. No flights, no dining out, and no over-priced Davos accommodation. And no more January weeks in the beautiful Swiss alps.

I was frequently media training at RAF Halton near Wendover in Buckinghamshire, one of the country's main military training centres.

Halton House, the officers' mess, was built for the Rothschild family in the 1880s. It really is truly magnificent and it's always a pleasure and a privilege to work there. It has also featured in many, many films and television programmes including *The Queen, The Crown, The King's Speech, Downton Abbey*, The James Bond film *The World is Not Enough, Poirot, Foyle's War, Miss Marple, Spooks* etc., etc., etc.

Since just about everything in the military became tri-service, training at Halton often produces a mixed bag of bedfellows. On this particular day, we trained an army doctor, an RAF pilot, a Royal Navy captain and a Royal Marines sergeant major.

At Château de Romainville they had a black Labrador called D'Artagnan, who became my best friend in all of France! Out of my work at the château arose a fabulous new opportunity. Steve Knight, who organised our work at Château de Romainville, was an adjunct professor of communications at INSEAD, the premier international business school with its main campus in Fontainebleau. So popular were his classes and workshops that he needed some help and, I'm delighted to say, recruited me. So, four or five times a year we would teach MBA and Executive MBA students to speak fluent human! We were aided and abetted by American voice coach and former opera singer Dory Grandia, who had also worked for the Democrats in Texas, often a thankless task. Bistrot Neuf in Fontainebleau became our favourite haunt in the evenings, talking American politics over the filet de boeuf and French red.

I was media training one day on Abingdon Green, opposite the Houses of Parliament. Andrew Neil was there making an election promo, and with an entourage of twenty-five! He joked that he was, "Making a documentary about over-manning at the BBC"!

When the country voted on that Thursday in May 2015, the exit poll was astonishing, and astonishingly accurate, predicting Conservatives 316, Labour 239, SNP 58 (out of 59 Scottish seats), the Lib Dems just 10 and UKIP 2. I don't think anyone could quite believe it but, as the night wore on, its accuracy gradually became apparent.

The SNP wiped out Labour in Scotland. Jim Murphy and Douglas Alexander were among those who fell. How would Labour every win another general election without any seats in Scotland?

The Lib Dems were in almost total meltdown. All their big guns were out. Vince Cable, Charles Kennedy, Danny Alexander, Ed Davey, Jo Swinson, Lynne Featherstone, Simon Hughes (until recently the party's deputy leader and an MP since 1983), Steve Webb, the list went on and on. They had been reduced from 57 MPs to just 8. Nick Clegg, who had held onto his Sheffield Hallam seat but only, it was clear, because of Tory tactical voting, described it as a "cruel and punishing" night. Angela Merkel had warned him about the fate of junior coalition partners, but no one had expected this almost total annihilation.

The final result gave the Conservatives 330 seats and a healthy enough overall majority. Labour actually lost seats, down 19 to 232. The SNP was now the third largest party in the House of Commons. The Lib Dems, devastated and a party in government only twenty-four hours earlier, had become irrelevant overnight.

UKIP got nearly 4 million votes and one MP. The SNP received 1.5 million votes and 56 MPs. This system is broken!

The morning after the night before, Ed Miliband, Nick Clegg and Nigel Farage all resigned as Party leaders.

Of course, it was immensely frustrating not to be reporting on election night, but I did the early morning paper review for LBC a couple of days later and that, of course, was all about the election and its aftermath. I had made my decision over two years earlier. I was where I was.

Which reminds me, Adam Boulton once said to an interviewee during a live programme, "Well, we are where we are."

"Oh no we're not", the guest replied.

I have no idea how you take a conversation like that any further.

On June 2nd, we lost Charles Kennedy. Charles was unfailingly courteous with an infectious sense of humour. He had been a highly-skilled debater since his days as an undergraduate at Glasgow University when I had been at Aberdeen. He was universally respected by political friend and foe alike. In his time, he had been the youngest MP at the age of twenty-eight. I felt I had lost a friend.

My new freedom meant I could now tweet or post on social media whatever I wanted. We had had a simple but very sensible rule at Sky News, do not tweet anything you wouldn't broadcast. Now I was free, for example, to tweet extremely rude things about Donald Trump.

Before that year's RCDS strategy game, working with Andy Reeds and our team, I did a live presentation to the RCDS members. I was now very relaxed about doing these and had even mastered PowerPoint. It had been a very different story the first time with a live audience in my television days. The camera was my friend and I could happily talk to millions of people, the trick being to talk to one person and never, ever to imagine you were addressing the nation. Suddenly, there were hundreds of them in the room, and they were all staring at me! And they were asking me questions! I soon got to love it almost as much as broadcasting.

It was 34 degrees in Bavaria that August, a heatwave. We were working at a US army base where Royal Anglian and Royal Irish troops were being put through their paces. We were reporting the scenario as if it was real, our 'fake news'. Although we had 5am starts, we also had some downtime when the British army HQ went into planning mode, so we got to spend some time at the lido in Parsberg, which certainly beat working for a living.

The scenario was a small town which had been taken over by the bad guys, played by American troops. In the centre of the town was a 'cafe' where the 'townspeople' had gathered. They were played by German civilians who took their roles extremely seriously. The Royal Anglians and Royal Irish were exemplary. We had an American army major with us called Doug but who I preferred to call Chuck, who kept asking us for our B roll as the British attack was "textbook". They first secured the cafe, protecting the civilians, before fanning out to find and kill the enemy. Doug, or Chuck, said American soldiers would have kicked the doors in, shot everyone and asked questions later! Their idea of hearts and minds, he said, was, "Bop bop bop, two in the heart and one in the head".

Next to the cafe was a wall, about nine or ten feet high. There were chairs scattered around outside the cafe. When the Americans had scaled this wall they had huffed and puffed, climbing over each other and shouting 'Yo!' a lot. It had taken them ages. When the British soldiers arrived, they simply lined the chairs up against the wall and were up and over in seconds.

Once the 'town' was secured, I decided I could duck behind one of the buildings to relieve myself. All that coffee. As I was doing so, I glanced down. Three feet to my left, lying prone on his stomach with his pointed rife guarding the perimeter, was a camouflaged British soldier! "All right sir?" he asked cheerfully as I emptied my bladder in his immediate vicinity.

I was teaching at INSEAD when Jeremy Corbyn was elected Labour leader that September with 59.5% of the first-round votes. A barely believable result. Tom Watson was elected deputy leader, a dream ticket but for the Tories not for Labour, which was now to be run by Tom and Jerry!

Jeremy Corbyn fielded a strong tactic in his first PMQs, asking questions he said had been sent to him by members of the public. This was disarming. David Cameron couldn't attack him without being seen to attack them. But it was a tactic that would quickly become tiresome and unconvincing.

I was interviewed for a TV documentary series, *Twenty moments that rocked the Noughties*, on the US presidential election, the Olympics, 7/7 and MPs' expenses. A remarkably large number of people saw it.

Al Jazeera asked me to do a paper review the next day but I couldn't. It was Sebastian's ninth birthday. My priorities had changed. For the third year running I got Christmas cards from former Sky News colleagues, including Adam, telling me how much they missed me. Very kind.

I had been to Kenya four times before, including on honeymoon. In the autumn of 2015 I went there for the first time to work, three weeks mostly spent in a three-man tent in the bush an hour or so by car on a dirt track from Archer's Post. Living in such close proximity you need team members you get on with. I was fortunate to have cameraman/editor Kevin Cook, not only supremely capable but also able to keep us laughing for three weeks. I was to work with some excellent cameramen/editors over the ensuing years, many of them, to my initial surprise, every bit as good as those at ITN or Sky News.

The third member of our team was a strange Egyptian-American radio reporter called Dan Brown. No, not that one, although he claimed to be writing a novel. Suffice it to say he hasn't worked with us since. There's an old joke in journalism. A young reporter takes his friend, also a young reporter, to meet his father who is also a journalist.

"What are you up to at the moment?" the father asks.

"I'm writing a book," replies the keen young thing.

"Yes, neither am I."

Kevin was not the fittest of men, he was as bad as me, and there was quite a bit of marching in very hot dusty conditions in full body armour and at six thousand feet, higher than Ben Nevis. These two unfit middle-aged men were being looked after by the regimental sergeant major of 2 Scots, John Curran. At one point, Kevin needed to stop, lie down and get his breath back.

"Just don't fucking die on me," was Sergeant Major Curran's less than sympathetic observation.

"Why?" I asked. "Too much paperwork?"

He laughed. "Damn right, too much fucking paperwork."

I have worked in Kenya for BATUK, the British Army Training Unit Kenya, several times since and always insist on a Land Rover. We are not fit nineteen-year-old paratroopers let alone Gurkhas who, in full kit, were running up hills I could barely walk up! We were not the ones being exercised.

For the first time, BATUK was using a new live-firing exercise area and we went up in a helicopter to film it. I do so love messing about in helicopters.

The Gurkhas slaughtered two goats they had bought from local Samburu tribesmen for a goat curry. Four Gurkhas hold the poor animal's legs while a fifth strikes the goat's neck with his Kukri knife. There is a technique to doing this, a simultaneous chopping and slicing motion which should decapitate the goat with one blow. Unfortunately, a novice was having a go and it took him five blows. The goat, his spinal cord severed, was dead after the first strike, his body convulsing in death. Meanwhile, the tethered second goat watched on! It's a cruel world, especially if you're a goat and anywhere near a Gurkha.

Back in Britain, replying to George Osborne's Autumn Statement, John McDonnell, who was now the Shadow chancellor, quoted from Chairman Mao's *Little Red Book* and brandished it at the despatch box. Unbelievable! An absolute gift for the Tories.

2016 started hideously. In January we lost both David Bowie and, just four days later, the supremely talented actor Alan Rickman, and both were only 69 years old. The nation was in shock. Well, I certainly was.

The year got worse, or better depending on your point of view, when the UK voted to leave the European Union.

Arsenal were still top of the league. This was the season that Leicester City became champions and Arsenal finished second. Leicester lost only three games all season, two of them home and away to Arsenal. At the start of the season, bookies were offering 5000-1 on Leicester City winning the Premier League. I wondered if anyone took those odds. Gary Lineker?

My working year began in Davos at the WEF annual meeting, hard work but in glorious surroundings and with the same brilliant team. We covered a press conference and, the next day, a speech by American Vice President Joe Biden. Iran's foreign minister, Mohammad Javad Zarif, was as smooth and persuasive as ever, a born diplomat. At the Congress Centre there were so many presidents and prime ministers it was like shooting fish in a barrel. Benjamin Netanyahu, Kofi Annan, the CEO of Microsoft, the Queen of Jordan, assorted African leaders etc. etc. We doorstepped the Turkish and French prime ministers. I bumped into the Sky News team and caught up on the gossip, and chatted to Gordon Brown who was as friendly as ever. David Cameron gave a rather parochial speech on the UK's forthcoming EU referendum. I tried to doorstep him but he only managed a quick, "Hello".

His director of communications, Craig Oliver, said, "Nice try Glen." I don't think he even realised that I was no longer with Sky News but was covering the event for the WEF. Other Downing Street aides with whom I had liaised for so many years, including Gaby Bertin and Liz Suggs, were a lot more pleasant. But then, they always had been.

The next morning was, once again, a turkey shoot, Grande Fromages everywhere. Bill Gates, Ban Ki-moon, Goldman Sachs president Gary D Cohn, Queen Máxima of The Netherlands, Prince Albert of Monaco, Gordon Brown, Christine Lagarde, the president of Lithuania and so on. And, oh look, there's Bono and Kevin Spacey. And over there, the presidents of Mexico and Argentina, John Kerry, Justin Trudeau etc. etc. It really is a truly unique event. I spotted David Miliband in the distance but didn't get a chance to ask him about his new life in New York. We filmed a meeting between Richard Branson and Kofi Annan, and adjourned after dinner to The Belvedere hotel for free champagne, but only for an hour. We were working hard with early starts.

CTTN, China's twenty-four-hour English language news channel, wanted me to work for them in Beijing. I would be a presenter and 'editorial advisor'. An exciting idea, and the money was very tempting, but Maddie and Seb needed me to be in London not halfway around the world.

I was back in Kenya for three weeks in March with a different team, Scottish journalist Linda Sinclair and RADA-trained actor turned cameraman Ian Williams. I hadn't worked with either before. Ian kept us laughing every single day. As usual, this involved 3am starts. It was too hot to work in the bush in the afternoons which were spent editing and attending exercise control meetings reviewing the last twenty-four hours and planning the next twenty-four.

We were looked after by a great character, Captain Tam Lindsay, who would ask us at the end of every briefing, which was usually about what we had to be doing at some ungodly hour the next morning, with "Happy?" Which is army-speak for I hope you have absorbed all that information.

My reply, at the prospect of getting up in the middle of the night, was usually, "Yes, Tam, fucking delirious."

Linda interviewed me for Glasgow's Radio Clyde, for whom she worked. It was twenty years to the day since the Dunblane massacre. We were in the bush in remotest Kenya but she was still managing to pull together a radio piece marking that appalling day.

The army had new tents which had a floor. Luxury! The dust was still a problem but didn't get into every nook and crevice as it had before. And it was forty degrees centigrade, too hot to sleep.

The animals were everywhere, of course, the magic of Kenya. One early morning we spotted a young leopard walking through the long grass near our camp, a very rare sight. We usually only saw leopards at a distance through binoculars, lounging on rocks or in a tree, and even then they were very hard to spot.

We had three companies exercising, two Gurkhas and one Royal Welsh, so each 'enemy position' had to be 'attacked' three times. The Gurkhas were, of course, uber-efficient. Their company commander, Major Ben Birkback, shouted. A lot. And very, very loudly. I nicknamed him 'Bellowing Ben'. One of the Kenyan 'actors' had once boxed for Kenya at the Olympic Games. He was playing a village pastor. All you could hear above the gun fire and people screaming, or pretending to scream, was Ben bellowing, "Priest! Priest!" I think he wanted a word with him.

A kingfisher flashed into the water outside my tent while two very bold vervet monkeys stole a pastry from my breakfast table right under my nose. At Laikipia Air Base, after interviewing the Gurkha CO Lt. Col. Jody

Davies, we filmed a Gurkha Kukri drill, another example of the privileged access I have enjoyed for so much of my working life.

Back in semi-civilization, in Nanyuki, meant a trip to a supermarket, fresh Kenyan coffee at Dorman's Café, and another trip to Nanyuki's animal orphanage where I once again got to pet another rescued cheetah cub. True civilization was afternoon tea at the Mount Kenya Safari Club on the equator. Next to an equator sign on the road was a huge billboard advertising Arsenal Football Club. Of course, I took photographs and posted them on Facebook.

Labour MP Jo Cox was murdered on June 16th, fatally shot and stabbed in Birstall, West Yorkshire. Her attacker, Thomas Mair, had a history of mental health problems and links with a neo-Nazi organisation. He had shouted, "Britain first", as he attacked. It happened in broad daylight. It was beyond shocking. MPs had been physically attacked before. Stephen Timms had been stabbed in 2010 and Ian Gow had been murdered by the IRA in 1990, but this was an entirely new nightmare.

Labour won the resulting by-election with 86% of the vote. Out of respect, the Conservatives, Lib Dems, Green Party and UKIP did not contest the seat.

Mair was sentenced to life in November 2016, but his conviction seemed almost irrelevant. It wouldn't bring Jo Cox back.

I was confident on EU referendum day, June 23rd, that we would vote to stay in the European Union. Why wouldn't we? But it had been a nasty and divisive campaign, the Leave campaign had told lie after lie while the Remain campaign seemed complacent, constantly reactive rather than proactive. No one realised just how deeply pissed off people were with the government, any government, the 'establishment'. In my view, it was the protest vote to end all protest votes. It was clear long before the votes were counted that the wounds inflicted during a vicious campaign would take years to heal.

I was teaching at the UK Defence Academy on that Thursday and then flew straight to INSEAD in Fontainebleau. My mobile phone went into meltdown from 4am on the Friday, as did Twitter and Facebook. My countrymen had actually voted to leave the world's largest trading block and an institution which, though deeply flawed, had rendered another European war unthinkable. The vote had been close, 51.9% to 48.1%.

Although the referendum was not legally binding, political reality said otherwise. What amazed me was that David Cameron had not set a higher threshold, at least 60% if not two-thirds rather than a simple majority for such a huge decision. In the previous such referendum, back in 1975, 67.2% had voted for the UK to remain in the EU. It felt to me like the country had been conned. It was the first time a British national referendum had resulted in a government defeat.

Dave resigned! Having claimed less than two weeks earlier that he would remain at the helm whatever the referendum result, the prime minister stood in Downing Street and said, "I do not think it would be right for me to try to be the captain that steers our country to its next destination". Many felt that destination would be straight onto the rocks, although the jubilant victors were already talking about 'Global Britain' and the fantastic trade deals just waiting to be negotiated.

I thought I understood the reasons why it had happened, people feeling ignored and disenfranchised for too long, but I had never seen a country shoot itself in the foot. I thought it would hugely diminish our influence in the world and might still lead to the break-up of the UK. The Leave campaign had lied and lied and lied again, a bunch of populists and political opportunists who, to their own amazement, had tapped into something, a massive disenchantment with our entire political system.

Something not entirely dissimilar seemed to be happening in some other European countries. Populist politicians throughout Europe opposed to the EU were, it seemed to me, doing Vladimir Putin's job for him if the end game was to be the demise of the EU. Their modus operandi was and remains simple enough. Amplify, exaggerate or simply invent problems (immigrants stealing our jobs), divide and polarise people, spread fear and then position themselves as the saviours, the only ones able to find a solution. In some ways it was straight out of the Goebbels playbook. In the Nazi Germany of the 1930s, every negative economic effect and every act of violence was blamed first on the Communists and later on the Jews. The only way to solve the problem was to jail political opponents, silence the press and control the judiciary. And we know where all that led to.

Needless to say, the reaction of my international MBA students at INSEAD was one of slack-jawed astonishment. Whatever country they were from, they were bewildered by the result. But they were the brightest of the bright and shared an internationalist view of the world.

I went straight from INSEAD back to the UK Defence Academy in Shrivenham. Here, there was a far more mixed reaction. It was clear that many military officers had voted to leave the EU for a variety of reasons. Chief among them seemed to be resistance to the idea of a European army, although we were members of NATO and worked extremely closely with our European allies, for example in the ARRC, the Allied Rapid Reaction Corps. Also much in evidence was the view, common among Brexiters, that they resented being 'dictated to' by Brussels.

Alarmingly quickly, attention drifted to football and the Euro 2016 championship. England lost 2-1 to Iceland which was not only humiliating but also very funny.

The next morning, Labour MPs passed a no confidence motion against Jeremy Corbyn's leadership by a huge majority, 172 votes to just 40. Corbyn said the ballot had 'no constitutional legitimacy' and he would not 'betray' the party members who had elected him by resigning. I had no doubt that, if it came to it, the party membership would re-elect him, but how can you stay as Party leader when such an overwhelming majority of your own MPs want you gone?

That day, David Cameron was at an EU summit in Brussels. Awkward? Not much! Nigel Farage gave the European Parliament both barrels, "you're not laughing now", and how they absolutely loathed him for it.

Two days later, Theresa May and Michael Gove announced their candidacies for the Conservative Party leadership and therefore Prime Minister. In a bizarre and astonishing twist, Boris Johnson appeared at his campaign launch to announce that he would not actually be standing. His support was already melting away, mostly towards Michael Gove. Like Corbyn, the party membership adored him, but the party's MPs did not.

No longer doing lives for Sky News, I had to content myself with writing about the events of that tumultuous week in a blog.

We had a new prime minister, and Theresa May wasted little time in selecting her new Cabinet. George Osborne was sacked, replaced as Chancellor by Phil Hammond. Amber Rudd was the new Home Secretary and, amazingly, Boris Johnson became Foreign Secretary. As expected,

David Davis became Secretary of State for Exiting the European Union, aka Brexit Secretary.

At INSEAD we joined in the French minute of silence for those killed in Nice when a truck deliberately drove into crowds of people celebrating Bastille Day. 86 had been killed and nearly 500 injured.

In Turkey, what looked like an attempted coup failed. Erdoğan cracked down and arrested anyone he thought opposed him, thousands of people including judges, university professors and journalists.

Donald Trump's wife, Melania, was widely derided for her speech to the Republican Convention, sections of which appeared to have been lifted straight from a Michelle Obama speech in 2008.

I was back in Kenya for three weeks with the army in September. With me were journalist Toby Gilles (Watford fan) and cameraman Alan Howard (Spurs). Alan is a dead ringer for Jürgen Klopp. In the market at Archer's Post one day two Kenyans, without any prompting from us, asked him if he was Jürgen Klopp. They also asked me if I was in the British army because "you look like a major". For some reason, the commanding officer of the exercising troops kept calling Toby 'Tim', so we became Jürgen, Tim and the major.

Our driver, Fantasu, known as Fanta, was speedy but also very careful. His Land Rover was filthy with the dust of the bush, so we couldn't resist writing on the dirty rear window: *Fanta cars: Better fast than safe*.

He and another of our drivers, Felix, were determined to be the fastest through the bush to our remote camp, trying to beat the record of forty-two minutes which resulted in some hair-raising though never quite white-knuckle driving. Forty-two minutes was the record for getting to Archer's Post and the nearest bar, the wonderful Omija bar beside a river from which we could watch hippos wallowing in the mud and elephants coming to drink and cross over to the other side. There was cold Tusker beer and, miracle of miracles, Wi-Fi! The nearest cup of cappuccino was another two-hour drive away in Nanyuki.

As well as exercising the soldiers, we made a wildlife safety film advising them on what they should do if confronted by a wild animal (walk backwards slowly but very deliberately and avoiding eye contact in most but not all situations). A soldier had been gored by an elephant just before we'd arrived. We met our wildlife expert Steve Carey, a white Zimbabwean, at the idyllic Laikipia wilderness camp. We filmed very close to a large pride of lions and an elephant seeing them off when they were in her way. Steve described for the soldiers the habitats of leopards and hyenas and what to do about snakes and scorpions. I felt like David Attenborough!

Steve had three dogs. My favourite, called Boris, was a cross between an African lion dog (which used to be called Rhodesian Ridgebacks) and something even larger. Steve said not to get too friendly with Boris as, "sooner or later a leopard will probably carry him off".

The best sleep I ever had was on a very uncomfortable army camp bed in a tent in the middle of the Kenyan bush. It only lasted forty-five minutes before we had lunch. We had been out filming the exercising troops since three a.m., and it was bliss. I remember how that forty-five minute deep sleep felt to this day. If I ever have trouble getting to sleep, which is extremely rarely, I just imagine myself back there.

We met an amateur football team who were all deaf and wearing a mixed bag of clothes. They too thought Alan might be Jürgen Klopp! At Toby's initiative, we bought them a football kit for each player. On our last night, dinner at the fabled Kongoni's restaurant in Nanyuki with Fanta and his splendidly and appropriately named pretty young wife Queen. Her second name was Elizabeth! She was from Arusha in Tanzania, the base for people climbing Kilimanjaro. Fabulous food, plenty of South African Merlot and Alan, Toby and I dissolved into a ridiculous fit of giggles. We were all completely exhausted.

Thinking about Fanta's Queen Elizabeth I'm reminded that my sister once had a Filipino boyfriend called Romeo. His sister's name was Juliet!

The actor David Harewood presented a TV programme, *Will Britain every have a black Prime Minister*? I thought it was time for Chuka Umunna to find his courage and stand for Labour leader, if his chance hadn't already passed.

2016, the year of Brexit, the year of Trump. A year in which, it seemed to me, nationalism had triumphed over liberalism, populism over evidence and expertise, paranoia over trust. It had been a battle between simple slogans ('Take back control', 'Make America great again') and complex truths, trade, jobs, influence in the world, the net EU immigrants' contribution of billions of pounds to the UK economy, the tens of thousands of immigrants working in the NHS.

On the way to the WEF in Davos in January 2017 I bumped into the lovely Hannah Pawlby, once special advisor to Charles Clarke at the Home Office. She was now working for a PR company and was to look after Jamie Oliver at the WEF annual meeting. I didn't have the heart to tell her that no one in Davos was likely to be even remotely interested in Jamie Oliver.

Because of our unique access, we got exclusive shots of US Vice President Joe Biden who greeted me with, "Hi. How are you sir?". In the front row of the opening ceremony, some of that year's star attractions, the beautiful singer Shakira, the wonderful Anne-Sophie Mutter, the supremely talented Forest Whitaker, the ubiquitous Al Gore, Máxima Queen of the Netherlands and Denmark's Helle Thorning-Schmidt. Quite a line up!

The main event on the first day was a speech by Chinese President Xi on free trade and protectionism, a brass-necked and very thinly-veiled attack on America's new president, Donald Trump. Star-spotting included the actor Matt Damon who was at the WEF to talk about Water Aid. The Dalian region of China hosted a charming reception with food, music and dancers. Great pictures! We were also treated to an equally exotic musical experience by four members of the Afghan National Women's Orchestra.

Theresa May spoke to the WEF the next morning. It was not a memorable speech. It was the eve of Trump's inauguration concert in Washington which was absolutely dire, no one wanted to perform for him. I watched his inauguration speech the next day. Many in Davos agreed with me that it was just another campaign speech, small-minded, mean-spirited and vindictive.

Within days, Trump was claiming that between three and five million votes had been fraudulent. He was clearly bonkers! If true, and it wasn't, it made his election illegitimate! He would try it on again when he lost in 2020.

I taught at INSEAD again in January, April, June and September, as stimulating as ever. Each year *The Financial Times* ranked the international business schools and INSEAD had again come first. Harvard had slipped from second to fourth, but Harvard is incredibly well-endowed and is part of the university rather than a stand-alone business school and would be back. Of the top ten, seven were normally American and two British, London and Cambridge business schools, usually mid-table. I was a mere visiting professor/executive coach but I took great delight in joining in the celebrations.

In February I was back in Cyprus. Once again, I went to too many briefings. The exercise was called Exercise Fusion. I called it Exercise Confusion. Happily, I had a couple of Bill Bryson's hilarious books to keep me going and, by way of total contrast, Janine di Giovanni's excellent *The Morning they Came for us: Dispatches from Syria*. If you read only one book on reporting a war, make it this one.

A few days in, they wanted a five-minute video on 'the story so far' to show at a VIP visit. Easy enough, except that the exercise director had written twelve pages of things that had to be included, which would translate into about half an hour of television. So, another lesson was needed in how television works, what is possible and what isn't, and why less is more. But the sun was shining and we were in Cyprus.

We filmed at the ruins of the ancient Greek city of Kourion, its acropolis perched one hundred metres above the beach at Episkopi Bay. The water in the eastern Mediterranean was freezing cold! We had the most splendid fish mezze at the beach cafe. Our team of eight were the only customers and it was not far off closing time. The cafe owner had a mountain of fish of various sorts to get rid of, so plate after plate piled high with seafood of all description arrived. And they were all equally fresh and delicious.

I taught at INSEAD three more times that year, 2017, and worked three more times at the UK Defence Academy as well as supporting the annual RCDS Strategy Exercise in July. I was offered the opportunity to take over Hillside media training, which was still going despite losing Hillside House. The brand had been kept alive. I could have my own company with several established clients. It would cost me of course, several thousand pounds, but the profit margins were slim and it would involve pitching for business. Touting for business was absolutely not what I wanted to be doing! I much preferred being the hired gun.

I had just returned from working in Prague where we stayed at the splendid Mandarin Oriental hotel, a former monastery. The training, with my friend and colleague Jacqui Harper, was very civilised. Our trainees, financial consultants, were used to plenty of coffee breaks and a proper one-hour break for lunch. I had two hours before my flight home to stroll around the city, climb the two hundred and fifteen steps to the top of St Nicholas' tower for the view, struggle through the hordes of tourists on the Charles Bridge, revisit Wenceslas Square and remember previous visits to that beautiful city.

While I was busy swanning around Europe on various assignments in June, the news at home was horrendous. Eight people were killed and forty-eight injured in the London Bridge terrorist attack. I know Borough Market well and could only imagine the horror as the three terrorists ran around randomly stabbing people. No sooner had we recovered from the shock of that attack when, just eleven days later seventy-two people died in a fire at Grenfell Tower in West London. It was the deadliest residential fire in Britain since the Second World War.

In between these two awful events, Theresa May made the mistake Gordon Brown might have made in 2007. Despite having a House of Commons majority, she went to the country to ask for her own mandate to govern. The result was to leave Mrs May and her government at the mercy of the DUP, the tail that would be wagging the Conservative dog.

The UKIP vote had collapsed. What was the point of UKIP now that we had left the EU? But a lot of their votes went to Labour and not just to the Conservatives. The SNP's Alex Salmond lost his seat, to a Conservative!

Lib Dem leader, Tim Farron, hung on to his West Moreland and Lonsdale seat but I was convinced that he would soon be replaced as Party leader by Vince Cable, or Jo Swinson, or maybe Ed Davey. He was gone a month later, replaced by Vince Cable who in turn was succeeded by Jo Swinson who held the position for just five months in 2019 before being replaced by Ed Davey. She had lost her own seat of East Dunbartonshire in the 2019 general election.

At INSEAD we had a new professor, an American Buddhist who had once been on a retreat of silence for six months. Imagine that, six months of not speaking. I can't keep quiet for six minutes!

Another of our colleagues, a woman, told us about her worst-ever dating experience. This man had persuaded her to go skiing with him. When she told him she had never skied before, he said not to worry he was an expert and would look after her. When they got to the Alps it turned out that he had never skied before either. "Two days later", she said, "I was bruised, mildly concussed... and single".

One evening, after supporting the RCDS Strategy Exercise in central London, we went to somewhere called the Big Easy where the gimmick was that, for a very reasonable set price, you could eat all the barbequed meat you could manage. There were nine of us, very jolly, but we ended up with a lot of food left over. Cameraman Dom Archer, being kind-hearted, suggested that we get it wrapped to take away and give it to the homeless people who were sheltering in doorways all around us in London's West End.

One of the intended recipients asked, "What's in there?"

"Chicken."

"I don't eat chicken!"

Fair enough. He obviously wasn't that hungry, perhaps our attempt at charity had been misplaced. It was gratefully received a few doorways along.

I got to do a voiceover with my friend, the actress Annie Cowan, for a dystopian movie, *Await further instructions*, starring David Bradley. I was impressed by Annie's acting. All I had to do was to play the role of a newscaster, so there was no acting involved. I really should do more voiceover work.

We were supporting an army exercise in Norfolk. One evening, we were in a country pub when a fight broke out, thankfully in the next bar. They took it outside, and I actually heard a girl screaming, "Leave it, Wayne, he ain't worth it." This in the middle of rural Norfolk! Nice pub, rough trade.

I did some media training for Global Witness. Trump's former presidential campaign manager, Paul Manafort, had just been charged with twelve offences including fraud, money-laundering, conspiracy against the United States and 'being an unregistered agent of a foreign country'. He had been working for Vladimir Putin's puppet, Ukrainian President Viktor Yanukovych. Global Witness was about to release what its lawyers claimed were money-laundering allegations against Trump himself, hence the need for some media training. Lawyers are always difficult. Television news is very simple and to the point, while lawyers seem to need at least twenty-four qualifying clauses for every statement or sentence.

The genocidal dictator, Robert Mugabe, was finally removed from office in Zimbabwe. A public advocate of illegal arrest and torture, his corrupt rule ended in what appeared to be a bloodless coup. The army simply placed him under house arrest. When he resigned, Mugabe managed to negotiate a deal to avoid any prosecution and which left his business interests and bank accounts, the proceeds of crime, untouched. Somehow, he also managed to get a severance payment of several million dollars!

In retirement, Mugabe was given full diplomatic status, a large, publicly-funded house and more than twenty members of staff. He died two years later. He had gone from being one of the heroes of the Zimbabwean and South African liberation movements to an internationally reviled mass murderer.

Tony Blair's relationship with Mugabe had always been fraught and often antagonistic. As the once resource-rich country, the breadbasket of Africa, slid further and further into economic disaster, hyperinflation, corruption and political tyranny, the Blair government had frozen all aid to Zimbabwe in 2000, as had the IMF. My senior military contacts at the time told me in confidence that Tony Blair had asked them to war game overthrowing Mugabe, but they had told him it was impractical and would cost too many lives, particularly Zimbabwean lives. In his book, *A Journey*, Tony Blair explains what I had been told at the time, that military intervention was impractical because:

> for reasons I never quite understood, the surrounding African nations maintained a lingering support for him and would have opposed any action strenuously.

My latest written feedback from our INSEAD MBA students included the gem that I 'cut through the BS to get to the point'. Yep, that's what spending years as a political correspondent does for you. Another remarked that my analysis of their performances was 'a bit tough'. Yes, kids, that's how you learn. Tough love!

After another training day in Amsterdam, my last major job of 2017 was in Rome training financial consultants with Jacqui Harper. The evening before the training day, I took Jacqui to the Pantheon, she hadn't been before, and we had dinner in the Piazza della Rotonda. I really should go and live in Rome. Before the year's end, I also trained some experts in international development which was far more within my comfort zone than financial consulting, fascinating though that is.

Before teaching at INSEAD in January 2018, the first of five trips to Fontainebleau that year, I did some corporate training at 4 Millbank. It was full on, seven people got four interviews each. So I did twenty-eight interviews in a day. I wondered who was being exercised! Because it was at Millbank, I bumped into some old Sky News colleagues. One of the cameramen told me that twelve members of the camera department had either been made redundant or got so fed up that they had simply left. I also bumped into Head of News John Ryley, and shook the hand he proffered. He was excited because the entire news operation was moving into a shiny new hangar at Osterley. It reminded me of ITN in its decline twenty years earlier. It was sad.

I was off to Kenya again at the end of the month, another three weeks in the hot, dusty but otherwise glorious Kenyan bush. Once again, I was working with cameraman/editor Kevin Cook. We were met at Nairobi airport by our driver Fanta. At the cafe they owned in Nanyuki, he and his wife Queen made us a feast of the fish in tomato and coriander sauce that I had complimented the last time we were there with spinach, salad and ugali, a mix of flour and maize and a staple diet of Kenya. It was their charming way of saying welcome back.

We didn't sleep much on our first night in our tent in the bush, a 'gun battle' was raging, mortars and machine guns, night training which continued into the next morning and furnished us with some great whizz bang pictures.

After that, the exercise fell into its familiar routine of very early starts, mock attacks, protecting 'civilians' and so on. We made a short film for the soldiers on how to deal with the heat and dust.

Chucka's chips at Kashima farm was our favourite pit stop on the road back to Nanyuki. They served chips and tea from a hatch, and had a small, very green English-style garden with geraniums galore. The air was cooler up in the highlands with their green rolling hills which reminded me of Devon. I could see why the first British settlers had fallen in love with this place. It was still well over 30 degrees but with a cooling breeze. Fanta complained that he was cold!

For our mid-exercise long weekend break we stayed at Kongoni's camp in Nanyuki, centred on its excellent restaurant. We stayed in individual circular huts, a traditional design but very upmarket. I returned to mine one evening to find a monkey had got into my hut through a window I had left only very slightly ajar. I looked at the monkey, the monkey looked at me. I don't know which of us was more startled, but the monkey was afraid. The Kenyans would whack them with sticks or wooden clubs if they got too close. It was panicking. It couldn't get out through the window it had used to get in. I opened the door wide and stood to one side, an open invitation. The monkey bolted. I have never seen a monkey move so fast.

There was no Wi-Fi but we had 4G. It took me hours to work through all the emails of the past ten days. I was reading Janine di Giovanni's *Madness Visible*. Kosovo. Grim but brilliantly written. For light relief I had Jonas Jonasson's *The Hundred-year-old man who Climbed out of the Window and Disappeared*. And I had Kevin to keep me informed and entertained with his litany of funny stories. He's the one who should be writing a book.

We had to drive in an army convoy from Nanyuki, we had become 'embedded', but only temporarily until I talked us out of it. It took seven hours to do what is normally a three-hour drive. We passed, as usual, through the town of Isiolo, a Muslim town in a largely Christian or Animist country. In every town and village there are shacks with corrugated tin roofs and a big sign celebrating Jesus, 'the church of the word', 'the church of redemption' and so on. Isiolo has mosques. The town would not have looked out of place in Somalia, but in Kenya it was an oddity. It is also very colourful, with fabulous photo opportunities everywhere you look but our army convoy wasn't stopping, least of all for us to do some filming and certainly not for me to take some tourist snaps.

What 'fake news' were we covering? Well, one day forty 'villagers' were massacred by bandits and, elsewhere, there was evidence of the use of chemical weapons. Two good 'stories'.

At an 'IDP camp' we met Maria, nineteen years old and already the mother of a two-year-old daughter called Angel Madeleine. I thought I was the only parent of an angelic Madeleine, my Maddie. Out here, we were told, it was perfectly normal, even expected, for a woman to have her first child at the age of seventeen.

Unfortunately, also very Kenyan was the text I got from the nineteen-year-old Maria who had got hold of my phone number. Apparently, I was 'sponsoring' her two-year-old daughter, and could I buy her a smart phone if I 'love' her? What do you do with that? I was mzungu, Swahili for white man, which really means rich white man. I didn't reply and never heard from her again.

After the work in Africa it was back to the more mundane business of earning a living which basically meant lots of media and communication skills training and the occasional message development brainstorming sessions which were far less energetic or exotic than working in Kenya with the army. I became very good at inventing slogans. Maybe I should have worked in advertising all along? Friends who had gone that route after university seemed very overpaid for not very much work with civilised hours and long lunches. But I had never wanted to sell widgets or soap powder for a living. While still at university I got had gone to see a recruiter from Proctor and Gamble who kept going on about some new project called, hush hush, 'Project X'. I thought, "You're not bloody MI6. It's just some new shampoo." They could keep their money!

I took Seb to Spain for a week and returned to Kenya, this time for a holiday, a week in Watamu, a beautiful Indian Ocean lagoon. It was a bit of a year of holidays, with a few days in early August in Barcelona where the biggest change was that you now had to pay to enter my favourite place, Parc Güell, followed by a week with Seb in Dubai. I had worked in Dubai, but it was never somewhere I wanted to go on holiday. We went for the water parks which Seb insisted we visited every day. There is little better for blowing away the cobwebs and leaving your worries behind than shooting down fast through a tube of water.

Our hotel was the spectacular Emirates Palace. The bathroom, complete with vast sunken marble bath, was bigger than most London apartments. The Dubai tourism department was working hard and was, of course, very well resourced. We went to the top of the Burj Khalifa. The last time I had been in Dubai it was still being built. Now it was the world's tallest building. However, while from the Empire State Building, or the London Eye, or the Eiffel Tower you got fabulous views of New York, London and Paris, here all you could see were hotels, shopping centres and building sites. But they were achieving superlatives. The world's largest shopping mall (of course), longest dry ski slope, biggest indoor theme park (recommended). They were even building a large Ferris wheel designed to rival the London Eye.

At INSEAD one of my MBA students, an English doctor, texted his father.

Do you remember Glen Oglaza?
I think so, is it in Scotland?

I had never been to Tilburg but I passed a pleasant two days in October media training in that pretty Dutch town. Nor had I ever been to Oman, although the Empty Quarter was definitely on my bucket list, but just three days after Tilburg I was off to Muscat for an army exercise.

We had an excellent team led by Andy Reeds and including Kevin Cook and Martin Chidlow who had both completely mastered the art of keeping us in fits of laughter. We produced plenty of 'news' every day. I was presenting in the classic extreme hot weather presenter outfit of a suit jacket, collar and tie and, under the table, shorts and sandals!

Kevin came up with the bright idea of working from our hotel instead of driving to and from the Omani military base every day. I concurred, arguing that this would actually be realistic if we were really in a war zone but the action was inaccessible, miles away somewhere in the desert, as was the case now. So we did, with me presenting from a hotel balcony, and it gave us plenty of time to see Muscat, the old town, harbour and fish market, the Grand Mosque and the beautiful Mohammed Al Ameen Mosque.

Back home, I was master of ceremonies at my friend Jacqui Harper's book launch at The Reform Club, a business book, *Executive Presentations*, her forte. It was lovely to see Jacqui and her family and other friends again. Although I had only been in Oman for two weeks it felt like I had been away for a lot longer.

My final significant job of the year was an army exercise in Thetford Forest, Norfolk with two of my funniest colleagues, Ian Williams and Toby Gilles. Both could easily do stand-up. The week went very well. The boss, Colonel Tom Marsden, showed us some of the comments on the feedback forms he had handed out. 'Really excellent', 'Hugely professional', 'Engaging and helpful'. This is what we liked to hear and a strong, positive note on which to end the year.

2019, the last year before the Coronavirus pandemic and a lot of interesting work both at home and abroad in Afghanistan, Kiev, Bydgoszcz in Poland, Tbilisi, Georgia and with a NATO fleet in the Mediterranean. I was supposed to go to Afghanistan in January but the job clashed with teaching at INSEAD to which I was already committed. In June, I was to experience going straight from Afghanistan to INSEAD in Fontainebleau, an almost surreal experience.

My working year began in January in Bydgoszcz, Poland's eighth largest city and home to NATO's Joint Forces Training Centre. A beautiful city with a typically tragic Second World War story to tell. In January it was covered in snow. After getting our accreditation we went to a supermarket to stock up on supplies, tea, coffee etc. I managed to order them in my very, very basic Polish. We were there for two weeks, a top team of journalist Mark Armstrong and cameraman Martin Chidlow and far too much vodka! And superb food, home-made bigos and pierogi in the city's finest restaurants which were still very reasonably priced though not as cheap as they had been during my family summer holidays in Poland as a child.

The work was 'real world' and, on the first day, we cut a six-minute package on the Afghan presidential election due in July. Mark and I had to give a talk one morning to three hundred NATO officers. We were followed by an American military strat com (strategic communications) advisor who told the assembled NATO officers that the United States would be pulling out of Afghanistan, and very soon. He said the official announcement would come within days. It was to take another two years.

Directly opposite the entrance to the NATO training centre was a huge billboard advertising a Polish online 'Spy Shop'. Someone had a sense of humour!

We media trained several officers, colonels and equivalent ranks, some very relaxed facing the camera others a lot less so. In his State of the Union address, President Trump announced not a withdrawal but the acceleration of peace talks with the Taliban. We included that in a long package on how life had improved in Afghanistan in the absence of Taliban control.

At the closing of the exercise, their boss, three-star British Lieutenant-General Stuart Skeates told the hundreds of assembled NATO officers, "I know from long experience that a training exercise is not over until Glen

Oglaza says it is!" He was referring to the Endex video we always produce to close an exercise, but my ego was suitably massaged by the name check.

On our last night, I embarrassed myself, hardly a first. We were in a bar and I had drunk far too much Zubrowka vodka. It was karaoke night. Some Polish skinheads had been singing nationalistic anti-Russian songs, some harking back to the days of Marshal Piłsudski and the war with Russia following the 1917 revolution. Fuelled by too much vodka, I was up for a bit of singing. The choice was very limited but I settled on Bruce Springsteen's 'Born in the USA' announcing to the assembled Polish throng, "This is an anti-war song. An ANTI-war song!" I knew it was a mistake as soon as I started. Attempting to imitate Springsteen's gravelly voice was hurting my throat! Fortunately, two American NATO officers we knew came to my rescue and joined in. The Polish drinkers laughed at these three old gits making fools of themselves.

Two days after returning from Bydgoszcz I was off to Inverness for three days of media training and a very different cuisine of delicious haggis, tatties and neeps. Haggis is very hit and miss. I was lucky to have found a really good one.

Working for the military is usually fantastic fun, extremely interesting and feels very worthwhile, but it pays poorly. Something to do with a sense of duty, serving Queen and country, and the fact that the MOD is a government department and has to account for every penny. To give you some idea, I normally charge half my corporate rate if the job is for a charity. Working for the military pays half as much again. But I have no complaints. I'm afforded unique access and insight.

A week later I was off to Kiev.

The BBC's Media Action is an international charity with a mission, to teach the value and practise of media and communications in some of the world's poorest and/or most politically vulnerable countries, underpinned by the BBC's editorial values. There is no doubt that it helps to challenge inequality and build more peaceful and democratic societies. It is not funded by the BBC licence fee, but depends on donations. The advice and training is usually delivered by senior former BBC journalists, so I was pleasantly surprised and rather honoured to be asked by the charity to go to Kiev and help a fledgling but already successful television station,

Hromadske. Its mission statement was 'to guarantee our audience objective and unbiased information'.

The young newsroom was led by the excellent Angelina Kariakina. And they were young, very young, but also extremely enthusiastic and occasionally overly exuberant. For example, one of their young anchors had cut off a Human Rights Watch guest when she had talked about civilian casualties in eastern Ukraine but had refused to blame the Russians. It is absolutely central to HRW's modus operandi that they never blame or apportion political responsibility. So, as well as the more general principles of television news (I had prepared a PowerPoint presentation, God help them!), I had to get into the detail of how best to conduct an interview.

It was a fascinating week. I worked with their presenters and their political editor who had to walk a tightrope between Ukrainian nationalism and political impartiality. There was a presidential election due just two months later. Volodymyr Zelensky, a comedian who played the president of the Ukraine in a popular TV comedy series *Servant of the People* which he was now calling his presidential campaign, was being dismissed as a joke in political circles. The incumbent president, Petro Poroshenko, who I had met at the WEF annual meeting in Davos, was expected to win. But Zelensky was immensely popular and his rants against political corruption went viral. He was elected in April, comfortably defeating Poroshenko.

The campaign had to be reported by Hromadske impartially, which is where my experience as a former political correspondent came in. At one point they turned the tables on me and interviewed me for forty-five minutes, my life and times and view of Ukraine and the world. I had done this many times before. I had often been collared on Abingdon Green after doing a live for Sky News by foreign broadcasters to do an interview for them, but forty-five minutes is a marathon!

The Ukrainian metro is very impressive, not quite the Moscow metro but not far off. My nearest station was called Arsenal. I don't suppose I need to tell you that I posted photographs on Facebook.

I was very grateful to be working in such a beautiful city with its stunning St Sophia's cathedral and the Monastery of the Caves, despite being caught in an occasional snow blizzard. Beside the Motherland monument is the most jaw-dropping collection of Soviet Second World War military hardware, including tanks and MiG fighters.

The Holodomor was the 'famine' of 1932-33, Stalin's genocide. I was moved to tears by the Holodomor Museum with its heartbreaking statue, *Bitter Memory of Childhood*, of a small, famine-skinny girl with hollow eyes clutching a handful of wheat. Picking up wheat left on the collective farm after reaping, as this starving girl had done, was punishable by death. As I sat and gazed at her, a group of students arrived and laid flowers at her feet. They probably wondered why this man was sitting on a bench gently sobbing. Or maybe not. Their own parents and grandparents had no doubt sobbed as they told them about Stalin's Ukrainian holocaust.

For more recent history, I visited Maidan, Independence Square, scene of the Orange Revolution of 2004-05. Subsequently two hundred thousand people had rallied there to support Yulia Tymoshenko. I could not be in Kiev and fail to do so. More recently, more than a hundred people had died in 2014 when another revolution overthrew Putin's puppet President Viktor Yanukovych. He was a Soviet-era dinosaur. Modernisers desperately wanted Ukraine to join the EU and NATO.

Two weeks later and work in another beautiful city I had also never been to: Tbilisi, the capital of Georgia. This was a NATO exercise. Like Ukraine, Georgia was very keen to join NATO and shake off so many years of Russian domination but, like Ukraine, they were victims of a potentially insurmountable problem, the occupation of part of their country by Russia. Crimea in the case of Ukraine, Abkhazia and South Ossetia in Georgia's case. As recently as 2008 Georgia had fought a short war with Russia in which Georgia's Defence Force was, of course, completely mismatched. But Georgia had contributed thousands of troops to the NATO coalition in both Iraq and Afghanistan, is a parliamentary democracy with a constitution that guarantees human rights and, since 2014, has had a joint Georgia-NATO training centre, which is where we came in.

With a change of planes in Istanbul, we arrived in Tbilisi as dawn was breaking. We stayed in a small, charming traditional two-storey hotel, the Khokhobi, which features in most tourist brochures and is located next to a complex of historic hot sulphur springs. Each room has a large balcony with views over the old town. I tried kuchapura for the first time, bread stuffed with cheese and with a fried egg on top. Tasty and very filling, and very fattening. Georgia also boasts some of the world's finest wine and prides itself on having more varieties of grape than France.

After our overnight flight our first day was to be spent settling in, which meant taking the cable car up to the Narikala fortress for great views of the city and getting a close-up view of the twenty-metre-high Mother Georgia statue, wine in one hand and a sword in the other. Wine for our friends, the Georgians say, and a sword for our enemies. We found a charming restaurant with live Georgian chanting, excellent food, jugs of delicious local red wine and cha-cha, the local rocket fuel. Our German colleague Norbert was a fan of the cha-cha, which must be at least 100% proof! The others in our excellent team, Steve Gravenor, Martin Chidlow, the erudite Tom Hill and I were more wary of it, but not for long. We laughed. A lot.

The work began early the next morning, a military coach with a police blues-and-twos escort for the forty-five-minute journey to the Georgia-NATO training centre and a lot of reading in. We were in Georgia for two weeks and the work soon fell into a pattern of getting the coach at 7.15 a.m., producing 'news' reporting the scenario the officers were practising interspersed with some basic media training. We would leave the hotel at 7 a.m., return at 8 p.m. and go out to eat. Work, eat, sleep.

My friend Teo, who I had met at the RCDS and who had previously been a member of Georgia's National Security Council and was now an MP, joined us for dinner one evening in our favourite restaurant. While she agreed that the ostri, beef stew, was good she was dismissive of our rustic red wine, 'for tourists'. In the following days she took us to less touristy restaurants where the wine was spectacular, including one featuring cuisine from her home region, which was basically delicious haggis!

One evening we found a restaurant for ourselves, without Teo. This was a mistake. Although the food was good, the live music was a middle-aged oaf singing very badly to a backing track turned up far too loud. You couldn't hear yourself think let along talk, and behind us a table full of Georgians on the cha-cha were trying to shout over the 'music'!

Tbilisi has more than 40,000 stray dogs. Forty thousand, an astonishing number. They were everywhere. The city authorities catch them, sterilise them and vaccinate them against rabies, put a numbered plastic tag in their ear and release them back to the street from which they'd been taken. They are well fed and well cared for. Each cafe and restaurant seemed to have its only small pack of dogs outside and fed them. I also gave them treats and was constantly followed by a small pack. My colleagues dubbed me 'The dog botherer of Tbilisi'!

The lunches at the Georgia-NATO training centre were almost inedible, hence all our evening meals. There was a stray dog living on the camp, a beautiful golden retriever or something very similar who I named Georgia. She got my lunch every day. She was such a lovely dog I even considered investigating whether or not I could take her home to be a companion for my labradoodle, Cookie. But I realised that she was very happy where she was, well fed and loved.

One of the sad effects of the 2020 Covid pandemic was that Tbilisi's cafes and restaurants closed and the dogs were going hungry. Nor were there any tourists (or dog botherers!) to feed them.

NATO Secretary General Jens Stoltenberg visited. Everyone was in a tailspin all morning preparing for this VIP arrival. Martin Chidlow and I filmed his short speech and followed him around for over an hour. It was like being a real reporter again! Lunch was disgusting but he ate it without complaint, as did the Georgian prime minister, the defence and foreign ministers and the head of the army.

Before we finished the exercise the UK's representative on NATO's military committee, General Sir George Norton, popped into our little office/studio for a chat and to say 'well done', which was very nice of him.

Tbilisi is a fine city, a mix of old and new, but the damage from earthquakes can be seen just a few streets up the hill from the city centre, abandoned buildings with huge cracks in their walls. The most recent had been in 1991, 1992 and 2002. But Georgia is ripe for tourism.

We had a day off and headed north-east to the mountains. Teo had recommended our driver and guide, Besara, who was incredibly helpful and informative. First stop was the sixteenth century fort and church at Ananuri, then along the Aragvi Valley, along the old military road, the only road leading to Russia. There were so many lorries heading to Russia we were stuck in a massive traffic jam in a snow blizzard. It soon cleared as the road reached 2, 395 metres at Jvari Pass. We had stopped in the small border-crossing town of Stepantsminda, St Steven's, just eight miles from Russia in the shadow of Kazbeg Mountain. We had lunch, delicious fresh trout, in the Rooms Hotel, once a Soviet sanatorium.

On the way back, a mad and very icy drive up to the fourteenth century Gergeti Trinity Church perched spectacularly at 2,170 metres. We had to walk to get right up to it on sheet ice. I very nearly injured myself coming back down and Besara had to help the struggling old man! I was wearing the wrong shoes, no tread. There are brown bears, wolves, lynxes and Caucasian leopards in the mountain forests. Sadly, we didn't see any.

I had loved our time in Georgia but, as always, was happy to be going home. Before we left, we visited the glorious Kashveti Church with its golden icons of St George slaying the dragon. The images of St George can be found in several churches and his golden statue, slaying the dragon, dominates Tbilisi's Freedom Square. Not English then! Of course, I couldn't make any sense of the explanation written in the churches. Georgian is a strange and unique language. It is neither Indo-European nor Turkic, Slavic or Semitic but truly unique. I had to read up to discover that St George was adopted as our patron saint in the Middle Ages. He was also adopted by Catalonia, Venice, Genoa and Portugal as the embodiment of the chivalric ideal. We had the Crusaders and later the Tudors to thank for our patron saint. He had replaced St Edmund, our original, home-grown patron Saint.

While I had been away the Conservatives and Labour had been playing politics with Brexit. An estimated one million people had marched in London against leaving the European Union, six million had signed a petition. A lost cause. I sympathised, but talk about flogging a dead horse.

In mid-April Notre-Dame Cathedral in Paris was burning. The spire collapsed and most of the Medieval wooden roof was destroyed. World leaders sent condolences and more than a billion pounds was pledged by donors to restore the cathedral. Some people, especially on social media, asked why we were so bothered about 'some old church' and why anyone would spend so much on it. Social media at its worst. Did I really need to explain?

For the first time English Premier League clubs contested both the Champion's League and the Europa League finals. Liverpool beat Spurs, Arsenal lost to Chelsea in Baku, Azerbaijan. The least said about that game the better, but Baku? Since when was oil-rich Azerbaijan in Europe? It's a question we would be asking again in 2021 during the European Championship when some games were played in Baku, and England lost the final at Wembley to Italy on penalties. An Italian fan had a banner, 'Football's coming Rome', cheeky but, as it turned out, accurate.

Still recovering from Arsenal's pathetic performance in the Europa League Final I headed to Afghanistan where Steve Gravenor and I were working at the NATO base near Mazir-i-Sharif, thirty miles from the Uzbek border. The Americans were out in the countryside doing most of the fighting, the base was being run mostly by Germans. Our liaison was Major Erich Gusenburger who we'd worked with in Bydgoczsz and who was immensely helpful.

There's an old joke about European heaven and hell. In European heaven the French cook, the police are British, the Germans organise and the Italians throw the parties. In hell the English cook, the police are German, the Italians organise and the French throw the parties. I have seen enough in my time to recognise the essential underlying truth of this, and here was another example of German organisational skill.

Steve and I went out in an armoured convoy with Montenegrin soldiers. It was very hot, about forty degrees, but this was the only safe way to travel. We saw a fair bit of Mazir-i-Sharif though not the famous Blue Mosque or the shrine of Ali, still a destination for Muslim pilgrims. We stopped just once, at an Afghan army checkpoint, where we were told there was nothing to report, the area had been quiet. We packaged the story and included an interview with the force protection commander.

We did see the Blue Mosque the next day when we flew over it in a helicopter on our way to Kunduz with American Special Forces soldiers who were straight out of central casting. At Camp Pamir we interviewed Afghan General Nabiullah Marzoi who gave us lunch and, for me, a gift, an Afghan chapor, or jailak, a colourful striped silk coat which looked more like a dressing gown and is to be worn on special occasions. You may have seen Hamid Karzai wearing one. We had the helicopter to ourselves for the one-hour return journey over the barren landscape of northern Afghanistan.

At that time, the Taliban controlled most of the countryside, the government held the cities but in some cases, like Mazir-i-Sharif with its population of half a million, only just.

We were off in a helicopter again the next day (it really is the only way to travel!) to Shaheen Afghan army camp to interview Major General Wali Muhammed Almadzi who was in charge of security across all of northern

Afghanistan. As we entered his office, he was concluding a meeting with the head of the secret police in the north. White-haired and with a kindly face he looked like everyone's favourite uncle, but I also found him rather sinister.

We carried out a few more interviews back in Mazir-i-Sharif, focussed on the Afghan presidential election due in September, and sat through a briefing which revealed that the Taliban appeared to be doing alarmingly well. We chatted to a couple of American military intelligence officers, definitely 'spooks' Erich assured us, who outlined some of the Taliban's recent successes. Donald Trump was on a state visit to London. We Europeans took great delight in mocking him and enjoyed the Trump balloons and other caricatures. We kept quiet in front of our American military friends, assuming that some if not most of them would be Trump supporters.

We flew back via Istanbul where Steve and I separated. I was off to Paris and straight to teaching in Fontainebleau. The contrast between northern Afghanistan and the comfort of academia at INSEAD could not have been greater, even just the weather, the cool and refreshing air of Fontainebleau Forest after the heat and dust of Afghanistan. They really were two totally different worlds.

At INSEAD I swapped one Steve for another, Gravenor for Knight. I seemed to have several significant Steves in my life. Steve (Knight) had found a fantastic clip of a David Attenborough speech to the previous year's UN Climate Change conference in Katowice, Poland: "Leaders you must lead". An example of rhetoric where every word carries weight. Leaders. You. Must. Lead. Look it up for a brilliant and very persuasive example of rhetoric. I taught at INSEAD twice more that year, in July and September.

I had done a DNA/genetic code test. The results revealed that I am 13% Jewish with, further back, some Punjabi, Bengali and even Han Chinese! Complete nonsense? Maybe we really had come over with Genghis Khan as the old family legend suggested.

As soon as I was back from INSEAD I gave a forty-five-minute lecture followed by a Q&A to the RCDS on the relationship between the military and the media, not for the first time. It seemed to go very well, the feedback was excellent. It was challenging given that I was speaking to around forty different nationalities, many with very different ideas about freedom of the press. This was ahead of our team spending a week supporting the RCDS annual strategy exercise.

While our heads were in international diplomacy and areas of potential conflict, the Conservatives were electing a new leader. In the first round of voting, Boris Johnson had a commanding lead. Dominic Raab came bottom and was eliminated. Rory Stewart's scrappy insurgency campaign was still alive.

Two days later, they were down to three:

Johnson – 160.

Hunt – 77.

Gove – 75 and eliminated.

The choice of the remaining two candidates would be put to the party's 160,000 members, many of whom were fully paid-up members of the Boris Johnson fan club.

I had been doing some work for the campaign to legalise medicinal cannabis through my friend and fellow Arsenal fan Steve Moore (another Steve!) and, in late June, chaired the inaugural policy summit of the CMC, the Campaign for Medicinal Cannabis, at Somerset House. Doctors and medical academics were extolling the virtues of medicinal cannabis and there were plenty of examples of how it had helped people, particularly children with epilepsy. It was legal to prescribe in the UK and had been for more than six months, but many doctors were reluctant to do so, and still are.

I also trained several clients that summer including a Jewish organisation which campaigns for a two-state solution in Israel-Palestine. They were young, highly educated, incredibly articulate and, in my case, were preaching to the converted even though I had to play devil's advocate to test their arguments and put them under pressure.

At INSEAD one of the exercises we got our MBA and Executive MBA students to practise was to argue a case for just sixty seconds. This was to teach them the value of being succinct. They had time to prepare. That July, a group in one of my workshops turned the tables on me and asked me to talk for sixty seconds off-the-cuff. I gave them an anti-Brexit rant structured with a beginning, a middle and a conclusion and lasting precisely sixty seconds. They were suitably impressed.

As expected, Jo Swinson was elected Lib Dem leader in July, defeating Ed Davey. She didn't last long! The next day we had a new prime minister. Boris Johnson had beaten Jeremy Hunt by 92,000 votes to 46,000. His acceptance speech was good, of course, but: Boris! Prime Minister!

He announced his Cabinet the next day. Sajid Javid was Chancellor, Dominic Raab Foreign Secretary and Priti Patel was Home Secretary. Priti Patel! I remembered her from her days as a Conservative Party press officer and thought she had some fairly extreme views even back then. It seemed to me at the time that Boris had probably packed his government with too many hardline Brexiters and had left too many potential enemies fuming, or at least smouldering, on the back benches.

By early September Ken Clarke, Phil Hammond and Nicholas Soames had been kicked out of the Conservative Party. They had rebelled in a Commons vote on taking back control of the House of Commons agenda from the government, which had lost the vote by 328-301. Twenty-seven Tories had rebelled and been expelled from the party, which had now it seemed become the Brexit party.

The next day, MPs voted to extend the EU departure date from October 31st, just over a month away, to January 31st, 2020. Boris Johnson wanted a general election before the end of October but lost that vote too. Earlier, he had been at the dispatch box for his first PMQs. It could have been his first and last had MPs agreed to an early general election. His performance was all bluster and very little if any substance.

Boris Johnson's brother, Joe, resigned as a minister and as an MP, Labour MP Luciana Berger defected from Labour to the Lib Dems. The Labour Party was in deep trouble over claims of anti-Semitism. Others had been expected to follow Luciana's lead but the exodus never happened.

By that September, wildfires had been burning unchecked in the Brazilian Amazon for nine months. Seven thousand square miles of forest was burning. Brazil's president, Jair Bolsonaro, not only did nothing but was actively encouraging the clearing of vast areas for farmland. The settlers were starting fires deliberately to clear more land. In my view this was a crime against humanity and every other creature sharing our planet and Bolsonaro should have been taken to The Hague in chains.

In October, Trump abandoned Syrian Kurds to their fate when he pulled US forces back from the Syrian-Turkish border after a phone call with Turkish president, Recep Erdoğan, and without consulting Congress or the Pentagon. The move endangered Kurdish civilians, emboldened both Turkey and ISIS and no doubt delighted the Kremlin. Turkish troops moved in. Within a week more than 100,000 Kurds had been forced to flee their homes. It was claimed that almost a thousand ISIS prisoners held by the Kurds had escaped. Trump's reaction? They will simply "escape into Europe"! His behaviour was little short of being complicit in a genocide. Turkish slaughter of the Kurds continued. It reminded me horribly of the nightmare plight of the Iraqi Kurds in 1990 after the first Gulf War.

Everything on a warship seems designed to hurt. I don't mean the armaments but the hunks of metal randomly protruding from walls and designed, it seems, for no other purpose than to keep you alert to avoid pain.

In October I did a two-week NATO naval exercise for the first time, thankfully in the western Mediterranean and not in the cold, rough waters of the North Sea. The NATO task force was led by the Spanish aircraft carrier the King Juan Carlos. Our small but superb team was led by journalist Mark Armstrong who lives in Majorca and is therefore fluent in Spanish. My Spanish was still rudimentary, although I caught him out one day describing me to some Spanish officers as his abuelo, grandfather. Cheeky bugger!

We flew to Madrid and then on to Jerez before driving to the town of Rota, near Cádiz. My luggage did not make it beyond Madrid! And we had to go. The airline, Iberia, assured me that it would arrive 'this morning' but by then we were at sea, first on the Spanish assault ship Castella and then on the Canadian frigate the Halifax. Without my suitcase or any change of clothes.

I was fortunate that my cameraman Clive Jackson is ex-Royal Navy and knew his way around a warship. The accommodation was basic, very, a system of three-tier bunk beds. I had the top bunk. I almost gave myself a hernia every time I got in or out of it. There was very little head room so you had to climb up and enter sideways, fine maybe for fit young marines, less so for an unfit, middle-aged man. To get out again involved rolling onto your side, grabbing hold of a pipe and jumping down. Cameraman Kevin Cook mischievously took some video of Mark attempting this inelegant manoeuvre. He looked awkward and struggled, though not as much as I did.

The flotilla of more than thirty ships from eighteen countries sailing in formation looked spectacular, especially at sunrise and sunset. We were blessed with good weather. Clive and I were producing 'news' packages and interviewed various senior officers including the Admiral of the Fleet. We transferred by a Belgian Alouette helicopter to the American destroyer USS Gridley. There was still no sign of my luggage. Thanks Iberia! The American public affairs team took me to the ship's shop for essential supplies, underwear, socks, a towel, toothpaste and a toothbrush, shaving kit and some T-shirts. They would not let me pay, very kind of them. Thank you, Emily and Audrey.

Transfers between ships were either by rib or helicopter. Even in the calm waters of the Mediterranean a rib transfer could be very dangerous as the rib drew alongside a ship and you had to catch and climb up a wet rope ladder. In the swell of the North Sea, I thought this could be potentially lethal. So, I insisted on helicopter transfers. I was pushing at an open door, they already had helicopters laid on for us.

We did another helicopter transfer to the Spanish aircraft carrier the King Juan Carlos. Getting around on warships is a tedious process, endless airlocks and incredibly steep, narrow metal stairs. The aircraft carrier was very different, wide staircases not unlike those on a cross channel ferry and luxury: A comfortable two-man cabin.

Filming the Harrier jump jets taking off and landing was not only spectacular but also deafeningly loud. We were producing 'news' pieces and did two long interviews, which we ran at full length, with Admiral Ruben Rodriguez Pena and the captain of the Juan Carlos, Francisco Jose Asensi Perez.

My bag finally arrived, by helicopter from the Castilla. It was only six days late! It was like being reunited with an old friend. A clean shirt at last!

We transferred on an Augusta Bell to the Spanish frigate Alvaro de Bazan and interviewed her captain, Ricardo Gomez Delgardo, and had dinner with him and his team of senior officers. They were utterly perplexed by Brexit.

We filmed various exercises, a ship-to-ship rescue, refuelling-at-sea, known as a RAS, an air defence exercise from the ops room, very rare access and, back on the Castilla I did a PTC beside a landing craft before they practised an amphibious assault.

We had flown back to the Castilla on a Sea King helicopter and were given a twenty-four-man dormitory, normally inhabited by marines, to ourselves. And we had tables to work on, editing our packages etc. And an en suite for the two of us, normally shared by twenty-four marines.

This was much more like it! Sadly, the food was almost inedible. It was hot so we spent a lot of our time on the flight deck, our sun deck! Dolphins were swimming, jumping and playing in front of and all around the ship. Beautiful. We sailed in Trafalgar Bay, close to the lighthouse. The battle of 1805 had been fought on this very spot.

The Spanish navy PR man on the Castilla was clueless. He was small, hunched over despite his height and constantly pulling on a cigarette cradled in his hand. We were supposed to interview the ship's captain, Vicente Cuquerello, one morning. The PR man, who we nicknamed Clouseau, eventually told us it would be impossible: 'No es possible', his favourite phrase. Eventually, four hours later we simply went to the bridge and did the interview. The captain was very happy to do it and wanted to do more for the practice.

Clouseau struck again the next day. He wanted us to go with him at once, 'inmediatamente', to interview the ops. officer. We hung around for an hour, no ops. officer. Clouseau was astonished that we had interviewed the captain the day before. It was the first he had heard of it.

We chatted to an intelligence officer. Clouseau was busy making himself a coffee, he hadn't offered us one. The intel officer didn't reveal much, only the top line for our next 'news', that a fishing vessel had struck a sea mine! Clouseau either didn't know or didn't care. He was due to retire soon anyway.

So, the game became doing our job despite Clouseau. The next morning the ship's siren sounded 'general quarters', action stations. We avoided Clouseau, filmed the crew preparing and climbing into their fire-resistant kit and filmed on the bridge where we interviewed several very helpful officers and did a PTC. Clouseau found us on deck a little later and took us somewhere where absolutely nothing was happening! He had no idea that we had already filmed more than enough on the bridge and below decks.

The next day, our last, we filmed another RAS. Clouseau hadn't bothered to tell us that one was scheduled, of course. He was supposed to be setting up an interview for us with a vice-admiral, Antonio Martorell. This is how Clouseau approached him.

"I know you're busy and don't have five minutes for an interview!"

"Not at all," replied the vice-admiral. "I have no problem." And, to us, "Take as long as you need."

If Clouseau had been intentionally undermining our efforts he could hardly have done a better job.

I had enjoyed being at sea but it was a relief to be back on solid ground and not constantly bobbing around on the ocean waves. We docked early in the morning and had a day in Rota which involved a lot of eating and drinking. It was my birthday and we were being paid to spend it in a resort popular with the urban Spanish but less well known to international tourists.

Back on dry land and back to media training, this time at Sellafield. Controversial, I know, but I felt sure the nuclear re-processing, waste storage and decommissioning people were doing their very best. They were also extremely knowledgeable. I learnt a lot.

There was plenty of other media training that autumn, including more days at RAF Halton, while Priti Patel was making ludicrous claims about cutting immigration. An election was only a month away. I watched Labour's campaign launch. I thought they were about to get absolutely hammered.

My working year ended where it had begun, back at the NATO Training Centre in Bydgoszcz, Poland. Our first day was full-on with seemingly endless briefings. Death by PowerPoint! Once again we had a great team led this time by Steve Gravenor who had to spend most of his time in meetings with the exercise directors. We were there for just over two weeks, worked hard but also enjoyed the city's Christmas market and lights. We were living mostly on bigos, goulash, dill potatoes, cabbage and beetroot. My vodka intake was a lot more moderate than it had been in January.

We arrived home in the wake of the general election which had given Boris Johnson a stonking majority. The first shock of the night had come when Labour lost Blyth Valley. Blyth Valley! This was soon followed by losses in Workington and Darlington. It was turning into a bloodbath. Bishop Auckland fell to the Conservatives with a big majority. Labour's heartlands were being destroyed. Labour's Leave voters had deserted the party. Chuka Umunna, now a Lib Dem, only managed second place in the Cities of London and Westminster constituency. Labour had put a huge effort into stopping him and they had cheered at Labour HQ when he lost to the Conservatives.

The DUP leader at Westminster, Nigel Dodds, lost his seat to Sinn Féin. Dominic Grieve failed in Beaconsfield, a great loss to the House of Commons. One tiny glimmer of hope for the Lib Dems came when they took Richmond Park from Zak Goldsmith.

Labour lost Sedgefield!

Caroline Flint lost in Don Valley due to Brexit party votes. The Conservative vote had remained static. Jo Swinson polled more than 11,000 votes but lost her seat to the SNP by just 149 votes. Maybe the Lib Dems could now find a better leader. A shame that they'd lost Chuka.

It had been a phenomenally successful night for the Conservatives, a landslide majority of 80, disastrous for Labour and dreadful for the Lib Dems, who were down to just 11 MPs. The SNP had 48. Jeremy Corbyn announced that he would not be leading Labour into the next general election.

Of course, I sat up all night in Poland watching history being made before flying home the next day. By the next morning, David Gauke was gone and so too was Remainer champion, Anna Soubry. Dennis Skinner, 'the beast of Bolsover', was defeated by the Tories. He had represented Bolsover since 1970! And Luciana Burger had failed to take Finchley and Golders Green.

Any doubts had now been dispelled. We were leaving the European Union. Labour and the Liberal Democrats had been smashed. 'Get Brexit Done' had proved to be a clear, powerful message which had resonated everywhere except, of course, in London, Scotland and Northern Ireland. A colleague suggested that London, Scotland and Northern Ireland should declare UDI and leave the rest of the country to stew in its own xenophobic Brexit juices.

Just before Christmas, MPs passed the European Union Withdrawal Agreement Bill by a majority of 124. This meant we would be leaving the EU by January 31st. Game over.

And so was the year, with stories of what looked like a serious outbreak of some kind of SARS virus in the Far East. We had no idea what was about to hit us.

2020 started well enough. I taught at INSEAD in January and again in March. We covered the WEF annual meeting in Davos remotely that January, from home via Zoom. A sign of things to come. It had been decided that this was a far cheaper way of covering the event. We made it work very well, but our January trips to the Swiss Alps were over. And, of course, it was no substitute for being there and rubbing shoulders with world leaders.

Towards the end of January, the world population reached 7.7 billion. And the population was ageing. Modern medicine allowed us to live longer, but at a cost. Some people were actually suggesting that 'nature' might fight back, there might be a cull, maybe another Spanish Flu-type pandemic. Be careful what you wish for!

I was back in Kenya for three weeks in February working with a great team of Kevin Cook, again, Jim Klass and, for the first time, former Royal Marine Sean Clee and Carla Prater.

Among the directing staff was the always charming Gurkha Major James Cartwright. Last time I had seen him, he had been almost swivel-eyed urging his Gurkha soldiers to 'win' against the Paras, even though the Paras were the troops being exercised with the Gurkhas helping them as part of their training. Now that he was on the directing staff he was the very voice of sweet reason, urging calm and restraint.

A plague of locusts, literally billions of them, hit northern Kenya. We saw swarms of them at Archer's Post. We had had heavy flooding in several parts of the world, disastrous bush fires in Australia and now a plague of locusts. It felt like the End of Days!

As well as the usual job of filming the exercising troops, including for the first time a Para drop from a Hercules and two Rapid Air Landings where troops jump out of the back of the aircraft almost as soon as it touches down and it takes off again after only just coming to a halt, we were making films for BATUK's outreach programme, Community Engagement, as well as producing our 'news' as usual.

There had been heavy rain before we arrived and, for once, Archer's Post was green, its river full and flowing strongly. Normally the town, more of a large village really, is enveloped in dust.

We had our mid-exercise break and headed straight to Kongoni's in Nanyuki. We arrived at 5.15pm. We were staying this time in newly-built and comfortable military accommodation. It was such a relief to be out of the relentless heat and dust of the bush that I suggested cold Tusker beers in the garden of Kongoni's was top priority. We had drivers Paul and Patrick with us. As team leader I bought the first couple of rounds before declaring, "Oh fuck it, let's just stay here and get drunk!" to general acclaim and cheers. We had food, a lot more beer, and we had music. Patrick had disappeared and returned with a large speaker. A party! But only until 9.30 p.m. as the drivers had to clock off and we didn't want to upset Kongoni's residents. Very sensible.

The new commander of BATUK was the legendary Paul 'Shove' Gilby, who had risen through the ranks after starting his army career as a private. He was very bloke-ish. For example, one day we came across a soldier with ginger hair crouching down in the extreme heat and dust guarding a position. "All right ginger nuts?" was his Commanding Officer's greeting. But Shove's first concern was always for the welfare of his soldiers, and his next instruction was to make sure 'ginger nuts' was drinking enough water.

Major Finlay (Fin) Bibby, now a Lt. Colonel and deputy commander of BATUK, liked to remind me that I had assured him early in 2016 that the country would never vote for Brexit and that Trump would never be US president. To this day, he takes great delight in introducing me to people as "This is Glen. He's really good at political predictions!"

We made several Community Engagement films. At a primary school, the British army was providing water tanks, desks and resurfacing classroom floors. They needed hard surfacing to suppress the wretched dust. We interviewed the head teacher and Major Jules Ward who was running the army's Community Engagement programme. We did the same at a dirt-poor secondary school. These were children from the slums who, if not in school, simply didn't get to eat. We gave them what we had.

We filmed at the tiny Vineyard church, little more than a shack, where we interviewed the parson and the BATUK padre who gave the sermon. The happy-clappy Kenyan congregation made for great pictures. Jim got surrounded by children eager, of course, to be filmed but also to look through his viewfinder and hit the record button themselves. Budding cameramen and women.

At Nanyuki's orphanage I gave them all the pens and T-shirts I had. T-shirts in Kenya are of notoriously poor quality. It wasn't enough but it was something. Kevin put together a road safety video based on the Green Cross Code public information films of our childhoods. Children being hit by cars was, and remains, a major problem in Kenya. One of our BATUK drivers, Joe, played the Green Cross Code man with two children from the orphanage acting out crossing the road safely. 'Look right, look left, look right again', etc. We also made a video on camp security for the benefit of the visiting, exercising soldiers.

We were also, of course, filming the exercising troops, producing 'news' and delivering media training. BATUK had certainly got their money's worth.

Back in London I watched the Sky News Labour leadership debate. Keir Starmer was clearly head and shoulders above the other candidates. I also watched Andrew Neil interviewing Starmer, who seemed prime-ministerial, and Rebecca Long-Bailey, who appeared to be completely delusional.

In early March I was teaching again at INSEAD. I was due to return to Kenya for three weeks later in the month, but then the curtain came down. Coronavirus lockdown. Kenya was cancelled/postponed as was everything else.

I started writing pieces for the politics section of the website, Reaction Life, which was fun because, unlike during my days at ITN and Sky News, I could say what I liked and be as rude as I wanted, proper opinion pieces. Donald Trump got both barrels! And, of course, there was plenty to say about the politics of the lockdown and how the government was handling or mishandling the pandemic. Also on how some high-profile broadcast journalists at the now daily government Coronavirus briefings were far too fond of the sound of their own voices and were not asking the right questions. A few days later the BBC put up Hugh Pym, their health rather than their political editor. Hugh asked one short and very poignant question. Unfortunately, he was followed by Robert Peston!

I also wrote pieces on the already disastrous effects of Covid on the economy. Like millions of others I could not visit elderly relatives for months, in my case my ninety-four-year-old father. And a piece on the Labour leadership contest and another on the shameful behaviour on wealthy Premier League football clubs who were applying for government funding to furlough non-playing staff and a piece arguing that garden centres should re-open, with mask wearing and safe distancing. Gardening and even nurturing house plants are good for the soul.

Boris Johnson led the Downing Street follies and refused to answer any questions about Dominic Cummings breaking the lockdown rules on his little jaunt to Barnard Castle or tell us when he, the prime minister, had known about it. Three days later he was still refusing to answer questions on the scandal, saying he had 'drawn a line' under it. No one else had.

The months were slipping by, the year was rapidly disappearing. If I was ever going to write this book, I had to do it now. If not during lockdown, then when?

Work was being cancelled left, right and centre but finally things began to ease and in mid-October I was off to Norway for a month.

Mark Armstrong and I were working at NATO's Joint Warfare Centre in Stavanger, but first we had to quarantine for ten days in a small but pleasant enough apartment. We went for long walks around the town each day, which was permitted. We also found a couple of coffee shops where we could sit outside, the weather was fine but it wouldn't last. A local old salty sea dog told us that once it started raining it wouldn't stop until February! It started on our fifth day. We also found a sports bar, big screen, Premier League football, outside seating with heaters. Probably not permitted during quarantine, but the tables were safe-distanced and there was plenty of fresh air.

I had been to Stavanger before but not since the early 1980s, a trip to Stavanger and Bergen when I had presented a weekly travel programme for Metro Radio. It seemed largely unchanged, at least in the old town and around the old harbour.

The highlight of the day was a trip to the supermarket. Thankfully, Mark is a good cook. I am not! By the end of ten days, we were sick of walking aimlessly up and down the steep hills of Stavanger, a charming enough city but limited and, frankly, a bit dull and extremely expensive. We were desperate to get to work.

A new rule came into force in Norway on our first day at the NATO training centre. The wearing of masks was now compulsory. There were very few cases of Covid in Stavanger but Oslo had been hit hard. The exercise was constantly curtailed by Covid fears. Part two of the exercise was supposed to be in Naples but that was cancelled. Rumours abounded that the entire exercise would end early.

The JWC in Stavanger had its own media centre, complete with TV studio. It was over elaborate and the permanent staff created a mystique around what they did and made the media support of the exercise appear far more complicated than was necessary. They were essentially doing what we regularly did on military exercises but with more than twice the resources and less than half as effectively. But the permanent staff in the media production office were pleasant and friendly and, best of all, they brought cakes into the office every day.

Now retired Royal Marines General Roger Lane was one of the exercise mentors and popped into the production office to say hello. The permanent staff in the room were surprised and possibly a little put out when they introduced me and Roger told them, "Glen and I go back years". As indeed we did.

With Covid still rampant, NATO announced a Europe wide travel ban. We would have to stay in Stavanger for part two, the 'execution phase' of the exercise. This would involve staying in Stavanger for an additional six weeks. Going home and returning to Norway was not an option. It would mean being away from home for far too long and it didn't take me too long to decide that this was not for me. Daughter Maddie told me to treat it as a holiday, explore the Fjords. Mark was happy to stay, but I really had had enough and had things to do at home and other work in the offing back in London. I didn't want to let people down but it emerged that they were drastically scaling down the exercise anyway and sending a lot of people home. And Seb was upset that I would be away for so much longer, which was decisive. Had the job involved relocating to Naples it might have been a different matter.

At our sports bar, the unlikely named Beverly Hills, we watched Arsenal beating the Norwegian team, Molde 4-1. In deference to the friendly Norwegians, only one of whom was actually a Molde fan, I suppressed my goal celebrations. Mark, with very little interest in football and none whatsoever in the fortunes of Arsenal, was very patient.

The US election was stuck at 253-213. Biden seemed on the brink of winning in both Georgia and Pennsylvania, but these two crucial swing states were still counting. This went on for days, unbelievably slow. We were glued to CNN.

Ten days after America went to the polls, Biden was finally declared the winner in both Arizona and Georgia, taking him to 306. What a long and tortuous process electing an American president can be.

There was no sign of Trump apart from highly toxic and utterly mad tweets. When he finally appeared on camera it was to take the credit for the development of a Covid vaccine, with no mention at all of the election. He seemed to be living in a parallel universe!

On a day off, I media trained Macmillan Cancer Support, a regular client, remotely on Zoom from Norway. There were five people to train and I gave them five interviews each, another of those twenty-five interview days. They were a great bunch and seemed to get a lot out of it but I was exhausted and ready for some cold beers.

The journey home, via Schiphol Airport, was painless. My taxi driver to the airport in Stavanger, a Somali man, was an Arsenal fan so we had plenty to talk about. In bed that night I had Coco the cat purring fiercely on the bed with me, Cookie the dog asleep on the floor next to us and Seb sleeping in the next bedroom. Home.

Only for a couple of weeks though. I was off to Lille, another NATO job, this time with the French Rapid Reaction Corps. I would have been unable to go had I still been in Stavanger. Tom Hill drove us, radio journalist Fiona Campion and I, to France via Dover. It had been many years since I had been on a cross channel ferry. The day was fine and cloudless and both the English and French coasts were clearly visible.

The French Rapid Reaction Corp is based in the huge Citadel of Lille, built between 1667 and 1670 and an historic monument. Once again, I felt privileged to have access to and be working in such a place. Sadly, the city of Lille was in Covid lockdown, the restaurants were all closed, but we had basic cooking facilities in our hotel rooms and a supermarket just two minutes away.

We had a great team of Tom and Fiona, Steve Gravenor and Norbert Horpel and the work was interesting, focused on the potential Russian threat to the Baltic States. We cut a 'road to crisis' video, the back story, and attended various briefings, some interesting others soporific. We soon settled into a pattern of interviews, producing 'news bulletins', writing fake newspaper articles and producing very realistic social media.

We interviewed a charming and very helpful retired Danish two-star general

Me: "We just need to get a level on your voice. What did you have for breakfast?"

Steve, on camera: "Yes, what do retired generals have for breakfast?"

The General: "Retired Generals can't remember what they had for breakfast!"

Covid struck again, six confirmed cases in the Franco-German Brigade who we were exercising. The entire brigade was being tested and might all be sent home, meaning we would lose our training audience and the purpose of the exercise. It ended three days early.

John Le Carré died. He was 89 and one of our greatest novelists. If you doubt that, just read *A Perfect Spy* for the most superb narrative of a father-son relationship.

The two Senate seats in Georgia would decide who controlled the American Senate. The Democrats needed to win both for a 50-50 Senate, with the vice-president having the casting vote. Both results were tight but the Democrats narrowly won both and had control of all three branches of government, the Senate, the House of Representatives and the White House. Trump supporters rioted in Washington and stormed the Capitol Building to prevent the Senate from endorsing Joe Biden's election victory. They had been egged on by Trump, for which he was impeached for the second time. Some were calling it an attempted coup, a subversion of democracy, but to me it simply looked like the dying throes of the Trump cult.

Among a raft of Executive Orders on his inauguration day, President Biden re-joined the WHO and the Paris agreement on climate change and cancelled spending on Trump's mad wall. And that was just for starters. I watched the new White House press secretary's first briefing, such a contrast to the Trump liars with their 'alternative facts'.

We covered the WEF annual meeting in Davos remotely from home again in January. It really wasn't the same as being there but we were still in full lockdown. Premier League football was being played in empty stadia. The games felt like training sessions. And I didn't get any other work, none, until April when jobs finally began to trickle in. First up was two weeks army training in Thetford Forest with my friend and colleague Kevin Cook on camera/edit. The town of Thetford was in lockdown like everywhere else, but there was army food. Chips with everything! Some takeaways were open, so on a couple of evenings we sat by the river, the Little Ouse, with fish and chips or pizza.

The work was interesting, once again training the latest British troops due to deploy to Mali. We produced 'news reports', a lot of backgrounders on the situation in Mali to inform the soldiers, and interviews with Nicola Griffiths of War Child and James Denselow of Save the Children, Mali experts, who were observing the exercise and advising where appropriate. We also gave the troops a lot of media training. The weather was uncommonly hot, almost Saharan, which added to the realism. The exercising troops were cavalry, roaring around the forest in their Jackals and Foxhounds, staging mock attacks, setting up roadblocks, dealing with IEDs etc. Great fun for us but for them Mali was likely to be a very tough deployment in extremely harsh conditions.

The Emirates Stadium admitted a limited number of fans, 10,000, for the final game of the season and I got to go. We tried to make enough noise to sound like a stadium at full capacity, 62,000. We beat Brighton 2-0 but we ended the season in sixth place, one point behind Spurs. For the first time in twenty-five years Arsenal would not be playing in a European competition the following season, not necessarily a bad thing at a time of transition and improvement.

Before the RCDS Strategy Exercise at the end of June, Andy Reeds and I delivered a lecture remotely, by Zoom, followed by three days of remote media training but our team supported the exercise itself, physically, in person. And what a relief it was to be among people again and working with familiar colleagues.

Opposite our hotel, The Millenium, was 'the only pub in Sloane Street', The Gloucester, perfect for our colleague Andrew Wise, a big Gloucester rugby fan. As usual I was the TV presenter and news editor. We had a great team, including the chuckle twins Kevin Cook and Martin Chidlow, and the postponed Euro 2020 football championships was on. The Gloucester had a big screen, good food and fine ale. Perfect.

Mostly, though, I was working on this book and its predecessor, *When I Stories*. I hope you have enjoyed the fruits of my labour. This is not the end. God willing, there are still plenty of stories and adventures to come. As I write, I'm due to go back to BATUK in Kenya, a NATO exercise in Spain and another in Tbilisi.

I've been very lucky in my life and I am very grateful. My fortune has been made not in financial wealth but in unique experiences, and in the people with whom I have shared those experiences and often powerful emotions. In my many loved ones and, above all, in my wonderful children.

All lives are incomplete, but I am so fortunate to still be doing things that are both interesting and (usually) fun. It is so important never to lose sight of the child's sense of wonder at our incredible world, to always remain positive and banish negativity. Sceptical, yes, but never cynical. I have tried to approach work, and life in general, with humour, humility and humanity. I hope that is reflected in these two books.

My pal, Tim Friend, who had also worked at both ITN and Sky News, once said to me, "When you're on your deathbed you won't be saying I wish I'd spent more time at ITN or Sky News but I wish I had spent more time with my family."

He was right, of course. Looking back, even though I now have a much healthier work-life balance, I wish I had had more time and energy for my marriage, my children and my friends. On the other hand, I would not have experienced the things I've experienced, seen the things I've seen, met the people I've met. I would not have heard their stories or been, in my own very small way, an eyewitness to history able to cover and sometimes uncover stories that needed to be told. Sometimes, even if only occasionally, we made a difference.

I have been so lucky. I am grateful beyond words for the opportunities I've had and for all the people who have helped me along the way.

Life is sweet. Treasure every moment of it.

Glossary of Terms

As Live: As it sounds, a live two-way recorded and used in later bulletins as if it was live.
Central Lobby: Between the House of Commons and the House of Lords and accessible to the public.
CCO: Conservative Central Office.
Doorstep: Waiting for someone in order to throw a question at them. Often involves hanging around in the cold and rain.
Doughnut: A live by the reporter before and after his/her package.
Embargo: A story that can't go to air or print until an agreed time.
Grab: Sky News jargon for a sound bite.
Live or Live Two-way: The reporter is answering the presenter's questions live.
Live at Five: Sky News flagship programme.
The Lobby: The parliamentary lobby, briefings usually conducted by the PMOS which political journalists with the correct accreditation as lobby correspondents, attend.
Millbank: 4 Millbank, the Westminster broadcasting centre where the Sky News, ITN and BBC political units and studios are based.
Package: A television news reporter's report.
PLP: The Parliamentary Labour Party.
PMOS: The Prime Minister's official spokesman/woman.
Pool or pooled: An interview or pictures shot by one broadcaster and shared with all other broadcasters.
PTC: Piece To Camera. The bit in the reporter's package where the reporter appears on camera.
RTS: The Royal Television Society which holds annual awards for the best of television news.
Sign-off: At the end of a package the reporter says his/her name, organisation and location eg. Glen Oglaza, *News at Ten*, Berlin.

Sound bite: The part of a recorded interview which gets on air, usually ten to fifteen seconds long.
Strap: Also called a Super or an Aston. The written text along the bottom of the screen identifying the person being interviewed.
Tease: A promo telling you what story or stories are coming up.
Ticker: Moving text along the bottom of the screen with the latest news headlines, also called a crawler.
Track and rushes: A reporter voice over and accompanying pictures to be edited together back at base.
Underlay: Video voiced over live by a presenter. Also called Overlay.
The Usual Suspects: Labour rebel MPs during Tony Blair's premiership. Jeremy Corbyn was invariably among them.
Vox Pop: Vox populi. When a reporter talks to members of the public, usually in the street.
VT Editor: Video tape editor.